THE MUSTARD SEED

Other books by Bhagwan Shree Rajneesh available
from Harper & Row:

The Book of the Secrets

I Am the Gate

Meditation: The Art of Ecstacy

THE MUSTARD SEED

Discourses on the Sayings of Jesus
taken from the Gospel According to Thomas

BHAGWAN SHREE RAJNEESH

Compilation :

SWAMI AMRIT PATHIK

Editor :

SWAMI SATYA DEVA

1817

Published in San Francisco by

HARPER & ROW, PUBLISHERS

New York   Hagerstown   San Francisco   London

Contents

Introduction

Jesus once said, "For this people's heart is waxed gross, and *their* ears are dull of hearing, and their eyes they have closed; lest at any time they should see with *their* eyes, and hear with *their* ears, and should understand with *their* heart, and should be converted, and I should heal them." King James, Matthew Chapter 13:15.

The Jesus that I was presented with as a child is a very different person from the Jesus that Bhagwan Shree Rajneesh introduced me to in *The Mustard Seed*.

My own heritage from organized religion has been a feeling, as Bhagwan says, that I was born wrong. Without rules and watchdogs to check the demon in me, torrents of poison and evil would naturally come gushing forth from my being to devastate and destroy all the good in my path. The conflict arose, 'me or God'; so I chose me, but very secretively. I was a sweet, acceptable hypocrite. But God being the cosmic spy that He was to me, and I deep down, knowing that I was wrong, I became a normal, modern day, guilty neurotic.

So I alighted from analysis, to drugs, to radical left groups, to encounter groups, to Reichian therapy to peace and love and flowers. I was trying to build a beautiful, high structure on a foundation of excrement, and all of my efforts were tantamount to curing cancer with antibiotics. I reacted to the original reaction to me in a vicious cycle.

In spite of all of the personal growth work, until two years ago, no one was ever able to help me to see my dilemma, other than intellectually, and to work with it.

For the last two years, everything seems to have become a journey from being 'because of' to being 'in despite'. The man responsible for this transformation is Bhagwan Shree Rajneesh.

I thought that I was self-searching and introspective, but I have discovered through him that even at my moments of deepest insight, I was not even wading in the shallows.

And such a man is bound to see deeper into everything.

And such a man is bound to understand the real message of Jesus.

Take the story of Genesis as an example. What I had been brought up to think was only a morality play about disobedience and sex, was transformed by Bhagwan into an enlightening parable of what falling from Grace really means, and that is, self-consciousness. There was no sin, only the separation from God, from Oneness. The ego was born; and the whole journey of life is back to that One-consciousness. Only inner ears could hear such a meaning.

Or when Jesus preached turning the other cheek, my reaction was, "I've had enough slavery and martyrdom." According to Bhagwan, the real message is 'the buck stops with you'. You become conscious of your responsibility for yourself, you become a responder rather than a push-button reaction machine.

And we are all reactors Bhagwan says. Even the love we know, the so-called love, is another reaction.

The subtleties of Bhagwan's words are enormous, and misunderstanding is the most likely thing, because we have not the eyes nor the ears. We only see and hear replays of our past experiences and future hopes.

So, someone is in the world today who has made Jesus' words not only intelligible, but who has made the teaching come to life again, throbbing with the realness and fire that the founder of Christianity must have intended.

Jesus has said, "The Kingdom of God is within you."

If through inner searching, someone could *realize* that he is also a Son of God, then such a one would understand what Jesus was indicating.

Bhagwan Shree Rajneesh is an Enlightened One. His being is a great emptiness, a clear mirror. Understanding and compassion radiate from him. As he speaks, one is left with a feeling of mystery, that somehow he has not said 'it', but all around him it is said.

In his ashram at 17 Koregaon Park in Poona, India, he speaks on numerous topics. He is not a scholar, although he is highly read in history and religion. He is not a theologian, a moralist, a logician or a psychotherapist, although these are roles that he can play beautifully. His depth of perception comes not from his intellect, but from his very being. I could go on and on, but I would only succeed in saying what he is not.

In the lecture hall in Poona, as you sit in his presence and listen, his eyes dancing and playing with the audience, his peace and serenity emanating from him like a shower of soft blue light to all present, unconditionally, you are struck with his silence, penetrated by it. And the gestalt changes: his words are no longer the issue, they have become a vehicle upon which one can glide into his being. The words come through him, he is undisturbed, untouched.

Only one who is so clear, so empty, can *know*. There is no ego there to collide with.

When he speaks of Jesus, Jesus has returned to set the story straight. Through Bhagwan, Jesus becomes real, relevant, helpful. It seems that these Masters have always been saying the same things. Bhagwan says that all Enlightened Ones are like the ocean, everywhere the taste is salty.

So if you can drop, for just a little while, all that you know, think you know, or have been taught about Jesus, and read *The Mustard Seed* openly, you may discover that religion is not at all what you thought, and that Jesus was perhaps the last Christian.

If you can read *The Mustard Seed* with your heart, it might very well blow your mind.

Ma Yoga Sudha

THE MUSTARD SEED

First Discourse

21st August 1974, Poona, India

THE FIRST SAYING

The disciples said to Jesus:
Tell us what the Kingdom of Heaven is like.

He said to them:
It is like a mustard seed—
smaller than all seeds,
but when it falls on the tilled earth
it produces a large tree
and becomes shelter for all the birds of Heaven.

Human relationships have changed a lot, and have changed for the worse. In all dimensions the deeper relationships have disappeared : the wife is no longer a wife, but just a girl-friend; the husband is no longer a husband, but just a boy-friend. Friendship is good, but cannot be very deep. Marriage is something which happens in depth. It is a commitment in depth, and unless you commit yourself, you remain shallow. Unless you commit yourself, you never take the jump.

You can float on the surface, but the depths are not for you. Of course, to go into the depths is dangerous—bound to be so, because on the surface you are very efficient. On the surface you can work like an automaton, no awareness is needed. But you will have to be more and more alert, the more you penetrate into the depths, because at every moment death is possible. Fear of depth has created a shallowness in all relationships. They have become juvenile.

A boy-friend or a girl-friend may be fun, but it cannot become a door to the deepest that is hidden in each and everyone. With a girl-friend you can be sexually related, but love cannot grow. Love needs deep roots. Sexuality is possible on the surface, but sexuality is just animal, biological. It can be beautiful if it is part of a deeper love, but if it is not part of a deeper love it is the most ugly thing possible; the ugliest, because then there is no communion—you simply touch each other and separate. Only bodies meet, but not *you*—not I, not thou. This has happened in all relationships.

3

But the greatest relationship has completely disappeared, and the greatest relationship is between a Master and a disciple. You will not be able to understand Jesus if you cannot understand the dimension of that relationship which exists between a Master and his disciples. That has completely disappeared. The wife is substituted by a girl-friend, the husband is substituted by a boy-friend, but the Master and the relationship that exists between him and his disciples has completely disappeared. Or, this relationship has been substituted by a very contrary thing that exists between a psychiatrist and his patient.

Between a psychiatrist and his patient, a relationship exists which is bound to be ill, pathological—because a patient comes not in search of truth, not really in search of health. This word 'health' is very meaningful: it means wholeness, it means holiness, it means a deep healing inside the self. A patient does not come for health, because if he comes for health he cannot be anything other than a disciple. A patient comes to get rid of the illness; his attitude is totally negative. He comes just to be forced to become normal again, just to become a working part of the normal world again. He has become maladjusted, he needs adjustment and the psychiatrist helps him to be adjusted again. But adjusted to whom? Adjusted to this world, this society, which is absolutely ill.

What you call the 'normal' human being is nothing but normal pathology or normal madness, normal insanity. The 'normal' man is also insane, but insane within the boundaries, the accepted boundaries of the society, of the culture. Sometimes somebody trespasses, goes beyond the boundaries—then he becomes ill. Then the whole society, which is ill, says that this man is ill. And the psychiatrist exists on the boundary to help this man back, back to the crowd.

The psychiatrist cannot be the Master, because he himself is not whole. And the patient cannot be the disciple, because he has not come to learn. He is disturbed, and he does not want to be disturbed; his effort is only for adjustment, not for health. The psychiatrist cannot be the Master, although he is pretending to be in the West, and sooner or later he will pretend that he is the Master in the East too. But he cannot be—he himself is ill. He may help others to be adjusted, and that is okay: one ill man can help another ill man—in some ways. But one ill man cannot bring another man, who is ill, to be whole; one madman cannot help another madman to go beyond madness.

Even your Freuds, your Jungs, and your Adlers are absolutely ill; not only ordinary psychiatrists, but the greatest of them are pathologically ill. I will tell you a few things so you can feel this : whenever somebody mentioned anything about death, Freud would start trembling. Twice he even fainted and fell down from his chair just because somebody was talking about mummies in Egypt. He fainted ! Another time too, Jung was talking about death and corpses, and suddenly he trembled, fell down and fainted, became unconscious.

If death is such a fear to Freud, then what about his disciples? And why should death be such a fear? Can you conceive of a Buddha being afraid of death? Then he would no longer be a Buddha.

Jung has reported that many times he wanted to go to Rome to visit the Vatican and particularly the library, the Vatican's library, which is the greatest one, holding the most secret records of all the religions that have existed—which is rare. But whenever he went tc purchase the ticket he would start trembling—just going to Rome ! What will happen when you go to *Moksha?* And he would cancel the ticket and come back. He never went, *never.* Many times he tried, and in the end he decided, "No, I cannot go."

What is the fear? Why should a psychiatrist be afraid of going to Rome? Because Rome is just the symbol, the representative of religion; and this man Jung had created a philosophy around his mind—that philosophy was afraid of being shattered. It is just like a camel being afraid of going to the Himalayas, because when a camel comes near the Himalayas, for the first time he comes to know that he is nothing. This whole philosophy that Jung has created is just childish, because man has created such vast, cosmic systems, and all those systems are in ruins now. The fear is that going to Rome means going to the ruins of the great systems that the past has created.

What about *your* small system? What about this small corner that you have cleaned and decorated? What about your philosophy?

Great philosophies have tumbled down and gone to dust: go to
Rome, see what has happened! Go to Athens, see what has
happened! Where are the schools of Aristotle, Plato and Socrates?
All have disappeared into dust. The greatest systems in the end
come to dust, and all thoughts finally prove to be useless, because
thought is just a man-created thing.

Only in 'no-thought' do you come to know the Divine. Through
thought you cannot come to know the eternal, because thought is
of time. Thought cannot be of the eternal; no philosophy, no
system of thought, can be eternal.

That was the fear. At least four or five times Jung made reser-
vations and cancelled them. And this man Jung is one of the
greatest of psychiatrists. If he was so afraid of going to Rome, what
about his disciples? Even you are not afraid, not because you are
better than Jung, but just because you are more unaware. He was
aware that in Rome his head would come down; that the moment
he looked at the ruins of all the great systems, a trembling, a
fear of death would grip him and he would ask himself, "What
will happen to my system? What will happen to me?" He trembled
and came back, and in his memoirs he writes: "Then finally I
dropped the whole project. I am not going to Rome."

The same thing happened to Freud many times, so it does not
seem to be just a coincidence. He also tried to go to Rome and
he also was afraid. Why? Freud was as angry as you can be, Freud
was as sexual as you can be, Freud was as scared of death as you
can be, Freud was as neurotic in his behaviour as you can be, so
what is the difference? He may have been a more intelligent man—
a genius perhaps—or he could help a little, but he was as blind as
you are as far as the Ultimate is concerned, as far as the secret-
most, innermost core of being is concerned.

No, psychiatry cannot become religion. It may become a good
hospital, but it cannot become the temple—it is not possible. And
a psychiatrist may be needed because people are ill, maladjusted,
but a psychiatrist is not a Master and a patient is not a disciple.

If you come to a Master as a patient then you will miss, because
a Master is not a psychiatrist. I am not a psychiatrist. People come
to me and they say, "I am suffering from this mental anxiety,
anxiety-neurosis, this and that."

I say, "It is okay, because I am not going to treat your anxiety, I am going to treat *you*. I am not concerned with your diseases, I am simply concerned with *you*. Diseases are on the periphery, and there is no disease where *you* are."

Once you come to realize who you are, all diseases disappear. They exist basically because you have been hiding self-knowledge, you have been avoiding yourself; you have been avoiding the basic encounter, because you don't want to look at yourself. Why don't you want to look at yourself? What has happened to you? Unless you are ready to encounter yourself you cannot become a disciple, because a Master can do nothing if you are not ready to face yourself. He can only help you to face yourself.

Why are you so afraid? Because something has gone wrong somewhere in the past. A child is born and he is not accepted as he is, many things have to be changed, forced, he has to be disciplined. He has many parts which the society and his parents cannot accept, so those parts have to be denied, repressed; only a few parts can be accepted and appreciated. So the child has to work it out. He has to deny many fragments of his being, which cannot be allowed manifestation. He has to deny them so much that he himself becomes unaware of them. This is what repression is, and the whole society exists on repression.

The greater part of the being of the child has to be repressed, completely thrown into the dark. But that repressed part asserts itself, tries to rebel, react; it wants to come into the light and you have to force it back again and again. So you become afraid to encounter yourself, because what will happen to the repressed part? That will come again, that will be there. What will happen to the unconscious? If you encounter yourself the unconscious will be there, all that you have denied will be there. And that gives you fear.

Unless a child is accepted totally as he is or she is, this fear is bound to remain; but no society has yet existed which accepts a child totally. And it seems that no society will ever exist which will accept a child totally, because it is almost impossible. So repression is bound to be there, more or less. And everybody has to face, some day, this problem of facing oneself. You become disciples the very day you forget about what is good, what is bad; you forget about what is accepted, what is not accepted. You only become a disciple the day you are ready to expose your whole being to yourself.

The Master is just a midwife. He helps you to pass through a new birth, to be reborn. And what is the relationship between a Master and a disciple? A disciple has to trust; he cannot doubt. If he doubts, then he cannot expose himself. When you doubt somebody, you shrink, you cannot expand. When you doubt somebody, he becomes a stranger, and then you close yourself. You cannot be open because you don't know what this stranger is going to do to you. You cannot be vulnerable before him; you have to protect yourself and create an armour.

With a Master you have to drop the armour completely—that much is a must. Even before a lover, you may carry your armour a little; before a beloved, you may not be so open. But with a Master the openness has to be total, otherwise nothing will happen. If you withhold even a little part of yourself the relationship is not there. Total trust is needed, only then can the secrets be revealed, only then can the keys be offered to you. But if you are hiding yourself, that means you are fighting with the Master, and then nothing can be done.

Struggle is not the key with the Master, surrender is the key. And surrender has disappeared from the world completely. Many things have helped it: for three or four centuries man has been taught to be individualistic, egoistic; man has been taught not to surrender, but to fight; not to obey, but to rebel; man has been taught not to trust, but to doubt. There has been a reason for it, because science grows through doubt. Science is deep skepticism. It works not through trust; it works through logic, argument, doubt: the more you doubt, the more scientific you become. The path is the very opposite of the religious path.

Religion works through trust: the more you trust, the more religious you become. Science has worked miracles and those miracles are very visible. Religion has worked greater miracles, but those miracles are not so visible. Even if a Buddha is there, what can you feel? What can you see? He is not visible—visibly, he is just a body; visibly, he is just as mortal as you are; visibly, he will become old and die one day—invisibly, he is deathless. But you don't have the eyes to see that which is invisible, you don't have that capacity to feel the innermost, the unknown.

That is why only trusting eyes, by and by, start to feel and become sensitive. When you trust, it means closing these two eyes. That is why trust is blind, just like love is blind—but trust is even more blind than love.

When you close both these eyes, what happens? An inner transformation happens. When you close these eyes, which see outwardly, what happens to the energy which goes through the eyes? That energy starts moving backwards. It cannot flow from the eyes towards objects, so it starts turning, it becomes a turning. Energy has to move, energy cannot be static; if you close one outlet, it starts finding another. When both eyes are closed, the energy that was moving through these two eyes starts turning—a conversion happens.

And that energy hits the third eye in you. The third eye is not a physical thing: it is just that the energy that moves through the eyes towards outside objects is now returning towards the source—it becomes the third eye, the third way of seeing the world.

Only through that third eye is a Buddha seen; only through that third eye is a Jesus realized. If you don't have that third eye, Jesus will be there, but you will miss him—many missed him. In his home town, people thought that he was just that carpenter Joseph's son. Nobody, nobody could recognize what had happened to this man: that he was no longer the carpenter's son, that he had become God's son—but that is an inner phenomenon. And when Jesus declared, "I am the son of the Divine, my Father is in Heaven," people laughed and said, "Either you have gone mad, or you are a fool, or a very cunning man. How can a carpenter's son suddenly become God's son?" But there is a way....

Only the body is born out of the body; the Inner Self is not born out of the body, it is born of the Holy Ghost, it is of the Divine. But first you have to attain the eyes to see, you have to attain the ears to hear.

And it is a very delicate affair to understand Jesus; you have to pass through a great training. It is just like understanding classical music. If you are suddenly allowed to hear classical music you will feel, "What nonsense is going on?" It is so delicate that a long training is needed. You have to be an apprentice for many, many years, only then are your ears trained to catch the subtle—and then there is nothing like classical music. Then, ordinary day-to-day music, like film music, is not music at all, it is just noise, and foolish at that.

Because your ears are not trained you live with that noise and you think it is music. But for classical music you need very aristocratic ears. A training is needed, and the more you are trained, the more the subtle becomes visible. But classical music is nothing before a Jesus because he is the cosmic music. You have to be so silent that there is not a single flicker of thought, not a single movement in your being; only then can you hear Jesus, can you understand Jesus, can you know him.

Jesus goes on repeating again and again, "Those who have ears should be able to understand me. Those who have eyes: see! I am here!" Why does he go on repeating, "Those who have eyes, see! Those who have ears, hear!" Why?

He is talking of some other dimension of understanding only a disciple can understand. Very few understood Jesus, but that is in the very nature of things and bound to be so. Very few—and who were those few? They were not learned scholars, no; they were not professors of the universities, no; they were not pundits or philosophers, no! They were ordinary people: a fisherman, a farmer, a shoemaker, a prostitute; they were very ordinary people, most ordinary, the most ordinary of ordinaries. Why could these people understand? There must be something extraordinary in an ordinary man. There must be something special which exists in an ordinary man and disappears in so-called 'extraordinaries'. What is this?

It is a humbleness, a trust. Because the more you are trained in the intellect, the less trust is possible; when you are not trained in the intellect, more trust is possible.

A farmer trusts, he has no need to doubt. He sows the seeds in the field and he trusts they will come up, they will sprout when the right season comes. They *will* sprout. He waits, and he prays, and in the right season those seeds sprout and they become plants. He waits and he believes. He lives with the trees, plants, rivers, mountains. There is no need to doubt: trees are not cunning, you need no armour around you to protect yourself from them; hills are not cunning—they are not politicians, they are not criminals—you need no armour to protect yourself from them. You do not need any security there, you can be open.

That is why when you go to the hills, you suddenly feel a rapture. From where does it come? From the hills? No! It comes because now you can put the armour aside, there is no need to be afraid. When you go to a tree suddenly you feel beautiful. It is not coming from the tree, it is coming from within you. But with a tree there is no need to protect yourself, you can be at ease and at home. The flower is not going to suddenly attack you; the tree cannot be a thief, it cannot steal anything from you. So when you go to the hills, to the sea, to the trees, to the forest, you put aside your armour.

People who live with nature are more trusting. A country which is less industrialized, less mechanized, less technological, lives more with nature, has more trust in it. That is why you cannot conceive of Jesus being born in New York—almost impossible. 'Jesus freaks' can be born there, but not Jesus. And these 'freaks' are just neurotic, Jesus is just an excuse. No, you cannot think of Jesus being born there, it is almost impossible. And even if he were born there, no one would listen to him; even if he were there, nobody would be able to recognize him. He was born in an age without technology, without science, the son of a carpenter. He lived his whole life with poor, simple people who were living with nature. They could trust.

Jesus came to the lake one day, early in the morning; the sun had not yet come up over the horizon. Two fishermen were there and they had just thrown their net to catch fish when Jesus came and said, "Look! Why are you wasting your life? I can make you fishers of men. Why are you wasting your energy on fishing? I can make you catchers of men, fishers of men. Come, follow me!"

If he had said that to you when you were sitting in your office or in your shop, you would have said, "Go away! I don't have any time. Don't waste my time!" But those two fishermen looked at Jesus; they looked at Jesus without any doubt. The sun was rising and the man was beautiful, this man Jesus. And his eyes—they were deeper than the lake; and his radiance was greater than the sun. They threw away their nets and they followed Jesus.

This is trust. Not a single question: "Who are you stranger?" They didn't know him, he was not of their village; they had never seen him, they had never heard him. But it was enough—the call, the invitation was enough. They heard the invitation, they looked at Jesus, felt his sincerity, and they followed him.

Just when they were going out of the town, a man came running and he said to those two fishermen, "Where are you going? Your father has died suddenly. Come back!" So they said to Jesus, "Can we go home and bury our dead father? And then we will come." Jesus said: "Don't worry about the dead. There are enough dead in the town. They will bury their dead. You come and follow me. You need not bother about the dead." And those two fishermen followed. This is trust: they heard, they saw Jesus.

He meant—and he was right: "When the father is dead, what is to be done? When somebody is dead, he is dead. There is no need to go. And there are enough dead in the town; they will do the remainder, they will do the ritual, they will bury your father. You come and follow me." So they followed and they never turned back, they never looked back. Trust means not looking back. Trust means not returning back.

A doubting mind is always looking back, always thinking of the alternative, always thinking of what he has not done, always thinking whether he has done right: "Should I go back or follow this madman? Who knows? He says he is the son of God, but who knows? Nobody knows about God, nobody knows about his sons—and this man looks just like us!" But the fishermen followed Jesus.

If you follow a man like Jesus, sooner or later he will become infectious. But you have to follow in the beginning. Sooner or later you will feel that he is the son of God, and not only that—through him you will realize that you are also sons of God. But in the beginning you have to trust. If in the beginning there is doubt, doors are closed.

This relationship between Master and disciple has disappeared because of three centuries of successful science. Science has succeeded so much. And it has achieved miracles—useless miracles of course—because they have not added a single bit to human happiness, and a miracle is useless if happiness has not increased through it. Rather, happiness has decreased. The more

technology, the more comfort—but the less happiness : this is
the miracle that science has achieved. The more things that can
be done by mechanical devices, the less you are needed. And the
less you are needed, the more you feel futile, useless, meaningless.
Sooner or later, the computer will replace you and then you will
not be needed at all. Then you can go and commit suicide because
the computer will do everything.

Happiness comes out of being needed. When you are needed
you feel happy, because you feel your being has meaning, you
feel your life has meaning; you feel that you are needed, and
that without you things would be different. But now, without
you, nothing will be different. Rather, things will be better without
you because machines can do everything better than you. You are
just a hindrance, just an out-of-date thing. Man is the most out-of-
date thing today, because every year everything comes in a new
edition : a new model of the Ford car comes out, a new model
of everything. Only man remains the most out-of-date model.
Amidst so many new things, you are the only old thing.

The modern mind continuously feels a meaninglessness, because
nobody needs you. Even children won't need you, because the
government, the Welfare State will take care of them. Your old
father and mother will not need you, because there will be homes—
government and state homes—which will take care of their needs.
Who needs you? And when you feel nobody needs you, that
you are just an unnecessary burden, how can you be happy?

In the old days you were needed. Somewhere, a Jewish mystic,
Hillel, who must have been a very trusting man, a very prayerful
man, said to God in his prayer, "Don't think that only I need
You—You also need me. You will be nothing without me. If
Hillel is not there, who will pray? Who will look up to You?
I am a must. So remember this: I need You, that is right, but
You also need me."

When the whole universe needed you—even God—then you
had a meaning, a significance, a fragrance. But now nobody needs
you. You can be disposed of easily, you are nothing. Technology
has created comfort and made you disposable. Technology has
made you better houses, but not better men, because for better

men some other dimension is needed—and that dimension is not of mechanics. That dimension is of awareness, not of mechanicalness.

Science cannot create a Buddha or a Jesus, but science *can* create a society in which a Buddha will become impossible. Many people come to me and they ask why there are no more Buddhas now, no more *Teerthankers*, no more Jesuses. Because of you! You have created such a society that it becomes more and more impossible for a simple man to exist, for an innocent man to exist. And even if he does exist you will not recognize him. It is not that Buddhas are not there—it is difficult to see them, but they are there. You may be passing them every day when you go to your office, but you cannot recognize them because you are blind.

Trust has disappeared. Remember this: Jesus lived in an age of trust, deep trust. His whole glory, his whole significance can be understood only through that dimension of trust.

Now, we shall enter this small piece of Jesus' saying:

"The disciples said to Jesus: Tell us what the Kingdom of Heaven is like."

They were not questioners, they were not curious people, they were not going to argue. Their question was innocent. When a question is innocent, only then can a Jesus answer it.

When is a question innocent? Do you know? If you already have the answer then the question is not innocent. You ask, "Is there a God?" and you already have the answer. You know that, yes, there is, and you have come to me just for confirmation. Or you know that there is none, and you have come just to see whether this man knows or not. If the answer is there then the question is cunning, it is not innocent. Then it cannot be answered by a Jesus because Jesus can answer only innocence.

When a disciple asks, there is no answer in his mind. He does not know, he simply does not know and that is why he is asking. Remember this: when you ask something, remember well, are you asking because you already have an answer, are you asking through your knowledge? Then there can be no meeting. Then even if I answer, the answer will never reach you. You are not empty enough to receive it. The answer is already there : you are prejudiced, poisoned, already.

There are two types of questioning : one is out of knowledge, and then it is useless because then a debate is possible, not a dialogue; but the other is when you ask out of ignorance, knowing well that you don't know. When you know that you don't know, and ask, you have become a disciple. Now it is not going to be an argument. You are just thirsty and you ask for water; you are hungry and you ask for food. You don't know and you ask; you are ready to receive. A disciple asks, knowing well that he doesn't know. When you don't know you are humble. When you know you become egoistic, and a Jesus cannot talk to egos.

"The disciples said to Jesus...", 'disciples' means those who are fully aware that they don't know, "...Tell us what the Kingdom of Heaven is like."

Jesus continuously talked about the Kingdom of Heaven, and that created much trouble. The very terminology created much trouble, because the word 'kingdom' is political and politicians became afraid. He was crucified because they thought, "This man is talking about some Kingdom which is coming on earth, and this man is saying, 'I am the King of that Kingdom'. This man is trying to create a revolution, an overthrow of the government. This man wants to create another Kingdom!"

The King, the Governor, the officials, the priests, they all became scared. And this man was influential because people listened to him; people not only listened to him—whenever they listened to him they were transformed, they became aflame, they were totally new, something happened within them. So the priests, Pontius Pilate the Governor, Herod the King, the whole government, both the secular government and the sacred government—all became scared of this man. He seemed to be dangerous. Such an innocent man there never was, and he looked dangerous. He was misunderstood.

But there is always the possibility of a Jesus being misunderstood. The problem is that he has to use your language because there is no other language, and whatsoever he says he has to say in your words. There are no other words and your words are already overburdened; they carry too much meaning already, they are too loaded. He was talking simply of the Kingdom of God, the Kingdom of Heaven. But 'kingdom'? That word is dangerous: 'kingdom' gives a hint of some politics.

Jesus was not a revolutionary of this world. He *was* a revolutionary, a master revolutionary—but of the inner world. He was talking of the Inner Kingdom. But even the disciples were not aware of what he was saying. When you come to a Master there is a meeting of two different dimensions, just like the meeting of sky and earth; the meeting is just at each other's boundaries. If trust is there you can move into the sky; if trust is not there you cling to the earth. If trust is there you can open your wings and move, but if trust is not there you cling to the earth.

This man brings a danger to you. What is the Kingdom of Heaven? What type of kingdom? This Kingdom is absolutely opposite, diametrically opposite the kingdom of this world. And Jesus explained and explained but it was difficult to make people understand.

He said: "In my Kingdom of God the poorest will be the richest, the last will be the first." He talked exactly like Lao Tzu, and he was a man like Lao Tzu. "The last will be the first in my Kingdom of God." He was saying that the humblest will be the most significant, the poorest will be the richest, and one who is not recognized at all here will be recognized there—upside-down!

It has to be so. If you stand near a river and the river is silent, there are no ripples, and you look at your reflection, it is upside-down. A reflection is always upside-down. In this world we are really upside-down, and if we have to be put right everything has to be put right-side-up. But that will look as if everything is going to be upside-down—a state of chaos is needed.

Buddha became a beggar—the last man of this world. He was a king, but the Kingdom of God belongs to the last. He left the kingdom of this world, because the kingdom of this world is just useless, it is a meaningless burden. You carry it but it is not a source of nourishment. It destroys you, it is a poison—although it may be such slow poison that you cannot feel it....

One man was drinking and another was passing, a friend. So the friend said, "What are you doing? That stuff is slow poison."

The man said, "It's okay—I'm not in a hurry."

Whatsoever you call life is a slow poison because finally it comes to death. It kills you, it never does anything else. You may not be in a hurry, but that doesn't make any change in the quality of the poison. It may be slow, you may not be in a hurry, but still it will kill you.

The kingdom of this world belongs to death, but the Kingdom of Heaven belongs to eternal life. So Jesus says: "Those who are ready, come to me. I will give you life abundant."

Jesus passed through a village. He was thirsty and then he came to a well. A woman was drawing water from the well and he said, "I am thirsty, give me a little water to drink."

The woman said, "But I belong to a very low caste and it is not allowed, I cannot give you water."

Jesus said, "Don't worry. Give me water, and in exchange I will also give you a water—from my well. And once you drink out of it you will never be thirsty again."

The disciples are asking, "What is this Kingdom of Heaven like?" Because that which is not known to us can be explained only in terms of 'like'. Hence all myth. Mythology means trying to explain things which you do not know, and cannot know in this state of mind, through something which you know. Trying to explain the Unknown in terms of the known is myth—bringing some understanding to you where you are.

The Kingdom of Heaven cannot be explained directly, immediately. It is impossible. Unless you enter it there is no way to say anything about it. Whatsoever is said will be wrong because the truth cannot be said. Then what are Jesus, Lao Tzu and Buddha doing continuously, for years? If the truth cannot be said, what are they doing? They are trying to explain something to you which cannot be explained, through some symbols which you know; trying to explain the Unknown through the known. This is the most difficult thing in the world—parables, myths, stories.

And there are foolish people who try to analyze a myth, dissect it and say, "This is a myth, this is not truth." They analyze and dissect, they do surgery on the myth and then they say, "This is a myth, this is not history." But nobody has ever said that myth is history. And myth cannot be dissected because it is simply symbolic.

It is just as if there is a milestone on which there is an arrow where it is written: "Delhi," and you dissect the stone, you dissect the arrow, the ink, the chemicals and everything, and you say, "Some fool has done this—there is no 'Delhi' in it!"

Myths are milestones, arrows towards the Unknown. They are not the goal, they simply indicate. That is the meaning of the disciples' question : "Tell us what the Kingdom of Heaven is *like*." We cannot ask what the Kingdom of Heaven *is*. Look at the quality of the question : we cannot ask what the Kingdom of Heaven is—that would be too much. We cannot expect the answer for that either. We can only ask what it is *like*, which means : "Say something which we know; make some indications through it so we can have a glimpse."

It is just like a blind man asking what light is like. How can you ask what light is when you are blind? If you ask, the very asking debars the answer. It cannot be answered. Light can be known—you need eyes. But, "What is light like? " means : "Say something in the language of the blind."

All parables are truths in the language of the blind; all mythologies are truths garbed in the language of the blind. So don't dissect them! You will not find anything there. They are just indications. And if you have trust, indications are wonderful.

In one temple in Japan there is no statue of Buddha. People go inside and they ask, "Where is the statue?" There is no statue, but just on the pedestal there is one finger pointing towards Heaven—and this is Buddha. The priest will say, "This is Buddha." I don't know whether the priest understands it or not—this finger pointing to the moon. What *is* a Buddha? Just a finger pointing to the moon!

The disciples ask what the Kingdom of Heaven is like : "Tell us, tell us in a parable, in a story that we children can understand. We don't know, we don't have any experience. Say something which can give us a glimpse."

"Jesus said to them : It is like a mustard seed—smaller than all seeds, but when it falls on the tilled earth it produces a large tree and becomes shelter for all the birds of Heaven."

Jesus has used this mustard seed very much, for many reasons :

one, the mustard seed is the smallest seed. God is invisible, smaller than the smallest, so how can you indicate Him? At the boundary of sight is the mustard seed, the smallest thing in the world of the visible. Beyond that you will not be able to understand because beyond is the invisible. The mustard seed is the boundary—you can see it but it is very small. If you go beyond you enter the world of the subtle, that which is smaller than the smallest. This mustard seed exists on the boundary.

And this mustard seed is not only the smallest visible thing, it also has a very mysterious quality : when it grows it becomes the biggest of plants. So it is a paradox : the seed is the smallest and the plant is the biggest. God is the invisible and the universe is the most visible; the universe is the tree, the plant, and God is the seed; God is the unmanifested and the universe is the manifested.

If you break down a seed you will not find the tree there; you can dissect it but you will not find a tree hidden there. And you can say there is no tree and people were just foolish, saying that a great tree is hidden in this seed when there is nothing.

This is what analysts have always been doing. If you tell them that this flower is beautiful, they will take it to the lab and they will dissect it to find where the beauty is. They will come upon chemicals and other things, they will dissect it and analyze it, and they will label different fragments of the flower in many bottles—but there will not be a single bottle in which they will find beauty. No, they will come out of the lab and they will say, "You must have been under some illusion, you were dreaming—there is no beauty. We have dissected the whole flower nothing has been left, and there is no beauty."

There are things which are known only in their wholeness. You cannot dissect them, because they are greater than their parts. This is the problem—a basic problem for those who are in search of truth. Truth is greater than all the parts joined together. It is not just the sum of the parts, it is greater than the parts.

A melody is not just the sum of all the notes, of all the sounds. No, it is something greater. When all the notes meet, a harmony is created, a harmony becomes manifest which was not there in single notes. I am speaking to you : you can dissect my words, they will all be found in a dictionary, but you cannot find me in the dictionary. And you can say, "All the words are here, so why bother?"

It happened once that Mark Twain went to listen to a friend who was a priest. The friend had been insisting for many, many days. He was one of the greatest orators, a very poetic orator, and he was very highly appreciated. Whenever he spoke the church would be overcrowded, but Mark Twain never came to listen to him. The friend insisted again and again until Mark Twain said, "Okay, I am coming this weekend." For the Sunday the priest prepared his best; he arranged all that was beautiful in his mind because Mark Twain was coming. Mark Twain sat just in the front and the priest delivered his best speech ever. He brought his whole energy to it and it was really beautiful; it was a symphony, it was poetry.

But by and by he became afraid, apprehensive, because Mark Twain was sitting there as if dead. Not even a glimpse of appreciation came to his face. The people clapped so many times, they were ecstatic, but Mark Twain just sat there not giving any indication at all that he had been impressed this way or that, neither negative nor positive. He remained indifferent—and indifference is more deadly than negative attitudes. Because if you are against something, at least you have some attitude towards it; if you are against, you give some meaning to it. But if you are indifferent you say that this is absolutely useless, not even worth being against.

When the speech finished, Mark Twain went back in the car with the priest. The priest could not ask and they remained silent. Just when Mark Twain was getting out of the car the priest said, "You have not said anything about my lecture."

Mark Twain replied, "It is nothing new. I have a book in my house and you have simply copied from it. This lecture is borrowed and you cannot fool me. You can fool those fools there in the church, but I am a man of letters and I study. By chance, only last night I was reading that book."

The priest couldn't believe it. He said, "What are you saying? I have not copied it from anywhere. It is impossible!"

Mark Twain said, "Every word that you said is there. And tomorrow I will send the book." The next day he sent him a copy of a big dictionary and he said, "You can find all the words here!"

This is the mind of the analyst. He can kill poetry immediately. He can say it is just words joined together. He cannot see between the words, he cannot see between the lines—and the poetry exists there. The beauty exists there, and the ecstasy and God and all that is significant always exists between the words, between the lines.

The mustard seed is the smallest and contains the biggest. You cannot see God because He is the smallest—the mustard seed—but you can see the universe. And if the universe is there the seed must be there. How can there be a tree without the seed? Can there be a tree without a seed? Whether or not you can see it is not the point. Can this universe exist without a final cause, a source? The Ganges is there—can the Ganges be there without a source? This vast universe—and you think it can exist without a source?

And this universe is not only vast, there is also such a harmony in it, such a universal symphony, such a universal system. It is not a chaos—so much discipline in it, everything in the right place. And those who know well say that this is the best of all possible worlds, that nothing can be better than this.

There must be a seed, but the seed is very small, smaller than the mustard seed. The mustard seed is used as a myth, to indicate. These men who were asking Jesus were fishermen and farmers and gardeners, and they would understand the parable, the parable of the mustard seed.

If you dissect it you miss. If you dissect religion you miss; either you can see it directly without dissecting it, or you cannot see it. There is one way which trust uses : in the seed you cannot see the tree, but you can go and sow the seed in the ground—this is what a man of trust will do. He will say, "Okay, this is a seed; I trust it will become a tree, and I will go and put it in the field. I will find suitable soil and I will protect this seed. I will wait and pray, I will love and hope, and I will dream...."

What else can you do? You can sow the seed and wait and dream, and hope and pray. What else can you do? Then suddenly one day, one morning, you awake and the seed has become a new thing, new sprouts are coming out of the earth. Now the seed is no longer a seed—it is becoming a tree, it is blooming.

What happens when a seed becomes a tree? That too is part of the parable. The seed has to die—only then does it become a tree. God has died into this universe; He cannot remain aloof, He is in it, He is lost in it. That is why you cannot find God. You can go to the Himalayas, to Mecca, to Kashi, or anywhere you like but you will not find Him anywhere, because He is here, everywhere!—just as the seed is now in the whole tree. You cannot find the seed because it has died into the tree and become the tree. God has died into this universe, into this existence and has become the cosmos.

He is not a separate thing. He is not like a carpenter who makes something and remains separate. That is not possible, for He is like a seed : the tree grows out of it, but then it disappears into the tree. You can find God again only when this tree disappears.

Hindus have been saying that you can find God either in the beginning of Creation or you can find Him at the end of Creation. In the beginning, when the world is not, the seed *is* there, but you are not there to find Him—because you are part of the tree, you are leaves of the tree. Or, He will be there in *pralaya* when the whole world dissolves, when the tree becomes old and dies. And this happens with every tree : when the tree becomes old, new seeds come again—millions of seeds.

In *pralaya* you will find millions of gods again—but then you will not be there, that is the problem. There is only one way to find God : you can find Him only if you can find Him here and now, on every leaf. If you are looking for a particular image, a Krishna, a Ram, then you will not find Him. They are also leaves—more beautiful, of course, more alive and more green, because they have realized God, realized that He is everywhere.

When Jesus says, "The Kingdom of God is like a mustard seed," he is saying millions of things. That is the beauty of a parable : you say almost nothing and yet you say many things. When the seed dies the universe is there; when the seed dies the tree is there. This is the Kingdom of *God*; here is the Kingdom of *Heaven*. And if you are looking for it somewhere else, you are

looking in vain. If you want to look into the Kingdom of God,
you also have to become like a seed and die : and suddenly the
tree is there—you are no more and God is there. *You* will never
encounter God. If *you* are there, God is not there because the
seed is there. When you disappear, God is there; so there is no
encounter really.

When YOU are not, God is there—emptiness in your hand,
then God is there. When you are no more, then God is there.
Again a paradox : the seed contains the tree, but the seed can
also kill the tree. If the seed becomes too egoistic, if the seed
thinks, "I am enough," and if the seed becomes afraid of death,
then the very container will become the prison; the very cell that
was protecting the tree before it reached the right soil will become
the prison—and then the tree will die in the seed.

You are like seeds which have become prisons. A Buddha is
a seed, a Jesus is a seed, which is not a prison : the seed, the
cell has died, and now the tree has sprouted.

"He said to them : It is like a mustard seed—smaller than all
seeds, but when it falls on the tilled earth it produces a large
tree and becomes shelter for all the birds of Heaven."

"...but when it falls on the tilled earth..." Right earth is
needed. Just a dying of the seed won't do, because you can die
on a stone and then there will be no tree, there will be simple
death. You have to find right soil, right earth—and that is the
meaning of discipleship. It is a training, discipleship is a training,
a learning to become a tilled, right earth. The seed is there but
the right earth has to be found. You have the tree within you,
the Master can only give you the right earth. He can till you,
he can throw the weeds out, he can make the soil worthy to
receive. He can make the soil rich with fertilizers—he is a gardener.

You contain all, but still you will need a gardener; otherwise
you will go on throwing the seeds anywhere. They may fall on
a cement road and they will die there, or they will fall on a path
and people will walk over them and they will die. Somebody is
needed when you are dying who can protect you. Look—when
a child is born you need a midwife. Nobody says that without
a midwife it would be good. A midwife is needed because the

moment is very delicate. But greater is the moment when the Truth is born; greater is the moment when God is born in you— greater than all births. The Master is nothing but a midwife.

Otherwise, without a Master many things are possible: a miscarriage may happen and the child may die before it is born. A Master is needed to protect you because the new sprout is very delicate, helpless—anything can happen to it. It is very dangerous. But if you trust—and trust is needed, there is no other way, for if you doubt then you will shrink and the seed will never die —but if you trust, the seed dies. The seed cannot know the tree, that is the problem. The seed wants to be certain that if it dies it will become the tree. But how can you make the seed certain?

This is the absurdity of faith. Faith *is* absurd. You want to be certain that you can become a *sannyasin*, that you can renounce all, you are ready to die; but what is the guarantee that when the seed is no more the tree will be there? Who can give you the guarantee and how can the guarantee be given? Even if the guarantee is given, the seed to whom it is given will not be there. And what guarantee can prove to the seed that when it is not there the tree will be there? No guarantee is possible.

That is why faith is absurd: believing in that which cannot be believed is the meaning of faith—believing in that which *cannot* be believed; there is no way to believe it and still you believe it. The seed dies in deep trust and the tree is born. But a "tilled earth" is needed, a right ground is needed. The whole of discipleship is just to become a tilled ground.

"...it produces a large tree and becomes shelter for all the birds of Heaven."

And when your tree has really grown, when it has become a 'Buddha-tree', then millions of birds who are in search come and take shelter. Under Jesus many "birds of Heaven" take shelter; under Buddha many "birds of Heaven" take shelter. To those who are in search of the deepest, that tree—the 'Buddha-tree', the 'Jesus-tree'—becomes a shelter and there they can feel the Unknown throbbing. There they can trust, there they can come to an understanding with the Unknown, and there they can take the jump.

"The Kingdom of Heaven is like a mustard seed..." *You* are

the Kingdom of Heaven, *you* are like a mustard seed. Be ready
to die, prepare for your death!

Of course there will be trembling and fear and apprehension.
The jump is going to be difficult. Many times you may come
back, many times you will go to the very brink and turn back
and escape, because there is an abyss. The seed can only know
the abyss, the seed cannot know the tree; there is no way that
the seed can witness the sprouting tree—there is no way. The
seed has to die and believe in the Unknown—that it will happen.

If you are ready to die, it happens. Go and sow seeds in the
ground: when the tree has come, then dig the ground again and
see where the seed is; it will have disappeared, it will not be there.
Go and dig in a Buddha, in a Jesus—you will not find the man,
the seed. This is the meaning of Jesus being the son of God, no
more the son of Joseph the carpenter. Because the seed came
from Joseph the carpenter and Mary, but now the seed has
disappeared, the shell has disappeared—and this tree never came
from the visible, it is from the Invisible.

Look at Jesus : the seed is no longer there, only God is there.
Be ready to die so that you can be reborn. Drop the mind, the
body, the ego, the identity—suddenly you will find that something
new is growing within you : you have become a womb, you are
pregnant. And to be spiritually pregnant is the peak of creation,
because you are creating yourself through it. Nothing is comparable
to it. You may create a great painting or a great sculpture, but
nothing is to be compared with when you create yourself, when
you 'self-create' yourself.

"...but when it falls on the tilled earth..." Be ready to die!
But before you are ready to take the jump, become "the tilled
earth"—become a disciple, become a learner, become humble;
become as if you are not. Soon you really will be not—but get
ready for it, behave as if you are not.

Then, "...it produces a large tree and becomes shelter for all
the birds of Heaven."

It has always been happening so : you are here near me; my
seed is dead—*that* is why you are here. It is not because of *you*
that you are here, it is because of *me* that you are here. But to
say "because of me" is not correct because there is *no* 'me'; the

seed has disappeared and now it is just a tree. And if you get a glimpse of your own possibility through me, the work is done.

"The Kingdom of Heaven is like a mustard seed..." You are the seeds, you are the possibility of that Kingdom. Get ready to die, because that is the only way to be reborn.

Second   Discourse

22nd August 1974, Poona, India

THE SECOND SAYING

Jesus said:
Men possibly think that I have come
to throw peace upon the world,
and they do not know that I have come
to throw divisions upon the earth—
fire, sword, war.

For there shall be five in a house:
three shall be against two
and two against three;
the father against the son
and the son against the father;
and they will stand as solitaries.

Jesus said:
I will give you what the eye has not seen,
and what the ear has not heard,
and what the hand has not touched,
and what has not arisen in the heart of man.

Jesus is very paradoxical but meaningfully so. To take in the meaning many things have to be understood. First, peace is possible if everybody is almost dead. There will be no war, no conflict, but there will be no life either. That would be the silence of the graveyard. But that is of no value, then even war is better because you are alive and vital.

Another type of peace—a totally different dimension of peace—exists when you are vital, alive, but centered inside your being: when self-knowledge has happened; when you have become Enlightened, when the flame is lit and you are not in darkness. Then there will be more life, more silence, but the silence will belong to life not to death. It will not be the silence of the graveyard.

This is the paradox to be understood: war is bad, hate is bad; they are the evils on the earth, they must go; disease is bad, health is good, disease must go but you must remember that a dead man never falls ill; a dead body can deteriorate but cannot be ill. So if you don't understand, all your efforts may create a dead world. There will be no disease, no war, no hatred—but no life either.

Jesus would not like that type of peace. That type of peace is useless—then this world, with war, would be better. But many have been endeavouring to bring about peace and their attitude is just negative. They think, "If war stops, everything will be okay." It is not so easy. And this is not only ordinary man's conception—even very great philosophers, like Bertrand Russell, think that if war is finished everything will be okay. This is negative.

Because war is not the problem, the problem is man. And the war is not outside, the war is within. And if you have not fought the war within you will fight it without. If you have fought the war within and have become victorious, then the war without will cease. That is the only way.

In India, we have called Mahavir 'The Conqueror', 'The Great Conqueror', the 'Jain'. The word 'Jain' means the conqueror. But he never fought with anybody so whom has he conquered? He never believed in violence, never believed in war, never believed in fighting. Why do you call this man Mahavir, The Great Conqueror? This is not his original name; his original name was Vardhaman. What has happened? What phenomenon has occurred? This man has conquered himself, and once you conquer yourself your fight with others ceases immediately—because this fight with others is just a trick to avoid the inner war.

If you are not at ease with yourself, then there are only two ways: either you suffer this unease or project it on somebody else. When you are inwardly tense you are ready to fight. Any excuse will do—the excuse is irrelevant. You will jump on anybody: the servant, the wife, the child.

How do you throw your inner conflict and unease? You make the other responsible. Then you pass through a catharsis: you can become angry now, you can throw your anger and violence and this will give you a release, a relief. Temporarily of course, because the inside has not changed. It will again accumulate, it remains the old. Tomorrow again it will accumulate—anger, hatred—and you will have to project it.

You fight with others because you go on accumulating rubbish inside yourself and you have to throw it out. A person who has conquered himself, who has become a self-conqueror, has no inner conflict, the war has ceased. He is one inside—there are not two. Such a man will never project, such a man will not fight with anybody else.

So, this is a trick of the mind to avoid the inner conflict, because the inner conflict is more painful—for many reasons. The basic reason is that every one of you has an image of yourself as being a good man. And life is such that without this image it will be almost impossible to live.

Psychiatrists say that illusions are needed to live. Unless you
have become Enlightened, illusions *are* needed to live. If you think
you are so bad, so devilish, so evil; if this image—which is the
truth, you are—gets inside, then you will not be able to live at all.
You will lose all self-confidence and you will be filled with such
condemnation towards yourself, that you will not be able to love;
you will not be really able to move, you will not be able to look
at another human being. You will feel so inferior, so bad, so
devilish, that you will die. This feeling will become a suicide, and
this is a truth—so what to do?

One way is to change this truth: become a man of God, not a
man of the Devil—become Divine! But that is difficult, arduous,
a long hard path. Much has to be done, only then can the Devil
become Divine. It *can* become Divine! You may not be aware
that the root of the word 'devil' is the same root from which the
word 'divine' comes: both 'devil' and 'divine' come from the same
Sanskrit root *'deva'*. The Devil can become Divine, because the
Divine has become the Devil. The possibility is there, they are two
poles of one energy. The energy which has gone sour, bitter, can
become sweet. An inner transformation is needed, an inner alchemy
is needed—but that is long and arduous.

And the mind always looks for the shortcut where the least
resistance is. So mind says, "Why bother about becoming a good
man? Just believe that you are good." This is easy because nothing
is to be done. Just *think* that you are good, just create an image
that you are beautiful, heavenly, that nobody is like you, and even
this illusion of goodness gives you energy to live.

If illusions can give you so much energy, you can conceive how
much will happen when the Truth is realized. Even the illusion
that you are good gives you life to move, gives you legs to stand
on, gives you confidence. You become almost centered even
with the illusion, and this center that happens in illusion is
the ego.

When you are really centered, *that* is the Self. But that happens
only when the Truth is realized: when your inner energies have
been transformed, the lower has been transformed into the higher,
the earthly into the heavenly; when the Devil has become Divine,
when you have become radiant with the glory that is yours; when

the seed has come to sprout, when the mustard seed has become a great tree.

But that is a long process, one needs the courage to wait, one needs not to be tempted by the shortcut. And in life there are no shortcuts—only illusions are shortcuts. Life is arduous because only through arduous struggle does growth come to you—it never comes easily.

You cannot get it cheaply; anything that is cheap cannot help you to grow. Suffering helps—the very effort, the very struggle, the long path, gives you sharpness, growth, experience, maturity. How can you achieve maturity through a shortcut? There is a possibility—now they are working with animals, and sooner or later they will work with human beings—there is a possibility: you can be injected with hormones. A child of ten can be injected with hormones and he will become a young man of twenty.

But do you think he will attain the maturity that he should have attained if he had passed through ten years of life? The struggle, the arising sex, the need to control, the need to love; to be free and yet controlled, to be free and yet centered; to move with the other, to suffer in love, to learn—all that will not be there. This man who looks twenty is really ten years of age. Through hormones you have only blown up his body.

But they are doing this with animals, with fruits, with trees. A tree can be injected, and a tree that would naturally come to flower in three years, will flower in one year. But those flowers will lack something; it is difficult to see because you are not flowers, but they will lack something. They have been forced, they have not passed through a seasoning. Fruits will come sooner but those fruits will not be so mature; they will lack something, they will be artificial.

Nature is not in a hurry. Remember: mind is always in a hurry, nature is never in a hurry—nature waits and waits, it is eternal. There is no *need* to be in a hurry; life goes on and on and on, it is an eternity. But for mind time is short, so mind says, "Time is money." Life never says that. Life says, "Experience!" not time. Life waits, can wait; mind cannot wait—death is coming near. There is no death for life, but for mind there is death.

Mind always tries to find a shortcut. And to find a shortcut the easiest way is to create an illusion: think that you are what you want to be—then you have become neurotic. That is what has happened to many people who are in madhouses: they *think* they are Napoleon, or Alexander, or somebody else. They believe this and they behave accordingly.

I have heard about one man who was being treated, psycho-analyzed, because he thought that he was Napoleon. After three or four years of treatment and psycho-analysis, the psychiatrist thought, "Now he is absolutely okay." So he said, "Now you are okay and you can go home."

The man said, "Home? Say, 'To my palace!' " He was still Napoleon. It is so difficult if you have become Napoleon; to be treated is very difficult because what is going to happen, even if you are treated and you become well, is that you are going to lose.

One General found a Captain who was always drunk, so he caught hold of him. The man was very good—drunkards are almost always good, they are beautiful people, just taking a short-cut. So the General said, "You are a good man and I appreciate you, and everybody loves you, but you are wasting yourself. If you can remain sober, soon you will become a colonel."

The man laughed and he said, "That's not worth it, because while I am drunk I am the General already. So that's not worth it: if I remain sober I am only going to become a colonel, and while I am drunk I am always the General!" There is too much involved in the illusion. How can this man let go of his illusion? So cheaply has he become the General!

Mind finds shortcuts and illusions are the shortcuts; *maya* is the easiest and the cheapest thing to achieve. Reality is hard, arduous: one has to suffer and pass through fires. The more you pass through fires, the more seasoned you become; the more seasoned, the more valuable. Your divinity cannot be purchased cheaply in a market, you cannot bargain for it; you have to pay with your whole life. When your whole life is at stake—only then does it happen.

You fight with others because this is an easy way. You think you are good, the other is bad, and the fight is outward. If you look at yourself then the fight becomes inward: you know you are bad, it is difficult to find a more devilish man than you. If you look within then you find you are absolutely bad, and something has to be done. An inner fight, an inner war starts.

And through that inner conflict—and it is a technique, remember, it is one of the greatest techniques that has been used through the centuries—if there is inner conflict then you become integrated. If there is inner conflict, then beyond the conflicting parties a new center of witnessing arises. If there is inner conflict then energies are involved, your total being is in turmoil: chaos is created and out of that chaos a new being is born.

Any new birth needs chaos; this whole universe is born out of chaos. Before you are really born chaos will be needed—that is the war of Jesus. He says: "I have come not to give you peace"— not that he has not come to give you peace, but not the cheap peace that you would like to be given.

Now try to understand his words:

"Jesus said: Men possibly think that I have come to throw peace upon the world, and they do not know that I have come to throw divisions upon the earth—fire, sword, war."

When you come to a Master like Jesus you come for peace. You are blissfully unaware that you have come to the wrong person. As you are you cannot get peace. And if somebody gives you peace, that will be death to you. As you are, if you become peaceful, what will that mean? That will mean the struggle has ceased before you have attained anything. As you are, if somebody makes you silent, what will that mean? You won't have achieved any Self, and you will be consoled by your situation.

This is the way you can know a false master from a true Master: a false master is a consolation, he gives you peace as you are, he never bothers to change you—he is a tranquillizer. He is just like sleeping-pills: you come to him and he consoles. But if you come to a true Master this is the criterion: whatsoever peace you have that too will be destroyed, whatsoever 'at-easeness' you have is going to the dogs.

A true Master will create more turmoil, more conflict. He is not going to console you because he is not your enemy. All consolations are poisons. He will help you to grow. Growth is difficult, you will have to pass through many difficulties. Many times you will want to escape from this man, but you cannot because he will haunt you.

Consolation is not the goal. He cannot give you a false peace. He will give you growth, and out of that growth some day you will flower. And that flowering will be the true peace, the true silence. Consolation is false. People come to me and I can see the way they come, the problems they bring: they want consolation. Somebody comes and he says, "I am in much difficulty, my mind is not at peace, I am very tense. Give me something, bless me so that I become peaceful." But what will that mean? If this man can be made at peace, what will that mean? Then this man is never going to change. No, that is not the way.

Even if a real Master consoles you, that consolation is just like a fishing net. You will be caught in the consolation and then, by and by, he will create the chaos. You have to pass through the chaos because as you are, you are absolutely wrong. In this state if somebody consoles you he is your enemy. With him you will lose time, life, energy, and in the end consolations won't help. When death comes all consolations will evaporate.

There was one old man whose son died. He came to me and he said, "Console me!"

I said, "I cannot do that; that is sin."

He said, "I have come for that."

I told him, "You may have come for that, but I cannot do it."

He said, "But I went to this *Shankaracharya* and he consoled me and he said, 'Don't bother, don't be worried; your son is reborn in a high Heaven!' "

I knew his son also, and that is impossible because he was a politician—they all go to Hell, they never go to Heaven. And not only was he a politician, but a successful politician—he was a Minister of State. With all the cunning of a politician, with all the ambition of a politician, how can he go to Heaven?

And this old man was also a politician. Basically he was not disturbed because his son was dead. The basic thing was that his ambition was dead, because through that son he was achieving more and more and more and more. He himself had become old, he had worked continuously his whole life but he was a little foolish, not very cunning, a little naive. He worked hard, he sacrificed his whole life, but he could not attain any post. And that was the deep hurt, it was a wound. And then through the son he had been trying, and the son had been achieving. Now that his son was dead his whole ambition was dead.

When I told him, "This is the reason why you are suffering so much; it is not your son," he was very much disturbed.

He said, "I had come for consolation and you are disturbing me more. It may be," he said, "whatsoever you say sounds true. It may be that my ambition has been hurt and it is not for the son that I am weeping—it may be for the ambition. But don't say such hard things to me, I am in such pain right now. My son is dead and you are saying such hard things to me. And I went to this *Mahatma,* and to that *Shankaracharya,* and to this *Guru,* and they all consoled me. They said, 'Don't worry, the soul is eternal, nobody ever dies. And your son—he was no ordinary soul, he has reached a high Heaven!' "

These are consolations, and if this old man goes on listening to these consolations he is missing a great opportunity. He is missing an opportunity in which he could face his ambition, which is his problem. He could have encountered the fact that all ambition is useless, futile, because you work and work and work, and then death takes everything. He could have penetrated to this. But no, he stopped coming to me. He used to come to me, but since that time he has never come. He went to others who would console him.

Are *you* here to be consoled? Then you are in the wrong place. That is what Jesus says.

He says: "Men possibly think that I have come to throw peace upon the world, and they do not know that I have come to throw divisions upon the earth—fire, sword, war."

Whenever a man like Jesus comes, the world is immediately divided between those who are for him and those who are against him. You cannot find a single person who is indifferent to Jesus. Whenever a type, a Jesus-type is there, immediately the world is divided. Some are for him and some are against him, but nobody is indifferent. It is impossible to be indifferent to Jesus. If you hear the word, if you look at the Jesus, immediately you are divided: either you become a lover or you become a hater; either you fall in line or you go against; either you follow him or you start working against him.

Why does this happen? Because a man like Jesus is such a great phenomenon and he is not of this world. He brings to this world something from the Beyond. Those who are afraid of the Beyond immediately become the enemies—that is their way of protecting themselves. For those who have a desire, a seed hidden somewhere, who have been searching and searching and longing for the Beyond, this man becomes charismatic, this man becomes a magnetic force—they fall in his love. For this man they have been waiting for many lives.

Immediately the world is divided: either you are for Christ or you are against him. There is no other alternative, you cannot be indifferent. You cannot say, "I'm not bothered," that is impossible, because a person who can remain in the middle will become a Jesus himself. A person who can stand in the middle, in neither love nor hate, will go beyond the mind himself. You cannot stand in the middle; you will fall, you will become a 'rightist' or a 'leftist', you will be on this side or on that. He creates great turmoil.

Not only in individuals but in society too, everything on the earth comes to be in a conflict, a great war starts. Since Jesus there has never been peace in the world. Jesus created a religion. He brought something into the world which created such a division, such a conflict in all minds, that he became the focus of all history. That is why we say 'before Christ', 'after Christ'; he became the focal point.

History is divided, time is divided with Jesus. He stands on the boundary. Before Jesus it is as if time was of a different quality; after Jesus time became of a different quality: with Jesus starts history. His attitude, his approach towards the human mind is very much different from that of a Buddha or a Lao Tzu. The ultimate goal is one, the ultimate flowering is going to be one, but Jesus' approach is absolutely different. He is unique.

What is he saying? He is saying that through conflict growth is achieved; through struggle centering happens; through war peace flowers. But don't take him literally—whatsoever he is saying is a parable. Christianity took it literally and missed the point. Then

Christians took the sword in their hands, and they have killed millions unnecessarily because that was not the meaning of Jesus. Then the Church, Jesus' Church, became a warring Church, it became a crusade.

Christians have been fighting Mohammedans, Hindus, Buddhists —they have been fighting everywhere. But they missed the point. Jesus was talking of something else. He was not talking of the swords of this world, he brought a sword of a different world. What is this sword? It is a symbol. You have to be cut into two because in you two things meet: this world—the earth—and Heaven, they meet in you. One part of you belongs to the mud, to the dirt; one part of you belongs to the Divine. You are a meeting-point and Jesus brought a sword to cut you asunder, so the earth falls to the earth and the divine enters into the Divine.

You cannot make any distinction as to what belongs to the earth. When you are hungry, you think *you* are hungry? Jesus says: "No, take my sword and cut it!" Hunger belongs to the body because it is bodily need. Consciousness has no hunger; it becomes aware because the body has no consciousness.

You may have heard one old *Panchtantra* story: It happened that a big forest accidently caught fire. Two men were there, one was blind and one was lame. The lame one couldn't walk, couldn't run, but he could see; and the blind one could walk and run, but he could not see. So they made a compact: the blind man took the lame man on his shoulders and as the lame man could see and the blind man could walk, they became one man. They came out of the forest—they saved their lives.

This is not just a story—this is what has happened in you. One part of you feels hunger, but cannot know it because it has no eyes to see. Your body feels hunger, your body feels sexual desire, your body feels thirst, your body needs comfort: all the needs are of the body. And your consciousness only sees, your Self is only a witness. But they have made a compact because without the body the consciousness cannot walk, cannot move, cannot do anything; and without the consciousness the body cannot realize what is needed, whether the body is hungry or thirsty.

Jesus' 'sword' means this compromise has to be realized knowingly, and then a distinction has to be made: what belongs to the earth belongs to the earth; fulfill it but don't become obsessed. If you are hungry, the body is hungry; know it well, fulfill the hunger but don't become obsessed. There are many people who become obsessed, who go on eating and eating and eating and then some day they become so frustrated with eating, that they go on fasting and fasting and fasting. But both are obsessions: too much eating is as bad as too much fasting.

A right balance is needed, but who will give the balance? You have to become two, you have to be completely aware that: "This is of the earth and I am not of the earth." This is the 'sword' of Jesus.

He says: "I have come to throw divisions upon the earth—fire, sword, war."

Why 'fire'? Fire is a very old kabalistic symbol, and also a very old Hindu symbol. Hindus have always talked about inner fire. They call that inner fire *tap* because it is heat. And to kindle that inner fire so that your fire is burning inside, they call *yagna*.

And there are techniques for burning that inner fire. Right now it is almost dead, covered with ashes. It has to be poked, discovered, rekindled; more fuel is needed and the fuel has to be given. When the inner fire burns in its totality, suddenly you are transformed—because there is no transformation without fire. You heat water and at particular degree, a hundred degrees, the water evaporates, becomes vapour; the whole quality changes.

Have you observed that when water changes into vapour, the whole quality changes? When it is water, it always flows downwards —that is the nature of water, to flow downwards. It cannot flow upwards, it is impossible. But when at a hundred degree heat it evaporates, its whole nature changes: the vapour floats upwards, never downwards. The whole dimension changes and it happens through heat. If you go to a chemist's lab what will you find? If you take fire out nothing will happen there, because every transformation, every new change, every mutation is through fire. And what are *you* except fire? What are you doing when you are living? When you breathe, what do you breathe? You breathe oxygen.

Oxygen is nothing but fuel to fire. When you run, more fire is needed so you breathe more deeply; when you rest, less fire is

needed so you breathe less deeply, because less oxygen is needed
—oxygen is fuel to the fire. Fire cannot exist without oxygen
because oxygen burns. You are fire—moment to moment, through
food, through air, through water, fire is created in you. When it
is too much you have to release it. When animals have the sexual
urge we say they are 'on heat'. It is meaningful because it *is* a
sort of heat. It is a sort of heat, and when you have more fire
than you can absorb, it has to be released and sex is an outlet.

Remember, in hot countries people are more sexual than in
cold countries. The first books on sexology appeared in hot
countries: Vatsayana's *Kamasutra*, Koka Pandit's *Kokashastra*,
they appeared first. The first Freudians were in the East and they
appeared before Freud, three thousand years before Freud. In the
West sex has just become important. In a cold country there is
not enough fire in the body to create much sexuality. Only within
the last three or four centuries has sex become very important
in the West, because now the country may be cold, but central-
heating is there. So people are not so cold; otherwise the fire
of the body continuously fights with the cold. That is why in the
East the population goes on growing and it is difficult to prevent it, but the West does not have so much of a population
explosion.

I heard it happened that when the first Russian astronauts
landed on the moon, they were very happy. But they were surprised
when they saw three Chinamen coming, walking there. So they
looked at them and they said: "You have reached before us? And
you don't have any means, any technology, any science! How did
you do it? It's a miracle. How did you reach here?"

Those Chinamen said: "Nothing like a miracle! A simple thing
—mathematics: we stood on each other's shoulders and reached!"
The Chinese can reach, the Indians can reach, there is no problem.
Once they decide they can reach anywhere!

Sex is a heat phenomenon, a fire phenomenon. Whenever the fire
is burning you will feel more sexual, and whenever the fire is not
burning so much you will feel less sexual. Because everything that
happens in you, whether it is a sexual transformation in the body,
or a spiritual transformation, it depends on fire.

Jesus was trained in a Essene community—in a very occult,

esoteric society he was trained, which, like Hindus, Kabalists, Jews and Sufis, knew many methods to create inner fire. So fire is not just the fire you know, it is the innermost fire upon which life exists.

If this fire can be raised to a particular level—then the transformation! But it is only possible to bring it to a particular degree if it is not released, and that is why all the religions which use this fire are against sex. If it is released through sex then it cannot be brought to a particular degree, because then you have an outlet.

Thus all the outlets have to be closed completely so there is no leakage of the fire and it reaches the one hundred degree point: a certain degree at which, suddenly, the transformation happens; the soul is separate and the body is separate—the sword has worked! Then you know what in you is earth and what in you is Heaven; then you know what has come from your father and mother, and what has come from the Invisible.

"...fire, sword, war..." A deep inner conflict is needed. You should not be lethargic, you should not relax unless the relaxation happens—and that is totally different. You have to fight and create conflict and *friction*. Friction is the right word for the inner war. Gurdjieff worked through friction, creating friction in the body. You may not be aware now but remember it: some day you will become aware that your body has many layers of energies. If you are not in friction then you use only the superficial layer. If much conflict arises, the superficial layer is finished and then the second layer starts functioning.

Try it this way: you always go to sleep at ten at night. At ten suddenly you feel sleepiness coming over you— don't go to sleep. Sufis have used this method—vigil—very much, and Jesus also used it: for a whole night he would not sleep; in the wilderness for forty days and forty nights he would not sleep; he remained on the hills alone without sleeping. What happens? If you don't sleep at ten, for a few minutes you will feel very, very lethargic, sleepier and sleepier and sleepier. But if you resist and fight, a friction is created, you become two: the one who wants to sleep and the one who doesn't want to sleep. Now there are two parts fighting. If you stick and don't yield, suddenly you will find all sleepiness has gone and you have become as fresh as you have never been in the morning. Suddenly all sleepiness has gone, you are fresh, and even if you want to go to sleep it will be difficult now. What happened? There were only two possibilities, and through the friction between them energy was created.

Energy is always created through friction. All science depends on creating friction which then creates energy. All dynamos are just friction techniques to create a fight, a war between two things. You create a war when your body wants to go to sleep and you don't want to go to sleep; friction is there, much energy is created.

If you yield that will be very bad, because if you yield, the body has won a fight and the consciousness has lost. So if you try, only try with a mind determined not to yield—otherwise it is better not to try. Friction methods are dangerous: if you try then you *have* to win. If you don't win you are lost, because then you lose your confidence. Your consciousness will become weaker and the body will become stronger. And if you lose many times, then there is less and less possibility of winning.

Once you use any friction method then make it a point to win. It is not to be lost, the battle must be won. And once you win you achieve a different layer of energy. Now you can see that if you win, the energy that was in the other part is absorbed by you so you become stronger. And then every fight will make you stronger, still stronger, until a moment comes when the whole energy of the body is absorbed by the Self.

Gurdjieff used friction very deeply and in such unbelievably dangerous ways. When he was very old, just within a few years of his death, he made a very dangerous motor-car accident happen. He did it—it was not really an accident. In the life of a person like Gurdjieff there is no accident. He is so aware that accidents are not possible. But he can allow an accident or he can even create one—and he did create one.

He was a fast driver and in his whole life there had never been a single accident. He was also a very dangerous driver; all those who sat with him would always be on edge, every moment. He was absolutely mad, didn't believe in any traffic rules or anything. He would go this way and that as fast as possible, and anything was possible at any moment—but it never happened.

One morning, when he went to Paris from his ashram in Fontainebleau, somebody asked, "When will you be back?"

He said, "If everything happens as I think it will happen, by the evening; otherwise, difficult to say." And in the evening when he was coming back there was an accident. And the accident was so severe and dangerous that the doctors said that nobody could have survived. Impossible! The whole car was crashed to bits.

But Gurdjieff was found. He had sixty fractures all over his body—almost dead. But he was found perfectly aware lying under a tree very far away from the car. He had walked to the shade and was lying there perfectly aware. He was not unconscious. He was taken to hospital perfectly conscious. He said that no anaesthesia should be given to him—he wanted to remain perfectly conscious. This was the greatest friction he ever created with his body: the body was just on the verge of death, he had created the whole situation and he wanted to remain absolutely alert.

He remained alert, and at this moment he attained the greatest centering that can happen to a man: he became centered in his consciousness—the earthly layer was completely separated. It became a vehicle: he could use it, but he was not identified with it.

This is the meaning of Jesus when he says: "I have brought fire, sword, war—although men possibly think that I have come to throw peace upon the world...

"For there shall be five in a house: three shall be against two and two against three; the father against the son and the son against the father; and they will stand as solitaries."

"For there shall be five in a house..." This is a parable: in your body there are "five in the house"—the five senses, the five *indriyas*. Really, deep down you have five bodies because each sense has its own center. And each sense goes on manipulating you in its own direction: the eye says, "Look at the beauty;" the hand says, "Touch, it is so lovable." The eye is not at all interested in touch; the hand is not at all interested in looking at a beautiful person, a beautiful body or a beautiful tree.

All the five senses exist as five separate centers and your mind is just a co-ordinator, which goes on co-ordinating between these five. When you look at me and you hear me, you hear from the ears and you look from the eyes—eyes never hear, ears never look; then how do you conclude that you hear the same person you see? How can you conclude? The mind goes on co-ordinating, it is a computer: whatsoever the eyes feed in, whatsoever the ears feed in, it combines and gives you the conclusion.

Gurdjieff used the method of friction, so did Jesus—and those who know the innermost secret of Jesus' life say that he was not crucified, but that he *managed* to be crucified just like Gurdjieff. He managed to be crucified—it was a drama that he arranged.

Those who crucified him thought they were killing him, but such a man as Jesus cannot be forced to die. He could have escaped very easily, for it was well known that he was to be caught. He could have moved away from the capital or away from the country, there was no problem—but he came to the capital. It is said that he enacted the whole thing, and that Judas was not his enemy but his friend who helped, who helped Jesus to be caught. The whole thing was managed and controlled by him.

What happened on the cross was the last inner war, the last and greatest friction: when he was dying, but not losing trust in the Divine; when the earth was falling back to the earth; when the division was absolute, total—he was not identified at all. He allowed it.

Gurdjieff used to say that this crucifixion of Jesus was a drama, and that really, the author of the drama was neither Pontius Pilate nor the high priest of the Jews, but Jesus himself. He managed it and he managed it so beautifully that even up to now it has not been discovered, not exactly discovered, what happened and how.

You cannot imagine managing your own crucifixion, but that is what religion is: managing your own crucifixion. Going to the cross means going to the climax of friction—where death is.

Jesus says, "For there shall be five in a house: three shall be against two and two against three..." A friction has to be created. The senses have to fight and the fight has to be made conscious. They continuously fight but the fight is not conscious; you are fast asleep and the fight goes on. The eye is continuously fighting the ear, the ear is continuously fighting the eye—because they are competitors.

Have you observed that a blind man has more listening capacity than a man who has eyes? That is why blind men become beautiful musicians and singers. Why does this happen? They have more capacity for sound, rhythm, more sensitivity in their ears. Why? Because the eye is no longer a competitor, the energy that was being used by the eyes is available for the ears—they are the competitors.

Your eyes are using eighty percent of your energy, leaving only twenty percent for the other four senses which are starved; they are continuously fighting. The eyes have become the supreme, the dictatorial force. You live through the eyes and some senses have gone completely dead: many people have no smell, that sense has gone completely dead; they never bother—they are not even aware that they cannot smell. The eye has completely exploited the nose, because it is so near that it can be exploited. Children have a sense of smell, but by and by it is lost because the eyes go on using more and more energy. The eye has become the center of your being, which is not good.

Methods of friction use the senses against each other. There have been methods and schools where seekers completely cut one sense against the other; a fight is created. In many methods the seeker remains with closed eyes for many months. The energy starts moving, you can feel it. If you remain completely with closed eyes for three months, you will be able to feel the energy moving continuously towards the ears, towards the nose—your smell may come back, you may start smelling! If you close the ears for three months and just see, don't listen, then you will see there is a constant movement of energy.

And if you can see your senses fighting, you will become separate because you become a witness. You are no more the eyes, no more the ears, no more the hands, no more the body— you are a witness. The fight goes on within the body and you are an onlooker. This is the meaning, the deepest meaning of the parable, but it is also true in another sense.

"For there shall be five in a house : three shall be against two and two against three; the father against the son and the son against the father; and they will stand as solitaries."

In another sense too this is true, that in a family of five, three will be against two and two will be against three; for whenever a religious person happens in a family, friction starts, because for a family a religious person is the most dangerous person. The family can tolerate anything—except religion, because once you become religious you will not be identified with the body.

The family is related to the body: your father is your father because of your body. If you think you are the body, then you are related to your father. But if you come to know that you are not the body, who is your father? How are you related to him? Your mother has given birth to your body, not to you. You are so identified with the body that you think your mother has given birth to you. When you are not identified with it, when the identification is broken, who is your mother? She has not given birth to you, but only to this body which is going to die. So your mother has not given you life—rather, on the contrary, your mother has given you one more death. Your father has not given you life, he has given you one more possibility to die. Once you are not identified with the body you have broken from the family, you are uprooted.

So the family can tolerate it if you go to a prostitute. It is okay, nothing is wrong; rather, on the contrary, you are getting more and more identified with the body. If you become an alcoholic, if you are a drunkard, it is okay, because you are getting more and more identified with the body. Nothing is wrong in this, but if you become a meditator, if you become a *sannyasin*, then it is not okay. Then it is difficult because you are being uprooted. Then the family no longer has power over you; then you are no longer part of the family, because you are no longer part of this world.

So Jesus says: "Father will be against son, son will be against father. And I have come to disrupt, to divide, to create conflict and friction."

This is true. You can worship a Buddha, but ask Buddha's father—he is against him; ask Buddha's relatives, they are against him—because this man has gone beyond their control. Not only that: he is also helping others to go beyond the control of the society, of the family.

The family is the basic unit of society. When you go beyond society you have to go beyond the family, but this does not mean that you should hate it—that is not the point; nor that you should go against it—that is not the point either. That is going to happen anyway : once you start to find yourself, all that has been before will be disrupted, there is going to be chaos. So what should you do? They will pull you back, they will try to bring you back, they will make every effort to do so. What should be done?

There are two ways: one is the old way which is to escape from them, not to give them any opportunity—but I think that is no longer applicable. The other is to be with them, but as an actor: don't give them the opportunity to know that you are moving beyond them. Move! Let that be your inner journey, but outwardly fulfill all formalities: touch the feet of your father and your mother and be a good actor.

The old way cannot be followed by many. That's why the earth could not become religious—because how many people can go out of society? And even if they go out of society, the society has to take care of them. When Buddha was here, or Mahavir, or Jesus, then thousands left their families. But still only thousands —millions were left behind and they had to take care of them. The whole earth cannot become religious if that is the only way, and it is not good either. It can be done in a more beautiful way, and that beautiful way is to be a good actor.

A *sannyasin* must be a good actor. By being a good actor I mean that you are not related at all, but you go on fulfilling the formalities. Deep down you are uprooted, but you don't even give a hint that you are uprooted. And what is the use of giving a hint? Because then they will start trying to change you. Don't give them any chance; let this be an inner journey and outwardly be completely formal. They will be happy then because they live in formalities. They live on the outside, they don't need your inner worship, they don't need your inner love—just the show is enough.

These are the two ways: one is that of Buddha and Jesus, the other is that of Janak and me. Be wherever you are. Don't create any outward show that you are changing and becoming religious, because that can create trouble and you may not be strong enough right now. Create the conflict inside but don't create it outside. The inner conflict is more than enough; it will give you the growth, the maturity needed.

"...the father against the son and the son against the father; and they will stand as solitaries."

This word 'solitary' has to be understood deeply. When you become religious you become solitary; then there is no society for you, you are alone. And to accept that you are alone is the greatest transformation that can happen to you, because mind is afraid of being alone, mind wants somebody else to hang on to, to cling to.

Alone you feel a trembling, a fear grips you; alone, immediately you rush towards society—to the club, the conference, the sect, the church; somewhere where there is a crowd, where you can feel that you are not alone, where you can lose yourself in the crowd. That is why the crowd has become so important: go to the racecourse, go to the cinema hall—but a crowd is needed in which you are no longer solitary, where you can relax.

A religious man, however, is a solitary because he is trying to reach his highest peak. He is not to lose himself in others. He has to remember, become more mindful, he has to become more aware and alert—and he has to accept the truth. This is the truth: that everybody *is* alone and there is no possibility of any togetherness. Your consciousness is a solitary peak, but that is the beauty of it and you are unnecessarily afraid of it. Imagine Everest in a crowd of Everests—then the whole beauty is lost. Everest is beautiful and challenging because it is alone, a solitary peak. A religious man is like Everest: he becomes a solitary peak, alone, and he lives and enjoys it.

That does not mean that he will not move in society, it does not mean he will not love. On the contrary, only he can love. On the contrary, only he can move in society because only he *is*. You are *not*—so how can you love? He can love but his love is not going to be like a drug, he is not going to be lost. He can share, he can give himself completely and still remain himself. He can give himself to you and still not be lost, because his mindfulness remains the innermost peak. There, in that shrine, he remains alone. Nobody enters there, nobody *can* enter there.

In the innermost core of your being you are alone—the purity of aloneness and the beauty of aloneness....

But on the contrary, you feel afraid. Because you have lived

in society—you are born in society, you have been brought up
by the society—you have completely forgotten that you can also
be alone. So to move for a few days into loneliness, just to feel
your loneliness, is beautiful. Then come to the market-place, but
bring your loneliness with you. Don't get lost there. Remain
aware and alert. Move into society, go into a crowd, but remain
alone. You can be alone in the crowd if you want; you can be
in the crowd even while you are alone if you want : you can go
to the Himalayas and sit there and think of the market—you are
in the crowd.

It happened that Junnaid came alone to his Master, who was
sitting in a temple. When Junnaid entered the Master was alone
and he said, "Junnaid, come alone! Don't bring the crowd with
you!" So Junnaid looked back, of course, because he thought
there was somebody else coming with him. But there was no one.
The Master laughed and said, "Don't look back, but look within."
And Junnaid closed his eyes and found that the Master was right.
He had left his wife but his mind was clinging to her; he had left
his children but their images were still there; and the friends who
had come to give him the last send-off, they were still standing
in his mind.

The Master said, "Go out and come alone, because how can I
talk with this crowd?" So Junnaid had to wait for one year
outside the temple to be freed of "this crowd". And after one year
the Master called, "Now Junnaid, you are ready, come in. Now
you are alone and a dialogue is possible."

You can carry the crowd; you can also be in the crowd and
yet alone. Try it : the next time you are moving in a big crowd
in the market, just feel alone—and you *are* alone so there is no
problem, you can feel it. And once you can feel that you are
alone, you have become a solitary. And Jesus says he has come
to make you solitaries, to stand alone.

*"I will give you what the eye has not seen, and what the ear
has not heard, and what the hand has not touched, and what has
not arisen in the heart of man."*

Your eyes can see that which is without, they cannot see within,
there is no way. Your ears can hear that which is without, they

cannot hear within, there is no way. They are outgoing, all senses are outgoing. There is not a single sense that is ingoing. So when all the senses stop functioning, suddenly you are in. There is no sense that goes in.

Jesus says: "I will give you what the eye has not seen—but first become a solitary." And that is what I mean by a *sannyasin*: a solitary. First become a sannyasin, first realize that you are alone —and be at ease with this aloneness. Don't be afraid. Rather enjoy it, rather see the beauty of it, the silence and the purity and the innocence. No dirt has ever entered there because nobody has entered into that shrine. It has remained eternally pure, it is virgin, nobody has been there.

Your virginity is hidden within you. Become a sannyasin, a solitary and then, Jesus says, "I will give you what the eye has not seen..."

When you become a solitary, totally alone, suddenly you realize that which no eye can see, no ear can hear, and what the hand has not touched. How can you touch your Self? You can touch the body, but that is not your Self. The hand cannot enter in, it cannot touch your consciousness—there is no way.

And the last sentence is the most beautiful uttered by any person on this earth :

"...and what has not arisen in the heart of man."

Because your soul is beyond even your heart. Of course, your heart is very deep within; but still, as far as your soul is concerned, it is also without, it is not within. The hands are without, the eyes are without, the heart is also without, on the periphery. The innermost core is not even the heart. Hunger arises in your body, love arises in your heart—not prayer.

Prayer is still deeper, deeper than the heart. Hunger is a bodily need; love is a need of the heart; God is a need of the Beyond, not even of the heart. One has to transcend the mind, one has to transcend the heart too. One has to transcend all peripheries so that only the center remains.

And what has not arisen in the heart of man? God has not arisen in the heart of man. In the mind science arises, philosophy arises; in the heart, art, poetry arises—but not religion. Religion

arises at a deeper layer, at the deepest beyond which there is no
go; at your very center, which is not even the heart.

"I will give you...what has not arisen in the heart of man."
That which is beyond and beyond and beyond. You cannot catch
hold of it, you cannot see it, you cannot hear it, you cannot even
feel it. Here Jesus transcends even those mystics who are of
the heart.

There are three types of mystics: first, mystics of the head—
they talk in terms of theology, philosophy, they have proofs for
God. There is no proof at all, or, everything is a proof. But
there is no need for a proof and you cannot prove God anyway
because all the proofs can be disputed and all the proofs can be
proved wrong. Then there are mystics of the heart: they talk of
love, of the beloved, the Divine, of Krishna; they talk in songs,
poetry— they are romantic. Their search is deeper than the head
but still not deep enough.

Jesus says: "I will give you something which has not arisen
even in the heart, something which no theology reaches and no
poetry has any glimpse of; neither logic nor love, where both
stop—I will give you that which has not arisen in the heart of man."

This is the deepest, the most profound possibility—and Jesus
opens it. But in Christianity it is lost. Christianity started to weave
theories around it, it became a head affair—not only a heart affair,
it became a head affair. Christians have produced great theologians.
Look at Thomas Aquinas' *Summa Theologica,* hundreds of
volumes of theology. But they missed because Jesus is not in the
head. And because of these head-oriented theologians, mystics
who were of the heart, who were a little deeper, were expelled
from the Church. Eckhart and Francis were expelled. They were
thought fools, or to have gone mad, or to be heretics—because
they were talking of the heart, they were talking of love.

But Jesus is missed by both theologians and mystics of the
heart, for he is neither head-oriented nor heart-oriented—he is
not oriented at all. He says simply throw all orientations, throw
all that is without and come to the innermost core where only
you are, where only the being throbs, where only Existence is.
You can come to this; and if you come to this, then every mystery

is revealed and all doors are opened. But even at the door you can miss. If you remain head-oriented you remain standing at the door, theorizing, or you may be standing at the door and poetizing —talking in poetry and singing.

I have heard that Mulla Nasrudin went to a psychiatrist and said, "I am very much puzzled, now do something. It has become impossible. Every night I have a recurrent dream that I am standing at a door and I am pushing and pushing and pushing. There is a sign on the door and I push and push to no end. Every night I wake up perspiring and the door never opens."

The psychiatrist started to note whatsoever he was saying. After half an hour's talk he asked, "Now tell me, Nasrudin, what is written on the door, on the sign?"

And Nasrudin said, "It says 'pull'."

If 'pull' is written on the door then don't go on pushing! Otherwise you will have a recurrent dream, you will push eternally! And there is no problem at all, simply look at what is written on the door. Jesus says neither head nor heart is written on the door—it is beyond both.

So do one thing : go beyond. Neither fall a victim of logic, of intellect, nor become a victim of emotions, of sentimentality. The head is in the body and the heart is also in the body—go beyond. What is beyond? There is simple existence, you simply are.

Being is without any attributes. That simple 'beingness' is *dhyan*, that simple 'beingness' is meditation—and *that* is written on the door.

Suddenly the door opens when you are a simple being—not emotion, nor thoughts; no cloud around you, unclouded; no smoke around the flame, just the flame—you have entered.

"...and what has not arisen in the heart of man I will give you."

Third Discourse

23rd August 1974, Poona, India

THE THIRD SAYING

Jesus said:
I took my stand in the midst of the world
and in flesh I appeared to them.

I found them all drunk,
I found none of them athirst.

And my soul was afflicted for the sons of men,
because they are blind in their heart
and they do not see
that empty they have come into the world,
and empty they seek to go out of the world again.

But now they are drunk.
When they have shaken off their wine,
then they will repent.

Jesus said:
If the flesh has come into existence
because of the spirit,
it is a marvel;
but if the spirit has come into existence
because of the body,
it is a marvel of marvels.
But I marvel at how this great wealth
has made its home in this poverty.

Jesus, or Buddha, or anybody who is Awakened, will find you all drunk. The drunkenness is of many types, but the drunkenness is there. You are not alert, you are not awake, you simply think that you are awake and alert—your sleep continues from birth to death.

Gurdjieff used to tell a short story: There was a man who owned thousands of sheep, and he was always in trouble because the sheep would go astray and they would become victims of the wild animals. So he asked a wise man, who suggested that he should keep watchdogs. So he had a hundred dogs to keep watch over the sheep. They would not allow the sheep to go out, and if any sheep tried to go out, they would kill it.

By and by, they became so addicted to killing that they started to murder the sheep—they became dangerous. So again the man came to the wise man and said, "It has become dangerous, the protectors have become murderers."

It always happens—look at your politicians: they are the protectors, the watchdogs, but once they are powerful they start killing.

So the wise man said, "Then there is only one way, I will come." So he came, and he hypnotized all the sheep and told them, "You are awake, alert, completely free. Nobody is your owner."

And then those sheep remained in that hypnotic state, and they would not go anywhere. They would not escape because this was not a prison, and they all believed that they were the owners, masters of their own selves. Even if some sheep was killed by the master, they would think, "This is her fate, not mine. Nobody can kill me. I have an immortal self and I am totally free, so there is no need to escape." Then there was no need for watch-dogs, and the master was at ease because the sheep were hypnotized.

They lived in a semi-sleep, and that is the state in which you are—in which Jesus finds you, in which I find you. But nobody has hypnotized you—this is an autohypnosis : you are both the wise man who hypnotized the sheep, and the sheep who was hypnotized—you have autohypnotized yourself.

There is a certain method of autohypnotizing yourself : if you think a particular thought continuously, you will be hypnotized by it; if you look at a thing continuously, you will be hypnotized by it; if you brood on something continuously, you will be hypnotized by it.

It happened that one French poet went to the United States. He was shown around New York, and the guide brought him to the Empire State Building. The poet looked amazed. He looked again and again, and then said, "It reminds me of sex."

The guide was puzzled. He had heard many types of reactions, but this was something new. Nobody had ever commented, looking at the Empire State Building, that it reminded them of sex. So he asked, "If you don't feel offended, please tell me why it reminds you of sex?"

The Frenchman said, "Everything does!"

If you continuously think of sex, you become hypnotized—then everything is sexual to you. Even if you go into a temple, the temple reminds you of sex. Where you move is not the question, because you carry your mind with you, and your mind goes on creating a world around you. One person is hypnotized through sex, one person is hypnotized through wealth, one person is hypnotized through power—but everybody is hypnotized. And nobody has done this to you—you have been doing this yourself, it is your work.

But you have been doing it so long that you have completely forgotten that you are both the magician and the sheep. Once a man realizes, "I am the magician and I am the sheep", then things start changing, because then the first spark of transformation has entered. Now you can never be the same again, because the hypnosis has started dropping. A breaking point has come—something of awareness has entered you.

You may have different objects of hypnosis—find out which is the main object of your hypnosis, which one attracts you most, which one has become the focal point of your being. And then look at it, at how you got hypnotized by it.

Repetition is the method of hypnosis : looking at anything continuously, or thinking about it continuously. If you go to a hypnotist he will say : "You are falling asleep, falling asleep, falling asleep, falling asleep." And he will go on repeating the same thing in a monotonous voice, and soon you will be fast asleep. And he was not doing anything but simply repeating something. Hearing it again and again and again, you will fall asleep—you have hypnotized yourself.

Remember this, because you are doing this continuously, and this is being done by society continuously. The whole mechanism of propaganda consists of repetitions. Politicians go on repeating certain things. They go on repeating them, and they don't bother whether you listen or not. Listening is not the point, because if they just go on repeating, by and by, you are convinced, persuaded; not logically, not rationally—they never argue with you—but just through repetition you are hypnotized.

Hitler went on repeating : "The Jews are the reason for the misery and fall of Germany. Once the Jews are destroyed, there will be no problem. You are the owners of the whole world, you are a special race; you have come here to dominate—you are the Master Race." Even his friends never believed it in the beginning, and he himself never believed it in the beginning, because this was such a patent lie.

But as he continued, by and by people started believing in it—they were hypnotized. And when other people were hypnotized by it, he too was hypnotized into thinking that there must be some truth in it : "When millions of people believe it, there must be something true in it." Then his friends started believing it, then it became a mutual hypnosis, and then the whole of Germany got into it.

One of the most intelligent races behaved very foolishly. Why?

What happened to the German mind? Just repetition, propaganda. Hitler has written in his autobiography *Mein Kampf*, that there is a simple process to transform a lie into a truth : just go on repeating it—and he knew by his own experience. If you go on repeating a particular thing : you smoke, you go on smoking every day, it becomes a hypnosis. Then even if you come to know that it is useless, futile, foolish, dangerous to health, nothing can be done, because now it is an autohypnosis.

Mulla Nasrudin's wife was reading an article to him against smoking. Experts were quoted that cancer and tuberculosis and other diseases are possible through smoking. He heard it and then said, "Stop this nonsense! This is all silly, and I tell you, I intend to continue smoking till I die!"

His weary wife said, "Okay then, have it your own way. But what makes you think that even then you will stop? What makes you think that even then, when you die, you will stop?"

Really, if you are under hypnosis, it never stops. Death doesn't make much difference: in the next life you start again the same way, because the next life starts from where the last was discontinued; it is a continuity. So when a child is born, he is not really a child, he is very, very old, very ancient. He brings all his ancient *karmas* with him, all the *samskaras* and conditionings. He starts as an old man—he already has his hypnosis. This is what Hindus call *samskaras, karmas*.

What are *karmas?* What is the deepest meaning of the theory of *karma? Karma* is a method of autohypnosis. If you repeat an action continuously you become hypnotized by it. Then the *karma*, the action, becomes the master and you are just a slave.

What have you gained through sex? Have you gained anything? Or is it just a repetition? But you have repeated it for so long, that now if you stop you feel you are missing something. If you continue you feel nothing is gained. If nothing is gained by continuing it, then you are not missing anything by stopping it. Then why do you feel something is missing? It is just the old habit, a *samskara*, a conditioning, a *karma*. You have repeated it too many times and you have become hypnotized by it. Now you have to repeat it, it has become an obsession, it is compulsive.

Look—a person goes on overeating: he knows it is bad, he suffers because of it, he is ill continuously; but still, when he sits down to eat he cannot help it, it is compulsive. Why is it a compulsion? Because he has been doing it so long, he has become hypnotized by it. He is drunk.

Mulla Nasrudin came home one night very late, it must have been three in the morning. He knocked, his wife was very angry, but Mulla said, "Wait! First give me one minute to explain, then you can start. I was sitting with a very sick friend."

His wife said, "A very likely story—but tell me the name of the friend."

Mulla Nasrudin thought and thought and thought, and then he said, triumphantly, "He was so sick, he couldn't tell me!"

The mind, if it is drunk, may find excuses but all those excuses are false, just like this one: "The friend was so sick that he couldn't tell me." For sex you will find excuses, for smoking you will find excuses, for your lust towards power you will find excuses, but all excuses are lame. The real fact is that you are not ready to recognize that it has become compulsive, that you are under an obsession, you are under a hypnosis.

This is what a Jesus finds: everyone drunk and fast asleep. You cannot find it because you yourself are asleep. Unless you are awake you cannot become aware of what is happening all around. The whole world is moving in a somnambulism. That's why there is so much misery, so much violence, so much war. It is unnecessary, but it has to be so because people who are asleep and drunk cannot be responsible for anything. If somebody came to Jesus to ask what he should do to change, Jesus would say: "You cannot do anything to change unless you become awake." What can you do? What can a man who is fast asleep do to change his dreams? What can he do?

People would come with the same question to Gurdjieff—and Gurdjieff is the man most representative of Jesus in this age, not the Pope of the Vatican. Gurdjieff is the most representative because he believed in, and worked out the same method of friction that Jesus was working with. He created many types of crosses for people to hang themselves on and be transformed. Gurdjieff also

used to say that you cannot do anything unless you ARE. And
if you are not awake, you are not there, you simply believe that
you are. This belief won't help.

Now look at these sayings. They are all very profound, deep,
very significant, and can become guidelights on your path.
Remember them !

*"Jesus said: I took my stand in the midst of the world and in
flesh I appeared to them. I found them all drunk; I found none of
them athirst."*

Jesus never renounced the world, he was standing in the midst
of us all. He was not an escapist, he moved in the market place, he
lived with the crowd. He talked to prostitutes, labourers, farmers,
fishermen. He didn't go out of the world, he remained here amidst
you. He knew the world better than anybody who has escaped
from it.

There is no wonder why Christ's message became so powerful—
Mahavir's message never became so powerful, but Jesus converted
almost half of the world. Why? Because he remained in the world,
he understood the world—its ways, the people, the mind. He moved
with them, he came to know how they function—asleep, drunk—
and he started to find ways and means to awaken them.

On the last night, when Jesus was caught— or managed to be
caught—when the last drama was enacted, one disciple was with
him. And Jesus said, "This is my last night, so I will go into deep
prayer. I have to pray, and you are to keep vigil. Don't fall asleep !
I will come and see—and remember, this is my last night !"

Jesus went and after half an hour he came again. The disciple
was fast asleep. He awakened him and told him, "You are fast
asleep, and I told you to keep vigil, because this is my last night.
Remain alert, because I will not be here again ! Then you can
sleep for ever and ever. But while I'm here at least, on my last
night, remain alert !" The disciple said, "Excuse me, I was feeling
so sleepy, that I couldn't help it. But I will try now."

Jesus went again into prayer. After half an hour he was back and
that disciple was fast asleep. He awakened him again and said,
"What are you doing? The morning is coming near and I will be

caught !" The disciple said, "Excuse me, forgive me, but the flesh is very strong, and the will is very weak, and the body was so heavy—and I thought, 'What is wrong in taking a little sleep? By the time you come, I will be awake again.'"

A third time Jesus came and the disciple was fast asleep. But this is the situation of all disciples. Many times I have come to you and I have found you fast asleep. Whenever I came to you I found you were fast asleep. Sleepiness has become just second nature. What does sleepiness mean? It means that you are not aware that you are—then whatsoever you do is irresponsible. You are mad, and whatsoever you do, you are doing just like a drunkard.

Mulla Nasrudin was caught kissing a woman, a stranger, on the road. When he came out of court he said to a friend, "It has been very hard: the judge first fined me fifty *rupees* for kissing—and then when he looked at the woman he fined me fifty more for being drunk !" Because the woman was almost no woman at all—she was so ugly that nobody could kiss her if he was in his senses !

And you have all been kissing the ugliest things possible. That is possible only because you are drunk and asleep. Have you ever thought about things that obsess you? How ugly ! Can you find anything more ugly than power? Can you find more ugly a man than Hitler, Napoleon, Alexander? But that is your ambition also; deep down you would like to be like Napoleon, Alexander, Hitler: successful in the world, powerful in the world. But have you found anything more ugly than them?

Power is the ugliest thing, but everybody wants power, domination. Have you seen the ugliness of wealth? It has to be ugly, it cannot be beautiful, because it depends on exploitation. Blood is there, death is there, because only after many have been deprived of their lives, does your bank balance go on increasing. You cannot find anything more ugly than that, but deep down, everybody is in search of wealth.

Whenever the Last Judgment Day comes, you will be fined fifty *rupees* first, and when God looks at the things you have been kissing you will be fined fifty more. Because you have been drunk, otherwise this would not be possible.

Says Jesus: "I took my stand in the midst of the world and in flesh I appeared to them."

And he was not a spirit. Many Masters go on continuously visiting you in their spirits. Buddha still knocks at your door, but in the spirit. And if you cannot see a person who has come into flesh, how can you recognize Buddha?

In this century, when H. P. Blavatsky discovered—or rediscovered—the existence of Masters who go on working and helping people who are on the path, in spirit, nobody believed her. They thought she had gone crazy, and people would say, "Give us proof—where are those Masters?" One of the greatest things that Theosophy achieved was the rediscovery of Masters, because anyone who has become Enlightened remains in the world, for there is nowhere else to go. This is the only existence there is. So he remains, but without the body, and his Being goes on functioning, helping, because that is his nature—it is not something he has to *do*.

It is just like a light: a light is there, and it goes on and on lighting everything that is around it. Even if the path is lonely and nobody passes, the light still goes on burning because that is its nature. If somebody comes to the path, then the light is there and the light guides him; not that it is something to be done on his part— it is just his nature. Whenever a being becomes Enlightened he remains a guide. But you cannot recognize a guide in the spirit if you cannot recognize a guide in the body.

Jesus says: "In flesh I appeared to them—I was in the body, they could see me, they could hear me, they could feel me, but still they missed. They missed because I found them all drunk. They were not there really, no consciousness at all. I knocked at their doors, but they were not at home."

If Jesus comes to your home and knocks, will you be there to receive him? You will be somewhere else, you are never at home. You go on wandering all over the world, except to your home. Where is your home? Inside you, where the center of consciousness is, is your home. You are never there, because only in deep meditation are you there. And when you are deep in meditation you can recognize Jesus immediately—whether he comes in the body or bodiless makes no difference. If you are at home you will recognize the knock. But if you are not at home, what can be done? Jesus will knock and you will not be there. That is the meaning of the word 'drunk': not at home.

Really, whenever you want to forget yourself, you take alcohol, drugs; whenever you want to forget yourself, you drink. Drinking means forgetfulness, and the whole of religion consists of remembering. Hence, all the religions insist against drinking. Not that there is something wrong in drinking in itself; if you are not moving on the path there is nothing wrong in it. But if you are moving on the path, then there cannot be anything more wrong than that, because the whole path consists of self-remembering—and drinking is forgetfulness.

But why do you want to forget yourself? Why are you so bored with yourself? Why can't you be alert and at ease? What is the problem? The problem is that whenever you are alert, alone, you feel empty; you feel as if you are nobody. You feel a nothingness inside and that nothingness becomes an abyss. You get scared, you start running from it.

Deep inside you, you *are* an abyss, and that's why you go on escaping. Buddha called that abyss 'no-self', *anatta*. There is nobody inside. When you look it is a *vast* expansion, but nobody is there—just inner sky, an infinite abyss, endless, beginningless. The moment you look, you get dizzy, you start running, you immediately escape. But where can you escape to? Wherever you go that emptiness will be with you because it *is* you. It is your Tao, your nature. One has to come to terms with it.

Meditation is nothing but coming to terms with your inner emptiness: recognizing it, not escaping; *living* through it, not escaping; *being* through it, not escaping. Then suddenly the emptiness becomes the fullness of life. When you don't escape from it, it is the most beautiful thing, the purest, because only emptiness can be pure. If something is there, dirt has entered; if something is there, then death has entered; if something is there, then limitation has entered. If something is there, then God cannot be there. God means the great abyss, the ultimate abyss. It is there, but you are never trained to look into it.

It is just like when you go to the hills and look into the valley: you get dizzy. Then you don't want to look because a fear grips you—you may fall. But no hill is so high, and no valley so deep as the valley that exists inside you. And whenever you look inside, you feel a dizziness, nausea—you immediately escape, you close your eyes and start running. You have been running for millions of lives, but you have not reached anywhere, because you cannot.

One *has* to come to terms with the inner emptiness. And once you come to terms with it, suddenly the emptiness changes its nature—it becomes the All. Then it is not empty, not negative; it is the most positive thing in existence. But acceptance is the door.

That's why there is so much attraction for alcohol, LSD, marijuana—drugs. And there are many types of drugs: physical, chemical, mental; wealth, power, politics—everything is a drug.

Look at a politician: he is drugged, he is drunk with power; he does not walk on the earth. Look at a man of wealth: you think he walks on the earth? No, his feet never touch the earth, he is very high, he has wealth. Only poor men walk on the earth, only beggars; a rich man flies in the sky. When you fall in love with a woman, suddenly you are on high; suddenly you never walk again on the earth—a romance has entered. The whole quality of your being is different, because now you are drunk. Sex is the deepest alcohol that nature has given to you.

Jesus said: "I found them all drunk; I found none of them athirst."

This has to be understood, a very delicate point: if you are drunk with this world, you cannot be thirsty for the other. If you are drunk with ordinary alcohol, with ordinary wine, you cannot be thirsty for the Divine Wine—impossible!

When a man is not drunk with this world, a thirst arises. And that thirst cannot be fulfilled by anything that belongs to this world; only the Unknown can fulfill it, only the Invisible can fulfill it.

So Jesus says a very contradictory thing: "I found them all drunk; I found none of them athirst."—Nobody was thirsty because they thought they had already found the Key, the Treasure, the Kingdom. So then there was no search.

God is a drunkenness of a different type. Kabir has said: *"Aisi tari lagi*—I have fallen into such a drunkenness that nothing now can disturb it, it is eternal." Ask Omar Khayyam, he knows, he talks about the Wine of the other world. And Fitzgerald totally misunderstood him, because he is not talking of the wine that you can get here; he is talking of the Divine Wine, which is the Sufi symbol for God. Once you are drunk with God, then there will be no thirst at all.

But this world and its wine can give you only temporary relief, can give you only temporary gaps of forgetfulness. And the difference is diametrical: when someone is drunk with God's wine, he is totally alert, aware, fully conscious; when somebody is drunk with this world and its wines, he is hypnotized, asleep, moves in a slumber, lives in a sleep—his whole life is a long dream.

"I found them all drunk; I found none of them athirst.
And my soul was afflicted for the sons of men, because they are blind in their heart and they do not see that empty they have come into the world, and empty they seek to go out of the world again."

"And my soul was afflicted. . ."—You cannot understand what suffering happens to a Jesus or a Buddha when he looks at you, drunk with this world, not thirsty at all for the Divine, for the Truth; living in lies, and believing in lies as if they were truths—and missing for nothing, missing all for nothing. Then it happens that the smallest things can become barriers.

Once it happened that a man was very ill. The illness was that he continually felt that his eyes were popping out and his ears were ringing—continually. By and by, he became crazy because it went on twenty-four hours a day. He couldn't sleep, he couldn't do his work, so he consulted doctors.

One doctor suggested, "Remove the appendix," so the appendix was removed, but nothing happened. Another suggested, "Remove all the teeth," so all his teeth were removed. Nothing happened, the man simply became old, that is all. Then somebody suggested that his tonsils should be removed. (There are millions of advisors, and if you start listening to them they will kill you.) So his tonsils were removed, but nothing happened. Then he consulted the greatest doctor known.

The doctor diagnosed and he said, "Nothing can be done because the cause cannot be found. At the most you can live for six more months. And I must be frank with you, because all that could be done has been done. Now nothing can be done."

The man came out of the doctor's office and thought, "If I only have six months to live, then why not live well?" He was a miser

and he had never lived, so he ordered the latest and biggest car;
he purchased a beautiful bungalow, he ordered thirty suits, he even
ordered shirts to be made to measure.

He went to the tailor who measured him and said, "Thirty-six
sleeves, sixteen collar."

The man said, "No, fifteen, because I always use fifteen."

The tailor measured again and said, "Sixteen!"

The man said, "But I have always used fifteen!"

The tailor said, "Okay then, have it your own way, but I tell
you, you will have popping eyes and ringing in the ears!"—And
that was the whole cause of his illness!

You are missing the Divine not for very great causes. No! Just
a fifteen collar—and the eyes cannot see, they are popping; and
the ears cannot hear, they are ringing. The cause of man's illness
is simple, because he is addicted to small things.

The things of this world are very small. Even if you get a kingdom, what is it? A very small thing. Where are the kingdoms that
existed in history? Where is Babylon? Where is Assyria? Where
is the kingdom of Pharaoh? They all disappeared, just ruins—and
the kingdoms were great. But what was attained by them? What
did Genghis Khan attain? What did Alexander attain? All kingdoms are just trivial things.

And you don't know what you are missing—you are missing the
Kingdom of God. Even if you become successful, what will you
get through it? Where will you get through it? Look at successful
people, diagnose them: where have they reached? Look at people
who sit on thrones of success: where have they reached? They are
also in search of mental peace—more than you. They are also
afraid of death, and trembling, just like you.

If you look at your successful people minutely, you will find that
those 'gods' also have clay feet. Death will take them and with
death all success disappears, all fame disappears. The whole thing
seems to be a nightmare: so much effort, so much misery, so much
hardship—and nothing is gained. In the end death comes and
everything disappears like a bubble. And because of this bubble,
that which is eternal is lost.

"And my soul was afflicted for the sons of men, because they are blind in their heart, and they do not see that empty they have come into the world, and empty they seek to go out of the world again."

Empty you have come, but not exactly empty: filled with desires. Empty you will go, but not exactly empty: again filled with desires. But desires are dreams, you remain empty. They have nothing substantial in them. You are born empty, and then you move in the world and accumulate things, just believing that these things will give you a fulfillment. You remain empty. Death snatches everything, you move again into the grave, again empty.

To what point does this whole life come? To what meaning and conclusion? What do you achieve through it? This is the affliction of a Jesus or a Buddha looking at men. They are blind, and why are they blind? Where is their blindness? It is not that they are not clever—they are too clever, more than they need, more than they can afford, more than is good for them. They are very clever, cunning. They think they are wise. It is not that they cannot see, they can see, but they can see only something that belongs to this world. Their HEART is blind, their heart cannot see.

Can you see with your heart? Have you ever seen anything with your heart? Many times you may have thought, "The sun is rising and the morning is beautiful," and think it is from the heart. No! Because your mind is still chattering, "The sun is beautiful, the morning is beautiful," and you may be simply repeating others' ideas. Have you really realized that the morning is beautiful—*this morning*, the phenomenon that is happening *here?* Or are you repeating words?

You go to a flower: have you really gone? Has the flower touched your heart? Has it reached to your deepest core of being? Or do you just look at the flower and say, "Good, it is beautiful, nice." These are words and almost dead, because they are not coming from the heart. From the heart no word ever comes; feeling comes, but not words. Words come from the head, feeling comes from the heart. But we are blind there. Why are we blind there? Because the heart leads into dangerous paths.

So nobody is allowed to live with the heart. Your parents have taken care that you should live with the head, not with the heart, because the heart may lead you to failure in this world. It does, and unless you fail in this world, you will not be athirst for the other.

The head leads to success in this world. It is cunning, calculating, it is a manipulator—it leads you to success. So every school, every college and university teaches you how to be more 'heady', how to be more 'headful'. And those who are 'headful', they get the gold medals. They are successful and then they have the keys to enter into this world.

But a man with heart will be a failure, because he cannot exploit. He will be so loving that he cannot exploit. He will be so loving that he cannot be a miser, an accumulator. He will be so loving that he will go and share, and whatsoever he has he will give, rather than snatch things from people.

He will be a failure. And he will be so true that he cannot deceive you. He will be sincere and honest, authentic; but then he will be a stranger in this world, where only cunning people can succeed. That is why every parent takes care that before the child moves into the world, the heart of the child should become blind, completely closed.

You cannot pray, you cannot love. Can you? Can you pray? You can pray—go into a church on Sunday : people are praying, but everything is false, even their prayer comes from their heads. They have learned it, it is not from the heart. Their hearts are empty, dead, they don't feel a thing. People 'love', they get married and children are born to them—*not out of love*. Everything is out of calculation, everything is out of arithmetic. You are afraid of love, because no one knows where love will lead you. No one knows the ways of the heart, they are mysterious. With the head you are on the right path, on the highway; with the heart you move into the jungle. There are no roads, no roadsigns, you have to find the path yourself.

With the heart you are individual, solitary; with the head you are part of the society. The head has been trained by the society, it is part of the society. With the heart you become a solitary, an outsider. So every society takes care to kill the heart, and Jesus says :

"...because they are blind in their hearts and do not see that

empty they have come into the world, and empty they seek to
go out of the world again."

Only the heart can see *how empty you are!* What have you
gained? What maturity, what growth has happened to you? What
ecstasy has come to you?—no benediction yet? Your whole past
has been a rotten thing. And in the future you are going to repeat
the past, what else can you do? This is the affliction of a Jesus,
of a Buddha. He feels miserable for you.

"But now they are drunk. When they have shaken off their
wine, then they will repent."

This is about YOU. Don't think "they"—"they" means YOU :
when you are shaken out of your drunkenness, you will repent.

This word 'repent' became very meaningful. The whole of
Christianity depends on repentance, no other religion has depended
so much on repentance. Repentance is beautiful if it comes
through the heart, if you realize that, "Yes, Jesus is right, we
have wasted our lives."

This wasting is the sin—not that Adam committed the sin—
this wasting of your life, of the possibility, the potentiality, the
opportunity to grow and become Godlike or become gods; wasting
this time, wasting it with futile things, collecting useless junk.
And when you become aware, you will repent. And if this
repentance comes through the heart, it will cleanse you. Nothing
cleanses like repentance. And this is one of the most beautiful
things in Christianity.

In Hinduism there is no secret about repentance. They have
not worked out that key at all. This is unique to Christianity.
If you repent totally, if it comes from the heart, if you cry and
weep, if your whole being feels and repents that you have been
wasting God's given opportunity—you have not been grateful,
you have misbehaved, you have mistreated your own being...
you feel the sin. *This* is the sin!—not that you have murdered
somebody or that you have stolen; that is nothing. Those are
minor sins which are born out of this original sin : that you have
been drunk. If you repent totally, you open your eyes, your heart
is filled with repentance, and then a scream, a cry, comes out of
your being. There is no need for words, you need not say to God,

"I repent, forgive me." No need, your *whole being* becomes a repentance. Suddenly, you are cleansed of all the past.

This is one of the most secret keys Jesus delivered to the world. Because Jains say that you have to work it out, it is a long process : whatsoever you have done in the past has to be undone. If you have done a wrong in the past, it has to be undone. It is mathematical : if you have committed a sin, you have to do something to balance it. And Hindus say that you have committed such sin, that you are in such ignorance, so many actions out of ignorance, and the past is so vast, that it is not easy to get out of it. Many more works will be needed, only then can you clean the past.

But Jesus has given a beautiful key. He says : "Just repent and the whole past is washed clean!" It seems to be a very unbelievable thing, because how can it happen? And that is the difference between Hindus, Buddhists, Jains and Christianity. Hindus, Buddhists and Jains can never believe that can happen just by repentance, because they don't know what repentance is. Jesus worked it out. It is one of the oldest keys.

But understand what repentance is. Just saying the words won't do, and saying them half-heartedly won't do. When your *whole* being repents, your whole being throbs and you feel it in every pore, every fibre, that you have done wrong—and you have done wrong because you have been drunk—and now you repent, suddenly there is a transformation. The past disappears and the projection of the future from the past disappears; you are thrown to here and now, you are thrown to your own Being.

And for the first time you feel the inner nothingness. It is not empty negatively, it is just that the temple is so vast, like space. . . . You are forgiven, Jesus says you are forgiven if you repent.

Jesus' Master was John the Baptist. His whole teaching was : "Repent! Because the Day of Judgment is near!" This was his whole teaching. He was a very wild man, a great revolutionary, and he went from one corner of his country to another, just with one message : "Repent! Because the Last Judgment is very near!" That is why Christians completely dropped the theory of rebirth. Not that Jesus was not aware of rebirth—he knew, he knew well that there is a cycle of continuous rebirths. But he completely dropped the idea just to give repentance totality.

If there are many lives your repentance cannot be total. You can wait, you can postpone. You can think : "If in this life I have missed, nothing is wrong, there's the next life." That is what Hindus have been doing. They are the laziest people in the world, because of this theory. And the theory is right, this is the problem; so they can always postpone, there is no hurry. Why be in such a hurry?

That is why Hindus have never bothered about time. They never invented watches, and, left to themselves, they would not invent them. So a watch, for a Hindu mind, is really a foreign element : a clock in a Hindu house doesn't fit. The clock is a Christian invention, because time is short, running fast—it is not a clock, it is life running fast out of your hands. This death is going to be the final one, you cannot postpone. This idea was created just to avoid postponement.

Jesus and John the Baptist, who was his Master, who initiated Jesus into the mysteries, their whole teaching depends on : "Repent! For there is no more time left, don't postpone any further, because you will be lost then." They bring the whole thing to an intensity.

If I suddenly say that this is going to be the last day, and tomorrow the world is going to disappear, the H-bomb is to be dropped, and then I say : "Repent!"—then your total being will be focused, centered, you will be here and now. And then there will come a scream, a cry, a *wild* scream from your being. It will not be in words—it will be more existential than that—it will be from the heart. Not only will your eyes weep, but your heart will be filled with tears, your whole being will be filled with tears because you have missed.

If this repentance happens, this intensity of becoming alert, all the past is cleaned. No need to undo it—no, because it has never been a reality. It was a dream, no need to undo it—just become alert. And with the sleep, all the dreams and nightmares disappear. They have never been there in reality in the first place, they have been your thoughts.

And don't be lazy about it—because you have been postponing for many lives. You can postpone for many : postponement is such an attraction for the mind. The mind always says, "Tomorrow"—always. Tomorrow is the shelter. Tomorrow is the shelter of all sin, and virtue arises at this moment.

I have heard, there was a school, a Christian missionary school, but with a few non-Christian boys as well, who were also taught the Bible, the parables and the stories—and they had to learn. One day, the school inspector came and he asked a small kid, "Who was the first man, and who was the first woman?"

The kid replied, "Adam and Eve."

The inspector was pleased and he said, "To what nationality did they belong?"

And the kid said, "Indian of course!"

The inspector was a little bit disturbed, but he still asked, "Why do you think they belonged to the Indian nationality? Why do you think they were Indians?"

And the kid said, "Easy! They had no shelter over their heads, no clothes to wear, nothing to eat except one apple between the two of them—and still they believed this was Paradise! They were Indians!"

The Indians are at ease with whatsoever is. They are not worried about doing anything, because they think : "Life is such a long affair, why worry? Why get in a hurry? There is no need to run."

Christianity created an intensity by the idea that there is only one life. And remember well : Hindus are right, as far as the theory is concerned, and Christians are wrong, as far as the theory is concerned. But theory is never a question for a Jesus. The problem is the human mind and its transformation—and sometimes truth can be poisonous, sometimes truth can make you lazy.

I will give you another example which will be helpful : Gurdjieff used to say that you don't have any eternal soul, remember. You can attain it, but you don't have it—you can miss. And if you don't attain it you will simply die, nothing is going to survive. And Gurdjieff said that only one in millions attains to the soul, and then the soul goes on moving. The body is left and the soul moves on. But this does not happen for everybody.

The soul is not given to you, it has to be worked out, it is a crystallization. If they work it out, then a Mahavir, a Buddha, a Jesus, they become eternal. Not you!—Gurdjieff used to say you are just vegetables! You will be eaten, you will dissolve; you don't have any center, so who can survive?

He was again using the Jesus tactics. He was not right because you do have a soul, an eternal soul. But the theory is dangerous, because when you hear that you have an eternal soul, that you are the *Brahma,* (Ultimate Reality), you go to sleep. This becomes a hypnotic thing : if you are already That, why worry? What need is there of *sadhana?* What need is there to meditate? "*Aham Brahmasmi*—I am God already." So you go to sleep because nothing is left to be done.

Theories can kill, even true theories can kill. Gurdjieff is not right, but he is more compassionate. And you are such liars that only lies can help you. Only lies can bring you out of your lies, just as when a thorn is in your flesh, another thorn is needed to bring it out.

Jesus knew well, he knew about reincarnation—nobody else knew so well. But he simply dropped the idea because he had been to India! He looked at the Indian mind, saw that the whole mind had become a postponement because of the theory of reincarnation, and he dropped that theory.

Gurdjieff also went to India and Tibet, and he looked at the whole nonsense that has happened because of the belief that you already have within you all that is needed, that you are Divine *already :* there is no need to do anything, so beggars think they are emperors—then why bother? Gurdjieff started teaching on the same line as Jesus, the essential note is the same : he said nobody has a soul already; you can create it, you may miss it, so don't take it for granted—work it out!

If you make much effort, only then will a center be born, and that center will live—but not you as you are, because you are just vegetables. And to say that you are just vegetables, he created a new myth. He said, "You are vegetables for the moon, food for the moon." He joked, but it is a very beautiful joke, and very meaningful.

He said everything in the world is food for something else :

this animal eats that, that animal eats something else. Everything is food for something else, so how can man be an exception? Man must be a food for something and Gurdjieff said, "Man is the food for the moon. And when the moon is very hungry, there are wars. When the moon is *very* hungry, there are wars because many people are needed. But he was joking about the moon, he was not serious. And followers are always blind, so they have taken even this joke as a truth. Gurdjieff's followers go on saying that this is one of the greatest truths he discovered—if he were to come back he would laugh.

He was joking, but when Gurdjieff jokes he jokes meaningfully. And the insistence was, the emphasis was, that you are vegetables —as you are. Only this much can be done with you : the moon can eat you. Can you find anything more stupid than the moon? Difficult to find! When the astronauts reached it, they thought that they were going to fulfill all the dreams and all the poetry of the world, because man has always been thinking about reaching the moon. But when they reached it, there was nothing. The moon is nothing—you are food for nothing. The moon is just a dead planet. And you are food for a dead planet, because you *are* dead!

Remember this : Christianity, particularly Jesus, knows well that there is incarnation, reincarnation, rebirth. Life is a long continuity, this death is not going to be the ultimate death. But once this is said, you relax. And the whole method of Jesus depends on friction : you are not allowed to relax, you have to fight, create friction, so that you can become crystallized.

"But now they are drunk. When they have shaken off their wine, then they will repent.

"Jesus said : If the flesh has come into existence because of the spirit, it is a marvel; but if the spirit has come into existence because of the body, it is a marvel of marvels."

I think Karl Marx missed this! I wonder what he would have thought if he had come to these saying of Jesus. Jesus says: "If the flesh has come into existence because of the spirit..." as all religions say—God created the world. That means : flesh has come out of the spirit, matter has come out of the mind;

consciousness is the source, the world is just a by-product. Then, Jesus says: "...it is a marvel!"—it is a mystery.

"But if the spirit has come into existence because of the body..." as atheists say, materialists say, Karl Marx, Charvak and others say....Marx says that consciousness is a by-product of matter. This is what all atheists say, that the world is not created out of the spirit, but the spirit is just a 'by-phenomenon', an epi-phenomenon of matter; it comes out of matter, it is just a by-product. ...then, Jesus says, "If the spirit has come into existence because of the body, it is a marvel of marvels." The first is just a marvel, that the God created the world. But the second is a marvel of marvels—if the world created God. Because to believe the first is difficult; to believe the second is almost impossible.

It is possible that the lower is born out of the higher, just as a man can paint a picture. We can say the painting has come from the painter, it is a marvel, a beautiful painting. But if somebody says the painter has come out of the painting, it is a marvel of marvels. How can spirit come out of matter if it is not already there? How can a flower come if it is not already in the seed? But Jesus says, anyway, both are marvels.

But the third thing is the greatest marvel, and that third thing is:
"I marvel at how this great wealth has made its home in this poverty."

You are poor, a beggar, because you are always desiring, always asking to be given more. Desire is begging, and a desiring mind is a beggar's mind. You may be an emperor, it makes no difference—you just become a big beggar, that's all, a great beggar, that's all. But you go on demanding.

It happened that a Mohammedan mystic, Farid, lived near Delhi in a small village. The Emperor, Akbar, was one of Farid's followers. Akbar used to come to him, and Farid was a poor fakir. The town came to know that Akbar used to come to Farid, and once when Akbar came the villagers gathered and said to Farid, "Akbar comes to you, so ask for something for us. At least a school is needed, a hospital is needed. And just by your saying it will be fulfilled, because the Emperor himself comes to you."

The village was poor, uneducated, and there was no hospital,

So Farid said, "Okay, but I am not very efficient at asking for anything because I have not asked for so long. But if you say so, I will go." So he went.

In the morning he reached the palace. Everybody knew that Akbar was his follower, so he was allowed to enter immediately. Akbar was in his shrine, a small shrine which he had made, where he used to pray. And he was praying, he was in prayer, so Farid stood just at the back and when the prayer was finished he would ask.

Akbar was not aware that Farid was standing behind him. He said the prayer, and at the end he said, "God Almighty, make my Empire still greater, give me more wealth."

Farid listened and he turned away. When Akbar had finished his prayer, he looked behind—Farid was going down the stairs. He called, "How did you come? And why are you leaving?"

Farid said, "I had come to meet an Emperor, but I find here also a beggar. So it's useless! And if you are asking God, why shouldn't I ask Him directly? Why an in-between? And Akbar, I thought you were an Emperor, but I was wrong."

Akbar has related the story in his autobiography, and he says, "At that moment I understood: whatsoever one gets makes no difference, because the mind goes on asking for more and more."

Jesus says this is the marvel of all marvels: "...how this great wealth"—of Divine Beingness, of Divinity of God—"has made its home in such poverty."

Drunken people, asleep, poor, begging continuously all their lives; asking for ugly things, fighting for ugly things, obsessed with disease and illness—and God has made it His temple, and God has made it His abode, His abode in you! Jesus says this is the best—impossible, incomprehensible—mystery. Marvel of all marvels! Nothing can transcend this.

This is the affliction of a Buddha, of a Jesus: looking at you—Emperors, who have the Kingdom of God, begging; asking for worthless things, wasting your time, your life, energy, opportunity.

Repent! Look at what you have been doing. It will look so foolish, you will not even be able to believe that you have been doing this. The whole thing will look nonsense!

Look at what you have been doing with your life, *look at what you have done to yourself*. You are just a ruin, and the ruin is growing every day. In the end you will be *just* a ruin, totally ruined. And in your begging heart, in your begging mind, there lives the King, the Supreme. This is a marvel!

And a Jesus feels very much, hence he is so sad, he cannot laugh. Not that laughter is difficult for him—he cannot laugh because of you. He is so sad, he feels so much for you that he goes on devising methods, devising keys to unlock you, to make you that which you already are, to make you realize who you are.

Go through these words and remember one key-word: *repent*. And if you can come to realize that repentance is the key, it will cleanse all your past. You will suddenly be fresh and virgin again.

And when you are fresh, God is there. Because God is nothing but your freshness, your virginity.

Fourth Discourse

24th August 1974, Poona, India

THE FOURTH SAYING

Jesus said :
Take no thought from the morning until the evening
and from the evening until the morning,
for what you shall put on.

His disciples said :
When wilt thou be revealed to us
and when will we see thee?

Jesus said :
When you take off your clothing without being ashamed,
and take your clothes and put them under your feet
as the little children and tread on them—
then shall you behold the Son of the Living One,
and you shall not fear.

Man lives not as he is but as he would like to be: not with the original face, but with a painted, false face. That is the whole problem. When you are born you have a face of your own—nobody has disturbed it, nobody has changed it, but sooner or later the society starts working on your face. It starts hiding the original, the natural, the one you were born with, and then many faces are given to you for different occasions because one face won't do.

Situations change so you need many false faces, masks. From the morning till the evening, from the evening till the morning, thousands of faces are used. When you see a man approaching who is powerful, you change the mask; when you see a man who is a beggar approaching you, you are different. The *whole* time, moment to moment, there is a constant change in the face.

One has to be alert about it because it has become so mechanical that you need not be aware of it, it goes on changing by itself. If a servant comes in the room you don't even look at him. You act as if he is not a man, as if he does not exist, as if nobody has entered. But when the boss comes in the room you suddenly jump, you have a smiling face, receiving, welcoming, as if God Himself has entered into the room.

Watch your face, the change that occurs continuously. Look in the mirror and think of the many faces that you can change. Look in the mirror and bring the face that comes when you approach your wife; look at the face that comes when you

81

approach your beloved; look at the face that comes when you are greedy, when you are angry; create the face that comes when you feel sexual; create the face that comes when you feel dissatisfied, frustrated. And watch in the mirror: you will find you are not one man—you are a crowd. And sometimes it will be difficult even to recognize that all these faces belong to you. A mirror can be a great blessing. You can meditate in a mirror, change your faces and look at them. This will give you a glimpse of how false your whole life has become. And none of these faces is *you*.

In Zen it has been one of the deepest meditations: to find your original face, the one you had before you came to this world—and the one you will have when you leave this world; because you cannot carry all these faces with you. They are gimmicks, techniques to deceive, techniques to defend yourself, they are armours around you. These faces have to be dropped, only then can you see Jesus, because when *you* see your original face, you have seen Jesus.

Jesus is nothing but your original face, Buddha is nothing but your original face. Buddha is not outside you, neither is Jesus. When you drop all the falsity and you are naked—just the original you, without any change, modification—you are Jesus, Jesus in his absolute glory is revealed. It is not in the son of Joseph that he is to be revealed. Suddenly you become Jesus. And only the like can know the like—remember that law always: if you are like Jesus, only then can you recognize him; otherwise how will you recognize him? When you feel your own inner being, then you can recognize the inner being of somebody else.

The light can recognize the light, the light cannot recognize the darkness. And how will the darkness recognize the light? If you are false you cannot recognize a real man, and Jesus is the most real man, the most real that is possible. He is not a liar, he is authentic, and if you are lying with your life continuously—your words, your gestures, everything is a lie—then how can you recognize Jesus? It is impossible. In your total nudity you will recognize the inner Jesus, and only then will the outer be recognized. The inner is the first to be recognized, because the recognition can come only from your innermost source of being. There is no other way.

One of the oldest Jewish sayings is that you start seeking God only when you have found Him. It looks paradoxical but it is absolutely true, because how will you start seeking Him if you have not found Him, found Him within yourself, realized Him within yourself? Only then does the search start, but then there is no need to search really. The search starts and ends at the same point, the first step is the last step.

Only one step exists between you and the Divine. There are not two steps so there is no path. Just one step: drop down all falsities that you have taken upon yourself, drop down all borrowed masks.

But why do we have faces? What is the need and what is the fear of dropping them? The whole mechanics has to be understood, only then will these words be clear to you.

First: you have never loved yourself—otherwise there would be no need. You hate yourself, and if you hate yourself you will hide your face. If you hate yourself how can you reveal your face to others? You yourself hate it, you yourself don't want to see it, then how can you reveal it to others? Why has it happened that you hate yourself? The whole conditioning of society depends on creating hatred in you about yourself, a self-condemnation, a guilt. Religions have existed, priests have existed, society exists— all types of exploitation exist on this basic seed that you hate yourself.

Why should you go to a priest if you don't hate yourself? What is the need? When you hate you feel guilty; when you hate you feel some transformation is needed; when you hate you think some help is needed—somebody is needed to change you, to make you lovable, worth loving. Your parents say to you: "You are wrong, this is wrong, that is wrong!" They go on continuously saying: "Don't do this, don't do that!"

I have heard: One small child wanted to play on the beach with the sand. His mother said, "No! Because the sand is wet and you will spoil your clothes." Then the small child wanted to go near the water. The mother said, "No, absolutely no! It is slippery and you may fall there." Then the small child wanted to run and jump around, and his mother said, "No! You may get lost in the crowd." Then the child asked for ice cream, because the ice cream vendor was near. The mother said, "No! Because that always creates a problem with the throat and it is bad for the health." And then she said to a person who was standing by, "Have you ever seen such a neurotic child?"

And the child is not neurotic—the mother is neurotic. To play with sand is not neurosis, to go near the water is not neurosis, to run around is not neurosis, but a neurotic mind always says, "No!" A neurotic mind cannot say, "Yes!" because a neurotic mind cannot allow freedom to himself or herself, so how can a neurotic mind allow freedom to you? And this mother, and almost all mothers are like that—and all fathers. Remember, when you become a mother or you become a father, they are all like that. Freedom is killed and the child is forced, by and by, to feel that he is neurotic, he is wrong; whatsoever he proposes to do he is told: "No!"

I have heard about a small child who went to school for the first day, came back, and his mother asked, "What did you learn there?" The child said, "For the first time I learnt that my name is not 'Don't'. I always feel that 'Don't' is my name—'Don't do that, don't go there, don't be like that!' So I was thinking that my name is 'Don't'. In school I learnt that that is not my name."

If you are neurotic—and this whole society is neurotic—there is a chain of neurosis from one generation to another. It goes on and on, and up to now no society has been able to create a non-neurotic society or a non-neurotic age. Only sometimes have a few individuals been able to get out of the prison, but that too very rarely happens because the prison is so big and has such strong foundations. The establishment is so old, it is supported by the whole past, and when a small child is born, it is almost impossible to think that he will be able to be healthy and not neurotic.

It is almost impossible because everybody around is mad and they will force him to be like themselves. They will kill his freedom and they will create the feeling that he is wrong, he is always wrong. That creates a condemnation, a self-condemnation—you start hating yourself. And remember: if you hate yourself you cannot love anybody else. Impossible! How can you love somebody when you hate yourself? If poison exists at the source, it will poison all your relationships. So, you are never able to love anybody.

And remember the second thing which follows as a logical consequence: if you hate yourself, how can you think that anybody is going to love you? If *you* cannot love yourself, who is going to love you? So you know deep down that nobody is going to love you; and even if somebody tries, you never believe him. You go on suspecting that he must be deceiving you. How can anybody love YOU? You cannot love yourself. Then even if someone loves you, you are skeptical about it, doubtful. You cannot trust, and you will find ways and means to prove that he doesn't love you. And when it is proved, you are at ease, then everything is right.

This hatred is the base of all false faces—you start hiding. Clothes exist not because of the climate, that is just a minor part of it. They exist to hide the body, they exist to hide the sexuality, they exist to hide the animal in you. But the animal is life—all that is alive in you is animal-like. Except for your head, everything is animal-like, so everything has to be hidden except the head. Only the head, thinking, is not animal-like, so that is allowed. The society would be very happy if your whole body were cut off and only the head existed.

They are trying to do this, and the experiments have been successful. It is possible for the whole body to be dropped and the mind to go on functioning. The brain goes on functioning just through mechanical help: a mechanical heart goes on beating, a mechanical blood system goes on moving the blood, circulating it in the brain—and the brain exists without the body. Scientists are doing many experiments, and they are in confusion as to what the brain should be thinking inside because the body is no longer there—the brain may be having dreams, thinking thoughts, creating systems.

They were successful in this just a few years back, but society has been successful with the same experiment in a different way: your whole body is cut off from your consciousness, only your head is allowed. If suddenly you come upon your body without the head, I am certain you will not recognize that this is your body. If suddenly you come upon your body without the head, will you be able to recognize that this is your body? You have never seen it; even in the bathroom you have never seen your body. Clothes have become too much. They are not just on the body, they are also on the mind.

Two small school children were passing a big wall and they wanted to know what was going on behind the wall. They found a small hole but it was very difficult to reach, so one boy stood on the other boy's shoulders, looked through the hole and said, "Wonderful! Many people are there and they are playing, but they are all nude. It seems to be a nudist club."

The other boy became excited and he said, "Tell me something more—whether they are men or women."

The small boy who was standing on top said, "I cannot say anything, because they have no clothes."

A man is recognized as a man because of his clothes, a woman is recognized as a woman because of her clothes. The small child is right. He says: "How can I say who they are? They have no clothes." Clothes are identity. That is why a king will not allow you to wear clothes like him—no! If ordinary people start wearing clothes like the king, then where will he be? It cannot be allowed because he should be something special.

Clothes are identities. And they become so heavy on you that even in your dreams you never see yourself naked, you always see yourself with your clothes on. This is something—it has gone very deep. Even in dreams you never see yourself naked, society naked. No! Clothes have gone into the very unconscious, because a dream is an unconscious phenomenon. At least in a dream you should be natural, but even there you are not natural; masks, faces continue.

This whole falseness exists, this pseudo-personality exists, because at the base you hate yourself. You want to hide, nobody should know your real self, because how will they be able to tolerate it if they come to know? How will they love it, how will they appreciate it? You have become actors. This is the base of Jesus' sayings.

"Jesus said: Take no thought from the morning until the evening and from the evening until the morning for what you shall put on."

Don't think about faces, clothes, falsities. Remain yourself as you are, accept yourself as you are. Difficult, very difficult, because if you think about yourself as you are, suddenly you feel uneasy.

From where does this uneasiness come? It comes because teachers have been teaching you, and these teachers are the great poisoners of life. They are not really teachers, they are enemies. They have been teaching: "This is animal, that is animal—and you are a *man*." What are they saying? They are saying: "Whatsoever is animal in you, deny it !" And I say to you that man is not something against the animal, man is the most supreme animal. Not something against—the highest, the very peak. If you deny animality, you deny your very source of life. And then you will always be false.

If you make love to a woman and you deny animality, what will you do? That is why many people have become almost incapable of loving. You may be surprised that in the East I think ninety-nine percent of women have never known any orgasm. The same was the case in the West also, but now it is changing. Ninety-nine percent of women have never known any sexual ecstasy, because they were never allowed to. Men were allowed to be a little animal-like, but never women. They have to be stiff while making love, dead, almost like a corpse. They should not show any emotion, they should not show that they are enjoying it—because only bad women enjoy sex. A prostitute is allowed to enjoy it, but not a wife.

If a wife enjoys sex and becomes ecstatic, then the husband will feel hurt and think that this woman is not very good because she should behave like a goddess, not like an animal. But to behave like a goddess without being a goddess is bound to create falseness. The woman lies down, dead, corpse-like, with no emotions.

Have you ever observed the word 'emotion'? It comes from the same root as 'movement', 'motion'. When you are in an emotion your whole being moves: it is thrilled, it throbs, it is alive—it is WILD. No, a woman is not allowed to be wild, to be alive. She has to remain corpse-like, dead; then she is a good woman, then she has transcended animality. But if you deny sex and you say that this is animal, then you will have to hide it.

In America, just three or four years ago, one manufacturer of toys got into deep trouble and the case went up to the Supreme

Court. And the trouble was this: that he created a few toys with penises and vaginas—real. A girl must have a vagina if she has a face, a boy must have a penis if he has a face. *Toys with sex organs* —he got into trouble ! And he had to cancel his productions. He did a beautiful thing, but the courts wouldn't allow it, society wouldn't allow it.

Why don't your toys have sexual organs when they have everything else? You want the child to be unaware of a fact? Then you are creating a false face. And why did people get so very mad against those toys? Toys are toys ! But priests, missionaries, so-called 'do-gooders', they got mad, and they brought the man into court. And he had done a beautiful thing, a historic thing. Children *must* know the whole body because the whole body is beautiful. Why hide it, why cut it? A fear, a deep fear of animality. But you are animals, it is a fact: you can transcend it but you cannot destroy it. Destruction means one thing: if you destroy the fact you will have a false face, your mask will be a false thing, your godliness will be just a mask.

If you transcend it, then your godliness will be something authentic. But transcendence means accepting it; passing through it with alertness, not being lost in it; passing through it and going above. And denial means never going into it, never passing through it, just bypassing it. In life nothing can be bypassed; and if you bypass it you will always remain immature, juvenile, you will never be a grown-up. Life has to be lived—only then do you grow. There comes a moment when you transcend sex, but that moment comes through knowing, that moment comes through experience; that moment comes through deepening of consciousness and love—not through denial, not through repression.

Jesus says : "Take no thought from the morning until the evening and from the evening until the morning for what you shall put on." Don't put on anything. I am not saying go and move naked in the town, but don't put on anything: just be yourself ! Whatsoever life has *made* you, accept it, enjoy it, welcome it ! Celebrate it ! Be thankful to the Divine that He has made you, whatsoever you are. Don't reject, because when you reject anything in you, you have rejected God; because He is the Creator, He created you this way.

Of course, He knows more than you. When you reject anything in you, you have rejected the Creator, you are finding fault with the universe, with existence itself. This is foolish, stupid, but such people have become very respectable. Jesus says don't think about what you are going to put on, just move spontaneously in life. Be responsive to life, but don't bring any falseness between you and the flow of life.

Live moment-to-moment without thinking, because thinking is the deepest mask. When you go to a woman, you rehearse in the mind what you are going to say: "I love you," or, "There is nobody like you." If you are making a rehearsal you are not in love. Otherwise, there is no need because love will speak on its own, love will flow on its own; of their own accord things will happen. Flowers will flower, but of their own accord—no rehearsal is needed.

Once Mark Twain was asked a question by a friend. He was coming from a lecture hall where he had delivered a beautiful talk. The friend asked, "How was it? Did you like your talk or not—you yourself?" Mark Twain said, "Which talk? Because there is the one I had prepared, and the one that I have delivered, and the one that I wanted to deliver—which talk are you asking about?" But this is your whole life: you prepare something, you deliver something else, and you wanted to deliver something else entirely.

Why does this happen? So much division? Because you are not spontaneous. One who is spontaneous will need only one thing, nothing else—that is being alert, mindful. Then he will respond out of his mindfulness. You prepare because you are unaware, not mindful. You are afraid, you are fearful, because who knows what situation will be there? "Will I be able to respond or not?" The fear! Then you become false. But Jesus says: "Don't think about what you shall put on."

"His disciples said: When wilt thou be revealed to us and when will we see thee?

"Jesus said: When you take off your clothing without being ashamed, and take your clothes and put them under your feet as the little children, and tread on them—then shall you behold the Son of the Living One, and you shall not fear".

Try to understand each single word. The disciples asked: "When wilt thou he revealed to us...?" Jesus was there, revealed in all his glory. He was present to them, before them. They were asking Jesus himself: "When wilt thou be revealed to us...?" They were thinking as if Jesus were hiding himself.

Once Buddha was asked the same thing. He was passing through a forest. Dry leaves were on the path, leaves were falling, wind was blowing and there was much noise in the fallen dry leaves. Ananda asked—there was no one else there, because some disciples had gone ahead and a few others were coming behind, following them, but at that moment only Ananda was near Buddha. He said, "I have always wanted to ask one thing: have you revealed everything that you have? Or are you hiding something from us?"

Buddha said, "My hand is an open hand—a Buddha has no fist. Look at this forest as it is revealed, nothing is hidden. I am just as open as this forest, and a Buddha has no fist." Then he took a few dry leaves in his fist and said, "Now my fist is closed, you cannot see those leaves." People who are greedy about their knowledge—those who would not like to share it—they are like fists.

Then Buddha opened his hand, the leaves fell down and he said, "But the hand of Buddha is not like a fist, he is open. I have revealed everything. And if you feel that something is still hidden, it is because of you, not because of me."

Jesus is there, present. The disciples are asking: "When wilt thou be revealed to us...?" He is revealed! "...and when will we see thee?" They think as if Jesus is hiding himself. No, Jesus is not hiding. Rather on the contrary, the disciples are not open, they are closed; their eyes are not open. They are hiding, not Jesus.

Truth is not hidden—you are closed. Truth is revealed everywhere, every moment. *Truth by its very nature cannot be hidden.* Only lies try to hide themselves, not truth. Only lies are secretive. Truth is always like an open hand, it is never like a fist. But you are closed.

"The problem is with you," said Jesus. "When you take off your clothing without being ashamed..." Because you can take off your clothing and still feel ashamed; then this nudity is not nudity really, this nudity is not innocent. Shame is cunningness.

In Christianity shame is the original sin. You have heard the

story, what happened to Adam and Eve? At which moment did
the sin happen? It has been a continuous search to find in exactly
what moment the sin happened. They were forbidden to eat the
fruit of the Tree of Knowledge, but they were tempted. It is
natural: whenever anything is forbidden, temptation comes—this
is how mind behaves. But mind has another trick also: it tempts
you, but it always makes somebody else responsible. Whenever
something is forbidden the mind becomes interested, it becomes an
invitation. The mind wants to know, to poke its nose in, inquire.

Adam and Eve were tempted by themselves, nobody else was
there. But the story says the Devil, Satan tempted them. This is a
trick of the mind: to throw the responsibility on someone else. And
this 'Devil' is nothing but a scapegoat, this 'Devil' is nothing but a
trick of the mind to throw all responsibilities. You are tempted,
but 'the Devil' is the tempter so you are not responsible. He has
persuaded you, he seduced you, so he is the sinner not you. But the
temptation came from the forbiddance, and this was a trick of the
mind. The story is beautiful :

God said: "Don't eat the fruit from this tree !" If they were
trusting, then they would have avoided the tree. But they were not
trusting. They said: "Why? Why does God forbid us this tree,
and this tree is the Tree of Knowledge?" The mind must have said
to them: "If you eat, you will become like gods because you will
be knowers. And He is forbidding you because He is jealous. He
is forbidding you because He would not like you to become like
gods. You will be knowers, then nothing will be hidden from you."
But the story says the Devil tempted them and said: "He has forbidden it because He is jealous and afraid." This was just a situation for Adam and Eve to prove whether they had trust or not—
nothing else.

But the mind persuaded them—mind is 'the Devil'. The Devil
came in the shape of a snake, and the snake is the oldest symbol
of cunningness—mind is the snake, the most cunning thing. Adam
and Eve both made the Devil responsible, threw the responsibility on the Devil—and Adam also threw the responsibility on
Eve. Man has always said that woman is the tempter, so men have
always been condemning women. In all the scriptures of the world

the woman is the tempter: she leads you into temptation, she seduces you, and she is the cause of all trouble. So your so-called saints go on condemning women.

This is the way of the mind: Eve says, "The Devil"; Adam says, "Eve"; and if you ask the Devil, if you get him somewhere, he will say, "God—because why should He forbid in the first place? That created the whole trouble. Otherwise, the Garden of Eden was so big and there were millions of trees, that by themselves Adam and Eve would never have come upon the Tree of Knowledge. 'Forbidden!' They knew this was the tree, and then the whole garden became uninteresting, their whole interest became focused—it was God's fault!"

But the story is beautiful and has millions of dimensions around it; it can be interpreted in many, many ways—that is the beauty of a parable. They took the fruit of the Tree, they ate it *and immediately they became ashamed of their nakedness.* Where did the sin happen? By disobeying God? If you ask the Pope of the Vatican, he will say: "By disobeying God," because priests would like you to always obey, never disobey.

If you ask philosophers, not theologians, they will say: "By eating the fruit of knowledge." Because when you start thinking, trouble arises. Life is innocent without thinking: children are innocent because they cannot think, trees look so beautiful because they cannot think. Man looks so ugly because his mind is always burdened and tense with worries and thoughts and dreams and reveries, and he is always burdened—the whole grace is lost. So if you ask existentialist philosophers, they will say that it is because of the Tree of Knowledge.

But if you ask the psychologists, whose approach is deepest, they will say: "Because of shame." Because when you feel shame, you have started to hate yourself. When you feel ashamed you have rejected yourself—but it came through knowledge. Children cannot feel ashamed, they move naked easily, there is no problem. You force them by and by to feel ashamed: "Don't be naked!" The more they become knowers, then the more they will hide themselves.

Jesus says: "When you take off your clothing without being ashamed..." But what did Adam and Eve do? They put fig leaves around their sex organs, the first clothing invented—the world started. How can you enter again into the Garden of Eden? Throw away your fig leaves! That is what Jesus says, he says this is the way back to Paradise. This is the way back: "When you take off your clothing *without* being ashamed..." Because you can take off your clothing and remain ashamed, then deep down the clothing is there: you are hiding, you are not open. So nudity is not nakedness; you may be nude, but not naked.

Nakedness has a deeper dimension: it means no shame, no feeling of being ashamed; it means accepting your body in its totality as it is. No condemnation in the mind, no division in the body—a simple acceptance, then it is nakedness. Mahavir is not nude, he is not a member of a nudist club; he is naked, he is naked like a child. In a nudist club you are not naked. Even your nudity is calculated, it is manipulation from the mind. You are revolting, you are rebellious, you are going against the society—because the society believes in clothes, you are throwing the clothes. But it is a reaction so you are not innocent, innocent like a child.

Says Jesus: "...and take your clothes and put them under your feet as the little children, and tread on them—then shall you behold the Son of the Living One, and you shall not fear."

First, you should accept your nakedness as you are before God, just like a small child before his father and mother, not ashamed. You should not be ashamed before the Divine—then you will be real. If shame is there then masks will be used, they are bound to be used.

And a second thing: if the feeling of being ashamed disappears, you shall not fear. They are joined together: if you feel ashamed, you will be afraid; if you don't feel ashamed, you will not be afraid at all. The fear disappears with shame. And when fear and shame both disappear, your eyes are open—and then you will see the Son of God, or "the Son of the Living One;" then Jesus will be revealed to you, then you can know a Buddha.

People come to me and they ask: "How can we recognize whether a master is Enlightened or not?" You cannot recognize an Enlightened Master as you are. It is just like a blind man asking how he can recognize whether the light is on or off. How can a blind man recognize this? Recognition needs eyes and the blind man's eyes are closed. You cannot recognize whether a man is Realized or not, Enlightened or not, whether he is really a Christ or not—you cannot recognize. Otherwise, how could Jesus have been crucified if people had recognized him?

They treated him very badly, they made him look foolish, they forced him to look foolish. The day when he was carrying his cross to Golgotha, there were soldiers, urchins, a mass of people all around, throwing stones and dirty things, enjoying themselves: "This is the 'King of Israel', this is the 'Son of God', this carpenter's boy—he has gone mad!" Jokingly they placed a crown of thorns on his head and said, "Look! Here is the 'King of Israel', here is the 'Son of God'!"

And then when he was crucified, the final joke was that they put two thieves on both his sides. He was crucified as a criminal with two thieves. And not only the crowd, even those thieves made a joke of Jesus. One of the thieves said, "Now we are all going to be crucified, remember us, don't forget us in your 'Kingdom of God'. We are also being crucified with you, so take note of us because you are 'the Son'! So when we reach the Kingdom of God, make some arrangements for us too. And you can do it—you can do anything!" They were also joking. Jesus was made to look like a fool.

How do we miss recognizing a Jesus? We have our eyes closed. And the eyes are closed because of your clothing—not just because of your clothes, but many types of clothing: clothes, shame, fear, self-hatred, self-condemnation, guilt—layers upon layers of clothing.

Jesus says: "When you take off your clothing without being ashamed, and take your clothes and put them under your feet as the little children..."

When in the beginning, a child is forced to put on clothes for the first time, he rebels. He is against it because it confines his freedom and it gives him a falseness. His resistance is natural, but you can force him, you can persuade him. You say: "When we go out you have to put on these clothes, when we come back you need not; because in society clothes are needed—otherwise you cannot come with us." And he wants to come so he has to put on the clothes.

But the moment he is back, this is what he will do: he will take off the clothes, and not only take them off, he will also jump on them. They are the enemies, they make him false. He is no more himself when those clothes are there. Now he is free again. He will celebrate this nakedness by throwing off the clothes and putting them under his feet, treading on them and celebrating the nakedness. If you do that like children: "...then shall you behold the Son of the Living One, and you shall not fear."

In your nakedness there is no fear, because fear is something that is added to you—fear is created through shame. Many religions have been creating guilt, so that you are guilty, feel shameful and then you become afraid. Then a neurosis is born, and then you go to the same persons who have been creating guilt and fear in you, you go to the same persons to learn how to transcend them! They cannot be helpful because they are the creators of fear. They will say: "Pray to God and be God-fearing." They cannot lead you beyond fear. Jesus can lead you beyond fear, but then the *whole* thing has to be demolished from the very foundation. This is the foundation: Don't accept yourself, and you will always be afraid.

Accept yourself, and there will be no fear. Don't think in terms of 'should' and 'should not', 'ought' and 'ought not', and you will never be afraid. Be real and trust reality, *don't fight* with reality. If sex is there, it is there, accept it; if anger is there, it is there, accept it. Don't try to create the opposite: "I am angry, this is not good; I must not be angry, I must be forgiving. I am sexual, this must not be there, I must be celibate." *Don't create the opposite end*, because if you create the opposite end you are trying to create masks. Anger will remain, your forgiveness will be just a false face; sex will be there, moving deeper and deeper in the unconscious, and on your face there will be a mask of *brahmacharya*. That is not going to help.

I have heard: One scientist was working to find the secret of diamonds. He worked hard and almost all the clues were revealed to him, except one single point. If he came to know that single thing he would become the richest man in the world. But he worked hard and couldn't find the single clue. Then somebody suggested : "You are wasting your life and time. I have heard there is a woman in Tibet, a very wise woman, and she knows all the answers. You go to her and just ask the simple question about this, your problem, and she will give you the answer. Why waste time here?"

The man travelled to Tibet, but it took many years. It was very difficult to reach the wise woman. He went through much hardship and many times his life was at stake, but he got there. In the morning he knocked at the door and the wise woman opened it. She was a very beautiful woman, such as he had never seen before. And not only was she beautiful, but her very being was inviting—in her eyes, the glimmer of "Come hither!" She said, "Okay, so you have arrived. My husband has gone out, and this is the rule: you can ask only one question and I will answer it. One question only, remember, no second question." The scientist blurted out : "When will your husband be back?"

This is the one question he had come to ask. Somewhere deep down in the unconscious, sex must have been the problem, the real problem. Working with diamonds, finding the secret of diamonds, must have been a distraction. Deep down in the unconscious he must have been thinking : "When I become the richest man in the world, all the women—all the beautiful women—will be mine" —somewhere, although he may not have been aware of it.

You can go on working on the surface without being aware of the unconscious, but at the right moment it will come, it will explode. Escape is futile. Only transformation can be helpful, and transformation needs deep acceptance of your being as you are. With no judgment, not saying : "This is good, that is bad"—with no evaluation. Don't be a judge! Just trust your nature and flow with it, and don't try to swim upstream—that is what nakedness means.

Move with life with a deep trust, wheresoever it leads. Don't create your own goal; if you create your own goal you will become false. *Life has no goal.* If *you* have a goal you are against life. Life moves, not like a business, it moves like poetry; life moves not from the head, it moves from the heart—it is a romance. Trust is needed, doubt won't be helpful. Life is not scientific, it is irrational. Life doesn't believe in Aristotles and the logicians, it believes in love, in the poets, it believes in the mystics. It is a mystery to be lived, not a riddle to be solved—it is not a puzzle, it is not a problem. The secret is open, only *you* are closed. It is revealed everywhere : on each tree, on each leaf, in every ray of the sun it is revealed—but you are closed.

Why are you closed? You don't accept life within you, how can you accept life without? Accept! Start from the center of your being. Accept yourself as you are and then you will accept everything as it is. And with acceptance comes transformation : *you will never be the same as you are* once you accept.

The transformation happens by itself, it comes of its own accord, but it always comes in a let-go. This is what Jesus says : Be naked so that you can be in a let-go. Drop all that the society has given to you—that is the meaning of the "clothing". The society has not given you life, it has given you only the "clothing". The society has not given you the Self, it has given you the ego. Drop the clothing and the ego disappears. Think of yourself walking on the street nude.

One man called Ebrahim came to his Master—Ebrahim had been a King, and then the search started—he came to the Master and the Master said, "Are you ready to accept *everything*?"

Ebrahim said, "I have come for that—you say and I will do."

The Master looked at him and said, "Okay, drop your clothes!"

The disciples became uneasy, because Ebrahim was a great King and this was too much and unnecessary. It was never asked of them, so why such a hard thing for the King? One disciple even whispered in the Master's ear, "This is too much, don't be so hard —you never asked it of us!"

But the Master said, "And take your shoes in your hands and go on the street and beat your head with the shoes! Move all over the town naked !"

This town was his capital, but Ebrahim followed. Nude, he went around the capital beating his head with his own shoes. And it is said that when he came back he was Enlightened.

What happened? He dropped his clothing. And he was a man with great potential, that is why the Master demanded so much. A Master demands only that much which is possible for you. The more potential you have, the more he will demand, but if you are just poor, he will not demand so much. Ebrahim was a man with much potential—he himself became a great Master in his own right. *What happened?* This happened : clothing dropped, as Jesus is saying to his disciples; ego dropped—all that society has given to you.

Many times the ego drops by itself because it is a burden, but again you put it on your head and carry on. Many times you are a failure, many times you don't succeed. Many times the ego falls by itself, but again, bruised, frustrated, defeated, a failure, you will carry the burden in some hope.

Here is one story I have heard : One day the lion came to the tiger and said, "Who is the boss of this forest?"

The tiger said, "Of course, master, you are the one, you are the King!"

Then the lion went to a bear, grabbed hold of him and asked, "Who is the master? Who is the boss?"

The bear said, "Of course, there is no need to ask—you are the King of all the animals, you are the boss!"

And then the lion went to the elephant and asked the same question : "Who is the boss here?"

The elephant grabbed the lion and threw him away, at least fifty feet. He was struck by a rock, bleeding, bruised, weak, but he stood and said : "If you don't know the right answer this is no way to behave!"

This is what you have been doing. But you will not drop, you will also say : "If you don't know the right answer this is no way to behave! Why be so rough? You can simply say : 'I don't know the answer.' "

If you can recognize that in failure all that society has given you falls, the failure can become the beginning of the greatest success that is possible in life. That is why only in failure does a man become religious—if he can recognize the failure. It is very difficult to become religious when you succeed. Then the clothing is giving you so much, why bother about being naked? Then the clothing is such a good investment. But in failure, suddenly you become aware of the nakedness that is there. Nothing can hide it, you can only deceive yourself.

Use your failures! And when you are thrown against a rock, bruised and bleeding, don't repeat the stupidity of the lion. Recognize that there is no success in this world. There cannot be, because this whole thing is so false and with false faces how can you succeed? Even your Napoleons, your Secundars, your Alexanders, your Genghis Khans, are all failures.

A Jesus succeeds because he stands in his originality, he stands in his nature. Try to understand this; and not only through understanding, but by gradually dropping your clothing become naked and you will be pure. Then you will have thrown that apple Adam and Eve ate; then the door of Paradise is open again.

Christians say that with Adam and Eve humanity was thrown out of Paradise; with Jesus the doors are again open—you can enter. But it will not happen just by being Christians. You will have to recognize Jesus, and that recognition comes only when you have recognized yourself as Jesus—nothing less can do.

Fifth Discourse

25th August 1974, Poona, India

THE FIFTH SAYING

Jesus said to them :
If you fast
you will beget sin for yourselves;
and if you pray
you will be condemned;
and if you give alms
you will do evil to your spirits.

And if you go into any land
and wander in the regions,
if they receive you,
eat what they set before you,
and heal the sick among them.

For what goes into your mouth
will not defile you,
but what comes out of your mouth,
that is what will defile you.

This is a very strange saying, but very significant also. It looks strange because man is not real, he lives in falsity. So whatsoever he does, it is going to be false.

If you pray you will pray for the wrong reasons; if you fast you will fast for the wrong reasons—because you are wrong. So the question is not what is right to do, the question is how to be right in your being. If your being is right, then whatsoever you do will be right automatically; but if your being is not right, not centered, not authentic, then whatsoever you do, it is going to be wrong.

Finally everything depends not on what you do, but on who you are. If a thief goes to pray his prayer is going to be wrong, because how can prayer be born out of a heart who has been deceiving everybody—stealing, lying, harming? How is prayer possible out of the heart of a thief? It is impossible. The prayer can change you, but from where will the prayer come? It will come from you. If you are sick, your prayer is going to be sick.

Mulla Nasrudin once applied for a job. In the application he mentioned many qualifications. He said, "I stood first in my university, and I was offered the vice-presidency of a national bank. I refused because I am not interested in money. I am an honest man, a true man. I have no greed, I'm not bothered about the salary; whatsoever you give me will be okay. And I love work— sixty-five hours per week."

When the superintendent who was conducting his interview looked at his application, he was surprised and said, "Lordy! Don't you have any weaknesses?"

Nasrudin said, "Only one: I am a liar!"

But that one covers all the rest. No need to have any other
weakness, one is enough. There are not many weaknesses in you,
you have only one weakness—out of that one all are born. And
you have to remember your weakness, because that is going to
follow you wherever you go like a shadow; whatsoever you do,
it is going to colour it.

So the basic thing in religion is not what to do, the basic thing
is what to be. 'Being' means your innermost core, 'doing' means
your surface activities on the circumference. 'Doing' means your
relationship with others, with the outer world, and 'being' means
you as you are, unrelated, as you are within.

You can be without doing anything, but you cannot be without
the being. Doing is secondary, dispensable. A man can remain
inactive, not doing anything, but a man cannot be without being
—so being is the essence. Jesus, Krishna, Buddha, they all talk
about being; and the temples, churches, mosques, organizations,
sects, the so-called gurus and teachers and priests, they all talk
about doing. If you ask Jesus, he will talk about your being and
how to transform it. If you ask the Pope of the Vatican he will
talk about what to do, about morality. Morality is concerned with
doing, religion with being.

This distinction has to be kept as clear as possible, because
everything else depends on it. Whenever a person like Jesus is
born we misunderstand him. And the misunderstanding is because
we miss this distinction : he talks about the being, and we listen
to him and interpret as if he is talking about doing.

If you understand this then this saying will be very clear, very
useful. It can become a light on your path. Otherwise it is very
strange and contradictory and will look anti-religious. When Jesus
spoke it must have seemed to the priests that his sayings were anti-
religious, that is why they crucified him. They thought he was
the man who was going to destroy religion.

Look at the saying—apparently it appears so :

*"Jesus said to them : If you fast you will beget sin for
yourselves..."*

And we have always heard that religion teaches fasting, because it has been told again and again that when you fast you are purified through it. The whole religion of the Jains depends on fasting. If they hear this saying from Jesus they will say: "This man is dangerous, and the Jews did well to crucify him!"

The Jews were also disturbed: such sayings are rebellious and their whole morality would be lost. If you say to people: "If you fast you will beget sin for yourselves," fasting becomes a sin! "...and if you pray you will be condemned." Have you ever heard that if you pray you will be condemned? Then what is religion? We think religion is going to church and praying to God, and Jesus says:

"...if you pray you will be condemned; and if you give alms you will do evil to your spirits."

Strangest of sayings, but very meaningful. Jesus is saying that as you are you cannot do anything right. The emphasis is not on fast or no fast; the emphasis is not on giving alms or not; the emphasis is not to pray or not—the emphasis is: whatsoever you are right now, as you are, everything will go wrong.

Can you pray? You can go to the temple because that is easy, but you cannot pray. Prayer needs a different quality—that quality you don't have, so you can only deceive yourself that you are praying. Go and look in the temple at people who are praying: they are simply deceiving themselves, they don't have that quality of prayerfulness! How can you pray? And if you have the quality of prayerfulness, what need is there to go to the temple or the church?

Wherever you are prayer is: you move, you walk—and it is prayer! You eat, you love—and it is prayer! You look, you breathe— and it is prayer! Because the quality of prayerfulness is always there, it is just like breathing. Then you cannot be in a moment of non-prayer. But then there is no need to go to the temple or to the church. Churches and temples exist for those who want to deceive themselves, for those who have no quality of prayer and still would like to believe that they are praying.

One man was dying, a sinner. He had never been to the temple, never prayed, never listened to what the priests say, but at the moment of death he became afraid. He asked the priest to come, he begged. When the priest came there was a crowd. Many people were around because the sinner was a great, successful man; he was a politician, he had power, he had money. So, many people had gathered.

The sinner asked the priest to come near because he wanted to say something in private. The priest came near and the sinner whispered in his ear, "I know that I am a sinner and I know well that I have never gone to church, I am not a church-goer. I am not a religious man at all, I have never prayed, so I know well that the world is not going to forgive me. But help me, and give me a little confidence, and tell me that God will forgive me! The world is not going to forgive me, that I know, and nothing can be done about it now—but tell me one thing: that God is going to forgive me!"

"Well," said the priest, "perhaps He will, because He didn't get to know you the way we have come to know you. Perhaps He *will*, because He does not know you the *way* we have come to know you." But if you cannot deceive the world, can you deceive God? If you cannot deceive ordinary minds, can you deceive the Divine Mind? It is just a consolation, a comfortable thing: "Perhaps." But that 'perhaps' is absolutely wrong; don't hang on such 'perhaps'!

Prayer is a quality that belongs to the essence and not to the personality. Personality is that which you have been doing, it is a relationship with others. Essence is that which has come to you— it is nothing of your doing, it is a gift of God. Prayer belongs to the essence: it is a quality, it is nothing you can do.

What is a fast? How can you fast? And why do people fast? Jesus' saying is very deep, deeper than any assertion of Mahavir about fasting. Jesus is relating a *very deep* psychological truth, and the truth is that the mind moves to the extreme: a person who is too obsessed with food can fast easily. This will look strange, paradoxical, that a person who eats too much can fast easily, that a person who is too greedy for food can fast easily. But only that type of person *can* fast easily. Someone who has always been balanced in his diet will find it almost impossible to fast—why? To answer this we have to go into the physiology and psychology of fasting.

First physiology, because that is the outer layer. If you eat too much you collect too much reserve, you collect too much fat. Then you can fast very easily, because fat is nothing but a reservoir, it is a reserve. Women can fast more easily than men, and you know it. If you look around at people who go on fasts, particularly Jains, you will find that if one man fasts, then five women can fast: that is the ratio. The husband cannot fast but the wife can. Why? Because the feminine body accumulates more fat, it is easier if you have much fat on you, because on a fast you have to eat your own fat. That is why you lose one or two pounds in weight every day. Where does that weight go? You are eating yourself, it is a sort of meat-eating.

So there is not much difficulty for women, they can fast easily, they collect more fat than men. That's why their bodies are more round. Fat people can fast very easily, they can go on diets, they are always in search of diets. A man, an ordinary healthy man, can collect so much fat that for three months he can fast and he will not die; ninety days—that much reserve can be collected. But if you are lean and thin—that means if you have been eating a balanced amount, only that much which is needed for the day-to-day activity of the body, and you have not collected much fat—you cannot fast. That is why the cult of fasting is always around rich people, never the poor.

Observe: whenever a poor man celebrates a religious day, he celebrates by feasting; and whenever a rich man celebrates a religious day, he celebrates it by fasting. The Jains are the richest people in India, hence their fasting. But a Mohammedan, a poor Mohammedan, or a poor Hindu, when the religious day comes, he has a feast because the whole year he is hungry, so how can he celebrate the day of religion with more fasting? He is already fasting the whole year, and the religious day *must* be different from the ordinary days. So that is the only difference: he will put on new clothes and he will have a good feast and enjoy himself, and give thanks to God. That is a poor man's religion.

Now, in America, fasting and the cult of fasting will develop rapidly. It is developing already because America has become so rich and people are eating so much that now, from somewhere, fasting has to come in. In America all the cults of fasting are growing rapidly—they may have different names but, physiologically, your body must have more fat than is needed, then fasting is easy.

Secondly, psychologically, you must be obsessed with food. Food must be your obsession: you must be eating too much, eating and eating, and *thinking* about eating more and more. That type of mind one day gets fed up with food and thinking about food. If you think too much about anything you will get fed up with it. If you get too much of anything you will get fed up with it. Then the opposite becomes attractive: you have been eating too much, now you need to fast. Through fasting you will be able to eat again with taste, your appetite will come back—that is the only way.

And mind has a basic law: that it can move to the opposite very easily, but it cannot remain in the middle. Balance is the most difficult thing for the mind, extremes are always easy. If you are an overeater you can become a faster, because that is another extreme—but you cannot remain in the middle. You cannot be on the right food, the right diet. No! Either this side or that—mind always leans to the extreme. It is just like the pendulum of a clock: it goes to the right, then to the left, then to the right; but if it stops in the middle then the clock stops, then there is no possibility for the clock to move.

If your mind stops in the middle then thinking stops, then the clock stops. But if you go to the extreme, sooner or later the opposite will again become meaningful, attractive, and you will have to go to it.

Jesus understands this well, very well. And he says: "If you fast you will beget sin for yourselves..."

What is sin? In Jesus' terminology the extreme, to move to the extreme is sin. To remain just in the middle is to be beyond sin. Why? Why is it sin to move to the extreme? To move to the extreme is sin because in the extreme you have chosen *half* and one half has been denied—and the Truth is whole. When you say, "I will eat too much," you have chosen half. When you say, "I will not eat at all," you have again chosen half, you have chosen something. In the middle there is no choice: you feed the body, and you are not obsessed either this way or that; you are not obsessed at all, you are not neurotic. The body gets its needs, but you are not overburdened by its needs.

This balance is going beyond sin. So whenever you have an imbalance you are a sinner. Jesus' idea is that a person who is too much in the world is a sinner, but if he moves to the other extreme, renounces the world, becomes too much against the world, then again he is a sinner. A person who accepts the world, without choosing this way or that, transcends it.

Acceptance is transcendence. Choice means you have entered in, your ego has come in, now you are fighting.

Whenever you go to one extreme you have to fight continuously, because at the extreme you can never be at ease—only in the middle can you be at ease. At the extreme you will always be tense, worried, anxiety will be there. Only in the middle, when you are balanced, is there no anxiety, no anguish, you are at home; nothing worries you because there is no tension. Tension means the extreme. You have tried many extremes, that's why you are so tense.

Either you are after women and then sex continuously moves in the mind, or you become against them and then too sex moves in the mind. If you are existing for sex, then sex will be the only thing in the mind, the smoke. If you are against it, an enemy, then again sex will be in the mind—because friends you remember, but enemies you remember more. Sometimes friends can be forgotten, but enemies never, they are always there; how can you forget your enemy? So people who go on moving in the world of sex are filled with sex. And go and look in the monasteries where there are people who have moved to the other extreme—they are continuously with sex, their whole mind has become sexual.

Eat too much, become obsessed with food as if your whole life exists to eat, then continuously there will be food in the mind. Then fast, then too continuously food will be in the mind. And if something is continuously on the mind, it becomes a burden. The woman is not the problem, the man is not the problem—*sex* continuously on the mind is the problem. Food is *not* a problem: you eat and it is finished; but food on the mind continuously, then it is a problem.

And if there are many things on the mind continuously, the mind is dissipating energy; the mind becomes dull, bored, so burdened that life seems just meaningless. When the mind is unburdened, weightless, fresh, then intelligence happens, then you look at the world with a fresh eye, with a fresh consciousness, unburdened. Then the whole existence is beautiful—that beauty is God. Then the whole existence is alive—that aliveness is God.

Then the whole existence is *ecstatic*, every moment of it, every bit of it is blissful—that bliss and ecstasy is God.

God is not a person somewhere waiting for you; God is a revelation in *this* world. When the mind is silent, clear, unburdened, young, fresh, virgin—with a virgin mind God is everywhere. But your mind is dead, and you have made it dead through a particular process. That process is: moving from one extreme to another, then again moving from this extreme to another, but *never* staying in the middle.

I have heard about one drunkard who was walking on a street, a very big street, very broad. He asked a man, "Where is the other side of the street?" It was so broad and the night was descending, the light was disappearing, and he was completely drunk. He couldn't see well so he asked, "Where is the other side?" The man took pity on him and helped him to move to the other side.

When he reached the other side he again asked another man, "Where is the other side?" The man tried to take him to the other side. The drunkard stood there and said, "Wait! What type of people are here? I was there and I asked: Where is the other side? They brought me here, and now I ask: Where is the other side? Now they say it is there! And you are taking me again to that side. What *type* of people are here? Where is the other side?"

Wherever you are it makes no difference: the opposite extreme becomes the other side and becomes attractive, because distance creates attraction. You can't imagine the attraction of sex for a man who is trying to be celibate—you cannot imagine! You cannot imagine the attraction of food for a man who is fasting. You cannot imagine because that is an experience: *continuously one thing* in the mind—food, sex. And this can go to the very end. Even when you are dying, if some extreme is there you will be obsessed.

How to be at ease and relaxed? Don't move to the extreme; that is the meaning of the saying: Don't move to the extreme! Jesus knows well that you are food addicts—don't go on a fast, that is not going to help:

"If you fast you will beget sin for yourselves; and if you pray you will be condemned..."

What *is* prayer? Ordinarily we think prayer is asking for something, demanding, complaining: you have desires and God can help you to fulfill them. You go to God's door to ask for something, you go as a beggar. For you prayer is begging, but prayer can never be begging; prayer can only be a thankfulness, a gratitude. But these are totally different: when you go to beg, your prayer is not the end, it is just a means. The prayer is not significant because you are praying to get something—that something is significant, not prayer. And many times you go and your desire is not fulfilled. Then you will drop praying, you will say: "Useless !" For you it is a means !

Prayer can never be a means, just as love can never be a means. Love is the end : you love, not for something else; love in itself has an intrinsic value—you simply love ! It is so blissful ! Nothing is beyond it, there is no result to be sought through it. It is not a means to some end, *it is the end !* And prayer is love—you simply go and enjoy it, not asking, not begging.

Prayer itself, intrinsically, is so beautiful, you feel so ecstatic and happy, that you simply go and give thanks to the Divine that He allowed you to be, He allowed you to breathe, He allowed you to see—what colours ! He allowed you to listen, He allowed you to be aware. You have not earned it, this is a gift. You go to the temple with a deep thankfulness, just to give thanks : "Whatsoever You have given me, it is too much. I never deserved it !" Do you deserve anything? Can you find that you are deserving in any way? If you were not here, could you say that some injustice had been done to you? No ! All that you have got is simply a gift, it is out of the Divine love. You don't deserve it.

God overflows with His love. When you understand this a quality is born in you : the quality of being grateful. Then you simply go to give Him your thanks, then you simply feel gratitude. Gratitude is prayer, and it is so beautiful to feel grateful that nothing can be compared to it, there is nothing in comparison to it. Prayer is the climax of your happiness, it cannot become a means to some other end.

Jesus says : "...and if *you* pray you will be condemned..." because your prayer will be wrong. Jesus knows well that whenever you go to the temple, you will go to beg something, to ask for something. It will be a means, and if you make prayer a means, it is a sin.

What is your love? Because through love you can understand what happens in prayer. Do you love a person—really? Do you love, or does something else exist there? A mutual gratification? When you love a person, do you really *love* the person? Do you give out of your heart? Or do you just exploit the other in the name of love?

You use the other in the name of love. It may be sexual, it may be some other use, but you use the other. And if. the other says : "No, don't use me !" will your love continue to be there, or will it disappear? Then you will say : "What is the use ?" If the other appreciates you, if a beautiful woman appreciates you, your ego is fulfilled. A beautiful woman looks up to you and you feel for the first time that you are a man. But if she does not appreciate you, does not look up to you, love disappears. If a beautiful man, a strong man, looks up to you as a beautiful woman, appreciates you continuously, you feel gratified because ego is fulfilled.

This is mutual exploitation—you call it love. And if it creates hell there is no wonder about it; it *has* to create hell because love is just the name, and under the name something else is hidden. Love can never create hell, love is the very quality of heaven. If you love, you are happy, and your happiness will show that you are in love.

But look at lovers : they don't seem to be happy—only in the beginning when they are just planning, unknowingly, unconsciously throwing nets to catch each other; but their poetry and their romance and all their nonsense is just to catch the other. Once the fish is caught then they are unhappy, then they feel as if they are in a bondage. Each other's ego becomes a bondage and both try to dominate and possess each other.

This love becomes condemnation. If your *love* is wrong your prayer cannot be right, because prayer means love to the Whole— and if you have been a failure in love, with an ordinary human being, how can you succeed in your love with the Divine?

Love is just a step towards prayer. You have to learn. If you can love a human being, you know a secret. The same key is to be used with the Divine, millions of times magnified and multiplied of course. The dimension is great but the key remains the same. Love is an end in itself and there is no ego in it. When you are egoless there is love. Then you simply give without asking, without any return. You simply give because giving is so beautiful, you share because sharing is so wonderful—then there is no bargain. When there is no bargain, no ego, love flows—then you are not frozen, then you melt. This melting has to be learnt because only then can you pray.

Jesus says to his disciples : "...if *you* pray," and the emphasis is on 'you', "you will be condemned..." He knows his disciples very well. "...and if you give alms you will do evil to your spirits."

Have you ever observed what happens inside you when you give something to a beggar? Is it out of kindness or is it out of ego? If you are alone on the street and a beggar comes, you say : "Go away !" because there is nobody to see what you are doing to the beggar, your ego is not in any way hurt. But beggars also know the psychology; they will never ask you if you are alone on the street and there is nobody around, they will bypass you—this is not the right moment. But if you are moving with some friends, they will catch hold of you.

In the market when many people are looking they will catch hold of you, because now they know that if you say : "No !" people will think, "You are so unkind, so cruel?" So then you give something *to save your ego*. You are not giving to the beggar, it is not out of kindness. And remember well that whenever you give, the beggar will go and tell other beggars that he deceived you, he befooled you. He will laugh because he also knows why you have given. It is not a question of kindness.

Kindness gives for a different reason : you feel the misery of the other, you feel it so deeply that you become part of it. Not only do you feel the misery, you also feel the responsibility that if one man is miserable, you are responsible somehow—because the whole is responsible for the parts : "I am helping a society which creates beggars. I am helping a society, a type of government, a structure, which creates exploitation; I am part of it and this beggar is a victim." You feel not only kindness, you feel responsibility : you *have* to do something. And if you give to this beggar, you will not want him to be thankful to you. Rather, you will be thankful to him *if* it is out of kindness, because you know this is nothing.

The society continues and you have much investment in the

society which creates this beggary. And you know that you are part of this establishment in which poor people exist, because the rich cannot exist without the poor. And you know well that you also have ambitions to become rich. You feel the whole guilt, you feel the sin—but then giving is totally different. If you feel that you have done a great thing because you have given two *paise* to this beggar, then Jesus says : "...you will do evil to your spirits ..." because you don't know what you are doing.

Give out of your love, give out of your kindness. But then you are not giving to a beggar, then it is not alms, then you are simply sharing with a friend. When the beggar becomes a friend it is totally different : you are not higher than the beggar, you are not doing something great to the beggar, the ego is not fulfilled. On the contrary, you feel : "I cannot do anything—just giving that little amount of money is not of much help."

It happened once : A Zen Master lived in a cottage on a far-away hill, many miles away from the town. One full moon night a thief entered. The Master became very worried because there was nothing that could be stolen except one blanket, and he was wearing that blanket, so what to do? He became so worried that when the thief came in, he put the blanket just by the door and hid himself in a corner.

The thief looked all around but in the dark he couldn't see the blanket—there was nothing. Dejected, frustrated, he was going to leave. So the Master shouted, "Wait! Take that blanket! And I am very sorry, because you came such a long way, the night is cold, and there is nothing in this house. Next time you come please inform me beforehand. I will arrange something. I am a poor man, but I will make some arrangements so you can steal. But *have pity on me*, otherwise I will feel very upset: you take that blanket—and don't say no !" The thief could not believe what was happening. He was apprehensive; this man seemed strange, nobody had behaved this way before. He simply took the blanket and ran away.

The Master wrote a poem that night. Sitting by his window— the night is cold, the full moon is in the sky—he wrote a poem, and the gist of the poem was: "What a beautiful moon! I would like to give this moon to that thief!" And tears were flowing from

his eyes, he was weeping and crying and feeling: "That poor man
came from so far away!"

Then the thief was caught. There were other crimes against
him, and this blanket was also found with him. That blanket
was very famous—everybody knew that it belonged to that Zen
Master. So the Zen Master had to go to court. The magistrate told
him: "Simply say that this blanket is yours, and it is enough.
This man has stolen this blanket from your hut—just say yes,
that's all."

The Master said, "But he never stole it, he is not a thief! I
know him well. Once he visited me, of course, but he has not
stolen anything—this is my gift, this blanket I have given to him.
And I still feel guilty that there was nothing else to give. The
blanket is old, almost worthless; and this man is so good, he
accepted it. Not only that, in his heart there was thankfulness
towards me."

Jesus says: ". . .and if you give alms you will do evil to your
spirits"—because you will give for the wrong reasons. You can
do a good thing for the wrong reasons and then you miss, then
you miss totally.

*"And if you go into any land and wander in the regions, if they
receive you, eat what they set before you, and heal the sick
among them."*

Two things Jesus says to his disciples: first, "Whatsoever they
give, receive it, don't make any conditions."

Buddhism spread so much—almost half the world became
Buddhist; but Jain monks could not go out of India, so Jains
remained confined to this country, no more than thirty *lakhs*
(three million). Mahavir and Buddha were of the same calibre,
so why couldn't Jains send their message outside? Because of the
Jain monk, he will not go, he has conditions: a particular type
of food, prepared in a particular way, given to him in a particular
manner. How can he go out of the country? Even in India he
can move only through those towns where Jains live, because he
will not accept food from anybody else. As a result of this food
addiction Mahavir became useless for the world, the world was
unable to use a great man.

Jesus says to his disciples: "...go into any land and wander in the regions, if they receive you eat what they set before you—don't make any conditions that you will eat only a certain type of food."

Your movement in the world should be unconditional. If you make conditions you become a burden. That's why Jesus' disciples have never been a burden: they will eat whatsoever· is given to them, they will wear whatsoever clothes they can get, they will live in all types of climate, with all types of people, they will mix with everybody. That's why Christianity could spread like a fire: it is because of the attitude of the disciple—he is unconditional.

Second, Jesus says to do only *one* thing: "... and heal the sick among them."

He doesn't say: "Teach them what truth is." No! That is useless! He doesn't say: "Force them to believe in my message. That is useless! Simply heal the sick! Because if a person is sick, how can he come to understand truth? How can he understand it? When his soul is sick, how can he receive my message? Heal the sick! Make him whole, that's all." Once he is whole and healthy he will be able to understand truth, he will be able to understand Jesus.

"Be servants, healers—just help people to be healed." Psychologically everybody is ill. Physiologically everybody may not be ill, but everybody is ill as far as mind is concerned, and a deep healing is needed in the mind. Jesus says: "Be therapists, go and heal their minds."

Try to understand what the problem is with the mind: divided it is ill, undivided it is healed. If there are many contradictory things in the mind, it is ill, it is like a crowd, a mad crowd. But if there is only one thing in the mind, it is healed—because through the one a crystallization happens. *Unless the mind is brought to one* it will remain ill.

There are certain moments when *your* mind also comes to the one. Certain moments sometimes accidentally happen: one morning you get up, it is early, everything is fresh and the sun is rising; the whole thing is just so beautiful that you become concentrated. You forget the market you have to go to, you forget the office you have to go to, you forget that you are a Hindu or a Mohammedan or a Christian, you forget that you are a father or a mother or a son—you forget *this* world. The sun is so beautiful and the morning is so fresh, you get into it, you become one. For a single moment, when you are one, the mind is whole and healthy, you feel a bliss surging all over your being. It can happen accidentally, but you can also make it happen consciously.

Whenever the mind is one, a higher quality expresses itself and the lower immediately settles itself. It is just like in a school: when the principal is in the school, then the teachers are working well and the students are learning well and there is order. But when the principal has gone out, then the teachers are the highest authority, and then there is not so much order because the teachers are at liberty. A lower energy starts functioning—they will start smoking, they will go and take tea and they will start gossiping. Still, if teachers are there, the students are disciplined. But a class becomes chaos if the teacher goes out; it is a crowd, a mad crowd. The teacher enters the class—suddenly everything changes, a higher force has entered, the chaos disappears.

The chaos simply showed that the higher force was absent. When there is no chaos, when there is harmony, it simply shows that the higher force is present. Your mind is in chaos—a higher point is needed, a higher crystallization is needed. You are just like school-children, a class, a mad class, and the teacher is not there. *Whenever* you become concentrated, immediately, a higher function enters.

So Jesus says: "Heal!" The word 'heal' comes from the same root as the word 'whole'; and the word 'holy' also comes from the same root as 'heal' and 'whole'. Heal a person and he becomes whole, and whenever a person is whole, he becomes holy. This is the whole process. Mind is in a disease because there is no center in it. Have you got a center in the mind? Can you say, "This center is me"? Every moment it changes: in the morning you are angry, then you feel that anger is you; in the afternoon you become loving, then you think: "Love is me;" by the evening you are frustrated and then you think: "The frustration is me." Is there any center in you? Or are you just a moving crowd?

There is no center as you are, there is no center yet—and a man without a center is ill. A healthy man is a man with a center. Jesus said: "Give people centers!" so whatsoever chaos is around you a center remains inside, you remain centered twenty-four hours a day; something remains continuous—that continuum will become your Self.

Look at it in this way: there are three layers of existence. One layer is of objects, the objective world; all around, your senses report about it—your eyes see, your ears hear, your hands touch. The objective world is the first layer of existence, and if you get lost in it you remain content with the most superficial. A second layer exists within you, the layer of the mind: thoughts, emotions, love, anger, feelings—that is the second layer. The first layer is common—if I have a stone in my hand you will all be able to see it—it is a common objectivity. But nobody can see what is inside your mind.

When you see me, you never see me, you only see my body; when I see you, I never see you, I only see your body. Another person can see your behaviour: how you act, what you do, how you react. He can see anger on your face, the redness, the cruelty that takes over, the violence in your eyes, but he cannot see the anger within your mind. He can see the loving gesture that you make with your body, but he cannot see the love. And you may only be making a gesture, there may be no love. You can deceive others just by acting, and that is what you have been doing.

Your body can be known by everybody else, not your mind. The objective world is common and that is the world of science. Science says that is the only reality because, "We can't know about your thoughts—whether they exist or not nobody knows. Only you say they do, but they are not common, objective; we cannot experiment with them, we cannot see them. You report them but you may be deceiving us, or you may be deceived—who knows?" Your thoughts are not things but you know well that they exist. Not only do things exist, thoughts also exist. But thoughts are personal, private, they are not common.

The outer layer, the first layer, the reality on the surface, creates science. The second layer, of thoughts and feelings, creates philosophy, poetry. But is this all? Matter and mind? If this is all then you can never be centered, because mind is always a flux. It has no center: yesterday you had certain thoughts, today you have other thoughts, tomorrow you will have other thoughts again—it is like a river, there is no center in it.

In the mind you cannot find any center: thoughts change, feelings change, it is a flux. So you will always remain ill, ill at ease, you can never be whole. But there is also another layer of existence, the deepest. The first is the objective world, science and its world; the second is the thought-world—philosophy and poetry, feelings, thoughts. Then there is a third world which is of religion, and that is the world of the witness—the one who looks at the thoughts, the one who looks at the things.

That one is one, there are not two. Whether you look at a house or you close your eyes and look at the picture of the house inside, the *looker* remains the same. Whether you look at anger or you look at love, the looker remains the same. Whether you are sad or happy, whether life has become a poetry or life has become a nightmare, makes no difference—the looker remains the same, the witness remains the same. The witness is the only center, and this witness is the world of religion.

When Jesus says: "Go and heal people," he is saying, "Go and give them their centers, make them witnesses. Then they will neither be involved in the world, nor involved in their thoughts, they will be rooted in their being." And once you are rooted in the being then everything changes, the quality changes—then you can pray.

But then you will not pray for the wrong reasons, then your prayer will be a gratitude. Then you will pray, not like a beggar, but like an emperor who has too much of everything. Then you will give, but you will not give for the ego, you will give out of compassion. You will give because giving is so beautiful and makes you so blissful. Then you can fast, but that fasting will not be an obsession with food, that fasting will be totally different.

That is what Mahavir's fast is, totally different. You will sometimes forget the body so much that you will not notice that there is hunger; you will move away from the body so much that the body will not be able to inform you that you are hungry. The word for fast in Sanskrit is very beautiful, that word is *upawas*.

The word carries no sense at all of food or no food, it has nothing of fasting in it, the word simply means 'living nearer to yourself'; *upawas* means 'living nearer to yourself', 'being nearer to yourself'. A moment comes when you are so centered that the body is completely forgotten, as if there is no body. Then you cannot feel the hunger, and fasting happens—but it is a happening, it is not a doing.

You can remain in this centering for many days. It happened to Ramakrishna: he would go into ecstasy and for six or seven days he would remain as if dead, his body would not move, it kept the same gesture; if he was standing he would continue standing. Disciples would have to make him lie down, and they would have to feed him forcibly with some water, some milk— but it was as if he were not there. *This is a fast:* because you are no longer in the body.

Being in the body, you are no longer in the body. But you cannot *do* this. How can you do it? Because all doing *is* through the body, you have to use the body to do anything. This fast cannot be done because this fast means bodilessness. This can happen—it happens to a Mahavir, to a Jesus, to a Mohammed. It can happen to you too.

Jesus says: "Go among the people, *eat what they set before you, and heal the sick among them. For what goes into your mouth will not defile you, but what comes out of your mouth, that is what will defile you.*"

This is a very significant saying. It means: Don't bother too much if the food is not pure, or if a *Shudra* (an untouchable) has touched it, or if a woman who is having her period has passed by and her shadow has defiled it. The question is not what you take in, the question is what you bring out—because what you bring out, *that shows* your quality; how you transform what you take in, that's the thing.

A lotus is born in the mud; the mud is transformed and becomes a lotus. The lotus never says: "I will not eat this mud, this is dirty!" No, that is not the question. If you are a lotus nothing is dirty. If you have the capacity of a lotus, if you have the transforming power, the alchemy, then you can remain in the mud and a lotus will be born. And if you don't have the quality of a lotus, then even if you live in gold, only mud will come out of you. What goes in is not the point. The point is that if you are centered in your being, whatsoever goes in is changed, is transformed; it takes your quality of being and comes out.

In Buddha's life he was once accidentally poisoned, it was food-poisoning, but it was an accident. A poor man had been waiting for many days to invite Buddha to his house. So one day he came early, at four o'clock in the morning, and he stood near the tree where Buddha was sleeping so that he should be the first one to invite him—and he was the first. Buddha opened his eyes and the man said, "Accept my invitation! I have been waiting for many, many days, and for many years I have been preparing. I am a poor man and I cannot afford much, but this has been a long longing that you should come and eat at my home." Buddha said, "I will come."

Just at that moment the King of the city approached with his chariot, his ministers, and a long retinue, and he prayed to Buddha: "Come, I invite you to my palace!"

Buddha said, "It is difficult; my disciples will come to your palace, but I have accepted an invitation—and this man was here first. The moment I opened my eyes he was the first to invite me, so I will have to go with him."

The King tried to persuade him that this was not good: "This man, what can he give you to eat? His children are starving, he has no food!"

Buddha said, "That is not the point. He has invited me and I have to go." So Buddha went.

What had that man done? In Bihar and in other poor parts of India, people gather many things in the rainy season; whatsoever comes up and sprouts on the earth they gather. A sort of flower, the *kukarmutta* (mushroom), a wide umbrella-shaped plant, comes in the rainy season and they gather it, dry it and keep it for the whole year. That is their only vegetable—but sometimes it goes poisonous.

So that man had gathered *kukarmutta* for Buddha. He had dried and prepared it, but when Buddha started eating it was poisonous, it was very bitter. But that was the only vegetable the man had prepared, and if Buddha had said, "This is bitter and I cannot eat it," he would have been hurt because he had nothing else. So Buddha went on eating and he never mentioned that it was bitter and poisonous. And the man was very happy. Buddha came back and the poison started working. The physician came and he said, "It is a very difficult case. The poison has entered into the blood stream and it is impossible to do anything—Buddha will have to die!"

The first thing Buddha did was this: he gathered his disciples and told them, "This man is not ordinary, this man is exceptional. Because the first food was given to me by my mother, and this is the last food—he is just like my mother. So honour him because this is something rare!

"In thousands of years a Buddha happens, and only two people will have this rare opportunity: the first is the mother, to help Buddha enter into the world; and the last is this man, to help me enter into the other world. So go and announce to the people that this man is to be worshipped—he is great!"

The disciples were very much disturbed because they were thinking of killing the man. When everybody had left, Ananda said to Buddha, "This is too much for us to do, to respect that man. He is a murderer, he has *killed* you! So don't say this. Why do you say this?"

Buddha said, "I know you, you may kill him—that's why I say this. Go and pay respect to him. This is a rare opportunity that happens only a few times in the world: giving Buddha his last food."

Poison is given to him, but love comes out. This is the alchemy: he feels compassion for this man who almost killed him. Even when poison is given to a Buddha, only love comes out.

Jesus says: "For what goes into your mouth will not defile you," even poison cannot defile you, "but what comes out of your mouth, that is what will defile you." So remember how you transform things: if somebody insults you, he feeds you with an insult, that is *not* going to defile you. What comes out of you now? How do you transform the insult? Does love come out of you or hate?

So Jesus says: "Remember what comes out of you, don't bother much about what goes in." And this has to be remembered by you too, otherwise your whole approach can go wrong. If you continuously think about what goes in, then you never develop that capacity of being which can transform things. Then the whole thing becomes outward: pure food, this type of food and that type of food; nobody should touch you, you are a *Brahmin*, a pure soul. Then the whole thing becomes nonsense! The real thing is not what comes in, the real thing is to remember that you have to transform it.

Once Shankaracharya was in Benaras, and one morning he went to take his ritual bath in the Ganges, thinking, with the old *Brahmin* type of mind, that the Ganges can make you pure. When he was coming back after taking his bath, one untouchable, one *Shudra*, touched him. He became very angry and he said, "What have you done? I will have to go and take another bath. You have defiled me!"

It is said that the *Shudra* replied, "Then your Ganges is worthless because if the Ganges purifies you, and right now, fresh, purified, you come and I touch you and you become defiled—I am greater than your Ganges?"

And the *Shudra* continued, "What *type* of knower are you? Because I have heard you say that in everyone the One exists. So allow me to ask a question: whether the touch of my body has defiled you? If so, that means my body can touch your soul. But you say the body is illusion, just a dream, and how can a dream touch the Reality? And how can a dream defile the Reality? That which is not, how can it defile that which *is*? Or, if you say that not my body, but my soul has defiled you, because a soul can touch a soul, then am I not *Brahma*, am I not that One you talk about? Then tell me who has defiled you?"

It is said that Shankara bowed down and said, "Up to now I was only thinking about the One, it was just a philosophy. Now you have indicated the right path, now nobody can defile me. Now I understand: One exists, only One exists, and the same is in me and the same is in you." Then Shankara tried very hard to find out who this man was. He could never find out, it was never discovered who that man was. It may have been God Himself, if may have been the very Source... but Shankara was transformed.

What goes in you cannot defile you because whatsoever goes in, goes into the body. *Nothing can go into YOU, your purity is absolute*. But whatsoever comes out of you carries your quality, the fragrance of your being—that shows something. If anger comes out of you, that shows that inside you are ill; if hatred comes out of you, that shows that inside you are not whole; if love and compassion and light come out of you, that shows that wholeness has been achieved.

I hope you will understand this strange saying. Misunderstanding is easy, and with persons like Jesus misunderstanding is always possible, understanding almost impossible—because they speak truths, and truths are always paradoxical because you are not ready to listen, not centered.

You understand through the mind and the mind gets mixed up, confused, and it interprets—then this saying becomes dangerous. I must tell you that this saying has not been recorded in the authorized version of the Bible. It has been left out— because what he is saying is dangerous! It is recorded, but not in the authorized version, not in the Bible Christians believe. But when Jesus was speaking many other people were recording and this record has survived. It was just found twenty years ago in a cave in Egypt.

All these sayings which we are discussing belong to that recording. They are not from the authorized version, because the authorized version can never be right—it is impossible. Once you organize a religion the spirit dies; organized, a thing is dead. And then there are also vested interests. How can the Pope of the Vatican say: "If you fast you will beget sin for yourselves"? Then nobody would fast. "And if you pray you will be condemned"? Then nobody would pray. "And if you give alms you will do evil to your spirits"? Then nobody would give donations. Then how could this big organization, the Church, exist?

Christians have the biggest organization : Catholic priests alone number twelve *lakhs* (one million two hundred thousand)—

thousands and thousands of churches all over the earth. The richest organization that exists is Catholic Christianity; not even governments are so rich because every government is bankrupt. But the Pope of the Vatican is the richest man, with the greatest organization all over the world, the only international state—not so visible, very invisible, but with millions of people working under it.

How can this happen? It all happens through donations, and if Christians learn that Jesus says: "Don't give, you will do evil to your spirits"...? And these churches are made for prayer, so if people come to know that Jesus says: "Don't pray, otherwise you will commit sin," who will go to pray there? And if there is no prayer, if there is no fasting, no ritual, no donations, then how can the priests exist? Jesus takes the very foundation out of all organized religion—then Jesus can be there, but there can be no Christianity.

This saying is not recorded in the authorized version, it must have been left out. You can also misunderstand it, but if you can *feel* what I am saying you will understand. He is not against prayer, he is not against fasting, he is not against giving and sharing—he is against your false faces.

The real must come out of your being. *First you must change* and be transformed, only then whatsoever you do will be good.

Somebody once asked Saint Augustine: "What should we do? And I am not a very learned man, so tell me in short, in as few words as possible."

Augustine said: "Then there is only one thing to be said: LOVE! And then whatsoever you do will be right."

If you love, of course, then everything becomes right; but if you don't love, then everything goes wrong.

Love means, be egoless! Love means, be centered! Love means, remain blissful! Love means, be grateful! This is what the meaning is: *live through your being, not through your acts.* Because acts are on the surface, being is in the depth.

Let things come out of your being. Don't manage and control your actions, transform your being. The real thing is not what you do, the real thing is what you *are.*

Sixth Discourse

26th August 1974, Poona, India

THE SIXTH SAYING

Jesus said :
The Kingdom is like a shepherd
who had one hundred sheep.

One of them went astray,
which was the largest.

He left behind the ninety-nine,
he sought for the one
until he found it.

Having tired himself out,
he said to the sheep:
I love thee more than the ninety-nine.

One of the most puzzling problems has been: what will happen to the sinners, those who have gone astray? What is the relationship between the Divine and the sinner? Is the sinner going to be punished? Is there going to be a hell? Because all the priests have been insisting that the sinner is going to be thrown into hell, he is to be punished. But can God punish anybody? Is there not compassion enough? And if God cannot forgive, then who will be able to forgive?

Many answers have been given, but Jesus' answer is the most beautiful. Before we enter into this saying many other things have to be understood, they will give you the background.

Whenever we punish a person, whatsoever rationalizations we may like to make, our reasons are different; and remember the distinction between reason and rationalization. You may be a father or a mother, and your child has done something of which you don't approve. It doesn't matter whether he has done something right or wrong, because who knows what is right and what is wrong? But you disapprove and whatsoever you disapprove of becomes wrong. It may be, it may not be, that is not the point— whatsoever *you* approve of is right. So it depends on your approval and disapproval.

And when a child goes astray, is doing something wrong in *your* view, you punish him. The deep reason is that he has disobeyed, not that he has done something wrong; the deep reason is that your ego feels hurt. The child has been in conflict with you, he has asserted himself. He has said no to you, the father, the authority, the powerful one, so you punish the child. The reason is that your ego is hurt and punishment is a sort of revenge.

But the rationalization is different: you say that it is because he has done wrong and he has to be put right—unless he is punished how is he going to be put right? So he should be punished when he moves in a wrong way, and he should be rewarded when he follows you. That is how he is to be conditioned for a right life. This is the rationalization, this is how you talk about it in your mind, but this is not the basic unconscious reason.

The unconscious reason is totally different: it is to put the child in his place, to remind him that you are the boss and he is not the boss, that you will decide what is wrong and what is right, that it is you who are going to give him direction; that he is not free, that you possess him, that you are the owner—and if he disobeys then he will suffer.

If you ask the depth psychologists they will say that in all behaviour this distinction between reason and the rationalization has to be understood well. Rationalization is a very cunning device—it hides the real reason and gives a false thing to you, but looks absolutely okay on the surface. And this is happening not only between a father and a child, a mother and a child, it is also happening between society and those children who have gone astray. That is why prison exists, the law exists—it is a revenge, a revenge taken by society.

Society cannot tolerate somebody who is rebellious, because he will destroy its whole structure. He may be right: Athens could not tolerate Socrates, not because he was wrong—he was absolutely right—but Athens could not tolerate him because if he had been tolerated then the whole structure of the society would have gone, been thrown to the dogs, and then the society could no longer have existed. So Socrates had to be sacrificed to society.

And Jesus was crucified, not because whatsoever he was saying was wrong—never have such true words been asserted on this earth—but he was sacrificed to the society because the way he was talking, the way he was behaving, was dangerous to its structure.

Society cannot tolerate this so it will punish you. But it also rationalizes: it says this is just to put you right, it punishes you for your own good. But nobody ever bothers whether that good is ever achieved or not. We have been punishing criminals for thousands of years, but nobody bothers whether those criminals are ever transformed through our punishment or not. Criminals go on increasing: as prisons increase, prisoners increase; the more laws, the more criminals; the more courts, the more punishments. The result is absolutely absurd—more criminality.

What is the problem? The criminal can also feel that it is a rationalization, that he is punished for doing wrong—he is punished because he has been caught. So he also has *his* rationalization: next time he has to be more cunning and more clever, that's all. This time he has been caught because he was not alert, not because he has done wrong. Society proved more clever than him, so next time he will see—he is going to prove himself more cunning, clever, intelligent, and then he will not be caught. A prisoner, a criminal who is punished always thinks that he is punished, not for the thing he has committed, but because he has been caught. So the only thing he is going to learn from the punishment is not to be caught again.

Whenever a prisoner comes out of prison he is a better criminal than ever: he has lived with experienced people inside the prison, with more advanced adepts who know much, who have been caught, who have been punished much and who have suffered long; and who have been deceiving in many, many ways—who are very advanced on the path of crime. Living with them, serving them, becoming a disciple to them, he learns; he learns through experience that next time he is not to be caught. Then he is a better criminal.

Nobody is stopped by punishment, but society goes on thinking that it is because the wrong has to be stopped that we punish. Both are wrong: society has some other reason—it takes revenge; and the criminal, he also understands—because egos understand each other's language very easily, howsoever unconscious—the criminal also thinks, "Okay, I will take revenge when my time comes, I will see." Then a conflict exists between the criminal's ego and society's ego.

Is God the same? Just like a justice, a magistrate, just like a father, or a boss? Is God also cruel in the same way as society is? Is God also the same deep down, an egoist as we are? Will He take revenge if you disobey? Will He punish you? Then He is no longer Divine, then He is just an ordinary man like us.

This is one of the profoundest problems: how will God behave with a sinner who has gone astray? Will He be kind? Then there are other things implied. And if He wants to be just, He cannot have compassion, because justice and compassion cannot exist together. Compassion means unconditional forgiveness, but it is not just.

It is possible for a saint to pray continuously his whole life, never do anything wrong; to always be afraid of moving beyond the boundary, to live in his own confinement, create an imprisonment for himself; to *never* do anything wrong, remain virtuous his whole life; to never allow himself any enjoyment of the senses, to be very austere. It is also possible for another man to live, indulge, to do whatsoever comes to his mind; go wherever his senses lead him, enjoy whatsoever the world gives; to do all types of things, all types of sins—and then for *both* to reach the Divine, for both to reach God's world.

What will happen? If the saint is not rewarded and the sinner is not punished, it will be very unjust. If both are rewarded, that too will be unjust, because the saint will think: "I have lived a good life, but nothing special is given to me for it." If the sinner is also rewarded in the same way, then what is the use of being a saint? The whole thing becomes futile. Then God may be compassionate, but He is not just.

If He *were* just, then the arithmetic would be clear in our minds: the sinner has to be punished, the saint has to be rewarded. But then He could not have compassion—a just man *has* to be cruel because otherwise justice cannot be done. A just man has to live in the head, not in the heart.

A magistrate should not have a heart, otherwise his justice will waver. He should not have any kindness in him, because kindness will become a barrier to doing justice. A man who is just *must* become like a computer, just a head: laws, rewards, punishments— no heart enters into it, no feeling should be allowed. He should remain a spectator, unfeeling, as if there is no heart in him. But then a difficult problem arises, because for centuries we have been saying that God is both just and compassionate; kind, loving, and yet just. It is a contradiction, a paradox—how to solve it?

Jesus has one answer, and the most beautiful. Now try to understand his answer. It will be difficult because it will go against all your preconceptions, against all your prejudices, for *Jesus is not a believer in punishment*. Nobody like Jesus can be a believer in punishment, because deep down punishment is revenge. A Buddha, a Krishna, a Jesus, they cannot believe in punishment. Rather, on the contrary, they can drop the very quality of justice from God. But compassion cannot be dropped, because justice is a human ideal, compassion is Divine. Justice has conditions attached to it: "Do this and you will achieve this. Don't do that, otherwise you will miss this." Compassion has no conditions.

God is compassionate. And to understand His compassion we have to start from the sinner.

"Jesus said: The Kingdom is like a shepherd who had one hundred sheep. One of them went astray, which was the largest. He left behind the ninety-nine, he sought for the one until he found it. Having tired himself out, he said to the sheep: I love thee more than the ninety-nine."

Absurd! Illogical!—but true. Try to understand : "The Kingdom of God is like a shepherd who had one hundred sheep. One of them went astray, which was the largest."

It is always so—the one who goes astray is always the best. If you are a father and you have five children, only the best child will try to resist and deny you, only the best child will assert himself. The mediocre ones will always yield to you, but the one who is not mediocre will rebel, because the very quality of his mind is rebellious. Intelligence is rebellious: the more intelligent, the more rebellious. And those who are not rebellious who are yea-sayers, are almost dead; you may like them, but they have no life in them. They follow you, not because they love you, they follow you because they are weak, they are afraid, they cannot stand alone, they cannot stand against—they are weaklings, impotent.

Look around : people whom you think are good are almost

always those who are weak. Their goodness does not come out of their strength, it comes out of their weakness. They are good because they cannot dare to be bad. But what type of goodness is this which comes out of weakness? Goodness *must* come out of overflowing strength, only then is it good, because then it has life, a floodlike life.

So whenever a sinner becomes a saint, his saintliness has its own glory. But whenever an ordinary man becomes a saint because of his weakness, his saintliness is pale and dead, there is no life in it. You can become a saint out of weakness—but remember, then you will miss. Only if you become a saint out of your strength will you reach. A man who is good because he cannot be bad is *not* really good. The moment he becomes stronger he will become bad; give him power and power will corrupt him immediately.

This happened in this country: Gandhi had a great following, but it seems that the goodness of his followers came out of weakness. They were good when they were not in power, but when they came to power, when they became the rulers of this country, then the power corrupted them immediately.

Can power corrupt a powerful man? Never! Because he is already powerful. If power could corrupt him, power would have corrupted him already! Power corrupts only if you are weak and your goodness comes out of weakness. Lord Acton has said: "Power corrupts and corrupts absolutely!" But I would like to make it conditional because this statement is not unconditional, not categorical, it cannot be: Power corrupts if goodness comes out of weakness; if goodness comes out of strength, no power can corrupt. How can power corrupt if you know it already, when it is there already?

It is very difficult though, to find from where your goodness comes. If you are not a thief because you are afraid of being caught, the day you become certain that nobody can catch you, you will become a thief—because then who will prevent you? Before, only your fear was the prevention; you were not going to murder your enemy because you knew you would be caught. But if a situation arises where you can murder the man and you cannot be caught, you cannot be punished for it, you will murder him immediately. So it is only through weakness that you are good.

But how can goodness arise out of weakness? Because goodness needs overflowing energy. Goodness is a luxury, remember. Saintliness is a luxury—it comes out of affluence. When there is too much energy, so much that you are flooded with it, then you start sharing it. Then you cannot exploit because there is no need. Then you can give out of your heart because you have so much that really you are burdened. You would like to share and renounce, you would like to throw everything and give all your life as a gift.

When you *have* something you would like to give it—remember this law: you cling to something only when you don't really own it; if you own it you can give it. Only when you can give something happily are you the owner. If you are still clinging to it, then deep down you are afraid and you are not the master of it. You know deep down that it does not belong to you, and sooner or later it will be taken away from you. That is why you cannot give. So only when a person gives his love does he show that he has love; only when a person gives his whole life does he show that he is alive. There is no other way to know it.

Out of weakness much goodness appears. It is an appearance, it is a false coin, and a false coin is just like a paper flower or a plastic flower. Whenever a tree flowers it flowers only because it is flooded with too much energy. Flowers are luxuries—a tree flowers only when it can afford to. If water is not given in the right proportion, if fertilizers are not given in the right proportion, if the soil is not rich, then the tree may have leaves but it cannot have flowers.

There is a hierarchy: the highest can exist only when there is energy to move to the highest. If you are not fed well, intelligence will disappear first because that is a flowering. In a poor country the real poverty is not of the body, the real poverty is of intelligence, because if the country is very poor intelligence cannot exist—it is a flowering. Only when all the bodily needs are fulfilled does energy move higher; when the bodily needs are not fulfilled, the energy moves to fulfill the bodily needs first. Because the base has to be protected first, the root has to be protected first. If there is no root there cannot be any flowering; if there is no body then where will the intelligence exist? And compassion is even higher than intelligence, and meditation still higher.

In India, Buddha and Mahavir were produced when the country was very rich. Since then so-called saints have existed, but not a man like Buddha—difficult, very difficult! Because such a flowering is possible only when there is *useless* energy, energy which cannot be used—only then does the energy start enjoying itself. And when energy starts enjoying itself it begins to turn inwards, it becomes an inner turning. Then it becomes meditation, then a Buddha is born, then ecstasy exists.

If you don't give water to the tree, first the flowers will disappear, then the leaves will disappear; then the branches will die and only at the last moment will the roots die—because with roots things can come up again, so the tree will protect its roots. A root is the lowest, but the lowest has to be protected because it is the foundation. When good days come, when the rains come and there is water, then the root can sprout again, the leaves will come again, and again there will be a flowering. And this same hierarchy exists in you.

Be good out of your energy, never be good out of your weakness. I am not saying be bad! Because out of weakness, how can you be either? Badness needs energy as much as goodness. You cannot be bad, you cannot be evil without energy, and you cannot be good without energy—because both are REAL. Then what can you be without energy? You can just have a false face: you will not be anything, you will just be a facade, a deception, a ghost, not a real person—whatsoever you do will be ghostlike. And this is what is happening. Then you will create a false goodness, a false saintliness. You will think you are a saint because you have not committed any sin, not because you have attained the Divine.

When you attain the Divine it is an achievement, a positive energy achievement. Then you become godlike, and then there is no effort to be godlike—it flows spontaneously. You can resist being bad, but that is negative. When you resist, the desire is there; and if the desire is there to do evil, you have committed it, it makes no difference. This is the difference between sin and crime.

Crime has to be an act. You can go on thinking about committing crime, but no court can punish you because no court has authority over the mind, only over the body—a crime has to be an *act*. I can go on thinking of murdering the whole world, but no court can punish me just because I go on thinking about it. I can say I enjoy it, but I have not murdered anybody, it has not become an act. Action comes under the law, not thought, and this is the difference between crime and sin.

Sin doesn't make any distinction between your acts and your thoughts : if you think, the seed is there; whether it sprouts in the act or not is not the problem. If it becomes an act then it will be a crime. But if you have *thought* it you have already committed the sin—for the Divine you have become a criminal, you have gone astray. But this is the point to be understood, a very difficult one : that those who go astray are always more powerful than those who remain on the path.

Those who go astray are always the best. Go to a madhouse and see: you will find the most intelligent people have gone mad. Look at the past seventy years of this century: the most intelligent people have gone mad, not the mediocre ones. Nietzsche, one of the best intelligences ever born, went mad, had to go mad—he had so much energy; so much energy that it could not be confined, so much energy that it had to become a flood; it could not be a gentle stream, he could not channel it—it was like an ocean, wild. Nietzsche went mad, Nijinsky went mad. Look at the seventy years of this century and you will find the best, the cream, the very best went mad, and the mediocrities were sane.

This looks very absurd : mediocrities remain sane and genius goes mad. Why does a mediocre person remain sane? No energy to move astray. A child becomes a problem child when he has overflowing energy, he has to do something or other. Only a bloodless child remains in the corner—if you say to him : "Repeat Ram, Ram, Ram," he will repeat it, if you give him a rosary he will do it. But if the child is really alive then he will throw away the rosary and he will say : "This is stupid ! I'm going to play and I'm going to climb in the trees, I'm going to do something!"

Life is energy. Only a bloodless, anaemic mind will not go astray, *cannot*, because it is difficult to afford that much energy, it is difficult to move to that extreme, to that abyss. But those who go astray—if they are ever found—they become Buddhas. If Nietzsche ever goes into meditation he will become a Buddha. He has the energy to become mad, so he has the energy to become Enlightened—it is the same energy, only the direction changes. A potential Buddha will become mad if he is not going to become a Buddha—where will the energy go? If you cannot be creative, energy becomes destructive. Go to the madhouse: you will find the most intelligent men there; they are mad only because they are not mediocre; they are mad because they can see further than you, deeper than you. And when they see deeper than you, illusions disappear.

The whole of life is such a puzzling thing, that if you can see deeper it will be very difficult to remain sane, very difficult. One remains sane because one cannot see : you see only two percent of life, and ninety-eight percent, psychologists say, has been closed; because if you come to see it, it will be such a flood that you will not be able to tolerate it—you will go insane, berserk.

Now a few psychologists, those who have been studying madness very deeply, like R. D. Laing and others, are stumbling on certain facts. One of the facts is this : that people who go mad are the best, people who go into crime are the most rebellious. They can become great saints and it is no surprise if a Valmiki becomes a saint.

Valmiki was a *dacoit,* a murderer, he lived by murder and loot. A sudden happening—and he became Enlightened.

One Enlightened person was passing, and Valmiki, a murderer, a man who lived by theft, caught hold of this Enlightened man. The Enlightened man said, "What are you going to do?"

Valmiki said, "I am going to rob you of all that you have!"

The Enlightened man said, "If you could do that I would be happy, because I have something very inner—rob it, you are welcome!"

Valmiki could not understand it, but he said, "I am concerned only with outward things."

The Enlightened man said, "But they won't help much. And why are you doing this?"

Valmiki replied, "Because of my family, for my family—my

mother, my wife, my children—they will starve if I don't do this; and I only know this art."

So the Enlightened man said, "Bind me to a tree so I cannot escape, and go back and tell your mother and your wife and your children that you are committing sin for them. Ask them if they are ready to share the punishment. When you are before God, when the Last Judgment comes, will they be ready to share the punishment?"

For the first time Valmiki started thinking. He said, "You may be right. I should go and ask."

He went back, asked his wife, and she said, "Why should I share the punishment? I have not done anything. If you do anything it's your responsibility."

And his mother said, "Why should I share it? I am your mother, it is your duty to feed me. I don't know how you bring the bread, that's *your* responsibility."

Nobody was ready to share the punishment—and Valmiki became converted. He came back, fell at the feet of the Enlightened man and said, "Now give me the inner, I'm not interested in the outer. Now let me be the robber of the inner, because I have understood that I am alone and whatsoever I do, it is my responsibility, nobody is going to share it. I am born alone, I will die alone, and whatsoever I do is my individual personal responsibility; nobody is going to share it. So now I must look inwards and find who I am. Finished! I am finished with this whole business!"—This man was converted in a second.

The same story happens with Buddha : There was one man who was almost mad, a mad murderer. He had taken a vow that he would kill one thousand people, not less than that, because the society had not treated him well. He would take his revenge by killing one thousand people. And from every person killed he would take one finger and make a rosary around his neck— one thousand fingers. Because of this his name became Angulimala: the man with a rosary of fingers.

He killed nine hundred and ninety-nine people. Wherever people came to know that Angulimala was near, nobody would move in those parts, the traffic would stop. And then it became

very difficult for him to find one man, and only one more man
was needed.

Buddha was approaching a forest, people came to him from
the villages and they said, "Don't go! Angulimala is there, that
mad murderer! He doesn't think twice, he simply murders; so
he will not think of the fact that you are a Buddha. Don't go
by that way, there is another way. You can move by that one,
but don't go through this forest!"

Buddha said, "If I don't go, then who will go? And he is
waiting for one more, so I have to go."

Angulimala had almost completed his vow. And he was a man
of energy because he was fighting the whole society : only one
man—and he had killed a thousand people. And kings were
afraid of him, generals were afraid, and the government and the
law and the police—nobody could do anything. But Buddha said,
"He is a man, he needs me. I must take the risk. Either he will
kill me or I will kill him." This is what Buddhas do, they stake,
they risk their lives. Buddha went. Even the closest disciples
who had said that they would remain with him up to the very
end, they started lagging behind—because this was dangerous!

So when Buddha approached the hill where Angulimala was
sitting on a rock, there was no one behind him, he was alone. All
the disciples had disappeared. Angulimala looked at this innocent
man, childlike; so beautiful that even he, a murderer, felt
compassion for him. He thought: "This man seems to be
absolutely unaware that I am here, otherwise nobody goes along
this path." And the man looked so innocent, so beautiful, that
even Angulimala thought : "It is not good to kill this man.
I'll leave him, I can find somebody else."

Then he said to Buddha, "Go back! Stop there now and go
back! Don't move a step forward! I am Angulimala, and these
are nine hundred and ninety-nine fingers here, and I need one
finger more—even if my mother comes I will kill her and fulfill
my vow! So don't come near, I'm dangerous! And I am not a
believer in religion, I'm not bothered who you are. You may be
a very good monk, a great saint maybe, but I don't care! I only
care about the finger, and your finger is as good as anybody else's.

So don't come a single step further, otherwise I will kill you. STOP!" But Buddha continued moving.

Then Angulimala thought : "Either this man is deaf or mad!" He again shouted : "Stop! Don't move!"

Buddha said, "I stopped long ago, I am not moving, Angulimala, you are moving. I stopped long ago. All movement has stopped because all motivation has stopped. When there is no motivation, how can movement happen? *There is no goal for me,* I have achieved the goal so why should I move? *You* are moving—and I say to you : you stop!"

Angulimala was sitting on the rock and he started laughing. He said, "You are really mad! I am sitting and you say to me that I am moving, and you are moving and you say that you have stopped. Your are really a fool or mad—or I don't know what type of, what manner of man you are!"

Buddha came near and he said, "I have heard that you need one more finger. As far as this body is concerned, my goal is achieved, this body is useless. When I die people will burn it, it will be of no use to anyone. You can use it, your vow can be fulfilled : cut off my finger and cut off my head. I have come on purpose because this is the last chance for my body to be used in some way; otherwise people will burn it."

Angulimala said, "What are you saying? I thought that I was the only madman around here. And don't try to be clever because I'm dangerous, I can still kill you!"

Buddha said, "Before you kill me, do one thing, just the wish of a dying man : cut off a branch of this tree." Angulimala hit his sword against the tree and a big branch fell down. Buddha said, "Just one thing more : join it again to the tree!"

Angulimala said, "Now I know perfectly that you are mad— I can cut but I cannot join."

Then Buddha started laughing and he said, "When you can only destroy and cannot create, you should not destroy because destruction can be done by children, there is no bravery in it. This branch can be cut by a child, but to join it a master is needed. And if you cannot even join back a branch to the tree, how can you cut off human heads? Have you ever thought about it?"

Angulimala closed his eyes, fell down at Buddha's feet, and he said, "You lead me on that path!" And it is said that in a single moment he became Enlightened.

Next day he was a *bhikkhu*, a beggar, Buddha's beggar, and begging in the city. The whole city was closed. People were so afraid, they said : "Even if he has become a beggar he cannot be believed. That man is so dangerous!" People were not out on the roads. When Angulimala came to beg nobody was there to give him food, because who would take the risk? People were standing on their terraces looking down. And then they started throwing stones at him because he had killed nine hundred and ninety-nine men of that town. Almost every family had been a victim, so they started throwing stones.

Angulimala fell down on the street, blood was flowing from all over his body, he had many wounds. And Buddha came with his disciples and he said, "Look! Angulimala, how are you feeling?"

Angulimala opened his eyes and said, "I am so grateful to you. They can kill my body but they cannot touch me—and that is what I was doing my whole life and never realized the fact."

Buddha said, "Angulimala has become Enlightened, he has become a *Brahmin*, a knower of Brahma (Ultimate Reality)."

It can happen in a single moment *if the energy is there*. If the energy is not there, then it is difficult. The whole system of Yoga is how to create energy, more energy. The whole dynamics of Tantra is how to create more energy in you, so you become a floodlike phenomenon. Then you can become good *or* bad.

Jesus says : "One of them went astray, which was the largest."

Only those who are great, who are the best, go astray. The sinners are the most beautiful people in the world—gone wrong, of course! They can become saints any moment. Saints are beautiful, sinners are beautiful, but the people who are just in between, they are ugly. Because impotence is the only ugliness : when you don't have any energy, when you are already a dead thing, a corpse; somehow carrying yourself, or having others carry you.

Why do the best, why do the great go astray? There is a

secret to be understood : the process of growth is that first you have to attain the ego. If you don't attain to a crystallized ego surrender is never possible. Looks paradoxical, but this is how it is. First, you have to attain a *very* crystallized ego, and then you have to drop it. If you don't attain to a crystallized ego, surrender can never happen to you How can you surrender something which you have not got?

A rich man can renounce his riches, but what should a beggar do? He has no riches to renounce. A great scholar can throw his intellect, but what will a mediocre person do? How can he throw it when he has not got it? If you have knowledge you can renounce it and become ignorant, humble; but if you don't have any knowledge, how can you renounce it?

Socrates could say, "I don't know anything." This is the second part : he knew much, then he realized that all knowledge is useless. But this cannot be attained by a person who has not moved like Socrates. The intellect has to be trained, knowledge has to be gained, the ego has to be crystallized; this is the first part of life. When you have the riches, then you can renounce them—the difference is great.

A beggar on the street and Buddha on the street are both beggars, but the quality differs absolutely : Buddha is a beggar by his own will. He is not forced to be a beggar, it is his freedom. Buddha is a beggar because he has tasted riches and found them futile; Buddha is a beggar because he has lived through desire and found it futile, useless. Buddha is a beggar because the kingdom of this world has failed. So Buddha's beggary has a richness about it—no king can be so rich, because he is still half way round and Buddha has completed the circle.

But a beggar who has never been rich also standing on the road: his begging is simply begging, because he does not know the taste of riches. How can he renounce a desire which he has not fulfilled? How can he say that palaces are useless? He has no experience of them. How can he say that beautiful women are worthless? He cannot say that because he has not known beautiful women. Only experience can give you the key to renounce. Without experience you can console yourself, and many poor people, poor in many ways, do that.

If you don't have a beautiful wife you go on saying: "What is there? The body is just the body, and the body is mortal and it is the abode of death." But deep down, deep down the desire remains, and desire can go only when experience has happened, when you *have* come to know—this is a consolation. A poor man can console himself that there is nothing in palaces, but he knows there is; otherwise, why is everybody mad for riches? And he himself is obsessed and mad: in his dreams he lives in palaces, in his dreams he becomes the Emperor. But in the daytime, when he is a beggar on the street, he goes on saying: "I don't bother, I don't care, I have renounced!" This consolation is of no use, it is dangerous, it is false.

The first part of life for a rightly maturing person is to attain the ego, and the second part—then the circle becomes complete —is to renounce it.

A child grows only when he resists his parents, when he fights with his parents; when he moves away from them, *against* them, he attains his own individual ego. If he goes on clinging to his parents, following them, he will never be an individual in his own right. He has to go astray—this is how life is meant to be. He has to become independent, and there is pain in becoming independent. There is a fight; and you can fight only if you feel you *are*. And this is a circle: if you feel you are, you can fight more; if you fight more, you become more, you are more— you feel: "I am". The child attains maturity when he becomes totally independent. Because of this independence he has to go astray.

The sinner may be seeking independence from the society, from the mother, from the father—but the sinner is seeking independence and ego in a wrong way. The saint is also seeking independence, but in a right way. The ways are different, but wrong ways are always easier. To become a saint is difficult, because to become a saint you must have been a sinner first. Try to understand this: to be a sinner you need not be a saint first, but to be a saint you *need* to be a sinner first. Otherwise, your saintliness will be poor, it will not be rich; it will be flat, pale, it will not be alive; it will be a summer stream, not a flooded river.

"One of them went astray, which was the largest."

As far as I know, the word 'largest', in the world of sheep, carries the meaning of 'the best'. Because the largest sheep is the best sheep : it carries more wool, it carries more fat, so it costs more to purchase; if you sell it you will gain more. The larger the sheep the better, the smaller the sheep the poorer. 'Largest' means the best—and the best went astray. It is symbolic.

"The shepherd...left behind the ninety-nine..." they were not worthwhile.

Why does Jesus always choose the shepherd and the sheep? It is very meaningful, his symbology is meaningful : the whole crowd of mediocre minds is just like sheep, they live in a crowd. Look at sheep moving on the road : they move as if they have a collective mind, not like independent beings—hugging each other, huddled, afraid to move alone. They move in a crowd.

I have heard: One school-teacher was asking a small boy whose father was a shepherd, "If there are ten sheep and one jumps over the fence around your house, how many will remain behind?"

The boy said, "None!" The teacher said, "What are you saying? I am giving you an arithmetical problem to solve—what are you saying? Ten sheep were there, one has jumped out; how many are left behind?"

The boy said, "You may know arithmetic, but I know sheep —none!" Because sheep have a collective mind, they move as a crowd : if one jumps, they will all jump.

The shepherd left the ninety-nine sheep behind and went in search of the one sheep who had gone astray.

Jesus always says that God will go in search of the sinner, not in search of the mediocre, the middle class—because the mediocre one is not worthwhile, he has not earned that much worth. And, moreover, he is always on the path, so there is no need to seek him, no need to search for him—*and he cannot go astray*. That is why the shepherd left ninety-nine sheep in the forest, in the dark night, and went in search of the one who had gone astray. Because this one had become individual, this one had attained the ego; the other ninety-nine were without egos, they were a crowd.

Look at your whole being : is it still a crowd? Or have you become an ego? If you have become an ego, then God will be in search of you because it is worthwhile—you have to be sought, you have to be found. You have gained half the circle, and now the other half is surrender; now the other half can be attained through God. Only you can attain the first half, the other half will be completed by the Divine. *When you have an ego,* then somewhere, in some form, God is in search of you because you have done your part, you have become an individual. *Now, if you lose individuality* you will become universal.

This is the difference : before individuality you are just a crowd, *not* universal; just a crowd, the local crowd. Then you attain individuality, you go astray; you become independent, you become an ego—and then when you *lose* this ego you become the Ocean, you become the Whole.

Right now you are not, so you cannot become the Whole. Right now the crowd exists, you are just numbers in the crowd. They do it well in the military, they give numbers to the soldiers : one, two, three, four—no names; because really you *don't* have any name, you have not earned it. You are just a number, a digit : one, two, three, four…so when any soldiers die, they can write on the board that such and such numbers have fallen. They are numbers and numbers can be replaced. When 'number one' has fallen he can be replaced by another person, and he becomes 'number one'. In the military there are sheep, and the military is the perfect society, the perfect antlike society, the crowd. If you want to know the crowd mind look at the military : they have to discipline you *completely,* in such a way that you lose all independence. An order is an order, you are not to think about it. They order : "Right turn!" and you 'right turn!' And this becomes *so* deep.

I have heard that the wife of one colonel was very much disturbed, because whenever the colonel slept on his left side he would snore. And it was difficult for her because it was not an ordinary snore—a colonel's snore. It was like a roar, so it was impossible for her to sleep. But whenever he lay on his right side, then he would not snore. So she went to a psycho-analyst and asked about it. He said, "It is simple: whenever he snores, turn him to the right."

She said, "That's difficult! He's a heavy man and then he gets angry. If I shake him and wake him up he gets angry; and it happens so many times in the night that my whole night would be lost doing this."

The psycho-analyst said, "Don't worry—simply whisper in the colonel's ear : 'Right turn!' and it will do." And it did! An order is an order—it goes so deep in the unconscious.

A society exists as a crowd. You can turn it into an army immediately, with no trouble. That's why Hitler could succeed in turning his whole country into an army camp. Mao has succeeded in turning his *whole* country into an army camp. The society lives just on the boundary; you can switch it immediately : a little discipline and the society can be turned into a military camp. There is no individuality because individuality is not allowed, you should not assert yourself. This is the sheeplike crowd, the sheeplike mind.

Have you got any consciousness of your own? Or do you simply live as a part of the society you were born in? You are a Hindu, a Mohammedan, a Christian, a Sikh, a Jain—but are you a *man*? You cannot say that you are a man, because a man has no society. A Socrates is a man, a Jesus is a man, a Nanak is a man—but not you! You belong, but a man belongs to no one, he stands on his own feet. That is what Jesus says : The best goes astray.

And once the best goes astray: "The shepherd...left behind the ninety-nine, and he sought for the one until he found it."

You go on praying for God but He is not in search of *you*, that's why you miss Him. First become yourself, then He will be in search of you. *There is no need to seek God*—and how can you *seek* Him? You don't know the address, you don't know His abode. You only know meaningless words and theories, they will not help.

I have heard that one priest arrived in a strange town. The taxis were on strike and he had to reach the church, because he had to deliver the sermon that evening. So he asked a small boy where the church was and the boy led him there. When he reached the church he thanked the boy and said to him, "I am very grateful that you helped me—not only did you show me, you came with me. If you are at all interested in knowing where God is, come this evening to my sermon, my talk. I am going to talk about the way to the abode of the Divine."

The boy laughed and he said, "You don't know the way to the church; how will you know the way to the Divine? I'm not coming!"

But I tell you, even if you know the way to the church it makes no difference. Everybody knows the way to the church, but that makes no difference because the church is not His abode, it has never been! You cannot seek Him because you don't know Him. He can seek you because He knows you—and this is one of the basic teachings of Jesus: that man cannot reach the Divine, but the Divine can reach man. *And He always reaches whenever you are ready.*

So the question is not to seek Him, the question is just to be ready and wait. And the first readiness is *to become individual, "to go astray."* The first thing is to be rebellious, because only then do you gain the ego. The first thing is to go beyond the crowd—that is what going astray means: to go beyond the clear-cut, formulated, limited scope of the society. Because beyond it is the wilderness, beyond it exists the vastness of God.

The society is just a clearing in the forest. It is not real, it is man-created. All your laws are man-created; whatsoever you call virtue, whatsoever you call sin, is just man-created. You don't really know what virtue is. This word 'virtue' from the Latin origin is very beautiful: the word from the Latin means 'powerful'; it doesn't mean 'good', it means 'virile', it means 'powerful'.

Be powerful, assert yourself, stand on your own! Don't fall a victim to the crowd! Start thinking, start being yourself! And follow your lonely path—don't be a sheep!

Ninety-nine sheep can be left in the forest—there is no fear about them, they will not be lost because they will huddle together, so they can be found any moment. The problem is not with them but with the one, the best, who has left the fold. Whenever a sheep can leave the fold it means power exists there, and the sheep is not afraid of the forest, not afraid of the wild animals, not afraid at all; the sheep has become fearless—*only then* can she leave the fold. And fearlessness is the first step of being ready.

Ego is the first step to surrender. It looks absolutely paradoxical. You will think that I am mad, because you think that humbleness is needed—I say, no! First ego is needed, otherwise your humbleness will be false. First ego is needed—*sharp*, sharp as a sword. That will give you a clarity of being, a distinctness, and then you can drop it; when you *have* it you can drop it. Then a humbleness comes and that humbleness is totally different : it is not the humbleness of the poor, it is not the humbleness of the weak—it is the humbleness of the strong, it is the humbleness of the powerful. Then you can yield, but not before that.

"He left behind the ninety-nine, he sought for the one until he found it."

And remember you need not go to seek God, he will come to you. Just become worthy and He will find you, He has to make a path towards you. The moment someone somewhere becomes crystallized, the whole Divine energy moves towards him. He may reach you as an Enlightened man, he may reach you as a Master, as a guru, He may reach you in millions of ways. But how He reaches you is not the point—that is for Him to worry about, it is not for you to worry about. First attain the ego, be ready, become individual, and then the universal can happen to you.

"Having tired himself out, he said to the sheep : I love thee more than the ninety-nine."

The one who has become rebellious, God loves him more. Priests will say: "What nonsense! One who has gone astray, God loves him more?" The priests cannot believe it, but this is how it happens. Jesus is the lost sheep. Buddha is the lost sheep, Mahavir is the lost sheep. The crowd goes on moving in its mediocrity, while a Mahavir, a Buddha and a Jesus are sought out—God rushes towards them.

This happened under the Bodhi Tree where Buddha was sitting, *perfectly individual*, with all the chains of society, culture, religion broken; *all* the chains broken, perfectly alone. Then God rushed from everywhere, from all directions, because He is in all directions—and Buddha became a God. And he had denied that there is a God, because that was one of the ways to go astray.

He had said : "There is no God, I don't believe in any God."
He had said that there is no society, no religion. He denied the
Vedas, he denied the caste-system—*Brahmins, Shudras*. He denied
the whole Hindu structure of thinking. He said : "I am not a
Hindu, and I don't belong to any society, and I don't believe
in any theories. Unless I know the truth I am not going to believe
in anything!"

He went on denying and a moment came when he was alone
and there was no link with *anything*, absolutely broken. He
became an island, *absolutely alone*. Under that Bodhi Tree,
twenty-five centuries ago, God rushed from everywhere to this
man, to this sheep who had gone astray. And, "Having tired
himself out, he said to the sheep : I love thee more than the
ninety-nine." This was also said to Jesus, this has always been so,
this is the foundational law. God seeks the man, not the man
God—man just has to be ready.

And how to be ready? Become individual! Be a revolutionary!
Go beyond the society, be fearless, break all chains, all relationships! Be alone and exist as if you are the center of the world!
Then God rushes towards you, and in His rush your ego is lost,
the island disappears into the Ocean—suddenly you are no more.

First the society has to be dropped, and that is the inner
mechanics : *because your ego can exist only with the society*.
If you go on dropping the society, there will come a moment when
the ego will be alone because the society has been dropped. But
then without the society the ego cannot exist, because society
helps you to exist as an ego. If you go on dropping the society,
by and by the base is dropped. When there is no 'thou', the
'I' cannot exist. At the *final* stage 'I' disappears because 'thou'
has been dropped. When there is *no* 'you', 'I' am not. The 'you'
has to be dropped, then the 'I' drops. But by dropping 'you'
first, the 'I' becomes sharper, crystallized, centered, beautiful,
powerful. Then it is consumed—this is the rush of the Divine.

Jesus was crucified because of these sayings. He was making
people rebellious, he was teaching them to go astray. He was
saying that God loves the one who has gone astray—the sinner,
the rebel, the egoist. The Jews could not tolerate it, it was too
much. This man had to be silenced: "This man has to be stopped

—he is going too far, he will destroy the whole society!" He was creating a situation in which the priests would not be able to stand, the Church would dissolve.

He was against the crowd—and the crowd is all that is around you—and the crowd became panic-stricken. They thought : "This man is the enemy, he is destroying the very base. Without the crowd how can we live?" By going and teaching the ninety-nine sheep to go astray, they will huddle together more. And if you go on teaching them they will take revenge, they will kill you, they will say : "Enough is enough!"

We live in the crowd, we are part of the crowd. Alone we cannot exist. We don't know how to be alone, we always exist with the other. The other is needed, it is a must. Without the other who are you? Your identity is lost.

This is the problem : ninety-nine sheep create all religions, and the real Religion happens only to the one sheep who has gone astray.

Be courageous! Move beyond the clearing, go to the wild! Life is there and only then will you grow. There may be suffering, because there is no growth without suffering. There may be a cross, crucifixion, because there is no maturity without crucifixion. Society may take revenge—accept it! That is bound to happen, because when the one sheep comes back the ninety-nine will say : "This is the sinner! This sheep went astray, this one is no part of us, this sheep doesn't belong to us!"

And those ninety-nine sheep will be absolutely unable to conceive that the shepherd is carrying that sheep on his shoulders —because this is the lost sheep and it has been found.

Jesus says the shepherd will go back to his home, he will call his friends, and he will have a feast because a sheep was lost and a sheep has been found. Jesus says whenever a sinner enters into Heaven there is rejoicing, because a sheep has been lost and a sheep has been found!

Seventh Discourse

27th August 1974, Poona, India

THE SEVENTH SAYING

Jesus said :
The Kingdom of the Father is like a man,
a merchant,
who possessed merchandise
and found a pearl.

The merchant was prudent.
He sold the merchandise
and bought the one pearl for himself.

Do you also
seek for the treasure which fails not,
which endures,
where no moth comes near to devour
and where no worm destroys.

If you look without, the world of the many exists; if you look within, then the world of One. If you go outside you may achieve much, but you will miss the One. And that One is the very center —if you miss it you have missed all . You may attain much but that much will not count much in the end, because unless one attains to oneself nothing is attained.

If you are a stranger to yourself, not even the whole world will fulfill you. If you have not got into your own being, then all the riches will make you even poorer. This happens : the more riches you have, the more poverty you feel, because now you can compare with outer riches, the inside in comparison looks poorer and poorer and poorer. Hence the paradox of the rich man : the richer he gets, the poorer he feels; the more he has, the more he feels that he is empty—because the inner emptiness cannot be filled by outer things. Outer things cannot enter into your being.

The inner emptiness can be filled only when you achieve yourself, when you attain to your being. Make a clear distinction : the world outside is the world of the many, but the One is absent there—and that One is the goal. That One *is* within you, so if you are searching outside you will miss. Nothing will be of much help; whatsoever you do, you will be a failure.

The mind will go on saying, "Attain that! Then you will be fulfilled." When you attain it, the mind will again say, "Attain something else! Then you will be fulfilled." The mind will say:

"If you are not succeeding it means you are not making enough effort. If you are not reaching, you are not running fast enough." And if you listen to the logic of the mind—which looks logical but it is not—then you will go on running and running and running, and in the end there will be nothing except death.

The many is the realm of death, the One is the realm of the deathless. The *seeker* has to be sought, not in outside objects but in your subjectivity; you have to turn within. A conversion is needed, a turning, an absolute about-turn is needed, so the eyes which see outside start seeing within. But how will this happen?

Unless you are *totally* frustrated with the world, this cannot happen; if even a slight hope remains, you will go on moving. Failure *is* great and with the failure of the many a new journey starts. The sooner you fail in the outside world the better; the sooner you get totally frustrated the better—because failure in the outside becomes the first step towards the inner.

Before we enter this sutra of Jesus, many more things have to be understood: who is the wise man? The one who is ready to lose all for the One. And who is the fool? The one who has lost himself and purchased ordinary things, who has sold what is most precious and filled his house with useless things.

I have heard, once it happened: A friend of Mulla Nasrudin became very, very rich. And when somebody becomes rich he wants to go back to his old friends, old neighbours, old village, to show what he has attained. So he came from the capital to his small village. Just at the station he met Mulla Nasrudin and he said, "Nasrudin, do you know? I have made it! I have become very, very rich, you cannot imagine! I have a palace with five hundred rooms, it is a castle!"

Mulla Nasrudin said, "I know a few people who have houses with five hundred rooms."

The friend said, "I have two eighteen-hole golf courses, three swimming pools and acres and acres of greenery!"

Nasrudin replied, "I know one man in the other town who has two golf courses and three swimming pools."

The rich man said, *"In the house?"*

Nasrudin said, "Listen—you may have made much money, but

I have also not done too bad: I've got donkeys, horses, pigs, buffaloes, cows, chickens."

The other man started laughing and he said, "Nasrudin, lots of people have donkeys, horses, cows, chickens..."

Nasrudin stopped him in the middle and said: *"In the house?"*

But whatsoever you get—whether it is eighteen-hole golf courses, three swimming pools, or five hundred rooms, or donkeys, horses and cows—whatsoever you can get outside will *not* make you rich, because really, the house remains empty, *you* remain empty. Nothing enters into the house, these things remain outside because they belong to the outside— there is *no* way to put them in. And poverty *is* within. Had it been outside, then there would have been no problem.

If you had felt the emptiness outside, on the periphery, then it could have been filled by houses, cars, horses or anything. But the emptiness is felt within, you feel meaninglessness within. What is creating the trouble is not that you don't have a big house, it is that inside you feel totally meaningless: why do you exist? Why this whole trouble of being in existence? Why be alive? Where is it leading?

Every day in the morning you wake up again to go—and nowhere to go! Every day in the morning you get dressed, but you know by the evening nothing is reached, no goal is achieved. Again you fall asleep, again in the morning the journey starts—the whole meaningless business of it! Inside you go on feeling empty, there is nothing. So with outside things you can at the most deceive *others*, not yourself. How can you deceive yourself?

The more things accumulate, the more life is wasted because they have to be purchased at the cost of life. You are less alive, death has come near, things are growing more and more, the pile goes on becoming bigger and bigger, and inside you are shrinking. Then comes the fear: "What am I achieving, where am I reaching? What have I done with my whole life?"

And you cannot go back, the time that is wasted cannot be returned to you, there is no way. You cannot get it back, you cannot say, "Sorry, I will start again;" that is not possible. Then by the time you become old, you become more and more sad.

That sadness is not because of physical age, that sadness is because now you realize what you have done to yourself: you have made a house, of course, you have succeeded, you are rich, you have attained prestige *in the eyes of others*—but what about your own eyes?

Now you feel the pain, the suffering of a wasted life, of a time lost. Death is coming nearer and soon you will dissolve with your hands empty. This emptiness is inner; you cannot fill it with anything that you can get *in* the world—unless you get yourself. Hence the insistence of Jesus that: "Even a camel can pass through the eye of a needle, but a man who is rich cannot pass through the gate of Heaven." Why? What is wrong with a rich man?

Nothing is wrong with a rich man. The emphasis is that one who has wasted his life in accumulating things of the world—that is what is meant by a rich man—cannot enter into the Kingdom of God, because *there* only one who has attained the inner enters. He cannot deceive at the gate of Heaven. He cannot enter because he will be too wasted, rotten, a ruin. He cannot dance at the door, he cannot sing. He cannot enter with a certain significance that he has attained in his life. He is uprooted: he possessed much, but he never possessed himself—and *that* is the poverty. If you possess yourself you are rich, *really* rich. If you don't possess yourself, you may be an emperor but you are poor.

The second thing to be understood is why we go on accumulating things. There must be some very deep reason because the truth is so clear, but still we go on. Nobody listens to Jesus or Buddha, and even if you listen, even if you feel that you understand, you never follow it. So Buddha and Jesus are neglected, you continue on your path. Sometimes a doubt arises, but that is all; again you get settled and you follow your own path. There must be something very deep-rooted which even a Buddha or a Jesus cannot shake, cannot uproot. What is that deep-rootedness?

We exist in the eyes of others: our identity consists of the opinion of others; others' eyes are the mirrors, we look at our faces in others eyes. *There* is the rub, the problem—because others cannot see your inner being. Your inner being cannot be reflected in any mirror whatsoever. Only your outside can be reflected; reflections are only of the outer, of the physical. Even if you stand before the best mirror, only the physical part of you will be reflected. No eye can reflect your inner part.

So others' eyes reflect your riches, your achievements in the world, your clothes; they cannot reflect *you*. And when you see that others think you are poor—that means you don't have good clothes, a good house, a good car—you start moving towards these things. You accumulate things just to see that you are rich in the eyes of others. Then others' eyes start reflecting that you are becoming richer and richer, you are gaining power and prestige. Your identity consists of your reflection, but others can only reflect things—they cannot reflect you. Hence, meditation is very very necessary.

Meditation means closing your eyes; not looking at the reflection, but looking at your own being. Otherwise, the whole day you are engaged with others. In the night also when you sleep, either you are unconscious when there is deep sleep, or you are again engaged with others in your dreams. Continuously living with the other is the problem: you are *born* into a society, you *die* in a society—your *whole* existence consists of the social. And society means eyes all around.

Whatsoever those eyes reflect, they impress you. If everybody says you are a good man, you start feeling good. If everybody thinks you are a bad man, you start feeling bad. If everybody says that you are ill, you will start feeling ill. Your identity depends on others, it is a hypnosis through others. Move into loneliness—live with the others, but don't exhaust yourself with the others.

At least for one hour a day just close your eyes. Closing your eyes means you are closed to the society; no society exists, only you, so you can face yourself directly. Move once a year for a few days to the hills, to the desert, where there is nobody, only you, and see yourself as you *are*. Otherwise, continuously living with others will create a hypnosis in you. That hypnosis is the reason why you go on influencing others, impressing others. The real thing is not how to live a rich life, the real thing is how to impress others that you are rich—but these are totally different things.

The others are impressed by whatsoever you possess, they are never impressed by *you*. If you meet Alexander in a beggar's garb you will not recognize him, but if you meet the beggar who

has always been begging on your street sitting on a throne like
Alexander, you will fall at his feet, you will recognize him!

It happened once: A great Urdu poet, Ghalib, was invited to
a dinner by the Emperor. Many other people were invited, almost
five hundred. Ghalib was a poor man, it is very difficult for a poet
to be rich—rich in the eyes of others.

Friends suggested, "Ghalib, you can borrow clothes, shoes and
a good umbrella, because your umbrella is so rotten, your coat
is faded, almost gone. And with these clothes and these shoes which
have so many holes, it won't look good!"

But Ghalib said, "If I borrow something I will feel very
uncomfortable inside, because I have never borrowed from anybody—I have lived on my own feet, I have lived in my own way.
To break the habit of my whole life just for a dinner is not good."

So he went to the Emperor's court in his own clothes. When
he presented his invitation card to the watchman, the man looked
at him, laughed, and said, "From where have you stolen this?
Escape from here immediately! Otherwise you will be caught!"

Ghalib could not believe it . He said, "I have been invited! Go
and ask the Emperor!"

The watchman said, "Every beggar thinks that he's been invited!
And you are not the first, many others have knocked at the door
before. Escape from here! Don't stand here because the guests
will be arriving soon!"

So Ghalib went back. His friends knew that this was going to
happen, so they had arranged a coat, some shoes, an umbrella
for him—some borrowed things. Then he put on those borrowed
things and went back. The watchman bowed down and said,
"Come in."

Ghalib was a very well-known poet and the Emperor loved his
poetry, so he was allowed to sit just by the side of the Emperor.
When the feast started Ghalib did a very strange thing, and the
Emperor thought that he looked a little mad—he started feeding
his coat and saying, "My coat, eat it! Because really you have
entered, not I."

The Emperor said, "What are you doing, Ghalib? Have you
gone mad?"

Ghalib said, "No—I had come before but I was refused entry. Now this coat has come—I'm just with it because the coat couldn't come alone—otherwise I could not have come!"

But this is happening to everybody: not *you* but your coat is recognized by others; so you go on embroidering your coat, dressing yourself.

Meditation is needed to give you a break from the others, the eyes of others, the mirror of others. *Forget* them! For a few minutes just look inside—then you will feel the inner pain and suffering, that you are empty there. Then a transformation starts: then you start looking for the inner riches, the treasury that exists within you—not for the treasures that are spread all around.

Many are the riches outside, only *one* is the treasure within. Many are the dimensions and directions outside; one, one-pointed is the goal within.

"Jesus says : The Kingdom of the Father is like a man, a merchant, who possessed merchandise and found a pearl.

The merchant was prudent. He sold the merchandise and bought the one pearl for himself."

The story is this: One man went to a far-away country to earn money. He earned much, he collected much merchandise, but at the last moment he came upon a pearl. He made an exchange: he sold all the merchandise and purchased the one pearl. When he was coming back, there was an accident and the ship sank. But with one pearl he could swim ashore and he reached his home with his entire treasure.

This is the story to which Jesus refers: that man purchased one instead of many, so even when the ship sank nothing was lost. The one can be saved, not the many. When death comes and your ship sinks, if you have one pearl you will be able to carry it to the other shore; but if you have many many things, you will not be able to carry them. A pearl can be carried, but how can you carry much merchandise?

Jesus says: "The Kingdom of the Father is like a man, a merchant, who possessed merchandise and found a pearl. The merchant was prudent." He was wise, because it is foolishness to sell the one and to purchase the many. This is wisdom; to sell the many and to purchase the one. The pearl is symbolic of the One, the Inner.

"The merchant was prudent. He sold the merchandise and bought the one pearl for himself.

Do you also seek for the treasure which fails not, which endures, where no moth comes near to devour and where no worm destroys."

Then be like that merchant, the prudent, the wise one. Whatsoever you can get in this world will be snatched away from you. Have you observed the fact that you cannot possess anything in the world, in reality? You simply feel you possess—but the thing was here when you were not, somebody else possessed it. Soon you will not be here, but the thing will be here and somebody else will possess it. Your possession is just like a dream: sometimes it is there, and sometimes it is gone.

It happened: There was a king, Ebrahim. One night he heard a noise on his roof, somebody was walking there. So he asked, "Who is there?"

The man said, "Don't be disturbed—my camel is lost and I am searching for it." On the roof of the palace his camel was lost!

Ebrahim laughed and said, "You madman! Get down! Camels are never lost on the roof of a palace. Go home!"

But then he couldn't sleep because he was a man of contemplation. He thought: "Maybe the man was not mad, maybe he was saying something symbolically; maybe he is a great mystic, because the voice was such that when he said, 'Don't be disturbed,' there was so much consolation and silence in it. The voice was so musical and harmonious, it cannot be that of a madman. And when he said, 'My camel is lost and I am searching for it,' the voice was so penetrating, it seemed to indicate something. . . . The man has to be found tomorrow morning! I must see who this man is— whether he is mad, or a madman of God; whether he was just on the roof in his madness, or whether he was sent for me particularly, to give me a message."

The King couldn't sleep the whole night. In the morning he told his courtiers to go and find this man with this type of voice. But the whole capital was searched and the man could not be found, because how can you find a man just by the tone of his voice? Difficult!

Then just in the middle of the day, there was much hustle at the door. A fakir, a beggar, had appeared and he was saying to the watchman, "Allow me to enter, because I want to stay here for a few days in this *sarai*, in this inn."

The watchman was saying, "This is not an inn, not a *sarai*—this is the King's own palace, his own residence!"

But the fakir said, "No! I know very well this is an inn: travellers come in, they stay and they go. Nobody is a resident here so let me in; I will talk to the King, who seems to be a foolish man."

This was overheard and the fakir was sent for. The King was very angry and he said, "What are you saying?"

The man said, "Listen! I came once before but then somebody else was sitting on this throne. And he was also the same type of foolish man as you are, because he thought this was *his* residence. Now you are thinking this is your residence!"

The King said, "Don't be stupid! And don't behave in such an uncivilized way—he was my father, now he is dead."

The fakir said, "And I tell you that I will come again and I will not find you here. Somebody else will be here. He will be your son and he will say, 'This is my residence!' What type of residence is this? People come and go—I call it a travellers' inn."

The voice could be recognized! The King said, "Then you are the madman who was looking for the camel on the roof!"

The fakir said, "Yes, I am the madman and so are you: if you are looking for yourself in riches, you are looking for a camel on the roof!"

The King came down from his throne and said to the fakir, "You stay in this *sarai*, but I am leaving it, because I was staying only believing that this was a residence, this was a home. If this is not a home, then I *must* go and search for home before it is too late!"

Ebrahim became a mystic in his own right. And when he became known, when he became a realized man, he used to live outside the capital—his own capital. Once it was his possession, now it was just a *sarai*, he used to live outside it. And people would

come and ask, "Where is the *basti?*" *'Basti'* means 'the city'; but
the word is very beautiful, it means, 'where people reside'. But
Ebrahim would show them to the cemetery. He would say, "Go
to the right and you will reach the *basti,* where people reside."

And then people would go. Later they would come back very
angry and say, "What type of man are you? We asked about the
basti, the city, where people reside—and you sent us to the
cemetery!"

Ebrahim would laugh and say, "So, we use terms in a different
way it seems—because there in the cemetery, once you enter
you are a resident forever. That is the real *basti,* the permanent
residence where your address never changes, because you *are*
there forever and forever and forever. So you are not asking for
the real *basti,* then you are asking for this city which is a cemetery
because people are standing in the queue just to die.

"Somebody's time has come today, somebody else's will be
coming tomorrow, somebody else's the day after tomorrow—but
everybody is waiting just to die! And you call it *basti?* You call it
the place where people reside? I call it *marghat,* the cemetery,
where people are simply waiting to die, where *nothing exists
except death."*

If life exists, it is nothing but a waiting for death, and how can
life be a waiting for death? How can life be momentary? How
can life be just like a dream? It is there—and it is gone and not
there! Life must be something eternal. But if you are looking for
the Eternal, then be like the prudent merchant: sell all that you
have got! Sell it and purchase the One, the one pearl of your
inner being which cannot be drowned, which cannot be snatched
away—because that pearl is YOU. You can possess only yourself,
nothing else can be really possessed. You can live in an illusion—
that's another thing.

You can live in the illusion that you possess this house, this
wife, this husband, these children, but this is an illusion; sooner
or later the dream will go away. You can possess only yourself
because that will never go away. The Being is permanent, eternal.
It is timelessly yours. It cannot be taken away from you.

This is the difference between a wordly search and a religious
search: the religious one means looking for the Eternal, the wordly

one means looking for the temporal. The world exists in time and religion exists in timelessness. Observe a clear fact: that whenever you close your eyes and thoughts have dropped, there is no time; whenever you close your eyes and thoughts are not there, time disappears. When thoughts are there, then there is time; when things are there, then there is time.

Around you exists time, the ocean of time. Within you exists eternity, timelessness.

That is why all the Realized Ones say that when you have transcended time, when you have gone beyond time, then you have reached yourself, you have come home.

Once it happened: A man worked in a factory. The man was very poor, and he used to come to the factory on his donkey. But he was always late coming back home and his wife was always angry. One day he said to her, "Try to understand my problem: when the last whistle, the quitting whistle goes, this donkey has become so accustomed to it that even if I am two or three seconds late, he goes on his own, he leaves for home without me. And there is such a rush! Everybody wants to leave the factory immediately, so when I get outside many times I have missed him, the donkey has gone! He waits two or three seconds at the most. If in that time I have jumped on him, it is okay; otherwise he goes without me and then I have to walk back! So this is the trouble." So he thought this would help, and then he asked his wife, "Do you understand the moral of the story?"

The wife said, "I understand it well! Even a jackass knows when it is time to go back home!"

Even a jackass knows when it is time to go back home—but you have not yet become aware of where your home is and when to leave for home. You go on wandering, you go on knocking at others' houses; you have completely forgotten where your home is. So if you are uneasy it is not strange. If you never feel at ease anywhere, it is not strange. You *go on* travelling from one corner of the world to the other. Why is there this madness to go from one town to another? What are you seeking? Whenever anybody can afford it he goes travelling. People work, then they save money just to go around the world—why? What are you going to gain?

I have heard that once an American hunter was looking into a Greek volcano, right into the center of the volcano. Then he said to the guide, "Heavens! It looks like hell!"

The guide said, "You Americans! You have been everywhere! Once you can afford it, you will even go to hell!"

But why does this uneasiness exist? Why is man a vagabond deep down? Because your home is missing and you are in search of it. Your direction may be wrong, but your uneasiness is indicative. *Wherever* you are it is not your home—this is the problem. So you go on searching for it, you can even go to hell in search of it, but you are not going to find it anywhere because your home exists within you. And even a jackass knows when it is time to go back!

It is time, it is already time, you have waited enough. Don't search for it in things, don't search for it in others, don't search for it outside—there you will meet the many, the multiple, what Hindus call *maya*.

Maya means the many, the multiple; *maya* means the endless. You go on searching and searching and there is no end to it. It is a magical world—*maya* means the magic of the many. The magic remains, you go on searching, but you *never get anything* because it is a magical world: whenever you come closer to it, it disappears like a rainbow. From a distance it is beautiful, it catches you, you become obsessed with it, it enters in your dreams, in your desires; you would like to have the rainbow in your fist. And then you go on and on, and the rainbow goes on receding.

Whenever you arrive you find there is nothing. The rainbow was a dream, an illusory reality. Hindus have called this world of the many *maya*—a magical world, as if created by a magician. Nothing exists really, everything exists through desire and dreaming. You create it through your desire; you are a creator through your desire—you create the world of the many.

There is a car, a beautiful car. If there is no man on the earth, what will be the value of the car? Who will appreciate it? Who will bother about it? The birds won't look at it, the animals won't bother. Nobody will pay any attention to it—it will rot, it will become junk. But when man is there it is valuable. Where does the value come from? It comes from your desire: if you desire

It, it is valuable; if you don't desire it, the value disappears. The value is not in the thing, it is in your desire.

The old law of economics was: wherever there is demand, supply follows. But now the law has completely changed: you supply and demand follows. Can you think of any person in Buddha's time dreaming about a car? There was no problem because the supply was not there, so how could you desire a car? Now the whole business world consists of creating new supplies. First they create supply, then they advertise, they create desire; then the demand comes in—then you *rush* because then you see: "Now here is the goal I was missing my whole life. Now here is the goal and once I achieve it, everything is achieved!"

But the businessman goes on inventing new things, advertisers go on creating new desires. Every year they create new cars, new houses, new goals. *Constantly* they supply you with ways of moving outwards—they don't give you a gap to think. Your car may be okay, but they say the new model has come. So now, moving with the old model hurts the ego. The new model may not be better— it may even be worse—but the new has to be purchased. You have to get it because the neighbours have got it, because everybody is talking about it.

One woman came to a doctor and said, "Do any operation on me!"

The doctor said, "What? Have you gone mad? Why an operation? You are completely healthy and okay!"

The woman said, "But it is very difficult—whenever I go to the club all the women are talking: somebody's appendix has been removed, somebody's tonsils have been removed, and only I feel somehow abnormal—nothing to talk about! Remove anything so that I can go to the club and talk about it!"

There is even competition in disease! You have to be ahead of each and everyone; whatsoever the consequence, you have to be at the top.

Three commuters were talking in a train. One bragged about his wife saying, "I have a wife. We got married ten years ago, and she still comes every night to meet me at the station when I come back home. Impossible!"

Another man said, "I can understand, because I have been

married for twenty years and the same thing is happening—my wife still comes to meet me at the station."

"I can beat that!" said the third. "My wife has been coming to meet me for thirty years—and I am not even married to her! She still comes to meet me, I can beat you!"

Even if people are telling lies, you have to top them, you have to be the first—whatsoever people are doing. If the style of dress changes, the new dress may look neurotic, but you have to follow it. Nobody is at home because everybody is knocking at each other's door.

Remember this well: nobody is a goal for you except your own Self. *You* are the goal, and *you* have to achieve *yourself*—nothing else is worthwhile.

This is what Jesus says:

"The Kingdom of the Father is like a man, a merchant, who possessed merchandise and found a pearl.

The merchant was prudent. He sold the merchandise and bought the one pearl for himself.

Do you also seek for the treasure which fails not, which endures, where no moth comes near to devour and where no worm destroys."

Look for the deathless and remain alert; don't waste your time with that which is not going to endure, don't waste your life for that which is going to change, which is part of the changing world.

Then what can you think of which is going to endure? Have you come upon any fact in your life which gives you a feeling that it is going to endure? The visible world is all around you—nothing endures in it. Even the hills will not endure forever; they also become old, they also die; even continents have disappeared .

The Himalayas were not there in the days of the Vedas, because the original *Rigveda* never talks about them. It is impossible not to talk about the Himalayas if they are there—impossible! How can you neglect the Himalayas? And the Vedas go on talking about other things, but they never talk about the Himalayas. Because of this, Lokmanya Tilak decided that the Vedas were created at least seventy-five thousand years ago. It looks meaningful, it may be so; they may not have been written so far back, but they must have existed in oral form for many thousands of years. That is why the Himalayas are not mentioned there.

Now, scientists say that the Himalayas are the latest addition to the world, the youngest mountains; they are the highest, but the youngest. They are still growing, they are still young—every year they go on growing higher and higher. Vindhya is the oldest mountain on the earth—maybe that's why it is bent like an old man dying. Hindus have a beautiful story about Vindhya.

One seer, Agastya, went to the south, and it was very difficult to cross Vindhya in those days, for no means existed. The beautiful story is that when the seer came, Vindhya bent down just to touch his feet, and the seer said: "I will be coming soon; you remain in the same posture so I can cross you easily!" So Vindhya has remained bent, and the seer never came back again—he died in the south. But the story is beautiful: Vindhya—the oldest part of the earth—is bent like an old man!

Even hills are young, old; they die, they are born. Nothing is permanent in the outside world. Look at the trees, at the rivers, at mountains: they give the feeling that everything is permanent, but look, a little deeper and the feeling disappears.

Then go within and look at your thoughts—they are even more temporary. They continuously go on moving, not a single thought stays: a moment ago you were angry and the mind was filled angry thoughts; a moment later you are smiling and those thoughts have disappeared completely, as if they never existed. Just like clouds in the sky they come and go; they are constantly changing their shape, just like the clouds—they are exactly alike.

Meditate on the clouds and you will see their form is constantly changing. If you don't look you may not become aware; otherwise you will see their form is continuously changing, not for a single moment is the form of a cloud the same. The same happens in your mind: the form of a thought is just like a cloud, it goes on changing. That is the reason why people cannot concentrate, because concentration means the form of the thought should remain constantly the same. That is the problem, because thought goes on moving and changing. Whatsoever you do it is changing: one thought changes into another, one form into another form. The world of thought is also not that which endures.

Hills change, clouds change, only the sky remains the same—it endures. The same is within you: things change around you and clouds, thoughts change within you—but the sky of the Self, the witnessing Self, remains the same. That is the pearl: the witnessing Self. It is formless so it cannot change. If there is form, change is going to happen. If there is no form, how can change happen? It is formless, *nirakar*.

If you go to this formlessness within you, in the beginning it will look empty because you don't know formlessness, you only know emptiness. But don't be afraid, don't get scared, enter into it. When you become acquainted with it, when you have settled in it, then the emptiness is no longer emptiness: it becomes formlessness. When this formlessness is achieved, you have the pearl. Then you have purchased One at the cost of the many. Right now, at the cost of the One you have purchased the many. And the One is the pearl, the many are just false stones. They may look very valuable but they are not, because they cannot endure.

Endurance, *nityata*, eternity, is the criterion of Truth, Remember this well: what is Truth? That which endures, and endures infinitely. What is a dream? That which begins and comes to an end; that which cannot endure forever. So look for that Pearl which nobody can snatch from you, not even death. In death the body will die, in death the thoughts will disappear—but YOU?—you will go on and on and on. . . .

Death *happens* near you, but *never* to you. It happens in the neighbourhood, but never at the center; it happens at the circumference. You have never died, you cannot die. Mountains disappear, clouds come and go, but the sky remains the same. And you are the sky. The nature of the Self is just like space: empty, infinitely empty, formless. Everything happens within it, nothing happens to it. This is what Jesus means.

"Do you also seek for the treasure which fails not, which endures, where no moth comes near to devour and where no worm destroys."

Eighth Discourse

28th August 1974, Poona, India

THE EIGHTH SAYING

Jesus saw children who were being suckled.
He said to his disciples:
These children who are being suckled
are like those who enter the Kingdom.

They said to him:
Shall we then, being children,
enter the Kingdom?

Jesus said to them:
When you make the two one,
and when you make the inner as the outer,
and the outer as the inner,
and the above as the below,
and when you make
the male and the female into a single one,
so that the male will not be male
and the female not be female,
then shall you enter the Kingdom.

This is one of the deepest sayings of Jesus, and one of the most basic to be understood by a seeker. It is also one of the most difficult to achieve, because if this is achieved nothing more is left to achieve. First try to understand a few things and then we will enter into the saying.

Man, if he lives with the mind, can never be innocent—and only in innocence does the Divine descend, or do you ascend to the Divine. Innocence is the door. Mind is cunning, calculating, it is clever, and because of this cleverness you miss—you miss the Kingdom of God. You may attain to the kingdom of this world through the mind, because here cunningness is needed. You have to be cunning: the more cunning, the more successful; the more calculating, the more efficient in the ways of the world.

But the door for the Kingdom of God is exactly the opposite. There, no calculation is needed, no cleverness is needed. Mind is not needed at all, because mind is just a mechanism to calculate, a mechanism to be clever. If you don't need any cleverness, any calculation, mind is useless. Then the heart becomes the source of your being, and heart is innocence.

Why do we go on being clever? Why does the mind go on thinking about how to deceive? Because that is the only way in this world to succeed. So those who want to succeed in this world will be failures in the Kingdom of God. If you are ready to accept your failure in *this* world, then you are ready to enter the other world. The moment one is ready to recognize that:

"The success of this world is not for me, I am not for it,"
immediately a conversion happens, a turning. Then the consciousness doesn't move outward, it starts moving inward.

Jesus emphasizes innocence very much. Hence, he goes on
talking about the beauty of children, or the innocence of the
flowers, of lilies, or the innocence of the birds. But that type of
innocence won't help, you have already lost that. So don't imitate
him verbally, don't try to understand literally, it is just symbolic.

You cannot be a child again—how is it possible? Once you
have tasted knowledge you cannot fall back. You can transcend
it but you cannot go back, there is no way to go back. You can
go ahead, you can go beyond it, but you cannot go behind it now
—there is no way. You cannot be an ordinary child again. How?
How can you lose that which you have known? But you can go
beyond, you can transcend.

Remember this, otherwise you may start imitating a child and
that imitation will be a cunningness, it will again be a calculation.
Jesus says, "Be like a child," so you start practising how to be
like a child—but a child never practises. A child is simply a
child, he doesn't even know that he is a child, he is not aware
of his innocence. His innocence is there, but he is not self-
conscious about it. But if you practice then self-consciousness will
be there. Then this childhood will be a false thing. You can act
it but you cannot be a child again—in the *literal* sense.

A saint, a sage, becomes like a child in a totally different sense.
He has transcended, he has gone beyond mind, because he has
understood the futility of it. He has understood the whole nonsense of being a successful man in this world—he has renounced
that desire to succeed, the desire to impress others; the desire
to be the greatest, the most important; the desire to fulfill the ego.
He has come to understand the absolute futility of it. The very
understanding transcends. The very understanding—and immediately
you are transformed into a different dimension.

Then there is again a childhood—that is called the second
childhood. Hindus have called that stage 'the twice-born', *dwij*.
Again you are born, but this is a different birth, not out of a
father and a mother. This is out of your own Self, not out of

two bodies meeting, not out of duality. It is through your Self that you are born.

This is the meaning of Jesus' birth—that he was born out of a virgin. But people take everything literally and then they miss. Out of the virgin means: out of the One. The other is not there, so who can corrupt it? Who can enter into it? The virginity remains absolutely pure because there is no other. When the other is there you have lost your virginity. If in the mind the other is there, you have lost innocence. So the consciousness of the other, the desire for the other, is losing virginity. This second birth can be virgin, but the first birth is bound to be out of sex— there is no other way, there cannot be.

Jesus is born out of sex like anybody else, and it is right that it should be so. Jesus is just like you—in the seed, but in the flowering he is absolutely different, because a second birth has happened; a new man is born. Jesus who was born out of Mary is no more there, he has given birth to himself. In the old Essene sect it is said that when a man is transformed he becomes his own father. This is the meaning: when we say Jesus has no father, it means Jesus has become his own father now. This looks absurd but this is how it is.

The second birth is a virgin birth—and then you are innocent again. And this innocence is higher than a child's, because the child *will* have to lose his innocence. It is a gift of nature, it is not earned by the child, so it has to be taken away. When the child grows he will lose his innocence— and he has to grow! But a sage remains innocent. Now this innocence cannot be taken away because it is the climax, the crescendo of growth; there is no further growth. If there is growth then things will change; if you have reached the goal beyond which nothing exists, only then will things not change.

A child has to grow every day: he will lose innocence, he will become experienced; he will have to attain knowledge, he will have to become clever, calculating. But if you get too obsessed with your calculating mechanism, then you remain born out of sex, out of duality. And then there is always a continuous conflict inside—because you are two.

When you are born out of two you are going to remain two, because both are there: a man is not only man, he is woman also; a woman is not only woman, she is man also—because both are born out of two. Your father goes on existing in you, your mother goes on existing in you, because they both participated, they both met in your body and their streams go on flowing—you are two. And if you are two, how can you be at ease? If you are two, there is going to be a constant conflict. If you are two opposite polarities together, a tension is always going to remain. This tension cannot be lost, yet you go on trying to find out how to be silent, how to be peaceful, how to attain bliss. It is impossible! Because you are two!

To be silent, oneness is needed, so you have to be born again—that is what Jesus said to Nicodemus. Nicodemus asked him, "What should I do?"

Jesus said, "First you have to be born again. Only then can anything happen. Right now, as you are, nothing can be done."

And the same I say to you: *Right now, as you are,* nothing can be done. Unless you are reborn, unless you become your own father, unless your duality disappears and you become one, nothing can be done.

When the woman within you and the man within you meet, they become a circle. They are not fighting, they disappear, they negate each other, and then oneness is left. This oneness is virginity.

That is what Jesus means when he says: "Be like children." Don't take it literally. But why "like children"? Because when a child is conceived, for the first few weeks he is neither male nor female. Ask the biologists, they will tell you that he is neither.

For a few weeks the child is neither male nor female—he is both or neither; the division is still not distinct. That is why medical science *is* now able to change the sex of the child. A few injections can change it, because both are there—the male and the female. The balance will soon be lost, either the male will predominate or the female will predominate. And whichever predominates will become the sex of the child. But in the beginning there is a balance, both are there. It will depend on hormones now.

If we inject male hormones the child will be male; if we inject female hormones the child will be female. The sex can be changed because sex is an outer thing; it does not belong to the being, it belongs only to the circumference, to the body; it is a hormonal thing, physical. The being remains totally different from it. But soon the distinction arises: the child starts becoming either a male or a female.

In the beginning the child is a unity. Then he is born: bodily now he is either a male or a female. But deep in the consciousness the distinction has still not penetrated; in consciousness he is still neither—the child does not know whether he is male or female. A few more months and then the distinction will enter into the mind. Then the child will have a different outlook—immediately he will become self-conscious.

In the beginning the body was one, then the body separated. But even when the body separates the child is one. Then the child also separates: the human being disappears because you are identified with being male or female—and that continues your whole life. That means you never reach the source again, the circle remains incomplete. But a sage reaches the source again, the circle becomes complete. And first the distinction disappears from the mind—just the reverse!

In the child the distinction first comes into the body, then into the mind. In the sage, first the distinction disappears from the consciousness, then from the body, and before he dies he again becomes one. This is the second childhood: again he becomes innocent—but this innocence is *very* rich.

The innocence of a child is poor because there is no experience; the innocence of childhood is just like an absence of something. But the innocence of a sage is a *presence* of something, not an absence. He has known all the ways of the world, he has moved, he has experienced all that was to be experienced. He moved to the very opposite and he became a sinner, he delved deep, he indulged, he experienced all that this world can give, and now he has come out of it. His innocence is very, very rich because experience is there. You cannot destroy it now, because he has known all that can be known—how can you destroy it now? You cannot motivate him any more, all motivation has gone.

If you reach this stage—in the beginning you were a child, in the end you again become a child—your life has been a circle, complete; this is what perfection is. If you don't reach the source again, your life has been incomplete. Incompleteness is suffering. That is what Buddha calls *dukkha*, misery. If you are incomplete there is misery, if you are complete you are fulfilled.

A sage dies fulfilled—then there is no more birth, because then there is no need to come back to the world of experience. *You* die incomplete, and because of that incompleteness you have to be born again. Your being will persist, again and again, to be complete; and unless you are complete you will have to move again and again into birth, into death. That is what Hindus call 'the wheel of life and death'. A sage jumps out of the wheel, because he himself has become a circle and now no wheel is needed.

But what happens to the ordinary mind? The distinction remains to the very end, sex remains to the very end. Even if the body becomes weak, the mind goes on—and sex is the basic duality. So unless sex disappears, the oneness, the non-dual, the *Brahma* is not going to happen. Remember, the non-dual—the *adwaita*, the *Brahma*, the One—is not a hypothesis, it is not a theory, it is not a doctrine. It is not a philosophical thing you can argue about, it is not a belief—it is a transcendence of sex. It is a very deep biological phenomenon, it is alchemical, because your whole body needs a transformation.

Three old men were sitting in a garden on a bench, discussing their miseries—because old men have nothing else to say. One old man, who was seventy-three, said, "My hearing is going. People have to shout into my ears, and even then I cannot hear rightly!"

Another, who was seventy-eight, said, "My eyes are becoming weak, I cannot see rightly, and moreover, I cannot even make a distinction between a blonde and a redhead!"

Then they asked the third man, they said, "Mulla Nasrudin, and what is your trouble?"

Nasrudin, who was ninety-three, said, "My trouble is deeper than both of yours. Last night it happened: we had dinner, then some wine, then I rested on the sofa and I fell asleep. About half an hour later I became aware that my wife had gone to bed. So

I went into the bedroom and I told my wife: 'Give me a little space, let me come into bed, and we will have a little fun!' My wife said: 'What? We had a little fun just twenty minutes ago?' "

And then Nasrudin tapped his head very sadly and said, "Gentlemen, my problem is that my memory is slipping!"

Sex goes on following you to the very end, to the *last*. And you may not have observed, you may not have thought about it, but if a man has not transcended mind, the *last* thing in the mind when he dies will be sex—because that was the *first* thing when he was born. It is bound to be the last thing, it is natural—try it!

When you go to sleep at night, just watch the last thought—the last, the very last; after that fall into sleep. Remember it, and in the morning you will be surprised: that will be the first thought in the morning—if you observe. Or do it the other way: in the morning, observe the first thought and remember it. In the night that will be the last thought, because life is cyclic. Sex is the first thing in life and it is going to be the last. If you don't transcend it, you are just victims, you are not your own masters.

Do you know what happens whenever a person is hanged? If a male is hanged, the semen is released immediately. This happens in every prison, wherever people are hanged. The *last* thing: when he is dying semen is released. What is the meaning of it? Why should it be so? Life is a cycle, it completes itself: that was the first thing, through which he entered life; that is going to be the last thing, through which he will again enter into another life.

A sage transcends sex—but a sage has not repressed sex, remember, because repression is not transcendence. If you repress something you are still in it: if you repress something you are still divided. A sage has not repressed anything. Rather, on the contrary, the male and the female energy within him have become a unity, now he is neither male nor female. That is what Jesus has said: "Eunuchs of God." That is what Hindus mean when they depict Shiva as *Ardhanarishwar*—half-man, half-woman—he has become One. And Hindus say Shiva is the most perfect god, the greatest—*Mahadeva*. Why do they call him *Mahadeva*, the greatest? Because he is half-man and half-woman, and when you are half-man and half-woman consciously, both become one circle and both disappear. The duality has disappeared, he has become One.

Jesus is talking about this Oneness—*Ardhanarishwar*, half-male, half-female. Then you are neither, then a new childhood has started, the second childhood—you are *dwij*, twice-born. A new world of innocence is discovered.

Now we will enter this sutra :

"Jesus saw children who were being suckled. He said to his disciples: These children who are being suckled are like those who enter the Kingdom.

They said to him: Shall we then, being children, enter the Kingdom?"

This is how disciples always miss: they take things literally, they understand words too much—and the message is wordless. They cling to the symbols too much, they make them too concrete, while when a Jesus speaks his symbols are not concrete, they are liquid. They show something, they don't say anything. They are like indications, fingers pointing to the moon, not saying anything.

Once Jesus says : "These children...are like those who enter the Kingdom," immediately we think that if we become like these children, then we will be capable, then we will be able, *then* we can enter into the Kingdom of God.

The disciples said: "Shall we then, being children, enter the Kingdom?"

Jesus said, "No! Just being children won't help."

"Jesus said to them : When you make the two one, and when you make the inner as the outer, and the outer as the inner, and the above as the below, and when you make the male and the female into a single one, so that the male will not be male and the female will not be female, then shall you enter the Kingdom."

This is what he means by being children again. Try to understand every sentence :

"When you make the two one..."

This is the *basic* problem. Have you observed that if a sun-ray enters a prism, immediately it becomes seven? Then all the colours

of the rainbow appear. That is how a rainbow happens: in the
rainy season, whenever the air is filled with vapour or tiny drops
of water, those drops of water hanging in the air behave like a
prism. A sun-ray enters and it is immediately divided into seven—
that is how a rainbow happens. In the rainy season, when the
sun is out of the clouds a rainbow will be there. The sun-ray
is white, pure white, but through a prism it becomes seven; the
whiteness is lost, seven colours appear.

Your mind functions as a prism; the world is one, existence
is pure white and through your mind it is divided into many.
Everything seen through the mind becomes many. If you are
very alert, you will see seven things in every mental concept. Mind
divides just like a prism—into seven. That is why we have divided
the week into seven. Mahavir, because of this attitude of the mind,
divided his whole logic into seven steps. They are called 'seven
aspects of logic,' and if you asked Mahavir a question he would
give seven answers.

You asked one question—he would immediately give you seven
answers. It was very confusing, because if you asked one question
and he gave seven answers, you left more confused than you had
come. And because of those seven, Mahavir could not be understood; it was impossible to understand him. But he was absolutely
correct, because he was saying, "You ask through the mind, so
I have to answer through the mind—and mind divides everything
into seven." And those seven contradict each other, they are bound
to because the Truth can only be one, the Truth canot be seven.

When you say seven things you have to make contradictions.
If you asked Mahavir whether God exists, he would say: "Yes,
God exists;" and he would say: "No, God doesn't exist." Then
he would say: "Yes and no, both—God exists and doesn't exist;"
and then he would say: "Neither...." And in this way he would
go on, up to seven answers.

Mind divides like a prism. Whenever you look through the
mind, everything becomes seven. If you look keenly, then seven;
if you don't look keenly, then two. If you ask an ordinary man
he will say: "Only two answers are possible. If you ask about God,
either God is or God is not—there are only two possibilities."
But he is missing five because he is not very alert. Otherwise,

the possibilities are seven, not two. So two is the beginning of the many, seven is the end of the many.

Jesus says: "When you make the two one..."

He is talking to very ordinary people, while Mahavir was talking to the greatest scholars and logicians. That is the difference between the audiences: Jesus is talking to very poor, ordinary people—just the mass; but Mahavir was talking to a very select few. He could talk about the seven, Jesus talks about the two—but they mean the same.

Jesus says: "When you make the two one, when the two disappear and one is left, you have attained." Mahavir says: "When you make the seven one, when the seven disappear and one is left, you have attained." The difference is in the audience, but they mean the same thing.

How can the two disappear? What should you do? Nothing can be done through the mind because if the mind is there the two will remain. How should the rainbow disappear? How can it disappear? You just throw the prism and there is no rainbow; just take away the drop hanging in the air and the rainbow disappears. Don't look through the mind and the world of the many disappears; look through the mind and it is there.

Don't look through the mind, put it aside and see! Children look at the world without the mind, because the mind takes time to develop. The body comes first, then later on mind follows—it takes many years really. When the child is born, on the first day he looks at the world and the world is one, he cannot make any distinctions. How can he make any? He cannot say, "This is green and that is red." He does not know red, he does not know green, he simply looks—the world is one. It is so 'one' that he cannot make a distinction between his own body and his mother's body.

Jean Piaget has worked very much on the developing mind of a child. He has been working on this his whole life, and he has come to reveal many truths: a child cannot make any distinction between his own body and things. That is why he will take his own toe and start eating it, because he cannot make distinctions. He cannot think that this is his own toe and it is useless sucking it, he catches hold of it as he will catch hold of anything—there is no distinction. He will defecate and start eating it—no bad, no good. We will say, "What dirtiness!" but for him there is no distinction, so what can he do?

Because of this, for centuries, in India many people have existed who have tried to imitate the child. So they will eat food in the same place where they defecate, and foolish people call them *Paramahansa*, those who have attained. They are simply imitating the child, they don't make any distinction—but they do! Otherwise, what need is there to do it? They make the distinction, but they *force* themselves not to make it. Buddha will not do it, Jesus will not do it, Krishna will not do it, but these so-called *Paramahansas*— you can find them, they are somewhere or other all over the country—they force themselves not to make distinctions.

But whether you make distinctions or force yourself not to make distinctions, mind remains the focus: the distinction is there, but you are repressing the distinction. You are behaving in a juvenile way, but you are not innocent.

"When you make the two one," when the two become one—just like the child. When the child is born, he opens his eyes—he *looks*, but he cannot *think;* the look comes first, thinking will follow. It will take time, sometimes years before the child will become able to make distinctions. A child will immediately snatch a toy from another child's hand, and you will say, "Don't do that! That's not good, that toy is not yours!" You are making a distinction of property because you believe in individual property. You think, "This is mine, and that is not mine." For a child no distinction exists—a toy is just a toy. He cannot think how it is not his: "If my hand can reach and snatch it, it is mine!" 'Mine' and 'thine' are still not clear-cut.

A child cannot make any distinction between a dream and a reality. So in the morning, a child may be weeping and crying because he had a beautiful toy in his dream: "Where has it gone?" He wants it to be given back immediately. He cannot make a distinction between the dream and the real, he cannot make any distinctions. His innocence exists because he is still unable to make distinctions.

And a sage's innocence comes when he has dropped making distinctions. Not that he cannot see that green is green and red is red, not that he cannot make the distinction that this is bread and that is a stone—but he has dropped the mind. Now he lives through the look and not through thinking. That is why Hindus have called their philosophies *darshanas*. *Darshan* means to look, not to think; and philosophy is not a right translation, because philosophy means to think, it is just the opposite.

Darshan means to look and philosophy means to think—they are just the opposite of each other, they cannot be joined together in any way. *Darshan* means a look like a child's, when distinctions have been dropped: "When you make the two one, and when you make the inner as the outer . . ." Because this 'inner' and 'outer' is also a distinction.

I myself have to say: Leave the outer, come to the inner, move within, drop the without! But you can misunderstand the whole thing, because when you drop the without, the within will be dropped automatically. When the outer is no more, how can the inner exist? They are relative terms: the inner exists only as the opposite of the outer; when there is no more outer, there is no more inner. First you drop the outer, and then the inner drops automatically by itself; there is no 'in', no 'out'—you have become one. *If* there is still inner and outer then you are still two, not yet one, you are still divided.

That is why Zen monks have said one of the most strange things ever asserted: they say this world is God; they say ordinary life is religion; they say everything as it is, is okay. Nothing is to be changed because the very concept of change creates the two: that which is has to be changed into something which ought to be; A has to be changed into B, the two comes in. They say *this* very world is Divine; God is not somewhere else, because that somewhere else creates a duality. God is not the creator and you are not the creature—YOU are God. God is not the creator—this *very* creation is Divine, the *very* creativity *is* God.

Mind always tries to make distinctions, that is mind's speciality. The more distinctions you can make, the more clever a mind you have. And mind will always say that these mystics are a little foolish, because boundaries are not clear. That is why they call religion mysticism, and by mysticism they don't mean a very good thing. They mean something vague like mist, something cloudy, something that is not a clear reality, but like a dream.

These mystics are fools for logicians because they don't make distinctions—and distinctions are everything you have to make; you have to know what is what! And logic thinks the more distinctions you can make, the nearer you come to the reality. That is why science—which follows logic, which is the application of logic and nothing else—has reached the atom; making distinctions, by and by, separating everything, they have reached the atom.

Religion, not separating but joining, *dropping* the boundaries, not drawing the boundaries, has reached the Ultimate, the One. Science has reached the atom, which means the many, the infinitely many; and religion has reached the One, the infinitely One. The approaches: science uses mind and mind makes boundaries, clear-cut distinctions; religion doesn't use mind and then all the boundaries disappear, everything becomes everything else, things are *meeting*. The trees are meeting the sky, the sky is dropping into the trees; the earth is meeting heaven, heaven is reaching the earth.

If you look deep into life, you will find that these mystics are right. All boundaries are man-made, there are no boundaries in reality. They are useful, utilitarian, but not true; they help in certain ways, but they hinder also in certain other ways.

Try to find distinctions: for the last week you have been unhappy—can you exactly pin-point the moment when you become unhappy? Can you draw a line? Can you say, "Exactly on this day, at nine-thirty sharp in the morning, I became unhappy"? No, you cannot draw a line! If you search, suddenly you will find everything is vague, you cannot say when you became unhappy. Then you become happy—watch when you become happy again. You may have missed because you were not aware in the past, but now you are unhappy and sometime you will become happy, because mind cannot remain in one state forever. You cannot help it. Even if you want to remain unhappy permanently, you cannot. Then watch: at exactly which moment do you become happy again? You will become happy and you will again miss the moment because it will be vague.

What does it mean? It means happiness and unhappiness are not two things. That's why you cannot make the distinction: they melt into each other, they mingle into each other, their boundaries merge into each other. There are *no* boundaries really, they are like a wave, they are like the hill and the valley: the valley follows the hill; the wave comes and the hollow follows the wave. *Where* does the hill start, and *where* does the valley end? Nowhere ! They are ONE !

It is your *mind* which says: "This is the valley and this is the hill." Can you have a hill without the valley? Can you have a valley without the hill? Can you have happiness without unhappiness? If you are trying to, then you are trying for the impossible. Can you have unhappiness without happiness? Drop it ! Difficult, because this happiness and unhappiness is more poetic. Health and illness are more physiological. Watch ! Exactly when did you become ill? Where can you draw the boundary? And when did you become healthy? Nobody can draw any line of demarcation: illness becomes health, health becomes illness; love becomes hate, hate becomes love; anger becomes compassion, compassion becomes anger—it may be uncomfortable to conceive, but mystics are true.

You were a child—when did you become young? When did youth enter in you? You are young, some day you will become old. *Watch,* and mark on the calendar that, "This day I have become old." And if you cannot distinguish when you become old, can you make the distinction between when you are alive and when you become dead? Even scientists are in much difficulty about when to declare that a man is dead. All that is known up to now is just utilitarian, not true.

When to declare that a man is dead? When he is not breathing? But there have been yogis who have demonstrated in scientific laboratories that they can remain without breathing even for ten minutes. So, the criterion of death cannot be that a man is dead whenever he is not breathing. He may not be able to breathe again, but this is not the criterion because people *have* demonstrated it, they can remain without breathing for ten minutes. This man may be a yogi. He may not want to come back, but you have no right to declare that he is dead. Still, we have to declare death because the dead have to be disposed of.

When is a man really dead? When his heart stops functioning? Or when his brain stops functioning? Now, in scientific laboratories there are brains without bodies—and they are functioning. Who knows what they are thinking? May be dreaming? They will not even be aware that they have lost the body. And scientists who have been observing brains which have no bodies, say they also have the same rhythm: they sleep, they are awake; they sleep, they are wakeful; they show signs that they are dreaming, and they show signs that now they are not dreaming; they show signs that they are thinking, and they show signs that they are sometimes angry and agitated and tense, and sometimes relaxed. Inside, what will they be thinking? They cannot be aware that the body is no longer there, but can you call those minds dead? They are functioning well. Which part can be the criterion? Which moment can be the criterion?

In the Second World War they experimented in Russia, and at least six persons are still alive who were declared dead because of a sudden heart failure. They were declared dead but they were pumped blood, they were revived, and six of them are still alive. What happened? They have been reclaimed !

Is there *really* a boundary where life ends and death begins? No ! Just a wave phenomenon. Life follows death just like a wave is followed by a hollow. They are not separate, they are one—the rhythm of the One.

Mystics say that for utilitarian purposes it is okay that you divide, but the reality is indivisible. What to do to know this indivisible reality? Just put aside the mechanism that divides—this is what meditation is. Put the mind aside and *look !* LOOK without the mind ! BE AWARE without the mind ! SEE ! And don't allow thoughts to stand as a screen between you and the universe. When the clouds, the thoughts, are not there, and the sun shines with full awareness, the world is one.

*"When you make the two one, and when you make the inner
as the outer, and the outer as the inner, and the above as the below,
and when you make the male and the female into a single one,
so that the male will not be male and the female will not be
female, then shall you enter the Kingdom."*

The greatest and the deepest distinction is between male and
female. Have you observed that you never forget that somebody
is male or female? You may forget the name, you may forget the
religion, you may forget the face *completely*, but you never forget
whether the person is a man or a woman. It is impossible, it seems,
to forget. That means the deepest impact on your memory is left
by the division.

Somebody you met twenty years ago; you cannot remember
anything—the face has disappeared, the name has disappeared—
but whether they were a man or a woman? That remains, that
sticks. That made the deepest impact on you, as if the *first* thing
you look for in the other is whether they are a man or a woman;
the first thing that you look for and the last thing that remains
with you. You may not be so consciously looking for it, but whenever you look at a person the first thing you note deep down is
whether they are a man or a woman. If she is a woman you behave
differently; if he is a man you behave differently. If she is a woman,
then your man inside you is attracted whether you know it or not.
You may be unconscious of it, but your behaviour becomes more
tender.

Now the people who run markets, they know it well, so all sales-
men are by and by replaced by saleswomen. It is bound to be so:
if the purchasers are men then it is better to have a saleswoman,
because then the purchaser cannot say *no* so easily as he can say to
a man. When a woman puts a shoe on your foot, touches your
feet—a beautiful woman—suddenly the shoe is not important, the
shoe becomes secondary. It may be pinching you but you say,
"Beautiful! It is good!" and you have to purchase it. You are
purchasing the woman not the shoe.

That is why with every advertisement—reasonably, unreason-
ably; related, unrelated; consistent, inconsistent; it makes no
difference whether you have to sell a car or shoes or anything—

you have to put a naked woman near it. Because the car is not purchased, the woman in the car is purchased. Sex is purchased and sold, everything else is superficial.

Deep down you are looking for sex—*everywhere!* Jesus says you will not be innocent if this looking for sex remains. Then you will remain divided: if you are a man, then you are looking for a woman; if you are a woman you are looking for a man. Then the looking will go on being concerned with the outer, it cannot become inner, you cannot move within, you cannot be meditative. The woman will disturb you, she will follow you. If you resist, if you fight, if you close your eyes, she will become more and more beautiful, she will tempt you.

What to do? How to transcend this duality? Many methods have been used. Most of them are just deceptions. People say: "Think of every woman as your mother," but it will not make much difference, it is a deception. "Think of every woman as your sister"—it makes no difference, because she *remains* a woman. Whether she is a sister or mother makes *no* difference, she remains a woman and you remain a man. A deep search goes on, and that search is so biological that it goes on behind your consciousness, it is a 'sub-stream'.

You watch! You are sitting in your room and a woman enters. Watch yourself, watch what happens. Suddenly you are a different person! And if she is beautiful then you are transformed even more. What happens? Immediately you are no more, just the man exists; you are no more, just the sex hormones. They start functioning, they put you aside, your consciousness is lost, you are almost unconscious, you behave as if you are drunk.

As yet, we have not been able to discover a greater alcohol than sex, a greater drug than sex: it immediately changes everything. If you take LSD things become colourful—sex is an in-built LSD. Whenever you are sexual things become colourful; everything has a different look, a different shine; you are more alive, you don't walk, you run; you don't say anything, you sing. Your life has become a dance, you are living in a *different* dimension.

Whenever sex is not there, suddenly you are back into the flat world, the world of things, uncoloured, no shine in them. You cannot sing, you cannot run, everything has become lazy. Again a woman or a man enters into your life and everything takes on colour, it becomes a romance to be, it becomes poetry to exist. What is happening? And if this goes on happening then you will remain in a duality—the deepest. This duality will not allow you to see the real. And the real is blissful, it is neither happy nor unhappy.

The real is beyond happiness and unhappiness. It is neither tense nor relaxed; it is neither dark nor light, it is *beyond*. When all duality has ceased then you are blissful. Hindus have called that *ananda*—it means 'beyond the two'. You cannot say that a sage is happy. He is not happy because happiness has to be followed by unhappiness. You cannot say a sage is unhappy. A sage is blissful, he has passed the duality. Now there are no hills and no valleys; he moves on the ground, he moves on one level. There are no ups and downs because 'up' and 'down' exist as a duality.

So Jesus says: "When there is nothing above and nothing below, no up and no down, when there are not two, then you cannot choose, you simply exist." And that existence is on one level: there are no waves, the ocean is absolutely silent and without any waves, not even a ripple, because nothing goes above and nothing goes down. The ocean has become a mirrorlike thing, no ripples, all agitation has ceased.

The whole agitation exists through duality, and sex is the base of all duality. You can leave all other things very easily, but the basic thing to leave is sex. And that is the most difficult because it is in every cell of your body, every cell of your being—you *are* a sexual being, you are *born* as a sexual being. That is why Jesus said, "Unless you are born again, nothing will be of any help." *As you are* you will remain tense; as you are you will remain miserable.

"And when you make the male and the female into a single one, so that the male will not be male and the female will not be female, then shall you enter the Kingdom."

So what is to be done? Inside, a circle has to be made. Jesus has not said exactly what is to be done because those secrets cannot be given openly, those secrets can be given only to disciples. Jesus must have given them to his disciples, because just by saying,

"Become one!" no one is going to become one. Just by saying that the male should be female and the female should be male, no one is going to become one, because this is the *goal*. What is the *method?*

Jesus must have kept that method secret. He must have given it to his disciples as a secret key, because those greater secrets which can make you one are also very dangerous. If you miss, if you apply them in even a slightly wrong way, you will go mad. That is the problem, and that is the fear.

Normally, as you are, you are a divided being: your male energy seeking female energy outside, your female energy seeking male energy outside—this is the normal human being. But to make you one the whole thing has to be transformed into your male energy seeking female energy *within*. The *man* within you trying to meet the *woman* within you is very dangerous, because nature has not provided this urge.

Nature has given you an urge to meet the woman, to meet the man, and that urge is natural. But to try for this happening to occur within you alone, is not natural. The key has to be applied very, very delicately. It can be done only under a Master, one who has travelled the path. That is why the deepest secrets of religion cannot be given through scripture, they can be given only through initiation.

I will give you a few hints though, how it can be done. But remember well: if you want to do them be careful not to move away from whatsoever I say, not to move astray, otherwise things can go wrong. It is better then to be normal, because many religious people become mad. This is the reason: you have the key but you don't know how to use it, you can use it wrongly. And if you once use a key wrongly the lock is disturbed; then it will be very difficult to repair the lock.

These methods are to be done only under a Master, so that the Master goes on continuously watching what is happening with you. I am giving you a few things because I am here, and if you want to work you can work.

The first thing: whenever you make love to a woman or a man, that is the right moment to look for the inner woman or the inner man. Whenever you make love to a woman, do it with closed eyes, make it a meditation. The woman outside always helps the inner woman to become awake. And when you make love your inner energies, both male and female, come to a peak. When the orgasm happens, it is not between you and the outer woman, it always happens between you and the inner woman.

So if you are alert you will become aware of the phenomenon that inside a meeting of energies is happening. And whenever *this* happens, the orgasm will be all over the body; it will not be local, it will not be confined to the sex center. If it is confined to the sex center it is just masturbation, nothing else. Orgasm means the *whole* body, every fibre of the body throbs with a new life, with a new energy, because much energy is released by the meeting. The meeting is happening within, but if you go on looking outside you will miss.

The outer woman or the outer man is just a representative of the inner. When you fall in love with a woman or a man, you fall in love only because that woman or man somehow corresponds with the inner. That is why you cannot give any reasons why you are in love with this woman, because it is not a rational thing at all.

You carry a woman within. Whenever any woman fits with that inner woman, suddenly you are in love. That love is not manipulated by you, it is not your mind that is falling in love, it is something very unconscious. In this woman you have a glimpse, suddenly you feel that this is the right person.

What makes this woman the right person? Because for others she is not the right person: there are people who will hate her; there are people who will be repelled, repulsed. There are people who will never look at this woman again; there are people who will not recognize that she has anything. And there are people who will laugh about you: "How have you fallen in love with this woman? Are you mad?" But this woman or this man, somehow fits with the inner. That is why love is an irrational thing: whenever it happens, it happens—you cannot do anything about it; if it is *not* happening you cannot do anything about it.

When you make love to a woman, the inner energy comes to a peak, it comes to a crescendo. At that crescendo, don't go on looking outside, otherwise you will miss something beautiful that is happening, something very mysterious that is happening inside:

you are becoming a circle. Your male and female are meeting, you are becoming *Ardhanarishwar*. In this moment, your whole body will vibrate from the toes to the head. Every nerve of the body will vibrate with life, because this circle spreads all over the body. It is not sexual, it is more than sex. Watch it! Watch the reaching of the peak, the meeting of the inner energies. Then watch when the tide has gone and the abyss starts. Watch, by and by, the separation of the energies again....

If you do it a few times, you will immediately become aware that the outer woman or man is not needed. This can be done without the outer because this is happening without the outer, the outer is just a trigger-point. That trigger-point can be created inside. And once you know how, you can do it inside. But this has to be experienced, only then do you know—I cannot say how. You have to observe, watch, and then you will know how the energies come, how orgasm happens; how they separate again, and again the two arise.

For a single moment the one happens in you. That is why there is so much attraction in sex, that is why so much pleasure is derived out of orgasm—because for a *single* moment you become one, the two disappears. And in the moment of orgasm there is no mind. *If mind* is there orgasm cannot happen. In the moment of orgasm there is not a single thought, the whole prism is put aside. You ARE, but without thoughts. You *exist*, but with no mind. This happens only for such a single moment that you can miss it easily, you have been missing it for many lives. It is such a small gap that if you are interested outside, you have missed it.

So close your eyes and watch what is happening inside. Don't try to make anything happen, just watch whatsoever is happening. By and by it happens, just like when you come inside a room after walking outside in the sun. You come inside the room and everything is dark, you cannot see anything because your eyes are still not accustomed to this dark room. Wait! Sit down and go on silently looking. By and by, the darkness will disappear and you will become aware of things now that your eyes are accustomed to it.

Coming from the outer to the inner is a great problem only because your eyes are accustomed to the outside. The inside looks dark—and by the time you are ready the moment has gone. So meditate more and more with closed eyes, and look inside so you can become attuned to the *inner* darkness. It is not dark, it just appears dark to you because you are accustomed to the outside light. By and by, a diffused light comes, things becomes clear; a moment comes when things become *so* clear that when you open your eyes, you will find the outside is darkness.

Arvind is reported to have said: "When for the first time I came to know what is inside, the light that is outside became like darkness." The life that is outside became like death, because now something higher, something greater, something of the source was happening.

Watch how the inner circle comes, how the two energies become one. In that oneness there is no mind and no thought. Look! By and by, you will be able to see what is happening. And once you know what is happening, the outer can be dropped—no need to drop it, but it can be dropped.

A woman is beautiful, a man is beautiful. Love is good, nothing is wrong, it is healthy and whole. There is no need to drop it but it can be dropped, and then you are no longer dependent on it. Then you can allow the phenomenon to happen inside, and a moment comes when this inner circle remains forever. With the help of the outer it cannot remain forever because the outer has to separate, the separation is a must. But with the inner there is no need to separate; if the inner marriage happens there is no divorce, there is no possibility because it is always there, both are there. Once they have met there is no question of any divorce. With the outer divorce happens continuously; one moment you are together, the next moment you have to be separate.

When this circle remains continuously within you, this is the state of *Ardhanarishwar*—and this is what Jesus means :

"And when you make the male and the female into a single one, so that the male will not be male and the female not be female, then shall you enter the Kingdom." Then you have entered: you have become perfect, you are not divided, you have become indivisible. *Now you have a Self:* now you have freedom and independence, now you lack nothing, you are complete in yourself.

Unless *this* circle happens you will lack something and you will depend on others to fulfill it.

That is why sex looks like a bondage—it is! It looks like a dependence and whenever you feel there is dependence you resent it. Hence the continuous fight with the lover: you feel resentment, you cannot go away from the other because you are dependent.

And nobody wants to depend on anybody, because every dependence is a limitation: the other tries to dominate, the other tries to possess—and if you are dependent, you have to allow the other a certain domination because you are afraid. This is a mutual agreement: "I will be dependent on you, you will be dependent on me, so we can both possess each other in certain ways, and we can both dominate each other in certain ways."

But nobody likes domination and possession. That is why love is such a misery. And if you love a person and also resent them, how can you be happy? Even the most beautiful person becomes ugly.

Mulla Nasrudin was sitting with a friend. His wife came and the friend said: "I suppose this is your most charming wife!" Mulla Nasrudin looked sad and said: "This is my *only* wife!"

That sadness is always present with lovers, because no woman can fulfill a man. Even if you get all the women of the world it will not be a fulfillment, because the inner is greater than the 'all'. All the men in the world will not be able to fulfill a woman—no! It is not possible! Something or other will always be lacking, because no man can be exactly like the inner man. And this is also a problem of time: because only for a single moment can the meeting happen, and then separation.

Unless you attain to the inner unity, you will move from one misery to another; from one woman to another, from one man to another; from one life of misery to another life of misery. The change may give you hope—but it is hopeless, the whole affair is hopeless.

When this circle happens you again become one, innocent like a child; *more* than the child, more than any child can ever be— you have become a sage.

Meditate on these words of Jesus, and what I have said, try. But if you want to try let me know. If you start working for the inner circle, then let me know continuously what is happening. Because if something goes wrong and two energies meet in a wrong way, you will go mad.

That is the fear of becoming a sage: if you fall, you fall to the very bottom, you become mad. If you reach, you reach to the very top, you become a sage. It is always like this if someone wants to walk on the heights, he has to have courage, because if you fall, you fall to the depth. Near the heights the abyss is always there.

So remember that a very balanced effort is needed, and many other things. If you want to work on it I will tell you, but that can only be done personally. That is why Jesus talks about the goal, but never talks about the method. The method is to be given personally, it is an initiation.

Ninth Discourse

29th August 1974, Poona, India

THE NINTH SAYING

Jesus said :
The mote that is in thy brother's eye
thou seest,
but the beam that is in thine eye
thou seest not.

When thou castest the beam out of thine eye,
then thou wilt see clearly
to cast the mote out of thy brother's eye.

Self-knowledge is the most difficult thing—not because it is difficult, but because you are scared to know about yourself. A deep fear exists. Everybody is trying to escape, escape from himself. This fear has to be understood. And if this fear exists, whatsoever you do will not be of much help. You may think that you want to know yourself, but if this unconscious fear is there you will continuously avoid self-knowledge, you will continuously try to hide, deceive. On the one hand you will try to know yourself, and on the other hand you will create all sorts of hindrances so that you cannot know.

Consciously you may think, "I would like to know myself," but in the unconscious, which is bigger, stronger, more powerful than the conscious, you will avoid self-knowledge. So the fear has to be understood. Why are you afraid? One thing: if you really penetrate within yourself, your image that you have created in the world will prove to be false. Your whole past will come to mean nothing, because it has been like a dream. And you have invested so much in it, you have lived for it, that now to know that it has been a false phenomenon you feel hurt—now your whole life has been wasted.

If whatsoever you have been living has been a pseudo-life, not authentic, if you have never loved but just pretended to love, how can you encounter yourself? Because then you will come to know that the whole thing has been a pretence: not only have you pretended that you love, you have also pretended that you are happy when you love. You have deceived nobody else but yourself. And now to look back, to look within, fear grips you.

You have been thinking that you are something unique, everybody does. That is the most ordinary thing in the world, to think oneself extraordinary, something special, 'the chosen'. But if you look at yourself you will come to know that there is *nothing*, there is nothing to be egoistic about. Then where will the ego stand? It will tumble down, fall down to the dust.

Fear is there, so you do not look at yourself. In not looking, you can go on creating dreams about yourself, images about yourself. And it is very easy and cheap to create an image, but it is very difficult and hard to *really* be something. One always chooses the cheapest—and you have chosen the cheapest. Now, to look at yourself is difficult.

In one house, the phone rang in the middle of the night—it was four a.m. The man got up, he was furious, and he shouted into the instrument, "What do you want?" The man at the other end said, "Nothing!" Then he was more furious, he said, "Then why have you phoned me in the middle of the night?"

The man said, "Because the rate is cheaper!"

If the rate is cheaper, you can even buy nothing. And that is what you have done. To create an image that you are unique is *cheap,* but to be unique is arduous, very hard. Many, many lives of struggle, striving, many lives of effort culminate into something when you become unique. But to believe that you are unique is just cheap, you can do it right now, there is no need to even move. And you have been believing in cheap things—that is why fear exists.

You cannot look at yourself. All that you have been thinking yourself to be you will not find there—and you know it well. Who else will know it as well as you know? If you think you are beautiful, then you cannot look in the mirror if this beauty is just an idea. And you know well! Rather than looking in the mirror, you will break all mirrors. Whenever an ugly man or an ugly woman looks into the mirror, he or she thinks that something is wrong with the mirror—because it is so painful to realize that you are nobody.

You are somebody in your eyes. Everybody else may know that you are nobody, but not you. Even a madman thinks that the whole world is mad. The whole world says to him, "You are mad!" but he will not listen because this is too painful. He will create all sorts of arguments, rationalizations to say, "I am not mad."

It happened: Mulla Nasrudin came running into a farm one evening and asked the farmer, "Have you seen a lunatic woman passing through here?"

The farmer said, "What did she look like?"

Nasrudin described her. He said, "She is six feet four inches tall, very fat, and weighs forty-five pounds."

The farmer looked a little puzzled and said, "If she is six feet four inches tall and is very fat, how can she weigh only forty-five pounds?"

Nasrudin laughed and said, "Don't be silly—didn't I tell you that she is a little crazy?"

It is always the other who is wrong, who is crazy. That's how you protect your own so-called sanity, this is a protection. And a person who cannot look at himself, basically *cannot* look, because he is not only afraid of looking at himself—the basic thing is that he is afraid of looking. For when you look at the other, the other can become the mirror; when you look into the other, the *other* can indicate something about *you*. In the other's eyes you are reflected, so you cannot look at the other. You create a fiction about yourself and then you create a fiction about others. Then you live in a dream world—that is how everybody is living.

And then you ask how to be blissful. Your nightmare is natural: whatsoever you have done, only a nightmare can come to flower from it. And you ask how to be at ease. No one can be at ease with fiction, only with fact. Howsoever hard it may be to accept, only fact can make you non-tense, only fact can lead you towards truth. If you deny the factuality then there is no truth for you, and then you go on moving around and around and never hit the center.

I have heard, once it happened: A doctor came to see a patient, a very ill woman. He entered the room and after five minutes he was out. He asked the husband who was waiting there, "Give me a corkscrew!" The husband was a little worried why a corkscrew should be needed. But then the doctor came again after five minutes, perspiring, and he said, "Now give me a screwdriver!" The husband got very much excited, but still kept silent—because the doctor knows what to do. After five minutes the doctor was back again and he asked for a chisel and hammer. Then it was too much, the distraught husband couldn't stand it any longer and he said, "What is wrong with my wife?" The doctor said, "I don't know yet, because I have not been able to open my bag!"

And I tell you, you are still struggling with the bag! And not only that—that you are not able to open it—but you don't even want to open it. All these corkscrews and screwdrivers and chisels and hammers that you carry with you are just phoney. You don't even want to open the bag, because once you open the bag then what are you going to do? Then the patient—which is *you*—then the patient has to be diagnosed, then you have to look into yourself.

So everybody is occupied with the bag—that is what your business is, your profession, your occupation. You may be a poet or a painter or a musician, but all your occupations are just ways to remain engaged outside. That is why nobody is ready to be alone, even for a single moment. It is so fearful, because when you are alone you may come across yourself. When you are alone what will you do? When you are alone you are with you—and the reality may erupt.

So everybody tries for continuous occupation, to be occupied twenty-four hours a day. When you are occupied you look a little happy, when you are not occupied you become unhappy. Psychologists say that if a man is left unoccupied for a long period, he will go insane. But why? Why if you are sane should you go insane if you are left unoccupied for a long period? If you are sane, then in a long fallow period, a long period where nothing is done, you will become more sane, you will grow! But why should you become insane if you are left alone for a long period? Because you *are* insane! Your occupation simply hides the fact.

Look around, because it is difficult to look at yourself, but look around, look at people! For example a man is constantly occupied with money. What is he really doing? Focusing his mind on money so he can avoid himself. He goes on thinking about money, morning, evening and night. Even on his bed he thinks about money and the bank and the balance. What is he *doing* with the money? That is why when he gets the money he is at a loss—what to do now? So the moment he gets the money he was thinking about, he starts thinking about more money—because money is not the thing he was asking for. Otherwise, when he gets it he should feel fulfilled, but not even a Rockefeller or a Ford is fulfilled.

When you get money you immediately demand more, because the basic motivation is not the money, the basic motivation is how to remain occupied. Whenever occupation is not there you are uncomfortable, a *deep* unease arises in you. What to do? If there is nothing to do, you will read the same newspaper again and again and again—the same newspaper you have already read completely. If there is no occupation, you may do anything which is not needed at all, but you cannot remain at ease. Hence the insistence of all the Masters, that if you can sit for a few hours without doing *anything*, soon you will become Enlightened.

An unoccupied state of mind is meditation. An occupied state of mind is the world, the *sansar*. It doesn't matter what type of occupation you have—whether you are interested in money or politics, or social service or revolution, it makes no difference—your sanity is the same. Even if you leave Lenin alone he will go mad: he needs the society and the revolution; if there is nothing to do, it will be impossible for him to exist, his sanity will be lost. He is sane through you. You work so much that the energy is lost in the work, you are exhausted, you can go to sleep.

Old men look almost crazy and eccentric, and the reason is that they have nothing to do. Old age is not the reason—they are now unoccupied, they are not needed, retired. Retired people always become a little eccentric. Something has gone wrong with them. The man was okay, he may have been a president or a prime minister of a country, but retire him and see what happens: immediately he deteriorates. His body and mind both deteriorate and he starts becoming a little eccentric, crazy, mad. Because now there is no occupation, nobody looks at him, nobody is interested in him. He has no work to do, nowhere to focus his mind. The whole turmoil goes in and in—he becomes a turmoil.

Psychologists say that retired persons die ten years earlier than they would have died if they had still been occupied. What happens? Why is it so difficult to be with yourself? Yet you always think that others should feel happy with you—your wife should feel happy with you, your husband should feel happy with you. You yourself never feel happy with yourself, so how can anybody else feel happy with you? If you are such a boring personality that you yourself get bored with yourself, how is it possible that others can tolerate you? They tolerate you for other reasons—not because you are such a loving person, no! They tolerate you because you give them an occupation. A husband is enough occupation for a wife, a wife is enough occupation for her husband. This is a mutual deception: they have agreed to deceive each other and help each other to remain occupied.

You cannot look at yourself, you cannot come to self-realization, because that is a very *far* goal. You cannot turn and see the 'facticity' about yourself, and the reason is: a false image, a false identity, a false idea that you are somebody very important, significant— the whole world will stop if you die. What will happen to the world when you are not there? When you were not there, what was happening? The world was a little more at peace, that's all. When you are not there, there will be a little less trouble in the world, that's all—because one uneasy person will have disappeared, and he was creating uneasiness in others. But to support the ego all these fictions are needed.

Napoleon became a prisoner in his last days. He was kept prisoner on a small island, St. Helena. He was nothing any more— nobody ever is, but now even to continue in the fiction was very difficult. He was an Emperor, one of the greatest conquerors: "What to do now? How can I allow this fact that I am nothing any more, just a prisoner, an ordinary prisoner?" But he would not look at the fact, he continued in the old fiction. He didn't change his clothes for six years, because the prison wouldn't give him clothes that suit an Emperor. His clothes were completely rotten, the colour faded, they became dirty, but he would not change them.

The prison doctor asked him, "Why don't you change this coat? It has become so dirty! We can give you better, cleaner clothes." Napoleon looked at him and said, "This is an Emperor's coat—it may be dirty but I cannot change it for an ordinary coat!" He walked as if he were still the Emperor, he talked as if he were still the Emperor, he gave orders—there was no one to listen to his orders, but he continued ordering. He would write letters and orders, and he had brought his letter-pad with him. In his mind he was still the Emperor.

What was happening to this poor man? And unoccupied, he began to be permanently ill. The doctor who was with him kept a diary, and in the diary he writes: "I feel that he is not really ill, now illness is just an occupation. Sometimes he says 'my stomach,' sometimes 'my head,' sometimes 'my legs'," and the doctor thought that nothing was wrong, the body was absolutely okay. But now he had nothing to remain engaged with, now the only other was the body. The whole world of others had disappeared, he was alone. Now the body was the other, so he remained occupied with the body.

Many people are ill as an occupation: in the world, fifty percent of illness exists as an occupation. If you remain occupied, then you need not face yourself. Otherwise, what would have happened to Napoleon? If he had faced himself, then he would have seen that he was a beggar—and that would have been too much! He died an Emperor. Before his death he ordered how he should be given the last send-off, every detail. Nobody was there to follow those details because nobody was interested. But he gave the orders, and he must have died at ease thinking that he was going to be given the last send-off like an Emperor.

With Napoleon the thing is so clear because he *had been* an Emperor. That too was a fiction—supported by the society. But nothing had changed, Napoleon was the same, only the support had disappeared. This is difficult to understand: there are fictions when the society supports you, there are fictions when nobody supports you. That is the difference between a sane and an insane person: a sane person is one whose fiction is supported by the society. He has manipulated the society to support his fiction. An insane man is one whose fiction is supported by nobody; he is alone so you have to put him in the madhouse.

But your support doesn't make anything real—if it is a fiction, it is a fiction. If you look at yourself, immediately you will feel you are *nobody*, nothing important. But then the whole earth, the base under your feet is withdrawn, you are in an abyss. Better not to look at it—just continue in your dreams. They may be dreams, but they help you to live in a sane way.

Not only can't you look at yourself, you cannot look at the other either, because the other is also representative. So you also create fictions about the other: through hate you create a fiction that the other is a devil; through love you create a fiction that the other is an angel, or a god. You also create fictions about the other; you cannot look directly, you cannot see through them, your perception is not immediate. You live in a *maya*, in an illusion created by yourself. So whatsoever you see it is exaggerated: if you hate a person, he immediately becomes the devil; if you love a person, he immediately becomes a god. You exaggerate: if you see bad, then you exaggerate and transform it into the ultimate badness; if you see good it becomes the ultimate good, a god.

But it is difficult to maintain these fictions, so you have to change again and again. Why are you so exaggerated in your perceptions? Why don't you see clearly what is there? Because you are afraid to see clearly. You want clouds around so everything remains in a mist. You want not to know yourself. And all those who have known, they insist: "Know thyself!" Buddha, Jesus, Socrates, they go on insisting: "Know thyself!" The whole insistence of religion is to know thyself.

And you insist not to know yourself. Sometimes you even play the game of knowing yourself. I come across many people who are playing the game of knowing themselves, and they don't want to know. This is a game: now they again want to create a new fiction, a religious fiction, and they come to me so that I can support them. They say, "I have realized this, I have realized that," and they look at me and their eyes are begging.

If I say, "Yes, you have experienced this," they are supported, they go away happy. And if I say, "No," they become unhappy, they never come back to me again. They simply disappear because they have to find somebody else, some other authority. But why are you in search of an authority? Why do you need a witness? If you have realized something, you have realized it—no need for any authority, because the experience in itself is self-evident.

If you realize your soul, you will not need anybody's recognition, a certificate. Even if the whole world says you have not realized, it makes no difference; a vote is not needed, you *know* it has happened. If a blind man has started seeing, he doesn't require anybody as a witness to say that now he can see—he can see, that is enough. But if the blind man is dreaming that he can see, then he will need some authority to seal the fact that this is true, that he can see.

People play games, even spiritual games exist. And unless you stop playing and become sober about the fact that fictions have to be dropped, and the hard truth has to be faced as it is, nothing is possible—because this is the door. And if nobody supports you, then you yourself support yourself. Then you stop talking with people, because they cannot understand you.

A man came to me a few months ago and he said, "You can understand, nobody else can understand me, because I have been receiving messages from God every night." And he had a big file with him—absolute nonsense! But he thinks he is receiving messages from God. And he thinks that this is the latest Koran, that since Mohammed nobody has received such messages—now the Koran is out of date. If Mohammedans come to hear of it they will kill him, because they believe in another fiction and he is trying to destroy their fiction. And this man who receives messages from God, he was so nervous and trembling, looking at me to see what I would say—because whomsoever he meets, they laugh and think, "You have gone crazy!" But he said, "I know that you are a Realized man." Now he is bribing me! And he was continuously begging: "Just say, 'Yes, this is right'."

But I said, "If God is giving you messages you need not come to me, God is enough."

Then he became a little doubtful, puzzled, and he said, "But who knows? It may be just my mind playing tricks." That he knew well. Whenever you are playing tricks, deep down you know it, and nobody is needed to show it to you—but you want to hide the fact.

I told him, "This is madness!" Then he never came back to me again—now I am not a Realized man! He wanted a mutual thing: if I had said, "Yes, you are receiving messages," he would have gone and said, "This man has become Realized!"

If I accept your fiction, then you can help my fiction; this is the mutual game that is going on. And this game is so satisfying that you don't want to break it. But a deep discontent also follows like a shadow. It is bound to be so because the whole thing is a fiction.

A beggar thinking that he is an emperor, knows that he is a beggar. This is the problem: he thinks he is an emperor, pretends he is an emperor, and knows deep down that he is a beggar. He feels very satisfied about the emperorhood, but a deep discontent follows like a shadow: "I am just a beggar." This is your problem: you think something about yourself, and you know it is not true.

You have never loved, you have pretended; you have never been honest, you have pretended; you have never been true, you have pretended—your whole life is a long series of pretences. And now, because you have wasted so much life in it, just to recognize that the whole thing has been only a fiction, is too much. Now you think, "Somehow I'll carry it to the very end." But if you don't finish it, even if you carry it up to the very end, it is not going to give you anything. It is simply a wastage; it is a *simple* wastage, and in the end the whole frustration will erupt.

That is why death is so difficult. Death has nothing dangerous in it, it is one of the most beautiful phenomena in the world—you simply go to sleep! And everything goes to sleep: a seed sprouts and then there is a tree; then again, seeds come and they fall down and go to sleep; then again they will arise. After every activity a rest is needed. Life is an activity, death is a rest. It has to be there so new life may arise out of it. Nothing is wrong in death, nothing is dangerous in death.

But why is everybody so afraid of dying? Because at the moment of death all your fictions will disappear; at the moment of death you will see that your whole life has been a wastage. Why do people say that at the moment of death, a person comes to see his whole life? It happens, it is true: at the moment of death a person *has* to face his whole life, because now there is no future and he cannot create any more fictions.

For fictions the future is needed, because fictions exist in hope, fictions are for tomorrow. *Death brings home the fact that now there is no tomorrow;* tomorrows are finished, now there is no future. Where can you dream? Where can you project your fictions now? Nowhere to go! Suddenly you are stuck. And your whole life you have been creating fictions in the future. Now you are stuck, there is no future—where will you look? You *have* to look at the past, and at the moment of death the society is disappearing;

you have to look at yourself, there is nothing left. Then you come to realize the pain, the anguish of a whole life wasted.

If it can happen to you before death, you become a religious man. A religious man is one who has realized before death that which everybody realizes in death. A religious man is one who has looked while still alive—looked into the past, seen through the whole game, realized the fictitiousness of his life—looked into himself.

If you look into yourself the change is certain, absolutely certain, because once the fiction is realized as a fiction, it starts dropping. To be retained, a fiction has to be retained as a fact; if it is to be carried, even an untruth has to be thought of as true. The moment you realize that this is untrue, and the thing penetrates, it starts dropping—it is already out of your hands, you cannot catch it. To continue the dream one has to believe that this is not a dream, this is reality. The moment you become aware that this is a dream, the dream is already disappearing.

But not to know is your whole effort, you avoid it; that is why you are never at ease when you are alone. Even if you go to the Himalayas, you take your radio set with you and the radio set carries the whole world; even if you go to the Himalayas, your wife, your friends, your children are with you. You go for a holiday but you never go—you carry the whole atmosphere *there* at the beach, in the hills, and again you are surrounded by the whole nonsense.

It happened once: A shipwrecked sailor reached a deserted island. For five years he had to live there because no ship passed. He built a small hut, he lived there, but he continuously thought of the world. Everything was so peaceful, as it had never been. He had never known, not even imagined that such peace was possible. The island was completely deserted, there was nobody—that was the only problem. Otherwise everything was perfect: the streams were beautiful, the trees were filled with fruit; he could eat, he could rest; there was no worry, nobody to worry about, nobody to create trouble. And he had always thought that some day, he would like to go to a peaceful place—and suddenly he was there! But it was unbearable. Silence *is* unbearable, one has to be capable of bearing it—it can kill you.

It was so difficult for this man, but he was an architect so he started building small things, just small models, just to remain occupied. He made a small street and he named the street; he made not only one church, he made two churches—one near his house, another at the other end of the town; he made small shops where one could go shopping. He created a whole town.

After five years, when a ship came and anchored in the bay, he was very happy. A man came in a small boat to the shore. He ran from his hut and reached the shore very excited that now he would be going back into the world again. But he became very puzzled: the man came out of the boat with a big bundle of newspapers. So he said, "What are these newspapers for, why have you carried them here?"

The man, who was the captain of the ship said, "First go through these, see what is happening in the world—and then tell us whether you still want to be rescued!"

The man threw those newspapers in the sea and said, "What nonsense! But before I come into the boat I would like to show you my town."

So he showed him the town, but the captain was puzzled when he showed him the second church. He said, "I can understand that you have made one church to pray in, but why this other one?"

So he said, "This is the church I go to, and that is the church I don't go to."

You need two churches, at least two religions, because the mind is a duality: "This is the church I say *yes* to, and that is the church I say *no* to. That is the wrong church; wrong people go there, those who don't belong to me." He was alone, but he had created the whole world. And he was eager to go back to the world, he was not ready to look at the newspapers. And he did well, because once you look at the newspapers you would not like to be rescued.

Look at your newspapers! What is happening in the world? Is it worth living in it? But you read, you don't look; your reading is not looking, you just read sleepily. You don't realize what is happening in the world, what man has done to man, what man is continuously doing to man: *such* violence, *such* foolishness, *such* a poisoning of every type of significance, of everything that is beautiful and true and good; everything poisoned. Would you like to live in it? If you *look*, then it will be very difficult to decide to live in it. That's why it's better not to look, just move as if you are in a hypnosis.

In order not to look at oneself, another technique has been used that Jesus talks about in this sutra, and that technique is: look in the other for all that is wrong so that you can infer you are good. There are two ways to be good: being good—that is difficult; then there is another way to be good and that is relatively: prove that the other is wrong. You need not be good, just prove that the other is wrong. That gives you a feeling that you are good.

Hence we all go on proving that the other is the thief, the other is the murderer, the other is the evil one. And then when you have proved that everyone is wrong, suddenly you have a feeling that you are good. This is a relative phenomenon: no need to change yourself, just prove that the other is wrong. And this is very easy—nothing is as easy as this. You can magnify the badness in the other; you can magnify and nobody can prevent you from doing it. And before that magnified, projected badness, evil, you look simply innocent. That is why if somebody says about someone: "He is a bad man!" you never argue against it, never; you simply accept it. Rather on the contrary you say, "I always knew that that was the case." But if somebody says something good about someone, you argue, you require proofs.

Have you observed the fact that there have been millions of people who have said: "We will believe in God but first give us proofs"? But nobody has yet written a book requiring proofs for the Devil—nobody! *Nobody* requires any proof for the Devil, nobody says, "I will believe in the Devil only when he is proved." No, you already know the Devil is there all around. Only God is missing, He is not there.

Why does good need proof and bad need no proof? Observe the tendency and you will come upon a beautiful phenomenon, one of the mysteries of the human mind, that deep down everybody seeks to be good. But it is difficult, so what to do? Prove that the other is bad: "You are worse than me—so then I am at least a little good!"

"Jesus says: The mote that is in thy brother's eye thou seest, but the beam that is in thine eye thou seest not.

When thou castest the beam out of thine eye, then thou wilt see clearly to cast the mote out of thy brother's eye."

You go on looking upon the other as darkness. This may give you an illusory feeling that you are light, but this cannot give you light. And if you try to make the other enlightened because you think he is in darkness, that is going to make things worse—that is adding insult to injury. Because in the first place darkness is projected by you, and in the second place you are not light yourself so you cannot enlighten the other.

So people who try to transform the society are the mischief-makers; people who try to change the other are always dangerous. They are murderers in a very subtle way, but their murder is so subtle that you cannot catch it. They don't kill you directly, but they cripple you, they cut you—and *'for your own good,'* so you cannot say anything against them. Your so-called saints are just trying to destroy the darkness which is not in you or may not be in you, but which they imagine to be there. They see a hell in you because that is the only way they can see and feel themselves as heavenly.

Mulla Nasrudin died. He knocked at the doors of Heaven. St. Peter opened the door, looked at Nasrudin and said, "But I am not expecting anybody today, because in my reservation list there is no name; nobody is to come today. So how...? You surprise me, how did you get here? Say your name loudly! Spell it, so I can check."

So Nasrudin spelled his name loudly, "M-U-L-L-A N-A-S-R-U-D-I-N." St. Peter went in and looked at his list, but there was nobody to come on that day.

He came back and he said, "Say! You are not expected to come here today, you are not due for ten years yet. So tell me, who is your doctor?"

Doctors can kill you before your time; do-gooders can kill you before you are due, and do-gooders are always dangerous. But you are all do-gooders in your own ways, small or big. Everybody wants to change the other because everybody thinks the other is wrong; everybody wants to change the world. And this is the difference between a political mind and religious mind.

A political mind always wants to change the world because he cannot think that he is wrong—the whole world is wrong. If he is wrong, it is *because* the whole world is wrong and the whole situation is so wrong. It has to be wrong—otherwise he would be a saint. A religious person looks from precisely the other end. He thinks, "I am wrong, that is why the world is wrong, because I contribute to the evil in it. Through me the world is wrong. Unless I change myself, there can be no change."

The politician starts from the world, but he never reaches any goal because the world is so big—and the world is *not* the problem. He creates more problems: through his medicine, many more diseases arise which were not there; through his efforts he creates more misery. A religious man changes himself. He only changes himself because that is the only thing that *is* possible.

You can only change yourself, and the moment you are changed the world starts changing, because you are a vital part in it. And when you are Enlightened—changed, totally changed—you become more vital; you now have the supreme energy in you. A Buddha simply sits under his Bodhi Tree and the world is transformed. And the world will never again be the same as it was before Buddha.

A Jesus is crucified, but that becomes a mark: history is divided from that day, history will never again be the same as it was. So it is good that we acknowledge and divide the years in the name of Jesus: we say 'before Christ, after Christ'. It is good, because before Christ a totally different humanity existed; after Christ a different humanity came into being. The phenomenon is so vital that whenever there is a Christ, whenever a consciousness rises as high as the consciousness of Jesus, all other consciousnesses are simultaneously affected. They also rise, they also have a glimpse—and they cannot be the same again, the same old level cannot be achieved.

A religious man simply transforms himself, but the transformation is possible only if you look; the transformation is possible only if you drop the fictions. If you come to realize your 'nobodiness,' if you come to realize your nothingness, if you come to realize your inauthentic life, immediately it starts dropping.

Knowledge *is* revolution—not knowledge that you gather through

the mind, but knowledge that you come to possess when you encounter yourself. Self-knowledge is a transforming force, nothing
else is to be done. This has to be understood: people think, "First
we will know, and then we will change." No! The moment you
know, change occurs. Knowledge itself is transforming; it is not that
first you know and then you do something to change. Knowledge is
not a method, it is not a means—knowledge is the end in itself.

But when I use the word 'knowledge', I mean self-knowledge. All
other knowledge is a means: first you have to know the know-how
and then you have to do something. But with self-knowledge the
quality is absolutely different: you know and the very knowing
changes you.

Drop the fictions! Gather courage to know yourself. Drop the
fear and don't try to escape from yourself!

And Jesus says: "When *thou* castest the beam out of thine eye,
then thou wilt see clearly..." Only when the fictions are dropped!
They are the beam in your eye, they have become a mist, a smoke,
a cloud in your eye. You cannot see clearly, you cannot see anything clearly, everything is blurred. When the beam is cast out from
thine eye, you will see clearly. Clarity must be the goal—just clarity
of the eyes so that you can look directly and penetrate to the fact
without creating any projection around it. But this is very difficult,
because you have become so automatic in it, so mechanized.

You look at a flower and immediately your mind starts talking:
"A beautiful flower, never seen before." Some poetry, borrowed of
course, arises. The flower is missed, the clarity is not there. Words
blur—can't you see a flower without naming it? Is naming a must?
Is your naming the flower going to help in any way? Will the flower
be more beautiful if you have the botanical knowledge about it?
That is the difference between a botanist and a poet: a botanist
knows *about* the flower, the poet knows the flower. The botanist is
simply ignorant—he knows much but it is about and about—the
poet sees.

In Sanskrit there is only one word for *rishi* and *kavi*, for the seer
and the poet. There are not two words, because they say whenever
there is a real poet, he is a seer; whenever there is a seer, he is a
poet. Clarity—then life becomes poetry. But then you have to look
at the flower without naming it— is it a rose or something else?

Why are words needed? Why do you say, "It is beautiful"? Can't you see the beauty without speaking? Is it necessary to repeat that it is beautiful? What do you mean by repeating it? It means the flower is not enough—you need a suggestion that it is beautiful, then you can create beauty around it. You don't see the flower, the flower is just a screen, you have to project beauty on it.

Look at the flower and *don't* say anything. It will be difficult, the mind will feel uneasy because it has become habitual. It constantly goes on chattering. Look at the flower and make it a meditation ! Look at the tree and don't name it, don't say *anything !* There is no *need*, the tree is *there*—why say anything?

I have heard it happened: Lao Tzu, one of the greatest Chinese mystics, used to go for a walk in the morning every day. A neighbour used to follow him, but the neighbour knew that Lao Tzu was a man of silence, so for years he followed him on the morning walk but he never said anything. One day there was a visitor at the neighbour's house, a guest, and he also wanted to come. The neighbour said, "Don't say anything, because Lao Tzu wants to live directly. Don't say anything !"

They went out and the morning was so beautiful, so silent, the birds were singing, that just out of habit the guest said, "How beautiful!" Just this much, nothing much; for a one hour walk, this is not very much: "How beautiful !" But Lao Tzu looked at him as if he had committed a sin.

Back home, entering his door, Lao Tzu said to the neighbour, "Never come again! And never bring anybody else—this man seems to be very talkative." And he had only said, "How beautiful!" —too talkative. And Lao Tzu said, "The morning *was* beautiful, it was so silent. This man disturbed the whole thing."

"How beautiful!" It fell like a stone in a silent pool. "How beautiful!" fell like a stone in a silent pool and the whole thing became rippled.

Meditate near a tree, meditate with the stars, with the river, with the ocean; meditate in the market with people passing—don't say anything ! Don't judge ! Don't use words ! *Just look !* If you can clear your perception, if you can attain a clarity of looking, everything is achieved. And once this clarity is achieved you will be able to see yourself.

Self-knowledge happens to a clear mind, not to a mind filled with knowledge, not to a mind filled with judgments of good and bad; not to a mind filled with beauty, ugliness, but to mind that is without words. Self-knowledge happens to a wordless mind. It is always there, you need only a clarity of mind to perceive it, so that it can be reflected; you need a mirrorlike mind so that the reflection becomes possible. Once this happens, *then* you can help your neighbour, never before. So don't advise anybody! All your advice is dangerous because you don't know what you are doing.

Don't try to change anybody, not even your son, not even your brother. Nobody is in need of your change because you are dangerous. You can cripple, you can kill, you can maim, but you cannot help transformation. Unless *you* are transformed don't move into another's life. When you are filled with light, you can help. Really, then there is no need to make any effort to help. Help flows from you just as light flows from a lamp, or fragrance comes out of a flower, or the moon shines in the night—no effort on the part of the moon, it just flows naturally.

Somebody asked Basho, a Zen Master, "Say something about your lectures. You go on talking and still you talk *against* words. You go on talking and in those talks you go on talking against words and against talking. So say something about it !"

What did Basho say? Basho said, "Others talk—I bloom !"

When there is no effort, then it is a blooming. Then it is just like a flower blooming, there is no effort to bloom. A Basho speaks, a Buddha speaks— no effort, it just happens ! It is a natural phenomenon when Buddha is speaking. When you are speaking it is not a natural phenomenon, other things are involved: you want to impress the other, you want to change the other; you want to control, manipulate the other, you want to dominate the other; you want to give the impression that you are a man of knowledge—you want to feed your ego. Many other things are involved. You are not blooming. It is a great political game when you talk, there is a strategy in it, tactics.

But when a Basho talks, he blooms. If somebody is there, then he will be benefited—but to benefit the other is not the goal, the benefit can happen effortlessly. The flower does not bloom for you. If you pass by the path the fragrance will reach you, you can enjoy it, you can feel ecstatic, you can be grateful—but the flower never flowered for *you*, the flower simply flowered.

A Buddha blooms, a Jesus blooms and the whole world is benefited. But you go on trying to benefit others and nobody is benefited, rather you do harm. The world would be better if there were less mischievous people around changing and transforming it. All the revolutions have simply done harm, and every reform has led into a deeper mess.

D. H. Lawrence once suggested that for a hundred years we should stop all revolutions, we should stop all universities, we should stop all reforms and all talk about them, and for a hundred years we should live like primitives. The suggestion is beautiful. Then humanity could come to be alive again, the energy could arise and people could attain to clarity.

Words have dimmed, they have become too burdensome, and you carry so much knowledge that you cannot fly in the sky. You are burdened so much that you are not weightless, your wings are not free. And you cling to the things that have become your prisons and bondages, because you think they are very valuable. They are valueless things, and not only valueless, but also dangerous to you: words, scriptures, knowledge, theories, 'isms'—they all cripple you. Clarity cannot be attained through them. Put aside all scriptures, put aside all judgment.

Look at life like a child, not knowing what he is looking at, just looking—and that looking will give you a new perception. That new perception is what Jesus is talking about. I will repeat the words:

> *"The mote that is in thy brother's eye thou seest, but the beam that is in thine eye thou seest not.*
> *When thou castest the beam of thine eye, then thou wilt see clearly to cast the mote out of thy brother's eye."*

Only that can be helpful. If *you* become a light unto yourself, you become a light unto others. But that is a blooming, and everybody is benefited—knowingly, unknowingly, everybody is benefited. You become a blessing.

Tenth Discourse

30th August 1974, Poona, India

THE TENTH SAYING

Jesus said :
It is impossible for a man
to mount two horses
and to stretch two bows;
and it is impossible for a servant
to serve two masters,
otherwise he will honour the one
and offend the other.

Everybody is already mounted on two horses, everybody is stretching two bows—not only two but many. That is how anguish is created, that is why you are constantly in anxiety. Anxiety shows that somehow you are mounted on two horses. How can you be at ease? Impossible ! Because the two horses are moving in two directions, and you cannot move anywhere.

With one horse movement is possible, you can reach somewhere. With two horses movement is impossible, they will negate each other and you will not reach anywhere. And this is the anxiety—that you are not reaching anywhere. Deep down this is the anguish: that life is slipping out of your hands, time is becoming less and less, death is coming near, and you are not reaching anywhere. It is as if you have become a stagnant pool, just getting dryer and dryer and dying. There is no goal, no fulfillment. But why is it happening? Because you have been trying to do the impossible.

Try to understand the mind *as it functions in you*, then you will be able to understand what Jesus means. You want to be as free as a poor man because only a poor man can be free—he has no burden, he has nothing to protect, you cannot rob him. He is unafraid. You cannot snatch anything from him because he has nothing; with nothing, he is at ease; with nothing as his possession, nothing can be stolen from him. Nobody is his enemy because he is not a competitor at all, he is not competing with anybody.

You want to be as free as a poor man, as a beggar, but you also want to be as secure as a rich man, as safe as an emperor. The rich man is safe, the rich man is secure, he feels more rooted. Outwardly, he has made all the arrangements, he is not vulnerable: he has protections against death, you cannot murder him so easily, he has an armour. And you would like to be free like the beggar and to be secure like an emperor—then you are mounted on two horses and it is impossible to reach anywhere!

You love a person, but you want the person to behave like a thing, completely in your hands. But you cannot love a thing, because a thing is dead and cannot respond to you. So if the other is really a person he cannot be possessed, he is like mercury: the more you try to keep him in your fist, the more he goes out—because to be a person means to be free. If he is a person, you cannot possess him; if you can possess him, he is no longer a person and you will not be able to love him. Then he is just a dead thing and who can love a dead thing?

You are mounted on two horses. You want a person like a thing, which is impossible! A person *has* to be free and alive, and only then can you love him. But then you will feel difficult, so you start possessing and then you start killing him; you are poisoning. If he allows you this poisoning, sooner or later he will be just a thing. So wives become decorative pieces in the houses, husbands become just watchmen—but love disappears. And this is happening in all directions.

There is doubt in you because doubt has its benefits: it gives you more calculating power, it gives you more protection, nobody can deceive you easily. So you doubt—but then doubt creates anxiety because deep down you are uneasy. Doubt is just like illness. Unless you have trust you cannot be at ease, because doubt means wavering and wavering is uneasy. Doubt means, "What to do? This or that?" Doubt means, "To be or not to be?"—and it is impossible to decide.

Not even on a single point is decision possible through doubt. At the most, you can decide with the part of the mind which becomes the majority. But the minority is there, and it is not a small minority. And because you have chosen against the minority, the minority will always be looking for the situation when it can say you have chosen wrongly. The minority is there to rebel—it is a constant turmoil within you.

With doubt there is uneasiness. It is an illness, it is just like any illness—it is a mental illness. So a man who doubts becomes more and more ill. But you cannot deceive him easily because he is more cunning, he is more clever in the ways of the world. You cannot deceive him, but he is ill. So there *is* a benefit: he cannot be deceived. But there is a loss, a great loss. The benefit is at a very great cost: he remains wavering, uneasy, he cannot decide. Even if he decides, that decision is just the major portion deciding against the minor. He is divided, there is always conflict.

Trust you also want. You also want to be in faith, because faith gives you health, there is no indecisiveness, you are completely certain. Certainty gives you happiness: there is no wavering, you are unwavering; you are whole, not divided—and wholeness is health. Trust gives you health, but then you become vulnerable, anybody can deceive you. If you trust you are in danger, because there are people all around who would like to exploit you, and they can exploit you only when you trust. If you doubt, they cannot exploit.

So you are mounted on two horses, doubt and faith—but you are doing the impossible. You will remain constantly in anxiety and anguish, you will deteriorate. In this conflict of the two horses you will die. Some day or other there is going to be an accident—that accident will be your death: you will be finished before you have reached anywhere; you will be finished before the flowers come; you will be finished before you come to know what life is, what it means to be. The being will have disappeared.

"Jesus said: It is impossible for a man to mount two horses..."

But every man is trying to do the impossible, that is why every man is in trouble. And I say to you, this is in every direction. So there are not only two horses, there are millions of horses altogether. And every moment you are living a contradiction. Why does it happen? The mechanism has to be understood, only then can you drop it. Why does it happen? The way every child is brought up is the cause. The way every child enters into this world of mad people all around is the cause. They create contradictions, they teach you contradictory things.

For example, you have been taught: "Love the whole of humanity, be brotherly to each and everyone, love thy neighbour as thyself." And simultaneously you have been educated, brought up, conditioned, to compete, to compete with everyone. When you

compete, the other is the enemy, not the friend. He has to be
defeated, he has to be conquered, really, he has to be destroyed. And
you *have* to be ruthless, otherwise the other will destroy you. If
you are a competitor, then the whole society is the enemy, nobody
is a neighbour, nobody is a brother. And you cannot love—you have
to hate, you have to be jealous, you have to be angry. You have to
be continuously ready to fight and win, and it is a hard struggle—
if you are tender-hearted you are lost.

So be strong and violent and aggressive. Before the other attacks,
you attack him. Before it is too late, you attack and win, otherwise
you will be lost because *millions* are competing for the same thing,
you are not alone. And how can a mind which is in competition be
in love with its neighbour? It is impossible! But both teachings have
been given to you: you have been taught that *honesty is the best
policy,* and also that *business is business!* Both things together, both
horses have been given to you together. And a child, unaware of
the ways of the world, cannot see and feel the contradiction.

To feel the contradiction a very mature intelligence is needed;
a Jesus, a Buddha is needed to feel the contradiction. A child is
unaware of the ways of the world, and the teachers—the father, the
mother, the family—are persons he loves. He loves them ! How can
he think that they are creating contradictions in him? He cannot
even imagine it because they are his benefactors: they are kind to
him, they are bringing him up. They are his source of energy, life,
everything. So why should they create contradictions? A father
loves, a mother loves, but the problem is that they were also brought
up in the same wrong way and they don't know what to do, except
to repeat whatsoever *their* parents taught them, which they now
teach their children. They are simply transferring a disease; from
one generation to another the disease is being transferred. You may
call it the 'treasure', the 'tradition', but it is a disease. It is a disease
because no one becomes healthy through it.

The whole society goes more and more neurotic. And a child is
so simple, so innocent, that he can be conditioned into contradictory
ways. By the time he realizes the contradiction it is too late. And
it happens that almost your whole life is lost, and you never realize
that you are mounted on two horses. Think about this contradiction

and find it, try to find it in your life. You will find millions of contradictions there—you are a confusion, a mess, a chaos!

When people come to me and they ask for silence, I look at them and I feel very much because it is almost impossible—silence can exist only when all the contradictions have been dropped. It needs arduous effort, very penetrating intelligence, understanding, maturity. Nothing is there, and you think that just by repeating a *mantra* you will become silent? If it were so easy, then everybody would have become silent. You think just by repeating 'Ram, Ram,' you will become silent? Riding on millions of horses, repeating the *mantra*, you will become silent? That *mantra* will be still one more horse, that's all—*more* confusion will come out of it. If one more horse is added, you will be more confused through it.

Look at the so-called religious man: he is more confused than the worldly because new horses have been added. The man who lives in the market, the world of the market, is less confused because he may have many horses, but at least they all belong to *this* world; at least one thing is the same, similar—they all belong to this world. And this religious man, he has so many horses: those which belong to this world and some new horses he has added which don't belong to this world. He has created a greater rift: the other world, God, the Kingdom of God, and he continues to move in this world. He becomes more confused, more conflict arises in his being. He is rent apart, he is not together; every fragment is falling apart, all his togetherness is gone—this is what neurosis is.

The way you are brought up is wrong, but nothing can be done now because you have already been brought up, you cannot move back. So you have to understand it and drop it through understanding. If you drop it because I say so, then you will add more horses. If you drop it through understanding—because *you* understand the whole thing and hence it is dropped—then no more horses will be added. On the contrary, old horses will be released to their freedom, so they can move and reach their goals, and you can move and reach your own goal.

For not only are you in difficulty, your horses are also in very great difficulty because of you; they cannot reach anywhere either. Have pity on yourself and on your horses—both! But this should be done through understanding—*your* understanding, not my teaching or Jesus' or Buddha's. They can show the path, but if you follow without understanding you will never reach the goal.

Now try to understand.

"Jesus said : It is impossible for a man to mount two horses and stretch two bows; and it is impossible for a servant to serve two masters, otherwise he will honour the one and offend the other."

Why is it impossible? And what is impossibility? An impossibility is not something which is very difficult, no! Howsoever difficult a thing may be, it is not impossible, you can achieve it. By impossibility is meant something which cannot be achieved whatsoever you do; there is *no* way, no possibility to do it.

When Jesus says impossible he *means* impossible, he doesn't mean very difficult—and you are trying to do the impossible. What will happen? It cannot be done, but you will be undone through it. It *cannot* be done! But what will happen to you who have been making an effort to do the impossible? You will fall apart. It is not possible to do it, but doing it, you are undoing your own life. This will happen, this has happened.

Look at people who doubt. Have you seen a man who has doubt and who does not have faith? If you see a man who only has doubt, you will see he cannot live, it is impossible to live. Go to the madhouses: there you will find people who have doubts about everything. Then they cannot even move, because they doubt even a simple action.

I knew a man who was so full of doubt that he could not go to the market—and the market was just a few yards away. He would come back again and again to check the lock. And when we were children we used to play tricks on that poor man. He would be going out and we would ask him, "Have you checked the lock?" He would be angry but he would go back to check it. And he was alone, there was nobody else—and so afraid! He would be taking his bath in the river and somebody would say, "Have you checked the lock?" He would be very angry, but half way through his bath, immediately he would come out and run to the house to check. This is the perfect skeptic. If doubt goes too far you will enter into a madhouse, because then you doubt everything. This is one type of man who is completely broken into fragments.

If you choose faith against this, you will become absolutely blind. Then anybody can take you anywhere, then you have no intelligence of your own, no alertness of your own. Around Hitlers you will find this type of person—they have trusted and through trust they have lost.

Because of this you are trying the impossible, to make a compromise: not to go to this extreme, because there neurosis comes; not to go to the other extreme, because there blindness happens. Then what to do? Then simple reasoning says: "Just compromise both, half and half—a little doubt, a little faith." But then you mount on two horses. Is it not possible to live without doubt and without faith?

It *is* possible! In fact, that is the only possible way to grow: to live without doubt and without faith; just to live simply, spontaneously, with awareness. And this is *really* what trust is—not trusting somebody else—this is trusting *life*, wheresoever it leads, without doubt, without faith; you simply move, you move innocently.

A man who doubts cannot move innocently. Before he moves he will think, and sometimes he will think so much that the opportunity is lost. That is why thinkers never do much. They cannot act, they become simply cerebral, because before action they must decide, they must come to a conclusion; and they cannot come to a conclusion, so how can they act? Then it is better to wait and not to act. But life will not wait for you. Or you become faithful, believing, a blind man. Then anybody, any politician, any madman, any Pope, any priest can lead you anywhere. But they themselves are blind, and when the blind lead the blind there is bound to be catastrophe. What to do? Reasoning says, ordinary reasoning says, "Make a compromise."

One scientist, B. F. Skinner, did an experiment worth remembering. A white mouse was the object of experiment: the white mouse was starved for two or three days so it was very hungry; really, it was just hunger, ready to jump and eat anything available. Then it was put on a platform. Just below the platform there were two similar boxes, the same colour, same size, and both boxes contained food. The white mouse could jump in either the right box or the left.

The mouse immediately jumped, not even a single moment of thought. But whenever he jumped into the right box, he would get an electric shock. And there was a trap-door, so he would fall inside another box through the trap door and would not be able to reach the food. Whenever he jumped into the left box, there was no shock and there was no trap-door, so he would reach the food. Within two or three days he learnt the trick: he would jump in the left box and avoid the right.

Then Skinner made a change, he changed the places of the boxes. The mouse jumped into the left box and found that there was an electric shock. Now it was disturbed, confused as to what to do and what not to do. So before jumping it would tremble and waver, doubtful. This is how a philosopher is—a white mouse, trembling, doubtful what to do: left or right, and how to choose? And who knows? But then it got accustomed again. Then Skinner again made a change. The mouse became so confused that although it was hungry it would wait, trembling, looking at this box and that—and how to decide? Then he decided the thing you have decided: he jumped betwen the two boxes—but there was no food, this was not going to help. And after a few weeks of experiment, the white mouse became mad, neurotic.

This is what is happening to you: you have become confused—what to do, what not to do? And the only thing that comes to the mind is that if it is difficult to choose this, difficult to choose that, then it is better to make a compromise, just jump in the middle. But there is no food. Of course, there is no electric shock, but there is no food either.

You miss life if you jump in the middle. If it were possible for the white mouse to mount both boxes, he would have done that. These are the two possibilities which open for reasoning: mount both horses or just jump in the middle. Intelligence, a very penetrating and keen intelligence is needed to understand the problem—*there is no other solution*. I am not going to give you any solution, no Jesus has given any solution to anybody, just the understanding of the problem is the solution. You understand the problem and the problem disappears.

Is it not possible to live without faith and without doubt? Not making a compromise? Because the compromise is going to be a poison: they are such contraries that your whole life will become a contradiction, and if contradiction is there you will be divided, split; schizophrenia will be the final result. Or if you choose one and deny the other, then you are denied the benefits that were possible from the other. Doubt gives you protection against exploitation, faith gives you certainty—drop one and the benefit of it is also dropped. If you choose both you mount on two horses; If you make a compromise you create a division within your being—you are two, you become a crowd. Then what to do?

Just understand the problem and get down from both horses—don't make any compromise. Then a totally different sort of being, a totally different quality to your consciousness happens. But why are you not doing that? Because *that* quality needs alertness, that quality needs awareness. Then you need not doubt anybody, you simply have to be fully alert. Your alertness will be the protection against exploitation.

If a fully alert man looks at you, you cannot deceive him, his very look will disarm you. And if he allows exploitation, it is not because you are cunning and cheating him, but because he is kind and *allows* you. You cannot cheat a fully alert man. It is impossible because he looks through you, you are transparent; he has such consciousness that you are transparent. If he allows you to cheat him it is because of his compassion. You cannot cheat him.

This consciousness seems to be difficult. That is why you have chosen the impossible. But the impossible *is* impossible—you only make-believe that it can happen; it has never happened, it will never happen. You have chosen the impossible because it looks easier. Compromise always looks easier—whenever you are in difficulty you compromise. But compromise never helps anybody, because compromise means two contraries will exist within you; they will always be in tension and they will divide you. And a divided man can never be happy.

This is what Jesus means, but Christians have misunderstood him. Christians have completely missed Jesus, because the mind goes on interpreting. What have they interpreted? They think Jesus is saying, "Choose one horse! Either this world or that—choose one! Don't mount two horses, because you will be in difficulty and it is impossible. So choose one horse." That is what they have come to conclude and interpret.

I have heard it happened: One night Mulla Nasrudin's wife was feeling hungry, so she went in search of a midnight snack. But she couldn't find anything—just a dog-biscuit. So tentatively she tasted it, found it good, it tasted good, so she ate it. And she liked it so much that in the morning she told Nasrudin to buy a big supply. Nasrudin went and purchased a lot of dog-biscuits. The local grocer said, "What are you doing? Because I know your dog is very small, you don't need such a large supply."

Nasrudin said, "It is not for the dog, it is for my wife."

The grocer said, "I must remind you that these biscuits are strictly for dogs, and if your wife eats them she will die—they are poisonous." And after six months his wife died.

One day Nasrudin admitted to the grocer, "My wife is dead."

The grocer said, "I told you before that those biscuits would kill your wife."

Nasrudin said, "Those biscuits didn't kill her—it was chasing behind the cars that killed her, not the biscuits!"

Our mind sticks to its own conclusions, because if one conclusion is lost, your confidence is lost. So whatsoever the situation you stick to your conclusions. That gives you ground for your ego and your mind to stand on.

One day, Mulla Nasrudin was walking with a very big stick which was too long for him. One friend suggested, "Nasrudin, why don't you cut a few inches off from the bottom?" Nasrudin said, "That would not help—because it is this end that is long."

Your reasoning can be suicidal. It is! You think it is reasoning, but it is not reasoning, it is just deceiving—deceiving yourself. But you don't want to lose ground, you want to be confident; and all confidence that comes through mind is false, because mind cannot give you confidence. It can only give you false things, it can only supply you with false things. It has not got the real thing with it, it is just a shadow. Mind is just thoughts, shadows, nothing substantial in it. But it can go on playing rationalizations, and you will feel good.

Christians miss the whole point. They think Jesus is saying, "Choose!" Jesus can never say, "Choose!" Jesus means choice-lessness. Because if *you* choose, the choosing mind is strengthened, not destroyed; the mind which is choosing becomes stronger through the choice. No, it is not a question of choice! And through choice you can never be total, because you have to deny something.

If you choose faith, you will have to deny doubt. Where will this doubt go? It is not something outward that you can throw, it is deep in you. Where will it go? You can simply close your eyes, that's all; you can simply repress it in the unconscious, that's all. But it is there, like a worm, eating your consciousness. It will be there, and some day or other it will come to the surface. What can you do? How can you drop it? If you choose doubt, where will your faith go? It is part of you! So a compromise will happen: you will become an amalgam of many things somehow put together; not a synthesis but a compromise.

Jesus means quite the contrary. He means, "Don't choose!"

"It is impossible for a man to mount two horses and stretch two bows; and it is impossible for a servant to serve two masters, otherwise he will honour the one and offend the other."

Look at the last phrase: "...otherwise he will honour the one and offend the other." If you choose one, you honour the one and offend the other—and the offended part of you will take revenge, it will become rebellious.

It happens—science depends on doubt, totally on doubt, no trust is allowed. So have you known, have you observed scientists? *Out* of their lab they are very faithful, you cannot find more trusting people than scientists. They are more easy to cheat than anybody else, because their doubt part functions in the lab and their trust part functions outside. They are simple people as far as the outside world is concerned, but in their lab they are very cunning and clever.

You can cheat a scientist very easily. It is not so easy to cheat so-called religious men. In the temple they are in deep trust, outside the temple they are very cunning. Look at the so-called religious people: outside the temple you cannot cheat them, but inside the temple is no possibility to cheat or to exploit them, inside the temple they are very simple. They use their trust part there, their doubt

part in the world. They are good businessmen, they accumulate
wealth—they exploit the whole world.

A scientist can never be a good businessman, he cannot be a
good politician. That is not possible, because the doubt part is
finished in the laboratory. Outside, the trust part functions. A
scientist at home is totally different from a scientist in his scientific
research work. You may have heard many stories about their
absent-mindedness. They happen, really happen, they are not
stories. Because he uses his attention in the lab, then outside the
lab he becomes inattentive—he has used one part, it is finished.
So he has a double life: in the lab he is very mindful, outside the
lab he becomes absent-minded.

There is a story about Albert Einstein: He was visiting a friend
and they took their dinner, they gossiped about this and that.
There was not much said because Einstein was not a man of gossip,
and he was not very talkative either. So the friend started feeling
bored. And it became darker and darker, until it was eleven o'clock
at night, and now he wanted Einstein to leave. But it was impolite
to say so to such a great man, so he waited and waited. Sometimes
he even gave hints, he said, "The night is very dark," and, "It seems
it is now about eleven-thirty." But Einstein would just look and
yawn, he wanted to sleep. Then it was almost twelve and the friend
said, "I think you are feeling sleepy, because you are yawning."
That was the final hint.

Einstein said, "Yes, I am feeling very sleepy, but I am waiting
for when you go, then I can go to sleep."

The man said, "What are you saying? You are at *my* home!"

Einstein stood up and said, "Sorry! Because I was continuously
thinking, 'When will this man go, so I can go to sleep?' "

In the lab, this man is perfect as far as attention is concerned,
presence is concerned. But that part is used up there; outside the
lab he is a totally different man, just the opposite.

That is why it happens that you find a contradiction in the life
of so-called religious people, it is natural. See them praying in the
temples, and look at their faces! They look so innocent, their eyes
filled with such deep emotion, tears flowing down. You cannot
imagine the same man outside, how he will look, how he will be at
his shop, how he will behave when you go to the shop. The

emotional part, the trusting part, is finished in the temple, in the mosque, in the church; when he comes out he is free of that part. Then he is as doubting as any scientist can be, as skeptical as possible.

This is how we live a double life, this is a compromise. Jesus is not saying, "Choose one against the other." If you choose one against the other, the other part will be offended, and the offended part of your being will take revenge. And it makes it very difficult, it makes life almost impossible to live. The more you try to live with one part, the more the other part disturbs all your planning, all your scheming; it comes up again and again. Then what to do?

The way, the thing to be done, is not to choose. The thing is to understand the whole contradiction of your being. Not choosing, but becoming choiceless; not dropping one against the other— because you cannot drop one aspect of a thing.

You have a *rupee*, it has two aspects. You cannot drop one aspect, you cannot drop one side of it. You may not like the other side, but you have to carry both; if you want to carry one you have to carry two, then the whole *rupee* will be with you. The only thing that you can manage is that you can hide the aspect you don't like, and the aspect you like you can put on the surface, that is all. That is how the conscious and the unconscious are created.

The conscious is that part, that horse that you like, and the unconscious is that horse, that part that you don't like. The conscious is that which you have chosen, the unconscious is that against which you have chosen. These are the two churches—the one you go to and the one you don't go to. Otherwise, in a man like Buddha, the conscious and the unconscious both disappear, because he has not chosen for, he has not chosen against. The whole coin drops. And only the whole coin can drop, half can *never* be dropped.

Doubt and trust are two aspects of the same coin, just like cold and hot; they look like contraries but they belong together. They are polarities in one whole, just like negative and positive electricity, just like man and woman. They look like opposites, but they are polarities of one phenomenon. You cannot drop negative electricity without dropping positive electricity, you cannot retain one and drop the other. If you do that, your being will be divided: the dropped, the repressed, the denied part will become the unconscious; the accepted, the welcomed part will become the conscious. And then there will be a continuous struggle between the conscious and the unconscious.

But you are still mounted on two horses. The only way is to drop the whole thing and the secret is: not dropping—because dropping can also become a choice. This is the most complex and subtle thing: you can drop, and choose dropping against not dropping—then again there are two horses. No, this is to be done through understanding. Dropping is not the thing, understanding is the thing.

Understand the whole madness: what you have done to yourself, what you have allowed to happen to yourself, what type of contradictions you have been accumulating—just see through the whole thing. Don't be for and against, don't condemn, don't judge—just look through the whole thing that you are. Don't hide, don't offend, don't judge: "This is good and that is bad," don't evaluate. Don't be a judge but just an onlooker, detached, a witness. Just see the whole thing that you are, whatsoever you are; whatsoever mess you are in, just see it as it is.

Suddenly, an understanding arises which becomes the dropping. It is just as if you have been trying to enter a wall, and suddenly you become aware that this is a wall and there is no door. Do you need to drop the effort now? You simply move! That movement is simple, it is not for and against—you simply understand that this is absolutely useless, impossible. That is the meaning of Jesus: you simply look, it is impossible, you move. There is no choice on the part of the mind, you don't make any effort.

Whenever there is understanding, it is effortless. And whenever something is effortless it is beautiful because it is whole. Whenever there is effort there is ugliness, because it is always the part, never the whole. Effort means deep down, you are fighting against something. But why are you fighting? Because that which you are fighting still retains meaning for you. The enemy also has meaning, just like the friend—the opposite meaning, but he carries meaning. And have you ever thought that whenever your enemy dies, something in you dies immediately? You not only suffer from the death of your friends, you also suffer from the death of your enemies—you cannot remain the same.

In India it happened: Mohammed Ali Jinnah and Mahatma Gandhi were constant fighters against each other. Then Gandhi was murdered, and Jinnah is reported to have said: "I feel very sad. Something in me has died." Now, against whom can Jinnah fight? Against whom can he be the fighter? Against whom can accept the challenge? The ego drops if the enemy is not there. You are constituted of your friends and of your enemies—you are a contradiction.

Only he is whole who has no enemies and no friends, who has not chosen, who has no leanings for this or for that; who simply moves moment to moment with a choiceless awareness, and whatsoever life brings, he allows. He floats, he is not swimming; he is not a fighter, he is in a let-go. If you can understand this, then you will be able to understand the meaning of Jesus:

"It is impossible for a man to mount two horses and stretch two bows, and it is impossible for a servant to serve two masters, otherwise he will honour the one and offend the other."

The ordinary meaning will be, 'choose one master, don't choose two'. But through choice you will never be whole, so it is not a question of choosing one master against another, because you will still remain a slave, you cannot be free. Only choicelessness can give you freedom. Then you don't choose you simply drop the whole effort—it drops by itself when you understand. *Then* you are the master.

In India, we have been calling *sannyasins*, '*swami*'. *Swami* means master of oneself, it means one who has dropped choosing, it means now he accepts no master. And this is not an egoistic understanding, this is a deep understanding that if you choose between contraries you are a victim, if you choose between the contraries you will remain divided in the contraries. A sannyasin is not against this world and for that one, a sannyasin is simply neither for nor against—he simply moves without friends and without enemies.

There is a beautiful Zen story: One sannyasin was standing on a hill-top alone in the morning. Just like the hill he was alone, standing unmoving, and three persons passed by who had come for a morning walk. They looked at this man and they had different opinions as to what he was doing. One man said, "I know that monk. Sometimes his cow is lost, so he must be standing there and looking around the hill for the cow."

The second said, "But by the way he is standing, he is not looking at all. He is not moving at all, his eyes seem to be almost fixed. That is not the way that a man looks for something. I think he must have come for a morning walk with some friend and the friend has got left behind—he is waiting for the friend to come."

The third said, "That doesn't seem to be the reason, because whenever somebody waits, sometimes he looks behind to see whether the friend has arrived or not. But he never moves, he never looks behind. He is not waiting, that is not the posture of a waiting man. I think he is in prayer or meditating."

They were so divided and they became so excited about the explanations as to what he was doing, that they thought it was better to go and ask the man himself. It was hard to go up the hill, but they went. They reached the man and the first asked, "Are you looking for your cow? Because I know sometimes it is lost and you have to look for it."

The man opened his eyes and said, "I don't possess anything, so nothing can be lost. I am not looking for any cow or anything." Then he closed his eyes.

The second man said, "Then I must be right—you are waiting for a friend who is left behind."

The man opened his eyes and said, "I have no enemies and no friends, so how can I wait for anybody? I am alone—I have not left anybody behind, because there is nobody. I am alone, totally alone."

Then the third said, "Then I must be absolutely right because there is no other possibility. I hope you are praying, meditating."

The man laughed and he said, "You are the most foolish because I don't know anybody to whom I can pray and I don't have any object to achieve, so how can I meditate?"

Then all three simultaneously asked, "Then what are you doing?"

The man said, "I am just standing. I am not doing anything at all."

But this is what meditation is, and this is what *sannyas* is: just being! Then you have a freedom—freedom from friends, enemies; freedom from possession, non-possession; freedom from this world and that; freedom from matter and mind—freedom from all choices and divisions. Then the impossible is dropped and you become natural, you become *Tao*, then you float.

When the impossible effort is gone, anxiety disappears, then you are no longer in anguish. And when you are no longer in anguish bliss arises. Bliss is not something to be achieved. You only have to create the capacity. When you are not in anguish, bliss happens. You have created the capacity, you have opened the door and the sun-rays enter and fill you. As you are, anxiety-ridden, divided, mounted on two horses, trying to stretch two bows together, you are schizophrenic, you are ill, you are wavering. Or at the most, you have made a compromise and you have become normally neurotic.

A normal being somehow carries on his work, the neurosis does not come in the way, that's all; an adjusted citizen, that's all. But it is not worthwhile! Even if you are an adjusted citizen, a good citizen, a normal human being, no ecstasy will happen to you. You will remain sad, and whatsoever you achieve in this world will give you more sadness. Look at the people who have succeeded, who are ahead of you, who have reached the top, and you will see they are *more* sad than people who are not so successful— because their hope is lost.

One morning, Mulla Nasrudin was walking towards the market very sad. And a friend asked, "What has happened?"

Nasrudin said, "Don't ask me! I am so sad and so depressed that I could cry."

But the friend insisted, "But what is the matter? We have never seen you so sad! You have been in so many difficulties, financial and otherwise, but we have never seen you so sad and depressed. What is the matter? What has happened? "

Mulla Nasrudin said, "Two weeks ago, one of my uncles died and he left one hundred thousand *rupees* for me."

The friend said, "Nasrudin, have you gone mad? If your uncle has left one hundred thousand *rupees* for you, you should be happy not sad!"

Nasrudin said, "Yes, that's so—but last week, my other uncle died and he has left two hundred thousand *rupees* for me."

The man said, "Then you are completely out of your mind—you should dance and rejoice and celebrate, because there is no reason to be unhappy! You are the happiest man in this town!"

Nasrudin said, "That I know—but I have no more uncles! That makes me sad."

That's what happens when a man succeeds: when you have no more uncles, then suddenly, no hope. A man who is a failure still hopes, can hope; there are still uncles, the possibility exists. The more success, the more anxiety, because the success will bring your neurosis up, the success will reveal you, your schizophrenia. That is why in America there is more schizophrenia, more madness than in any other country, because America has succeeded in many ways.

In a poor country, there is not so much madness. People can still hope. And when you can hope, nothing comes up—you go on running and running. When the goal is achieved, then you stand still and you have to look at yourself and at what a mess you have created in your being, what chaos. You suddenly go out of your mind. You have always been out of your mind, but it is revealed when you succeed, because when there is no more to dream about, you *have* to encounter yourself. As you are, bliss is not possible, happiness is impossible. You can only hope for it and tolerate the pain, the suffering that you have brought upon yourself.

But bliss *is* possible, it has happened to a Jesus, to a Buddha, it can happen to *you*—but then you have to leave the impossible aside. Think of the natural, the possible, the easy. Don't think of the impossible, the difficult, the challenging. The ego always likes to do the impossible, but it is a failure, it *has* to be a failure. But the ego likes to take the challenge of the impossible, because then you feel you are something. Against an impossible goal you become a great fighter.

And religion is simple, easy, natural—it is not riding on a horse at all! It is just a morning walk, not going anywhere; just walking is the end, not doing anything in particular, just enjoying the morning breeze, the sun, the birds—just enjoying yourself.

Eleventh Discourse

31st August 1974, Poona, India

THE ELEVENTH SAYING

Jesus said :
A city being built on a high mountain and fortified,
cannot fall nor can it ever be hidden.

Jesus said :
What thou shalt hear in thine ear and in the other ear,
that preach from your housetops;
for no one lights a lamp and puts it under a bushel,
nor does he put it in a hidden place,
but he sets it on the lampstand
so that all who come in and go out may see its light.

Jesus said :
If a blind man leads a blind man,
both of them fall into a pit.

The whole human problem consists of choosing between the momentary and the eternal. If you choose the momentary you are building your house on sands—it is going to fall. If you choose the eternal, then something is achieved which is going to be forever and forever.

And nothing less can satisfy you, only the eternal can satisfy you. The momentary cannot satisfy you. Rather, on the contrary, it will make you more hungry and more thirsty. It is like someone throwing butter in the fire to put it out—it will become food for the fire and the fire will increase. The momentary is just like butter in the fire of your mind's desire; it helps it, it is a food. Only the eternal can quench the thirst, there is no other way.

But when I say, "If you choose the eternal, only then do you build your house on a mountain-top, on something rock-like which will endure and your effort will not be wasted," what do I mean when I say, "If you choose the eternal"? Because the eternal cannot be chosen. If you choose you will always choose the momentary, because choice *is* of the momentary. Then what do I mean when I say, "Choose the eternal"? I mean: if you can understand that the momentary is useless—by the next moment you will be thirsty again, and this water is not going to destroy your thirst—if you understand this then the momentary drops. It becomes useless, you simply come to understand its meaninglessness. It simply drops and the eternal is chosen—you never choose it.

When the momentary drops, the eternal enters into your life.

But the momentary *must* become *absolutely* fruitless, meaningless; with the momentary your failure must be total. "Blessed are those who fail in this world"—this beatitude must be added to Jesus' other beatitudes.

Be a failure in this world! You are trying to do just the opposite: to succeed in it. If you succeed, that will be the real failure because then you will remain with the momentary—but no one ever succeeds. Fortunate we are because no one ever succeeds. At the most, you can go on postponing the failure, that's all. You may postpone it to a further life, you can postpone it for millions of lives. But no one ever succeeds in this world, because how can you succeed with the momentary, that which is fleeting? How can you make a house on it? That which is passing moment to moment, going out of existence, how can you make a house, an abode on it? By the time the house is ready, the moment is gone. That is why every moment you feel frustrated—but again you start doing the same thing.

It seems you are not aware, it seems you are not alert to what you are doing—it seems you have not learnt *anything* from life. You have remained ignorant of life, you have not attained to any experience. You may have much knowledge, you may know how to build the house—you may be an engineer, an architect—but you have not learnt through experience that on the momentary the house cannot be built. This is the first thing Jesus says.

"Jesus said : A city being built on a high mountain and fortified, cannot fall nor can it ever be hidden."

Many things: first, "A city being built on a high mountain..."

You always make something in the valley! These are symbols: 'valley' means the dark night; 'high mountain' means more conscious, more aware; the more aware you are, the higher you go. When you become perfectly aware, you are on Everest. That is why Hindus have been saying that Shiva lives on *Gaurishankar*, the highest mountain-top: Shiva is the highest consciousness; Shiva is not a person, Shiva means the *perfect* consciousness. Perfect consciousness lives on *Gaurishankar*.

When you are unconscious you fall down into the dark valley— your night is a valley, your sleep is a valley. When you are aware, you start moving towards the height; when you are completely unconscious, that is the lowest point of existence. Rocks are existing there, at the lowest rung of the ladder, because rocks are perfectly unconscious. They are not dead—they are alive, they grow; they are young, they become old, they die. They pass through all the phases you pass through, but they are not conscious—the lowest rung of the ladder. Sometimes you are like a rock: when you are fast asleep what is the difference between you and a rock? When not even a single ray of consciousness is there, what is the difference between you and the earth? You have fallen back.

In sleep, you go towards the valley. The 'sinner' means one who lives constantly in sleep; the 'saint' means one who is not asleep even in his sleep. Krishna has said to Arjuna: "When everybody is asleep, the yogi is still awake. When everybody is in slumber, the yogi is still alert." The totality of the yogi never goes to sleep. A point of witnessing always remains there; he witnesses his own sleep. In sleep you fall down, in awareness you rise high. When nothing is asleep in you, when your whole consciousness has become a light, when not a single fragment is unconscious, when your complete being is filled with light—that is what we mean by a Buddha, a Christ: no unconsciousness exists—this is the highest peak. Hence the symbolic meaning of "A city built on a high mountain."

You are building your cities, your houses, in a valley, and ordinary sleep alone is not enough for you, you also seek drugs to fall more asleep; you seek methods of hypnosis to become more sleepy, more unconscious—because consciousness is pain, it is anguish. Why is it anguish? And Buddha and Jesus say it is the greatest bliss that is possible! But for you, why is consciousness painful? And why do you want to forget everything? Why is consciousness painful?

It is painful if only one percent of you becomes conscious and ninety-nine percent of you remains unconscious, then that one percent suffers seeing the mess all around. Seeing that ninety-nine percent in a state of madness, that one percent of consciousness suffers, that one percent of consciousness seeks alcohol, drugs, LSD, marijuana or something else—sex or music or a *mantra*—to create an autohypnosis. So that one percent also falls back and becomes part of the whole. Then you are not worried because there is nobody to know, then there is nobody to be alert and conscious—then there is no problem.

This is what they call the logic of the ostrich. Whenever an ostrich finds that some enemy is coming, he will hide his head in the sand. For the moment he cannot see, and his logic is: "When I cannot see the enemy, how can the enemy be there?" The ostrich seems to be a perfect atheist, for that is what atheists have been saying. They say: "If we cannot see God, how can He be there? Something exists only when *we* see it," as if existence depends on your seeing; and if you don't see then the thing disappears.

The ostrich hides his head, closes his eyes, and immediately he is unafraid because the enemy is no more. But the enemy does not believe in your logic. On the contrary, you are playing into his hands when your eyes are closed; you are playing into the hands of the enemy, you are asking to become a victim. You could have escaped, but now there is no escape because you think there is no enemy. You may feel a momentary happiness because the enemy is not there—not that the enemy is not there, but because you feel as if he is not. That's how you feel a momentary happiness when you become unconscious through drugs: no problems exist, all the enemies disappear, there is no anxiety—because for anxiety you need to be alert, aware.

When one hundred percent of your being becomes conscious, then there is bliss because the conflict disappears—Buddha is right. You are also right because your experience says that the more you become alert, the more you feel problems around you. So it is better to remain in a long slumber, in a life-long sleep. That is why we build our cities in the valleys, not on mountain-tops.

Then there is another reason.

"A city being built on a high mountain and fortified, cannot fall nor can it ever be hidden."

We build our cities in such a way, on such a fleeting existence, on the momentary, the temporal, that by the time they are ready they are falling; by the time they are ready they have already become ruins. Why? Because we can see only the momentary, we don't have a total vision. We can see only that which is nearest, just very close. Only the moment is close—you see one moment, then it passes, then another moment, then it passes. You see these passing moments, you cannot have a total vision.

For the total vision a perfect consciousness is needed. In a total vision, you can see the whole of life; not only the whole of life, you can see the whole world. That is what Jains mean when they say that when Mahavir became Enlightened, he could see past, present and future—the whole of time. What do they mean? They mean that the *wholeness* of existence becomes clear to you, and when the wholeness is clear, only then can you make a fortified city. Otherwise, how can you make one?

You don't know what is going to happen the next moment. Whatsoever you do, the next moment may undo it. And whatsoever you do depends on the momentary, not on the whole. The whole may reject it, it may become absolutely meaningless in the whole.

It happened once that a Chinese Master had an American disciple. When the disciple was going back the Master gave him a present, a small carved wooden box, and he said, "One condition *always* has to be followed; if you give this box to somebody else, then the condition has to be fulfilled. Promise! Because I have been fulfilling this promise, and this is not a new thing, it's a very ancient thing and for many, many generations the condition has been fulfilled."

The disciple said, "I will fulfill it." It was such a beautiful thing, so valuable, so ancient, he said, "Whatsoever the condition I will fulfill it!"

The Master said, "The condition is simple: you have to keep it in your house facing east. And this has always been done, so be respectful to the tradition."

The disciple said, "This is very simple, I will do it."

But when he put the box facing east, then he came to understand that it was very difficult, because his whole arrangement in the drawing-room became absurd. That box facing east would not adjust. So he had to change the whole arrangement of the drawing-room—to be harmonious with the box. But then the whole house became absurd, so then he had to change the whole house. Then the garden became absurd! Then he felt exhausted. He wrote to the Master: "This box is dangerous! I will have to change the whole world—because if I also change my garden, then next it will be the neighbourhood...." And he was a man of sensitivity, that is why he felt like this.

If you build your life on the momentary, you are going to be in difficulty with the whole because it will never adjust. It will never be harmonious, something or other will always be wrong. The whole has to be looked to before you make your city, before you make your abode; the whole has to be consulted and referred to. With the vision of the whole you should create your life and the pattern of your life; you should live with the vision of the whole. Only then will your life be a harmony, a melody—otherwise, you will always be somehow outlandish, eccentric.

Every man is eccentric. This word is beautiful. 'Eccentric' means out of the center, somehow missing the center, not exactly as it should be. Why is every man eccentric, out of the center, out of focus, *out of step with life?* Because everybody is trying to make life according to the moment, and the moment is not the whole. The moment is a *fragment,* such a small, trivial fragment of eternity. How can you adjust to eternity if you make your life according to the moment? That is why Jesus says, "Make your life, create your life according to the whole, the eternal, not the momentary."

"A city being built on a high mountain and fortified, cannot fall nor can it ever be hidden." Your city will always be falling, your city will always be in ruins. It is so! You need not ask Jesus, you can just look at your life: it is a ruin; before you have built it, it is already a ruin. You are a ruined city. Why is it happening? Because of the momentary. Have a vision of the eternal, of the timeless.

How will this vision come? The higher your consciousness, the greater your vision; the lower your consciousness, the smaller your vision. Go and stand on the street under a tree and look: you have a vision—you can see to the nearest corner of this road, then there is a turning and the vision stops. Climb the tree and have a look from the tree—then you have a greater vision. Move in an aeroplane—then you have a bird's-eye view of the whole city. Go higher and greater becomes the vision; go lower, smaller is the vision. There are rungs in the ladder of consciousness. If you are at the peak of your consciousness, look from there: eternity is revealed.

Have you observed a very small thing? You are standing under a tree, you look to the east—you don't see anything. Somebody is sitting on top of the tree and he says, "I can see a bullock cart coming."

You say, "There is no bullock cart! I can't see it—and when I can't see it, how can it be?" The bullock cart is in the future for *you*, but for the man who is sitting on top of the tree the bullock cart is in the present. So don't think that the present means the same to everyone. Your present is confined to you, it may not be present for me; my present is confined to me, it may not be present for you. It depends on the ladder of consciousness.

For Buddha everything is present because there is no future—his vision is complete. For Jesus everything is present: there is no past because he can see, there is no future because he can see. From the highest peak of consciousness the whole is visible, so nothing is past, nothing is future; *everything is here and now!* The future exists because of your confined vision, *not* because the future is a necessity in the world, in existence. It simply shows that you have a narrow vision: something that goes out of your field of vision becomes the past; that which has not yet come into it becomes the future. But things in themselves are in eternity.

Time is your invention because you live in the valley. Hence, all the traditions of the world have been emphasizing that when you move into *samadhi*, ecstasy, deep meditation, time disappears. What do they mean? They mean that the division of past, present, future, disappears; existence is, but without divisions—timeless. Build your city on the timeless, don't build it on the momentary. Otherwise it will always be a ruin, because the present is fleeting and becoming the past. Why do I say it will be a ruin before you have even built it? Because the *moment* you build, that moment is past, it is already gone, it is no more in your hands! The earth below your feet is moving continuously.

"A city being built on a high mountain and fortified..."

And why does he use the word 'fortified'? As you are, in the valley, you are always in fear, insecurity, always in danger. The valley is filled with ghosts, shadows, enemies, hatred all around.

I have heard about a house-fly who was passing by a supermarket. In one window insecticides were on display. She read the sign; in big red letters it was written: "New spray guaranteed to kill flies immediately!" She read the sign and as she flew away, muttered to herself, "There is too much hatred in the world!"

You live in the world of the valley. There, everything is guaranteed to kill—*immediately*. You live in the valley of death—nothing else is guaranteed there, only death is guaranteed.

Have you ever observed the fact that in life, everything is uncertain except death? It should be otherwise, but the only certainty that you have is a guarantee to die, that's all. This much can be said in the valley: you will die; that much *is* certain. Everything else is uncertain and accidental—it may happen, it may not happen. What type of life is this where only death is guaranteed? But it is so, because in darkness only death can exist; in unconsciousness only death can exist. Unconsciousness is the path towards death.

Whenever you want to be unconscious, you want to die. A *deep* urge to die is in you, otherwise you would start moving towards the height. Freud, in the last phase of his life, stumbled upon a very deep fact: he called it 'thanatos'—the wish towards death. His whole life he was thinking around 'libido'—a theory which says that man exists as a will to live; but the more he penetrated into the will to live, the more uncertain he became. The more he started to understand the will to live, he found that deep down there is a will to die.

It was very difficult for Freud because he was a linear thinker, one-dimensional, he was an Aristotelean, a logician. This was very contradictory that behind the libido—the lust to live, the will to live—there is a will to die, thanatos. He became very much disturbed. But that is what Buddha has always been saying, and that is what Jesus has been saying: that *as* you are, you are *so* useless, your whole life is so futile, just full of frustrations, that you would like to die.

When you take something to become unconscious, the wish to die is there—because unconsciousness is a temporary death. You cannot live without sleep even for a few days, because sleep is a sort of temporary death. You need it, you need it very deeply. If you cannot die every day for eight hours, you will not be able to live the next day—because your whole life is such a mess, and to be is *not* bliss; rather, not to be seems to be blissful. So wherever you can lose yourself, you feel blissful. If you can lose yourself in a political movement, if you can become a Nazi and you can lose yourself in a crowd, you feel good because this is a death—you are no more there, only the crowd exists.

That is why dictators succeed—because of your wish to die. Even in the twentieth century dictators succeed, because they give you a chance to die so easily. That is why wars have always existed, and they will continue to exist because you are not in any way changing. Man is not transforming himself. Wars will exist because they are a deep will to die. You want to kill and you want to be killed. Life is such a burden that suicide seems to be the only solution. If you have not committed suicide up to now, don't think that you are truly a life-lover. No! You are simply afraid. You are not a lover of life, because a lover of life will always move towards the heights—the higher the peak, the more life. Hence Jesus can promise: "Come to me, and I will give you life in abundance!"

Hence Jesus says: "I am life, great life. Come to me!" But to come to Jesus is very difficult because you have so much investment in the valley, in the dark ways of life. And you are so afraid of being alive. You make many arrangements in order not to be too alive, you exist with the minimum of life. You exist like an automaton, you turn everything into a mechanical thing so that you need not bother about it—you need not *live* in it.

Wars will continue, violence will continue, and men will go on killing each other. The whole effort has been to create a device which can become a global suicide, and now we have discovered it—the H-bomb. Why are scientists continuously working, devoting their whole lives to create destructive things? Because that is the deepest desire in man: to die, somehow to die. It is not very conscious, because if it becomes conscious you will start transforming yourself. Many times you assert: "It would have been better if I had not been born!"

One Greek philosopher, Philo, is reported to have said: "The first blessing is not to have been born; the second blessing is to die as soon as possible." And he says these two are the only blessings. First, not to have been born—but no one is that fortunate because everybody is already born. So only the second is available—

to die as soon as possible. Philo himself lived to be ninety-seven. Somebody asked him, "But you have not committed suicide?" So he said, "I have just been tolerating life to give the message to others—the message that to die is the only solution."

Suicide is a deep-rooted instinct. Immediately you feel anything going wrong, you feel you want to commit suicide, to destroy yourself. A religious man is one who becomes alert that a deep death-wish is hidden inside. Why is it there? You have to bring more light into yourself so that you can become aware of the corner where death is hidden and eating you continuously. It is not that suddenly one day you die—you die slowly for seventy years. Death is not a phenomenon that comes in the end, it starts with birth. Then every breath and every moment is simply nothing but a continuity of dying and dying and dying. It completes itself in seventy years because it is a very slow process.

But you have been dying, and you are waiting deep down to be finished—the sooner the better. You have not committed suicide because you are very afraid, scared: what will happen? So you tolerate life, you are not enjoying it as a gift of God. You are simply tolerating it, you are simply carrying it somehow, waiting for the moment when you can get out of the train.

Once it happened: Thomas Edison was invited for a dinner at which a few friends had gathered. He was a man of few words and he was always disturbed whenever there was a crowd. He was a lonely worker in his laboratory; he was a researcher, a contemplative man; the presence of the other was always a disturbance for him. And at the dinner there were many people, and they were so much engaged in eating, gossiping and discussing, that he felt: "Now this is the moment I can escape!" So he just started to look for the door through which he could escape—and then he was caught. The host caught him and asked, "Mr. Edison, what are you working on now?" He said, "The exit!"

But everybody is working for the exit. Become alert to it!

But why can't you enjoy life—which is a gift? You have not earned it, that is why I say it is a grace. Existence has given it to you—you can call it God—it is a simple gift, a pure gift; you have not done anything to achieve it, to gain it. Why can't you be blissful and thankful and enjoy it? It should be enjoyed dancing.

But what is the problem? It is because to enjoy bliss, greater awareness is needed; to suffer anguish there is no need to be aware. To suffer anguish, more darkness is needed, *less* consciousness is needed—night is needed, not day. But to enjoy bliss, *more* alertness is needed.

So if you see a saint who is sad, know well that he is not a saint. Because awareness will give a blissfulness, awareness will give a deep laughter to his whole being, awareness will give him something so that he will become childlike: he can run after a butterfly, he can enjoy simple food, and he can enjoy the ordinary things of life so much that *everything* becomes a gift. Everything becomes a grace from God and he can be thankful moment to moment—even for his breathing. He can even enjoy his breathing, simple breathing—it is *so* blissful! If you find a saint who is sad, know well something has gone wrong; he still lives in the valley, he has not moved to the peak. Otherwise, he has a radiance, a lightness, a childlike enjoyment, unworried, unafraid—he is fortified in his consciousness.

Why does consciousness fortify you? Because the more conscious you become, the more you know you cannot die, there is no death. Death exists only in the dark valley. And if you are fortified against death, you are fortified. The more conscious you are, the more you know you are the eternal, the Divine. Right now you don't know who you are. This is the valley of ignorance, and there only death happens, nothing else; and you live trembling, shaking with fear. If you *look* within, you will find only fear and nothing else because around you there is only death, nothing else. So this is natural: with death all around fear inside is a natural counterpart.

If you move to the heights, love will be within and eternity all around. There will be no fear—there cannot be, because you *cannot* be destroyed, you are indestructible. There is NO possibility of your death, you are deathless. This is the fortification Jesus talks about.

"A city being built on a high mountain and fortified..." but remember the high altitude is the fortification "...cannot fall nor can it ever be hidden."

This is very paradoxical: in the valley you constantly fall, on the top never. This is paradoxical because we see people falling from the top. In the valley, why should one fall? One is walking on level ground, people fall from heights—that is a myth! In the inner world nobody falls from the heights; once the inner height is achieved, one never falls from it. Nothing can be taken from you if you have achieved it in the within. But without, your myth is true.

People fall whenever they are on the heights, but those heights belong to the valley, they are not real heights. If you have fame, you can be certain that sooner or later you will be defamed; if you are on the throne, sooner or later you will be dethroned. Whatsoever you achieve in *this* world will be taken away. But in the inner world, whatsoever you achieve you achieve forever, it cannot be taken away. Knowing cannot go back; once achieved, it becomes part of you. It is not something you possess—it becomes your being and you cannot unknow it.

Once you have known that you are deathless, how can you unknow it? There is no way to unlearn it—you have learnt. And only that which cannot be unlearnt is real knowledge. That which can be unlearnt is just memory, not knowledge; that which you can forget is just memory, not knowledge.

Knowledge is that which you *cannot* forget, there is no way to forget it. It has become your being, it is part of *you*, your very existence. You need not remember it—you need remember only those things which are not part of you.

"Fortified, a city being built on a high mountain cannot fall nor can it ever be hidden."

You cannot hide it. A city built on the top will be known—for eternities it will be known, there is no way to hide it. How can you hide a Buddha? It is impossible! How can you hide a Jesus? It is impossible! The phenomenon is so *tremendous*, their existence is so *penetrating*, that the impact will last.

You can crucify a Jesus, but you cannot neglect him. And those who crucified him still suffer for that crucifixion. Just a single man, an ordinary son of a carpenter was killed—nothing important. The Jews must have thought that way because nobody was bothered: if you kill a carpenter's son and you kill according to the law, there is no problem. But Jews have suffered for two thousand years because of that crucifixion, generation after generation. They have been continuously crucified, just for this one man. It looks very illogical, and Jews go on saying, "We have not done anything!" They are right in a way, because those who did it, they died long ago.

But a person like Jesus moves with the timeless. As far as Jesus is concerned, the crucifixion is going to remain forever and forever. It is not past, because a person like Jesus is never past—it is a fact right now: he is crucified. Jews may think, "We did it in the past, but those who did it are no more. We never did it—we may belong to those who did it, but we never *did* it!" but Jesus' crucifixion is now going to be an eternal fact. Now it cannot be moved into the past, it is going to be a live wound; the wound is going to remain there in the heart. And Jews have suffered, they have suffered too much it seems, because just for one man millions of Jews have been killed these twenty centuries. Just for one man, millions of Jews? It seems unjust.

But you don't know this man, that is why it seems unjust. This man is worth more than millions of men. The day they crucified this son of a carpenter, they played with a tremendous fire. They tried to hide it, but it cannot be hidden. They tried to hide it: there exists no Jewish record in which Jesus is crucified. Christian records exist, but Jews have not even recorded the fact that he was crucified. But you cannot hide it, and Jews started to disappear, they suffered because they tried to close their eyes against the sun. And this is the misery of the whole thing: that they gave birth to Jesus.

Jesus was a Jew and he remained a Jew up to the very last moment—he was never a Christian. And the Jews had been waiting for this man for many thousands of years. Their prophets in the past had told them: "A man will come who will deliver you. Soon a man will be there who will become your salvation." From the housetops, for thousands of years, prophets had been telling this to the Jews and the Jews had been waiting, waiting. They prayed and they waited and they waited—and this is the irony: when the man came, they refused him! When the man came and knocked at their door, they said, "No! You are *not* that promised one." Why?

It is easy for the mind to wait, because the mind can go on

hoping, desiring, dreaming. But when God knocks at your door, remember, you will also refuse—even though you may have been praying. But when God knocks at the door, what is the problem? Why do you refuse? Because only one can exist in the house. When God knocks at the door, you have to disappear—that is the problem.

Waiting, you exist, your ego exists. The Jews were very egoistic about the promised man to be born in their race. They were the chosen few, God had chosen them and the son of God was going to be born in a Jewish family—the ego felt very good about it. But when this chosen man came and knocked at the door and said, "I have come to fulfill the promise," they said, "No, you are not that chosen man! And if you try to say that you are, we will kill you!" What was the problem?

The problem is human. The problem is that if Jesus exists, then you have to disappear, you have to dissolve in him—you have to surrender. It was good for the ego to think that the promised man will come to *us*, the chosen race of the world, but it was very difficult to accept the man when he came.

They killed Jesus, but they have not even recorded it. They wanted to forget this whole thing so that they could hope again—and they are hoping still. The Jews are still hoping for the promised man. And I tell you, if he comes again—he will not come, because he must have learnt by experience—if he comes again, they will crucify him again. And they have suffered a lot, just because they tried to ignore the city built on the mountain-top.

They tried to hide a city built on the mountain-top, they tried to hide the sun—they tried to hide the Truth. They *crucified* the Truth. But Truth cannot be crucified, you cannot kill it; it is eternal, it is deathless. And still they have not become aware why they have suffered so much. The guilt! They still feel guilty deep down; a Jew is never without guilt—the guilt follows like a shadow. The guilt is that they refused the promised one when he came. And Jews know deep down that they have committed the greatest sin that is possible: to refuse God when He knocks at your door.

And He is not going to fulfill your expectations—whenever He comes He will be a stranger. Because if He fulfills *your* expectations, then he is no longer God. God is always a stranger, always the

unknown, knocking at the door of the known. He cannot come in
the form of the known, it is not possible—He remains always the
unknown, the mysterious. You would like Him to come according
to the formula. No! He follows no formula, He is not dead—only
dead matter follows a formula. Life lives as a mystery.

*"Jesus said: A city being built on a high mountain and fortified,
cannot fall nor can it ever be hidden.*

*Jesus said : What thou shalt hear in thine ear and in the other
ear, that preach from your housetops; for no one lights a lamp
and puts it under a bushel, nor does he put it in a hidden place,
but he sets it on the lampstand so that all who come in and go out
may see its light."*

Jesus said to his disciples, "Whatsoever you have heard, go and
shout it from the housetops so that others can hear it... for no
one lights a lamp and puts it under a bushel, nor does he put it
in a hidden place..."

Jesus says, "Go and tell the good news! Go and tell that the
unknown has entered into the known; go and tell that in your
routine world the mysterious has entered! Go and tell it from the
housetops so that people can hear, and people can come and
know and be benefited—don't be shy about it!"

There is a deep problem about this. It is very difficult—it must
have been very difficult for Jesus' disciples, it is always so—to tell
others that the son of God has come.Very difficult! Because people
will laugh, they will say you have gone crazy. They will not believe
that Jesus is the Christ—they will believe you are crazy. If you
say, "Jesus is God," they will think you have gone completely
mad: "You need some psycho-analysis—go and visit a doctor, take
some medicine, rest and relax! Because if you think this, something
is wrong with you! Something has gone wrong in you!"

It is *very* difficult to tell people that someone has become Realized.
Why? Because whenever someone becomes Realized it becomes a
deep wound in you, it becomes a deep hurt—you could have become
the same, but you have missed. A comparison enters, your ego
feels hurt: "Jesus is the son of God? Why am I not? The case
should have been otherwise. How has Jesus become the son of
God?" And it is easier to deny this than to change yourself and

become the son of God. It is easier because *no* is always the easiest thing in the world: nothing is to be done, you say *no,* and it's finished! If you say *yes* everything starts, nothing is finished. *No* is always the end, *yes* is always the beginning.

If you say, "Yes, Jesus is the son of God," then you have to transform yourself. Then you cannot remain with this *yes,* you have to move, you have to *do* something. If you say *no,* the problem is solved. Then whatsoever you are, wherever you are—in the valley, in darkness, in death—you are at ease. Jesus creates an unease in you; Buddha moves amidst you and he creates an unease, and we take revenge—because if one man can reach such a height, how is it that you have missed? It is better to say that there is no height, nobody has ever reached it. Then you are at ease in your darkness, then you can be comfortable.

Jesuses and Buddhas, they are very great tensions, because they uproot you from the valley, they shake you from your sleep and they say, "Move on—this is no place to stay!"

There is a saying of Jesus: "This world is just a bridge. *Move on!* This is no place to make a home. Cross it, but don't stop on it. Nobody makes a house on the bridge." This world is just a bridge and you have made a house on it. You would not like to know the fact that this is a bridge, because then what will happen to all your effort and labour and all your investment and your whole life devoted to making this house? And now somebody comes, a vagabond, who says, "What are you doing? This is a bridge!" So it is better not to look down into the river.

Why is it a bridge?—because Jesus, or people like Jesus, never use a single word without deep meaning. It is a bridge because it is on a river, and the river is of the momentary. Time is just a momentary river—it goes on flowing and flowing. Heraclitus has said: "You cannot step in the same river twice"—because if you come to step twice, the river has gone; it is some other water that is flowing now, the same water is not there. The river gives you the appearance that it is the same river, but there is no fixed river-like thing. A river means change—it is going, going, going, flowing. Why does Jesus call this world a bridge? Because you have made it on the temporary: time, the river of time, everything moving. Move from this bridge! This is no place to make a house.

But if somebody comes and tells you this, when for fifty years you have been making the house and now it is almost ready... and remember, it is always almost ready, never ready! It cannot be, that is not the nature of it. When it is almost ready and you were just going to rest from the whole effort and tension of building the house, if this man comes and he says, "This is on the river," rather than believing in this man and looking down, you would like to say, "Go away, you are a fool!" Or if this man insists, as Jesus goes on insisting and hammering, you will become angry. Hence he was crucified—it was too much trouble.

Socrates was poisoned, because the whole of Athens was in discomfort because of this man. He would catch hold of you anywhere in the market place and ask uncomfortable questions—destroying your comfortable lies. He became such a nuisance! In the valley, a Buddha is always a nuisance. Socrates created so much anguish and anxiety. People could not sleep, they could not do their work well because he created doubt. He said: "What are you doing? This is a river and this is a bridge—and you are building your house here, in this market? Seek the Eternal, the Truth!" Socrates became such a nuisance that they had to poison him.

In the valley, that has always been happening. If a man with eyes comes to a town of blind men, they will kill him—or if they are kind, they will operate on his eyes. But they will do something, because simply coming there that man *makes them blind!* They think they have never been blind—they never knew it—and this man comes and he says, "You are blind, you are mad!" He makes them aware of things they don't want to be aware of. Those things create anxiety.

Jesus says to his disciples: "Go, and cry from the housetops!" Why from the housetops? Because people are almost deaf, they don't hear, they don't want to hear. Even when they listen they are not hearing, they are somewhere else. Even when they nod they are simply bored. They may tolerate it, but they never enjoy the truth. For truth will always make you uncomfortable, bound to do so—because you live in the valley of lies.

Your whole life is such a lie: you have been lying to others, to yourself, and you have made everything around lies. Now somebody comes and speaks the truth. Somebody comes to a man who

believes that he is healthy when he has all sorts of diseases and
says, "What nonsense you are talking—you are ill!" That man
thinks, "This man is a bad omen—he is making me ill. I was
absolutely okay." To make you alert, to make you aware of the
truth, destroys your palaces, dream palaces you have made out
of cards, out of playing cards.

Jesus says: "Go, and whatsoever you have heard me telling you...
preach from your housetops; for no one lights a lamp and puts
it under a bushel..."

Don't be shy, and don't be afraid! The light is there, now don't
hide it: "...nor does he put it in a hidden place, but he sets it
on the lampstand so that all who come in and go out may
see its light."

This has always been a problem: Buddha, Mahavir, Lao Tzu,
Jesus, Mohammed, Zarathustra, they always have to insist
continuously that the disciples go and tell others. Because the
opportunity will not be forever, Jesus will not be there in his
physical body forever. And if you cannot realize him when he is
in his physical body, how will you be able to realize him when
he is not? If his physical presence cannot become a revelation to
you, how can it become a revelation to you when he has disappeared
into the universal?

Only rarely does someone become Enlightened, only rarely does
someone's darkness disappear. It is such a rare phenomenon and
it is not going to last forever—hence Jesus is always in a hurry.
He knows well. And Jesus had the most limited time on earth.
He died when he was thirty-three. He started preaching when he
was thirty, he died when he was thirty-three—only three years—
he was in a great hurry. He knew this crucifixion was going to
happen, so he said, "Go and make as many people aware and
alert as possible. The door is open now, they can enter into
the Divine."

But the disciples always remained wavering. They started
preaching only when Jesus died, because when Jesus disappeared,
then they realized what had happened to their lives. That too always
happens: when Jesus is there you become accustomed to the light
that Jesus is; when he disappears—*then* darkness, and then you feel
what light you have missed; and then you go on preaching from

the housetops. When Jesus was there something was possible, but now nothing is possible.

You go on for centuries—the Church is doing that: all over the world they go on preaching, preaching that Jesus is the light. But now it cannot be very helpful because the door has disappeared, now Jesus has become invisible. He can help, but if you cannot see the light when it is visible, how can you see it when Jesus becomes invisible? If you cannot enter the door when it opens just in front of you, how will it be possible for you to enter a door which is not visible at all? Difficult!

But disciples *themselves* become alert when the light disappears. Then they start crying and weeping, and then they know. Because only through contrast do you come to know; you only become aware that you were alive when you are dying; when you come to the moment of death, then you become aware what life was and how you have missed it. It is said that only when people die do they come to know that they were alive—otherwise they miss.

"Jesus said: If a blind man leads a blind man, both of them fall into a pit."

So don't be shy! Go and tell others that there is a man who has eyes—otherwise people will be led astray, because people have a need to be led. If you cannot find a Buddha or a Jesus, you will still follow someone because there is a great need to follow. There is a great need because you don't know where to go. And if somebody says, "I know," what to do?

Jesuses are not available every day, Buddhas are not born every day. But the need is there! If you cannot get the right food you will eat the wrong food, because the hunger is there every day. And it is very easy to find a blind man because you are blind—you understand the language. It is very easy to follow a blind man because you both belong to the same world of darkness, the same valley. It is much easier to be convinced by a blind man that he is the master, than to be convinced by a man who is not blind—because he uses a different language, he talks about a different world; he is so strange, you cannot understand him.

It is always easy to follow a wrong master, because *you* are wrong; something is similar between you and the master. But, "If a blind man leads a blind man, both of them fall into a pit."

It happened: Mulla Nasrudin died and his two disciples committed suicide—because without the master, what could they do? Mulla leading, the disciples following, they all three knocked at the door of the other world, a beautiful gate. Nasrudin said: "Look! This is what I promised—and I always deliver whatsoever I promise. We have reached Heaven!" They entered.

The guide took them to a beautiful palace and he said, "Now you are going to live here for eternity, and whatsoever you need, you just tell me and I will fulfill it immediately." Mulla said, "Look! This is what I promised and I have delivered it!"

For seven days they lived in rapture, because whatsoever they needed, immediately the demand was fulfilled—whatsoever it was. All their desires of millions of lives were fulfilled within seven days, because there was no effort to be made, no time to be wasted. But by the seventh day they became very frustrated, because when you get something too easily, you cannot enjoy it. And when you get it so immediately that there is no gap between the desire and the fulfillment, you become fed up—that is why rich men are so fed up. A poor man can have a little dance in his life, but not a rich man. Look at kings: they are *dead,* fed up with everything, because everything is available. Availability is such a great problem —greater than poverty, greater than scarcity.

By the seventh day they were fed up, because they enjoyed the most beautiful women, the most costly wine, the best food, the costliest clothes—they lived like emperors. But then what to do? By the seventh day Mulla asked the guide: "We would like to have a look down on the world. We would like you to open a window so we can look at the earth." But the guide said, "Why?" Mulla said: "Just to regain our interest, it will be helpful to regain our desire." So the guide opened a door, they looked down at people on the earth, they looked at us struggling our whole lives and not achieving much—and they regained their hunger by contrast.

They enjoyed seven days again, but again they became fed up. Now the same medicine wouldn't do; just looking at the world would not be of much help, they had become immune. So Mulla said, "Now I have another ridiculous demand: we would like you to open a door unto Hell, so we can look at Hell and regain our taste. But we have become afraid—because what will we do after it?"

The guide started laughing and he said: "Where do you think you are?" *They were in Hell!*

If all your desires are fulfilled you will be in Hell, because you don't know the bliss of desirelessness, you know only the struggle. That is why poets say that the pleasure is in the waiting, not in the meeting; the pleasure is in desiring, not in fulfillment. And they are right about you! Whenever everything is fulfilled, what will you do? Then you will come to know that you have been in Hell.

But this happens if you follow a blind man: even if you reach Heaven, it will turn out to be Hell, because blindness can never reach Heaven. Heaven is not really a place to reach, it is a state of consciousness; it is not somewhere in geography, it is not geographical—it is something in *you*. Hell and Heaven both exist in you. But if you follow a blind man, how can a blind man lead you towards the heights? He will lead you into the valley. But there is a need to be led—be aware of that need.

You want to be led, because then the responsibility goes to the other. It is better to have a blind leader than none—this is your state of mind. Hence Jesus says, "Go and tell people from the housetops that the Master is here!"

Jesus has appeared, and the chance is rare, and there is every possibility you may miss the opportunity. Run and catch hold of this man, because few are the moments when the door of Heaven opens! Those are the moments when a man becomes Enlightened. Then he is a door: then you can look through him and you can realize the whole truth.

A Master is not a man who teaches you, a Master is a man who awakens you. A Master is not a man who has some information to give to you, a Master is a man who is going to give you a glimpse into your own being. But this became a problem: if Jesus had remained silent, nobody would have crucified him. But he was in a hurry, and he started moving around the country and telling people. That created a problem because nobody understood him —everybody misunderstood him. This is going to be so, because between two different dimensions communication is impossible. He talked about the Kingdom of God and people thought he was talking about some kingdom here.

He said: "I am the King," and people thought that he was going to dethrone the King here. He said: "Those who are meek shall inherit the earth"—he was talking about something else, but people thought he was promising his disciples: "You will inherit the earth." Then politicians became afraid, because 'kingdom', 'king', 'inheritance of the earth'—all these terms are political. Priests also became afraid because whatsoever he said was beyond law.

Love is always beyond law. Love cannot follow any law because it is a superior law, the highest. When you love, everything is okay because love cannot do anything wrong. There are no regulations and rules for it—rules and regulations exist because you can't love, because you are incapable of love. That is why there are so many rules: so that you cannot harm the other, so that you are prevented from harming the other. But when you love, why should you harm the other? Rules disappear!

And Jesus talked about the Ultimate Law, love. Then priests became afraid, then the judges, magistrates, the legal system became afraid that he would make a chaos, he would create anarchy. He was crucified because he became a trouble-maker.

This need not happen—it has happened in the past, but this need not happen now. Because now, after thousands of years, experiencing Buddhas, Mahavirs, Zarathustras, Jesus', Mohammeds, we *must* become more alert!

But no! It is still the case—as if man never learns. His stupidity seems to be ultimate, final, and he goes on rationalizing his stupidity. He fortifies his stupidity, his ignorance, and whosoever comes to take it away looks as if he is the enemy. Friends look like enemies, enemies look like friends. Those who can lead seem to be leading you astray, those who are blind are your leaders.

Understand first your need to be led. It is beautiful, because that shows a search—but don't be in a hurry to follow *anybody*. How will you decide? What is the criterion? For the seeker this is one of the most puzzling things: how to decide who is Jesus and who is a blind man? Certainty seems to be impossible, but glimpses of certainty are possible. You cannot be absolutely certain from the very beginning, because the very nature of the thing is such: how can a blind man decide that the other has eyes? The only decision, the only certainty possible is when *he* starts seeing. Then he will be able to decide—but then there will be no need! When *you* become a Buddha, there is no need to recognize a Buddha; when you are like Jesus, there is no need to know Jesus or follow Jesus. This is the paradox.

You are blind and you have to choose—how will you decide? By the words? Then you will be deceived, because scholars, pundits, priests, they are very clever with words. Nobody can defeat them, because they have been in the business for a long time. Jesus will look poor in his words—the high priest of the Jews could have defeated him easily. That would not have been a big problem. Kabir or Buddha can be defeated easily through argument, through logic. But you cannot judge through words, you will be deceived— don't use that criterion.

A Jesus can be judged only by his being: be near him—don't try to listen to what he is saying, try to listen to what he is. That is the key: just be near him! Hindus have called it *satsang*, just being near the Truth. Just be near—don't listen to what he is saying, don't get engaged intellectually—just listen to what he is.

Being vibrates, being blooms, being has a fragrance about it. If you can be silent near a Jesus, you will start listening to his silence. And that silence will make you so blissful, and that silence will make you so fulfilled, so overflowing with love and compassion— that is the criterion. If you do that with a pundit, with a man of knowledge, then you will simply be filled with misery—because he is as miserable as you are. If you listen to the words, he will look very great. If you listen to his being, to his vibrations, to the throbbing of his life, he is as miserable as you are—maybe more. That's why he has become a man of words: to hide his misery. That's why he talks theories, philosophies, systems; that's why he argues— because he does not know.

A man who knows does not really argue, he simply states, he simply says.... Look at these sayings of Jesus—he is not arguing, he is not giving any reasons, he is simply making statements, simple statements: "A city being built on a high mountain and fortified, cannot fall nor can it ever be hidden." No argument, just a simple statement of fact. "What thou shalt hear in thine ear and in the other ear, that preach from your housetops; for no one lights a lamp and puts it under a bushel, nor does he put it in a hidden place. but he sets it on the lampstand so that all who come in and go out may see its light."—No argument! Not trying to prove anything, simply making a statement.

"Jesus said: If a blind man leads a blind man, both of them fall into a pit."—Simple statements of fact! These words can be used more beautifully by a man of knowledge, but there you will be deceived.

Whenever you are in search of a Master, listen to his being. Learn the art of listening to his being; just be near him, feel him— through the heart. Suddenly you will feel you are changing, because he is a magnetic force. Suddenly you will feel something is going, a deep change within you. You are no more the same, your room is filled with an unknown light—as if your burden has dropped for a moment, as if through him you have got wings, you can fly. *And this is an experience.* Only this experience will give you a right person, a man with eyes who can lead you.

Where is he going to lead you? He is going to lead you to yourself. A man of knowledge will always lead you to somewhere else, to a heaven somewhere in the sky, to a goal somewhere in the future. But a man of being, a Jesus, a Buddha, leads you nowhere else, just to yourself—because there is the goal. You are the target, you are the goal.

And listen through the heart, *satsang,* that is the criterion. Otherwise, blind men have been leading you for many lives, and again and again the blind leader and you have both fallen in the pit.

The last thing about the pit: whenever Jesus says, "They fall into the pit," 'the pit' is the womb. Whenever a blind man leads, both fall into the womb again—that is the pit. They are born again into the same miserable life, the same anguish starts in new forms. Nothing substantial changes, the story remains the same; the whole thing remains the same, just outer forms change. You are again in hell, again in misery—the womb is the pit.

When a man of being leads you, you never fall into the pit. Then you are born in another dimension, and it is no longer worth being born again into this world. You disappear from here, you appear somewhere else. That somewhere else is God, that somewhere else is *Nirvana.*

Twelfth Discourse

1st September 1974, Poona, India

THE TWELFTH SAYING

Jesus said to his disciples:
Make a comparison to me and tell me who I am like.

Simon Peter said to him:
Thou art like a righteous angel.

Matthew said to him:
Thou art like a wise man of understanding.

Thomas said to him:
Master, my mouth will not be capable
of saying whom thou art like.

Jesus said:
I am not thy Master, because thou hast drunk,
thou hast become drunk from the bubbling spring
which I have measured out.

And he took him, he withdrew,
he spoke three words to him.

Now when Thomas came to his companions,
they asked him:
What did Jesus say to thee?

Thomas said to them:
If I tell you one of the words he said to me,
you will take up stones and throw at me;
and fire will come from the stones and burn you up.

Whenever there is a man like Jesus or Buddha, you try to escape from him in every way possible—because he is just like a death to you. Of course, you will rationalize your escape, you will find clever reasons why you are escaping. You will argue in your mind, "That man is not a Christ, that man is not yet Enlightened." You will find something wrong in that man, so that you can feel at ease. You will avoid that man. It is dangerous to encounter him, because he can live, he can see through you; you become transparent to him. You cannot hide yourself from him, you cannot hide the falseness that you are—before him, you are just like an open book. And your whole life you have been hiding.

Your whole life you have been trying to live a false, inauthentic life; you have been living in *lies!* And he will see through you. Before him, you will become a trembling leaf; before him you will be reduced to your truth; before him, you cannot manage your false image—he will be a catastrophe. So only those who are very courageous can come near to a Jesus. The greatest courage is needed to come near a man like Jesus. That means you are ready to take the jump into the abyss, you are ready to lose yourself.

In the insecurity of the unknown, in the uncharted, in the ocean where the other shore is not visible—to move with Jesus, tremendous courage is needed. And this is the problem: very few will follow Jesus. Those who escape, they will miss him, and they will miss the very meaning of their own lives. Because deep down, when you try to escape Jesus, you are trying to escape from your own

truth. He is nothing but your future—you are a seed, he is the tree;
he has come to bloom, he is your future, he is your possibility.
Escaping from him, you are escaping from your own ultimate
possibility.

But it is not certain that those who come near will encounter
Jesus just by coming near. Those who escape, they have escaped—
finished! But those who come near, live near, even living near
they can avoid Jesus, because they can be near him for the wrong
reasons. So, out of thousands, few will choose him. And those few
who choose him, they will not all be with him for the right reasons.
And those who are with him for the wrong reasons will also
miss him.

You can be with an Enlightened person for the wrong reasons.
Look for the reasons why you seek: why do you go to a Master?
What are your real reasons? Are you seeking truth? Rarely is a
man seeking truth! You may be seeking happiness, but not truth.
Happiness happens when truth is achieved. But if you are seeking
happiness you cannot achieve truth, because happiness is a by-
product; you cannot achieve it directly, there is no way to it—it
comes via truth. If you reach the true, happiness *will* happen; it
is a shadow, it comes with the truth. But if you *seek* happiness,
then happiness is not possible and truth is missed.

Out of one hundred seekers, ninety-nine *are* for happiness. They
have suffered much pain, life has been a misery: they are seeking
the antidote, they are seeking the opposite. To be with a Jesus or
Buddha in search of happiness is to miss him again, because your
eyes are closed! Happiness can never be the goal; it is achieved, it
comes automatically, you need not bother about it. It is *always* a
by-product: you simply take care of the tree, and flowers come! You
need not go directly to the flowers—if you do, you will miss. If
you are after flowers, you will miss; but if you take care of the tree,
flowers come in their own time! You need not worry, you need not
even think about them.

In your ordinary existence also, this is known, but you never
make it a deep experience. You have been happy for a few moments
—it is difficult to find a man who has not been happy even for a
few moments—because if you have never been happy for a few
moments, if you have never tasted happiness, then you cannot

seek it. Without having tasted it, then why would you search for happiness, how could you make it a goal? You *have* tasted it. It was momentary, a glimpse—and then again darkness; a glimpse—and then again anguish. The morning comes only for a moment, and then midnight again. You have tasted it, but you have not *entered* into it. How does it happen? Try to enter into it.

Whenever you have felt happy, you were not looking for it. That is the first basic thing about happiness: it happened when you were looking for something else. For example, you have heard the story of Archimedes: he was in search of a scientific truth. He worked, experimented, thought, pondered over it many days and nights. He forgot himself. Then suddenly, when he was in his bath one day, lying down in his tub, it happened, it bubbled up—he realized it! He was naked, but he forgot that he was naked. When you are happy, you forget yourself; if you cannot forget yourself, you are not happy. Happiness means you are no more there; it happens only when you are not.

Archimedes' problem was solved, the whole tension relaxed. He ran into the street shouting, *"Eureka, Eureka! I have found it, I have found it!"* People thought he had gone mad. They had always been suspicious of this man, this Archimedes, and now their suspicion was proved right. "Too much thinking is bad"—they had always been of this opinion, and this man was thinking too much. Now he had gone mad and was crying, *"Eureka!"* on the street—*"I have found it!"*

What happened? How ecstatic he was in that moment! And it was not the Ultimate Truth, it was just an ordinary problem. Now it is ordinary—once discovered, scientific truths become ordinary, common. But he discovered it. In that moment of discovery, all tensions relaxed, and he was so happy, so ecstatic, that he forgot himself. Whenever you are happy, the first basic thing is to remember that you were searching for something else, not for happiness. If you search for happiness directly, you will miss it forever and forever. It is a by-product: you are engaged in search of something else, and then that something else is discovered. The discovery makes you so fulfilled, the whole effort relaxes, the whole tension goes; you are at ease, at peace, at rest, and you feel filled with happiness.—Happiness is a by-product.

Second thing to remember: if you seek after it, how can you lose yourself? The seeker can never lose himself; the ego remains, you remain a point of reference. Whenever happiness happens, you are not there. Remember moments of happiness: you were *not* there. It may have happened in a deep love, it may have happened in a discovery, or it may have happened just when you were playing cards—but you became so lost...suddenly the upsurge! *Anything* can trigger it, but a direct search is dangerous because you will miss it.

If you come to a Master in search of happiness, you are near him for the wrong reasons. Then you remain hidden in your wrong reasons. You remain close physically; spiritually there is much distance. Your eyes are blind, you will not be able to know this man, Jesus or Buddha. It is impossible, because your eyes are filled with the wrong goals.

Or you may not even be in search of happiness, there are even lower goals. You may be near a Master to attain power, you may be near him to attain some *siddhi*—you may be near him to attain a more egoistic state. Then you will miss him completely. There are even lower aims. And the lower the aim, the more possibility there is of missing because then you are more blind. You may be near him just for very ordinary reasons like seeking health. You are ill and Jesus will cure you; or you are poor and Jesus will give you money—his blessings will become money to you; or you don't have a child and he can give you a child.

The lower the aim, the more you will miss, because the lower the aim, the more you are in the deep valley—and Jesus exists on the top of the hill; the distance goes on becoming more and more. Many have escaped, but those who have come near, not all of them have come near either—only one who comes for the right reason. And that right reason is truth. But why do you never seek it?

Truth seems to be so bare, truth seems to be so dry, there seems to be no urge to seek it. Happiness seems worthwhile, and if I insist, "Seek truth and happiness will be the by-product," you may even agree to seek the truth because the by-product happiness will be there. But you are still seeking happiness. If you come to know that to seek happiness, truth has to be sought, you may start seeking truth—but you are not seeking truth, your mind remains focused on happiness. That focusing is wrong.

Only when you are a truth-seeker do you come near Jesus, Buddha, Zarathustra; otherwise you never come near! For *any* other reason you are near physically; spiritually, you are very, very far away—*vast* spaces exist.

Now look at this saying of Jesus:

"Jesus said to his disciples: Make a comparison to me and tell whom I am like".

Why has Jesus asked this question? Is he not aware who he is? Is it to be known through the disciples who he is? Why does he want to know through the disciples who he is? Because whatsoever they say will show why they are near Jesus. You create the image of your Master according to your desire. If you are near Jesus because you are ill, Jesus will be the healer. You look through your desire, you project your desire. If you are there to seek power, then Jesus is the omnipotent, the most powerful, because only when he is the most powerful can he give it to you. If you are seeking immortality, if you are seeking a state of deathlessness, if you are afraid of death, then the image of Jesus will reflect your search.

Why has Jesus asked his disciples, "Tell me who I am?" He has asked just to know what they are projecting. If you project anything you will miss, because to know Jesus or Buddha, non-projecting eyes are needed. You should not project anything, you should simply look at the *fact*.

Jesus is a *fact*, the most vital fact that is possible in the world. Look at him directly, immediately. Don't bring your desire in between; don't make a screen of Jesus. Otherwise, you will see but you will see your own desire reflected.

"Jesus said to his disciples: Make a comparison to me and tell me whom I am like.
Simon Peter said to him: Thou art like a righteous angel."

This man must have been a moralist, a puritan. This man must have been guilty of his immorality, because whatsoever you say about others *never* shows anything about others, it simply shows something about you. Whatsoever you judge is not a judgment about others, it is a judgment about you. Jesus says again and again, "Judge ye not!" because all your judgments are going to be wrong—*you* will be there. A thief is a sinner for you. Why? Because you are too much attached to your private property. It does not show anything about the thief, it simply shows your possessiveness.

I have heard that one Englishman died and he reached Hell. The Devil asked him, "Which hell would you prefer? Because we have all sorts of hells here: the English, the German, the Chinese, the Russian, the Indian...."

The Englishman said, "The Indian of course!"

The Devil was puzzled. He said, "You look like an Englishman, so why do you choose the Indian?

He said, "I am an Englishman, but I have been in India and I know well that in the Indian hell the heating won't work!"

Your mind accumulates experience. Whatsoever you say about Hell or Heaven or other persons, it is your experience speaking; it is you reflected in each word you assert.

This Simon Peter said: "Thou art like a righteous angel."

Two things he is saying, first: 'righteous'—he must have always been afraid of wrong, he must have been afraid of sin, he must have been afraid of being immoral. The opposite he projects on Jesus—that is why he is with Jesus.

Remember one thing: opposites attract each other. If you are a man, you are attracted to a woman—and that is the trouble! Because she is the opposite, that is why she is attractive. But to live with a woman will be difficult, because she is the opposite. This is how the misery of marriage arises: it begins in the attraction for the opposite, but when you have to live with the opposite, then there is trouble because in every way she is opposite. Her logic is totally different from yours. A man never comes to understand a woman. It is impossible to understand her, because a man thinks like a man and a woman thinks like a woman; they have different dimensions. A woman is more intuitive; she is not logical, she jumps to conclusions—and almost always she is right! That makes more trouble. She cannot *convince* you; she cannot convince you whatsoever she says, because she has no logic about it. But she has insight, she looks immediately.

Once, Mulla Nasrudin was caught in a legal case. He looked in the court: twelve woman jurists. And he said to the judge, "I confess! Because I cannot deceive one woman at home, so twelve in the jury—impossible! I have committed this sin, simply give me the punishment."

Every husband knows it is difficult to deceive a woman. Howsoever you plan, everything goes wrong the moment you reach home. The wife simply catches you, she hits exactly right at the wound. She is not aware either how she functions; her functioning is different.

A woman can never understand a man. This is also the reason why they attract each other, because only mysteries attract. But to live with someone you cannot understand is bound to create trouble, then there is going to be fighting. So wherever there is love, continuous fighting happens, each moment a fight.

The opposite attracts: if you are a greedy person, you will be attracted by a man who has renounced; you will go to a saint who has renounced all if you are a greedy person. This is very difficult because this creates many troubles.

Look at the Jains in India: they are the most rich—and riches don't come without greed, you have to be greedy—but they worship saints who have renounced all. They will not allow their saints to even wear clothes. No! That too is not allowed. The authentic *Digamber* Jain saint remains naked with no possessions, not even clothes. He possesses only his body, that's all. He has to take his food in his hands; he is not allowed to take food twice, once is enough. He sleeps on the ground, and that is why he is called *Digamber:* the sky is his only covering, the sky is his only house, his only roof. But why this phenomenon? Why does this happen?

Mohammed talked about peace: the word 'Islam' means peace. But look at Mohammedans—they have been the *most* violent people on earth. Why were they attracted to Mohammed and to the religion of peace? The opposite attracts. The opposite is always attractive because this is the basic pattern of sex, and this basic pattern of sex follows you everywhere, whatsoever you do.

This Simon Peter said to Jesus: "Thou art like a righteous angel." This man must have been guilty about his immorality—rightly or wrongly, but he was guilty. He was attracted to Jesus because Jesus looked like an angel: pure, innocent, he had never committed a sin. That is why Christians go on insisting that he was born of a virgin mother, which is absurd! Why do they insist that he was born of a virgin mother? Because sex looks immoral. And if you are born out of immorality, how can you become absolutely moral? Impossible! If the very source is poisoned then how will you be moral? You can try but you can never be perfect. At the very source the immorality should be cut. Hence their insistence that Jesus was born of a virgin mother.

Nobody is born of a virgin mother—it is absolutely wrong, it cannot happen! But they insist, they depend on it. If it is proved finally that Jesus had a father, then Christians will desert him, they will immediately escape: "This man is just like us! We are immoral, we are born in sin, and if he is also born in sin then what is the difference?"

The second thing he is saying: 'angel'—"Thou art like a righteous angel."

Angels are just symbols of absolute perfection, purity, innocence. This shows something about Simon Peter, and Simon Peter became the rock of the whole Christian Church, he became the base. Hence, the Christian Church is continuously involved with what is moral, what is immoral. The whole Church has become a morality, not a religion. This Simon Peter is the root cause: he created guilt, because whenever you are too concerned with what is wrong, what is right, you become guilty. And life knows neither.

Life is absolutely amoral. It is neither moral nor immoral, it is amoral. It knows nothing of what is wrong and what is right. It moves in both directions, it is both together. A river in flood: what will you call it, moral or immoral? Thousands of villagers are drowned, hundreds of people dead, thousands homeless. What will you call this river in flood—bad? No, you will not use that word, because you know the river does not know what is good, what is bad. And God exists in the river as much as in you. A tree falls down where a saint is meditating, he is killed. What will you call this tree—a sinner, a murderer? Will this tree have to be forced to appear in a court? No, you will simply say, "This is a tree. Our morality—sin or non-sin— doesn't apply to this tree."

Morality is man-created, God seems to be amoral. The whole of existence is amoral. Amoral means neither—or both. But if you go to Jesus with a moralistic attitude, you will miss him. Saint Peter, this Simon Peter, missed Jesus completely. He was in search of a moral man; he was in search of a saint, not in search of a sage.

And this is the difference between a saint and a sage: a sage is as amoral as life, he has become one with life, he doesn't think in terms of opposites; a saint has chosen the right, denied the wrong, he is half-alive, he has not taken the whole of life. A saint is really not religious, because a religious man will accept life as it is. He will not deny, because whatsoever you deny it is a denial of God. Then you try to prove that you are *better* than God! Look, God creates sex—otherwise, who will create it? And you deny it; then you can become a saint but your sainthood will be just moral, it cannot be religious.

Hindus understood it very well. If you go back to the days of the Vedas, the *rishis* used to live a very ordinary life: they had wives, children; they were householders, they had not renounced. Renunciation entered with Jains and Buddhists. Otherwise, Hindu *rishis* always lived in a very ordinary way, because they knew, they came to know that life has to be accepted in its totality; nothing has to be denied, everything has to be accepted. This is what theism will really mean: *astika* means one who says *yes* to the whole of life, he is not a no-sayer. This Saint Peter can become a good priest, he can become a saint, but he cannot become a sage. He has his own conceptions, that's why he has come to Jesus.

When you are filled with too many moral concepts, what do you do? You condemn yourself, because there are things that are not dissolved just by saying they are wrong, they remain. This man will become attracted to women; they are beautiful, and the desire exists—it is a gift of God. It is deep in your every pore, every cell of your body. Scientists say there are seventy million cells in the body, and each cell is a sexual being. Your whole body is a sex phenomenon! Whatsoever you do—you can close your eyes, you can escape to the Himalayas, but always beauty will attract you.

A flower looks so beautiful—have you observed? That too is sexual. A bird singing in the morning near a saint's cottage or hermitage, looks beautiful, but have you observed that this singing of the bird is a sexual invitation? He is inviting the partner, seeking the partner, the lover. What is a flower? A flower is a sexual phenomenon, a flower is just a trick; because the tree cannot move, its sexual cells have to be carried by bees, butterflies and others to other trees. Remember, there are female trees and male trees, and they cannot move because they are rooted in the earth. The flower is a trick to attract the bees, butterflies, other insects: they will come on the flower, and with the bees the sexual seed will go; then they will go to the female plant and that seed will fall there.

Wherever there is beauty there is sex. The whole of life is a sexual phenomenon. What can you do? You can reject it, that is in your hands, but when you reject you feel guilt, because deep down the suppressed remains. You continuously feel guilty; something is wrong. You cannot be happy with guilt, remember, you cannot dance with guilt. Guilt will paralyze you: wherever you go, you cannot laugh, you cannot move in ecstasy, because you will always be afraid of the suppressed.

If you dance, sing, if you feel blissful, what will happen to the suppressed? It may come up, so you have to be constantly on watch. You become a watchman, not a master of your life, not an enjoyer of your life; you become just a watchman. And the whole thing becomes ugly because there is conflict, continuous conflict. Your energy is dissipated in inner struggle. And this type of man, who has suppressed his own being somehow, will always look at others with condemning eyes—it is bound to be so!

A moralist is very difficult to live with, because his eyes are continuously condemning you: you are wrong because you have taken tea. Are you drinking tea? Then you are thrown into hell—you cannot drink tea. Really, anything that can give you any enjoyment the moralist condemns. In Gandhi's ashram, you were not allowed to taste food—aswad, tastelessness, was the principle to be followed; you could eat, but you should not taste. Why? Why be against taste? Because taste is enjoyment, and saints are against enjoyment. You cannot find a saint laughing or smiling—

impossible! He looks sad, always condemning himself and others. His whole life is ill, he cannot be happy.

This Simon Peter is symbolic. He said: "Thou art like a righteous angel." He is saying, "I have come to you because you are pure: born of a virgin mother, never married, never enjoyed life, never lived. You are pure, so I see you as an angel."

"Matthew said to him: Thou art like a wise man of understanding."

This Matthew is not in search of morality, this Matthew is in search of knowledge—more scientific. And Jesus looks like a man of understanding, he thinks he can get some clues about the mystery of life from this man: "This man carries some keys. He knows, I can gather information from him." Matthew is in search of knowledge.

But when you come to Jesus or a man like Jesus, don't come in search of knowledge. Jesus looks a wise man, because whatsoever he says hits directly, whatsoever he says sounds true. Whatsoever he says is very meaningful, but you are paying too much attention to his words and not to his being. This Matthew is a pundit, a scholar; he is in search of principles, theories, systems, philosophies. If you come to Jesus with such a mind you will miss him, because Jesus is not a man of knowledge—he is a man of *being*. And what is the difference?

Knowledge is superficial, borrowed, dead. *This man is alive*, absolutely alive! This man has not borrowed anything from anybody—he has come to realize himself. He can share his being with you, and you are foolish if you just carry words from him. These words can be carried from books, there was no need to come to Jesus. A library would have been better; there is more knowledge in a library, accumulated for centuries.

You come to this man where your being could have quenched its thirst and you simply carry away words. You come to an Emperor and he is saying, "Ask, and it shall be given to you," and you ask only for one piece of bread and go away happy. The whole Empire was at your feet, just for the asking—you carry words, you learn theories, you become a theologian. This Matthew is the root theologian for Christians.

And then the whole Church got entangled in two things—that is why these two are mentioned: Peter became the base of Church morality, antisexuality, and he continues to be the base; and Matthew became the base of theology, and he continues to be the base. Christianity is involved with two things, not with Christ at all: with morality—what is wrong and what is right; and with theology, theories about God. Theology means theories about God—and there can be no theory about God.

God is not a theory, He is not a hypothesis which has to be proved or can be disproved, you cannot argue about Him. And when Jesus was there, you could have *encountered* God. God was there, He had penetrated this man—but a search for knowledge is a barrier. You should not ask Jesus for knowledge, you should ask for being. But to gather knowledge is easy, because you need not transform yourself. You simply listen to the words and gather; no transformation is required on your part. But if you ask for *being*, then you have to be silent, then you have to be in deep meditation, then you have to become just a silent presence. Only then can Jesus pour his being into you.

This Matthew said to him: "Thou art like a wise man of understanding."

Jesus is not a wise man. He is wisdom itself, but not a wise man—because you can be wise without becoming Enlightened. There are wise men: Confucius is a wise man, but not Enlightened; Manu is a wise man, but not Enlightened. Buddha is Enlightened, Lao Tzu is Enlightened. Their wisdom comes from a totally different source. They have reached the very center of life—they have *known*. Their knowledge is not through intellect, their knowledge is through being. That is why I will call Jesus a man of being, not a man of knowledge.

Wisdom you can gather through experience—every old man becomes wise. Even a foolish man becomes wise, because they say if you persist in your foolishness you will become wise. Just time can give you wisdom; just living through life, committing the mistakes, going astray, coming back, many experiences gathered, you become wise.

Jesus is not wise in that way: he was not an old man, he was just thirty, he was a very young man. He did not really have much experience of life, he is not wise in that way. But he has known something, something that is the very base of life. He has not moved on the branches of the tree of life, he has reached to the root. This is a totally different thing—and Matthew will miss it. He will gather notes; whatsoever Jesus says, he will gather. He will create a gospel out of it, he will spin theories. Both these men miss him totally.

Thomas, the third, who has reported these sayings, he is the disciple closest to Jesus. But his sayings are not included in the Bible, because Jesus and his closest disciples have to be excluded—they are dangerous.

"Thomas said to him: Master, my mouth will not be capable of saying whom thou art like."

"It is impossible to say. You are so many things, and so much you are—you are so overflowing, you are so multi-dimensional, my mouth will not be able to say it. I am unable to say anything, words are not enough. You cannot be compared to anybody, you are incomparable. And whatsoever I say will be wrong, because it will not be enough. Words are very narrow, you are *vast!"*

So says Thomas: "Master, my mouth will not be capable of saying whom thou art like. No, impossible! I will not say anything, because it cannot be said. You cannot be caught in words, you are inexpressible!"

Thomas comes nearest, but even the nearest is far away, the gap exists.

A similar story exists with Bodhidharma. He lived in China for nine years. He taught people, many meditated, many came nearer and nearer, and when he was leaving he asked his four disciples to say something about *Dharma*, to say something about Truth. The first three are just like these three: Simon Peter, a man of morality—the most superficial; then Matthew, the man in search of knowledge—a little deeper than Simon but still very far away; then Thomas who said, "I cannot say anything."

But Bodhidharma was more fortunate than Jesus, because there was a fourth who really remained silent. He didn't even say this: "I cannot say." Because when you say, "I cannot say," you have said something! This has to be understood: the fourth remained absolutely silent. He simply looked in Bodhidharma's eyes, bowed down at his feet, and Bodhidharma said: "One has my bones, another has my flesh, another has my blood—and you are my very marrow!" This fourth one would not say even as much as Thomas has said. He came closest, he became the marrow.

Jesus was not so fortunate. There are reasons: the climate was not good, the situation was absolutely different. China had known Lao Tzu, but the Jews have never known a man like Lao Tzu. Lao Tzu created the very soil in which Buddha's seed could sprout beautifully. When Bodhidharma went to China the soil was ready. It had been tilled by Lao Tzu, Chuang Tzu—rare phenomena!—and then Buddha's seed was carried by Bodhidharma. It flowered beautifully, it blossomed beautifully. Jesus was not so fortunate, the soil was not ready. There have been prophets in the Jewish culture, but not sages like Lao Tzu and Chuang Tzu, no. There have been saints, so Simon Peter was available. There have been moralists, because Moses put morality at the very base of Jewish culture: the Ten Commandments—they are the base.

There were men like Simon Peter because nothing exists without cause, nothing exists without a long tradition. A Simon Peter is not just an accident, a long history is needed behind him. Moses is the deepest cause, the root from where Simon Peter came: the Ten Commandments, the moral attitude towards the world, towards life. But there was no man like Lao Tzu who says, "All distinctions are false: the moment you say, 'This is good and that is bad,' you have divided life and killed it;" a man who was for the whole, not for the division. Bodhidharma was fortunate, and that is the reason he had four disciples, not three.

In a Jewish culture, at the most Thomas was possible. Look at the phenomenon of Thomas, what he is saying—and this is one of the basic problems. There are people who say, "Nothing can be said about God," but they have said something. Even if you say, "Nothing can be said about God," you have said something. If you are correct then you have made a mistake. If you are correct— nothing can be said—then this should not be said either; you should remain completely silent. Otherwise you create a dilemma: on the one hand you say nothing can be said, but if this much can be said then why not a little more? What is the problem? If this much can be asserted, then why not more? If assertion is possible, then more assertion becomes possible.

That is why Buddha remained *absolutely* silent. He would not even say, "Nothing can be said about God." He would not say even this much. You asked about God and he would talk about something else. You asked about God and he would not listen—as if you had not asked about God—he would simply drop the subject, he would talk about something else. He would not even say this much that nothing can be said, because this is absurd. Then why are you saying it? Even through negation we indicate. Not only is positive assertion an assertion, negative assertion is also assertion.

You say, "God has no form." What do you mean? Have you known Him? And have you known Him so totally that you can say, "He has no form"? If you have known Him totally, then He *has* form. For example, you say that this ocean cannot be measured; it is so deep, it cannot be measured. Then there are only two possibilities: either you have measured it, because only then can you say it is so deep that it cannot be measured; or you have not measured it, otherwise how can you say it is so deep it cannot be measured? Even depth is measurable—*has* to be, it cannot be immeasurable; howsoever deep, it can be measured.

When you say, "God has no form," have you come to His boundaries and seen that there is no form? If you have come to the boundaries, He *has* form. And if you have not come to the boundaries, then don't say He is formless, because He may have form. When you come to the boundaries, only then can you know. So those who have really stumbled upon God—it is a stumbling—who have fallen into Him, will not say anything, not even this, because this is contradictory.

One of the keenest logicians of this century, Wittgenstein, has written a beautiful sentence. In his book *Tractatus Logico Philosophicus*, he has many beautiful statements. This is the best: he says, "Nothing should be said about something which cannot be said. If nothing can be said about a thing one should remain silent."

Thomas comes closest, but remains distant. He has still tried to say, tried to express the inexpressible.

"Thomas said to him: Master, my mouth will not be capable of saying whom thou art like."

Jesus said: "I am not thy Master, because nobody understands me, so how can I be thy Master?"

If you understand, only then can you be a disciple. If you understand, only then can you enter into the temple. If you understand, only then can you enter the being of the Master.

"Jesus said: I am not thy Master..."

To all the three he says, "I am not thy Master." Thomas came closest but still missed. He is the best, but still not perfect—just approximately the best; he comes closer but a barrier remains: he still believes in words, because he tries to express that which cannot be expressed.

"I am not thy Master, because thou hast drunk, thou hast become drunk from the bubbling spring which I have measured out."

Here he is stating a very profound truth. He is saying, "All three of you are talking from the mind, 'the bubbling spring which I have measured out,' which I have gone beyond, 'measured out.' You are still talking from the mind: one is talking through the moralist mind, another is talking through the theological mind, the third is talking through the mystic mind—but still, all are part of the mind. And if you talk from the mind I am not thy Master, because the whole emphasis is: drop the mind!"

That is what a Master goes on insisting: Drop the mind! And you play a trick: you start talking about the Master from the same mind he has been insisting to drop. That is why I say Bodhidharma was more fortunate: he had a disciple who remained really silent, he would not answer.

There have been even more fortunate Masters. One of them was Rinzai. He asked the same thing—because really it is the same story again and again: Buddha and his disciples, Jesus and his disciples, Bodhidharma and his disciples, Rinzai and his disciples— the story is the same. It cannot be different because the relationship is the same, the phenomenon is the same. Rinzai was even more fortunate. What happened? When he asked his chief disciple, "Say something about Truth," what did the disciple do? You know?

You cannot even conceive. He slapped the Master! And the Master laughed and he said, "Right, you did well, because how can one answer when the very question is wrong?"

And this is the most fortunate Master! How can you answer a question when the very question is wrong? The disciple is saying, "Don't be foolish, don't play games with me, don't try to put me in a puzzle, don't throw me in illogical nonsense! Because if I answer it will be wrong, and if I don't answer, that will also be wrong—because a Master is asking. If I answer it will be wrong, because the very nature of Truth is such that it cannot be expressed. If I don't answer, that will be impolite—a Master is asking, I have to answer." This is what he said when he slapped the Master. And Rinzai laughed and he said, "Right! When a disciple can slap the Master, he has become a Master in his own right. Now you go and teach others."

"Jesus said: I am not thy Master, because thou hast drunk, thou hast become drunk from the bubbling spring which I have measured out."

You are all still drunkards, drunk with the same madness of the mind!

Mind is the source of all madness—there can be degrees, but everyone who has a mind is more or less mad. Mind is equivalent to madness. You may not be too much, you may be just lukewarm mad, so you are not boiling, not evaporating—nobody is thinking of sending you to the madhouse. You are just lukewarm mad, workably mad; you can work, you can move around and keep your madness inside. A man goes beyond madness only when he goes beyond mind. That is why Jesus says you are drunk.

"...thou hast become drunk from the bubbling spring which I have measured out. All three of you are speaking from the mind. You have not looked at me, because when you look there is no mind."

Don't carry a mind to a Master. It is stupidity, because if you carry a mind to a Master, you are not going nearer to him. You will not attain to *satsang*, you will not be in his presence; you will be filled with your mind, you will be drunk with your mind. When he is there you will be thinking, chattering. Inside, the mind will go round and round and round and will create a wall, and it will be impossible for Jesus to penetrate you.

And, *"He took Thomas,"* because he was the nearest, the best, "he *withdrew* into loneliness and *he spoke three words to him."*

"Now when Thomas came to his companions, they asked him: What did Jesus say to thee?"

He had to work with the second best, the best was not available. Thomas was chosen, he took him and said three words to him.

"Now when Thomas came to his companions, they asked him: What did Jesus say to thee?" They are still interested in what Jesus says, not in what Jesus is. They are still interested in knowledge, words, not interested in the being.

"Thomas said to them: If I tell you one of the words he said to me, you will take up stones and throw at me; and fire will come from the stones and burn you up."

This is very mysterious. Those three words have not been recorded, and Thomas never told the other disciples what those three words were. But he gives indications—because when you are not ready, only indications can be given; when you are not ready, only hints can be given. If you are *really* an inquirer, through the hints you will reach the secret. The final secret cannot be given, you have to be ready for it. The more ready you are, the more it becomes revealed. He gives hints, so first try to understand the hints.

"If I tell you one of the words he said to me, you will take up stones and throw at me; and fire will come from the stones and burn you up."

One thing he says : "If I say even a single word," Jesus has said three, but, "If I say even a single word, you will immediately start to throw stones at me." What does he mean?

Man lives in lies, every man, because lies are very convenient, comfortable. Truth is hard, inconvenient, uncomfortable. Lying is just like going down—you go easily, with dancing feet. Truth is going high, up—it is difficult, arduous, you perspire, it is not comfortable. Lies are convenient, comfortable, because you can make them, you can invent them. You can invent your own lie to fit you, but you cannot invent truth. This is the problem, the rub.

You can invent lies: you just go to a tailor and he makes a garment for you; you can make lies for yourself like garments, lies that fit you. But truth is not going to fit you, you cannot invent it, you will have to fit with the truth—you will have to cut yourself. Truth cannot be cut like a garment; to fit truth, *you* will have to change. Lies are beautiful because you need not change—you simply change the lie, and it fits you. It is very cosy, it clings to you, it never forces you to change, you can remain static, stagnant.

The lie is always with you, never against you. And truth—truth does not bother: if you want to be true, you have to change yourself. Truth cannot be invented, it has to be discovered—it is already there. That is why man lives in lies, because you can invent your own lies.

Each country has its own lies, each race has its own lies, each religion, church, temple, *gurudwara* has its own lies. And they are very cosy, they cling to you—they protect you from the truth. That is why whenever truth is asserted, you will start throwing stones at the man who asserts it: because if he is true, your whole life is false. That's very difficult to accept—you have invested so much in it, you have lived for it. Your dreams are all that you have got, your lies are all that you have got, and somebody comes and throws a truth...? So there are only two possibilities: either you are ready to collapse completely, or you throw stones at this man, because throwing stones at this man will not allow his truth to shatter your lies—you can move again in your lies.

Psychologists have come to understand that man cannot live without lies. And as far as ninety-nine percent of people are concerned, they are right; the one percent remaining we can leave —they are exceptional. Freud, Jung, Adler, all three great discoverers of the mind of man, are absolutely in agreement on one thing: that as man is, he cannot live without lies, he needs lies; they are a basic necessity like food, even more basic. You can live without food for three months, you cannot live without lies for even three seconds—it is like breathing.

See what type of lies you live in! And whenever somebody

supports your lie and makes it appear to be a truth, you bow down to him. You are afraid of death, so you believe in the immortality of the soul. That is a lie for you—you don't know anything, not even the ABC about the soul; you don't know whether the soul exists or not, but you believe in its immortality. And when somebody argues and proves that the soul is immortal, you bow down to him, you pay respect and you say, "Here is a man who has known!" What has he done? He has simply supported your lie; now he has given more life to your lie. You remain the same: you don't know what the soul is, you never *bothered* to know it. But the lie helps you to live. Then you are not afraid of death because there is no death—the soul is immortal.

Hence, a very strange phenomenon has happened: this country, India, is the most cowardly on earth. Otherwise, how was it possible to make such a vast country a slave for hundreds of years? And to small races like the English, not even equal to a province! Fifty *crore* (five hundred million) people being enslaved by three *crore* (thirty million) people—looks illogical. But whosoever came— Huns, Moghuls, Turks, the English—whosoever came, India was always ready to be a slave. Why so much cowardice? And these people are the "Knowers of the Self," and they say that they have the root knowledge and they know that the soul is immortal!

If the soul is immortal, how can you be a coward? If the soul is immortal then nobody can be braver than you, because nothing is going to die; even when somebody is murdering you, you will not be afraid, because nothing is going to die. But this is not the thing— just the contrary is the thing: the soul is immortal, and yet Indians are the greatest cowards. Really, because they are cowards they hide their cowardice in the philosophy of the immortality of the soul. This immortality is not their knowledge. Buddha may have known, Yajnavalk may have known, but this is not a knowledge which can be transferred.

Self-knowledge remains individual. No country can possess it, it cannot become a heritage, it is not a tradition. A man knows and when that man dies that knowledge disappears from the world. It has to be discovered again and again and again, you cannot make it a possession.

This country is cowardly, but they have a beautiful theory. They are afraid of death, you cannot imagine how very much afraid of death they are. Even to conquer Everest, foreigners have to come. Indians won't bother because everybody will say, "What foolishness are you going to do? And what are you going to get there? Why put yourself in danger?" Indians are always afraid of dangers; wherever there is danger, they will not move. And these people think that they know that the soul is immortal. No, that is a lie! Not that it is not true—for *you* it is a lie, and you are protecting your cowardice by it.

Look! India is a phenomenon—look around. You cannot find such a greedy people, miserly people, anywhere in the world. And they call the whole world materialist—a beautiful trick of the mind. They are spiritualists and the whole world is materialist; whenever they look at a Western man, deep down they say, "You materialists!" And you cannot find a more materialistic man than the Indian. He lives for money, is greedy for possessions; it is impossible for him to give anything, he has forgotten how to give, he clings to everything. But he calls the whole world materialist, "And we are spiritualists," a lie, a patent lie, but repeated so many times it looks like truth. It is false.

Everybody invents his private lie also. These are public lies, then you invent your private lies, and you live in them. They help you in a certain way: you may be a coward, but you think yourself a brave man, and you try to act like a brave man. That helps a little, because really, if you are a coward and you feel that you are a coward you will stop moving in life. You will say, "I am a coward"; you will be paralyzed.

So psychologists say that without lies man cannot live—even a coward moves into life. And this happens almost always: whatsoever you are, you will create the opposite lie, and you will over-act it to make others believe and to make yourself believe. You will overact it—a coward will overact: he will become a daredevil, but he is a coward, otherwise there will be no overacting. He may move into danger even where there is no need to move, just to show others and to convince himself that, "I am not a coward." But deep down he is afraid of his cowardice, afraid. So he projects the opposite.

A greedy man can renounce the world, become naked, just to

convince himself that, "I am not greedy." But this is not going to
help. This is a lie. Just by throwing clothes and leaving the house,
you cannot leave greed, because greed is not outside. It is not part
of the house, it is not part of your treasures, it is part of *you*.
Wherever you go—naked or in clothes—makes no difference. Now
greed is trying to hide itself by overacting, by moving to the opposite
extreme of renunciation.

A man who is without greed will be without renunciation, because
he doesn't need to overact. A man who is without fear will be without so-called bravery, because he doesn't need to overact. A man
who has come to understand his being will be neither on this extreme
nor the other. He will be balanced, his life will be a balance.

What do you think? A Buddha is moving and a snake comes.
What will he do? He will simply jump out of the way! What will
you call him? A coward or a brave man? He is just a sensitive man,
a man of understanding. You will like that man who remains there,
doesn't bother what the snake is doing—the snake even bites him
and he remains there—you will call that man brave. But he is
foolish, not brave. And deep down, he must be a coward; to hide
this cowardice he remains there.

But if you see Buddha jumping out of the way of the snake, you
will feel, "What type of man have I been following? This is a
coward!" He is *not* a coward. When a snake is there, one has to
move out of the way. This is simple intelligence. It is just as if somebody is honking his horn and you are standing in the middle of the
road and you think you are a brave man. You are simply stupid!
And standing there, whom are you convincing? Yourself, deep
down, that "I am a brave man."

A man of understanding never moves to the opposite—he moves
with understanding. Whatsoever the situation that arises, whatsoever the situation is, he responds with his awareness; he is neither
brave nor a coward. You are either a coward or brave, but the
other is hiding there: even a cowardly man can become brave in
certain situations, even a brave man proves to be a coward in
certain other situations.

Look at this problem: the bravest man when he comes home,
becomes a coward—even a Napoleon before Josephine is a coward.
Why does it happen that a husband who is such a great fighter

in the world, in competition, in the market, before his poor wife simply becomes a coward? What happens? And don't think that this is about others, that you are not the man—*every* husband is henpecked! This seems an exaggerated statement. It is not, because out of sheer necessity, every husband has to be henpecked: the whole day he is brave, so at home he wants to relax from the bravery; and if even at home he is not relaxed, then where will he find the relaxation? So the moment he enters his home, he puts aside his armour.

He has been brave in the market, fighting continuously—competition, enemies. There is war, a continuous war in the world; the whole day he fights. When he comes home he is tired of fighting, tired of bravery—you cannot be brave twenty-four hours a day. Remember, nobody can be anything twenty-four hours a day—you can only be alert twenty-four hours a day. Except that everything moves with the opposite.

You come home, you are tired, you want rest; now you cannot fight—you have been fighting the whole day. And what has your wife been doing the whole day? She has no competition, she has no war going on around her; she is just in the home, protected; the whole day she has been resting. In a way, there was no point during the whole day where she could show her bravery. So she is tired of being a coward, just a wife. You come home—she is ready. She will jump on you!

Once it happened: There was a lion-tamer, a very brave man. But he was always afraid of his tiny wife. And whenever he was late there was trouble. One night with friends, he forgot completely, drank too much, and then by midnight he became aware, remembered that he had a wife and a home. And to go back home now would be very difficult, so where to hide? Not finding any place—because it was a small town and if he went to any hotel, his wife would come and catch hold of him—not finding any place open, he went to the lions' cage in the zoo where he was a tamer. The key was with him, he opened the door: six big ferocious lions in the cage! He slept—he used a lion's back as a pillow.

His wife searched all over the town. In the early morning, not finding him anywhere, she went to the place where he was working as a lion-tamer. He was sleeping, fast asleep, snoring. She poked the man inside the cage with her umbrella and said, "YOU COWARD! Come out, and I'll show you!"

This is bound to happen: if you choose one extreme, the other follows you. You may be a brave man in one place, but you will be a coward somewhere else. It has to be so, because cowardice will be a relaxation. So that is why I say, out of sheer necessity, a husband has to be henpecked. There is only one way that a husband is not henpecked: if he functions as a wife at the house, and the wife goes out and works. Then he is not henpecked, because then he is no longer a husband—he is really a wife, and the wife is the husband.

Every extreme hides the other in it, and you have to show it somewhere. Otherwise it will be too burdensome, it will be impossible to live under it. Only intelligence, awareness, what Buddhists have called *prajnyan*, a meditative state which is of balance, is always relaxed. A state of awareness is just like a cat: even when she is asleep, she is alert. Just a little sound in the surroundings, and she will jump on her feet, fresh, alert, awake. The mind of someone who has remained in the middle, balanced, even if he is asleep, remains alert. There is no relaxation, because relaxation is not needed—he has never been tense, he has never been a brave man nor a cowardly man. He has understood both and gone beyond.

Man lives in lies. He has to because he is trying not to accept the whole of his being, only part is accepted. Then what to do about the other part? He has to create some lie to hide it.

"Thomas said to them: If I tell you one of the words he said to me, you will take up stones and throw at me..."

Truth has always been welcomed that way. It is not easy to assert truth: those who listen to it will become your enemies, they will start throwing stones. They are not really against you, they are only protecting themselves, their lies: "...you will take up stones and throw at me..."

And then he says a very beautiful thing: "...and fire will come from the stones and burn you up."

"You will throw stones at me, you will throw stones at the Truth —but from the stones a fire will come up and burn *you*."

You cannot burn Truth, you cannot crucify Truth. You crucified Jesus. That is why I was saying yesterday that when Jesus was crucified by the Jews, he was not crucified—they crucified themselves. And the fire has been burning since then, and they avoid and they escape from the fire—but it follows. You can throw stones, but Truth is never *hurt*.

The moment you throw stones at the Truth, it means that *you* will be hurt finally, you will burn; a fire will come out of your own stones. And this is the whole history of the Jews: for twenty centuries continuously, they have been burning. And I am not saying that those who have been torturing them are right. No! I am not a supporter of Hitler, or others who have been burning and destroying Jews; no, they are not doing right. The Jews are carrying their wound within themselves—they create their Hitlers. This will look very, very difficult to understand.

A guilty man moves around to find someone who will punish him. When nobody is punishing him, he feels living more difficult. When someone punishes him, he feels at ease. Have you watched children? If you don't punish them, they will punish themselves; they will slap their own faces—that relaxes them. A child has done something wrong and he looks to see whether father or mother or somebody has come to know or not, he is in search of that. If they have come to know, they can beat the child, and the child is at ease because now he has been punished. Finished! The account is closed; he did wrong and he has been punished. But if nobody knows, then he is in difficulty: something remains incomplete. He will move into a corner and slap his own face. Then he is at ease.

That is what is happening with people who move into austerities: they have done something wrong—whether it is wrong or not is not the question, they *think* they have done something wrong— then they go on punishing themselves. You think they are moving into a deep *tapascharya*, austerity, they are great saints. They are simply guilty people punishing themselves. They may fast, they may beat their own chests; they may even burn themselves alive, but they are simply guilty children, immature, punishing themselves; they have done something wrong, and they want to create the balance. They want to say to God, "I have punished myself enough, now You need not punish me." This is what Jews have been doing. This is one of the very deepest complexities of the human mind.

Jews are always in search of their Adolf Hitlers, somebody who can kill them—then they feel at ease. When nobody bothers about them, then they are uneasy, the guilt follows. When you throw stones at Truth this is bound to happen, and even after twenty centuries of suffering, the Jews have not confessed that they did wrong. No! Jesus is still unaccepted, they go on behaving as if Jesus never existed; Jesus is still not part of them. And I tell you, unless they reclaim Jesus they will remain in trouble. And trouble is not being created by others—they seek it. They are guilty people, and their guilt is very great.

Can you conceive of anything more criminal than to crucify a Buddha, to crucify a Jesus, to crucify a Krishna? Jesus who was to be followed and worshipped, Jesus who was to be followed and lived—and you did just the opposite. Jesus who should have become your life, very life, your throbbing heart—you did just the opposite: you killed him! Rather than making him your life, you destroyed his life. This wound will follow the Jews. It is difficult to get rid of it—unless they reclaim Jesus.

The Hindus are better. That is why they are less guilt-ridden: they never killed Buddha. Buddha was more dangerous than Jesus: he tore up the whole of Hinduism from its very roots. Jesus said, "I have come not to destroy the tradition, but to fulfill it." Never Buddha! He said directly, "I have come to uproot the whole tradition. All the Vedas are rubbish!" But Hindus never killed him, that is why Hindus could live without guilt. Not only did they not kill him—they are very clever and prudent people—they even made him an *avatar*. They accepted him—just a little gone astray, but nothing much to bother about. They integrated him into the tradition. They say, "He is our tenth *avatar*," and they created a story around him—that is why I say they are very clever and prudent people.

No other race is so clever, it has to be, because Hindus are the oldest, most wise. Experience has taught them much: that if you crucify Buddha, you will never be free of him because he will follow you, haunt you, so don't crucify—neglect. But even if you neglect him, something of you will again and again look back. The man is there, so it is better to accept him—and they accept him in such a rejecting way! This is prudence.

They created a story: God created Hell and Heaven, but for millions of years nobody reached Hell, because nobody was sinning. Everybody was religious, righteous; everybody was going to Heaven. Then the Devil went to God and said, "Why, what have you created Hell for? This is useless. Nobody comes, and I am tired of waiting and waiting. So *do something*—otherwise close it down!"

God said, "Wait, I will send a man, Gautam Buddha, to the world. He will confuse people. And when people are confused they go astray, they will start entering into Hell." And since then, Hell has been filled to overflowing. But Hindus accepted Buddha as an *avatar* sent by God—and they rejected him in a very subtle way. They have never been guilty.

The Jews have remained guilty; the wound follows them and they are still not reclaiming Jesus. They should reclaim him— he was a Jew: born a Jew, lived a Jew, died a Jew; he was never a Christian—they can reclaim him. And no other Jew has come of that calibre. Many great Jews have been born, even in this century. The greatest in this century have been Jews—Jews are people of very great potential: Freud is a Jew, Marx is a Jew, Einstein is a Jew—all the three great men who have created this whole century. But nothing to compare with Jesus! They have rejected the greatest of the Jews. Once they reclaim him, they will be at ease, their wound will heal. They will be healthy and whole, and then there will be no need for Adolf Hitlers.

They create their Hitlers, and when I say this to you, you also remember: whenever you feel guilty, you create the punisher. You seek for punishment, because the punishment will make you guilt-free, then you can come to rest. Don't feel guilty, otherwise you will seek punishment.

Enjoy life in its 'totalness', otherwise you will feel guilty. Accept

life as it is, and be thankful for it as it is; have a deep gratitude—
that is what makes a religious man. And once you accept the
Whole, you become whole. All divisions disappear, a deep silence
ascends in you... you are filled with the unknown; because when
you are whole, the unknown knocks at your door.

Thirteenth Discourse

2nd September 1974, Poona, India

THE THIRTEENTH SAYING

Jesus said:
If those who lead you say to you:
'See, the Kingdom is in heaven,'
then the birds of Heaven will precede you.

If they say to you:
'It is in the sea,'
then the fish will precede you.

But the Kingdom is within you
and it is without you.

If you will know yourselves,
then you will be known
and you will know
that you are the sons of the Living Father.

But if you do not know yourselves,
then you are in poverty
and you are poverty.

The Kingdom of God has been preached as if it is always somewhere else: in time, in space, but always somewhere else—not
here and now. Why has this happened? Why is the Kingdom of
God not here and now? Why in the future, or why somewhere else?

It is because of the human mind. The human mind disappears
in the present. It lives in the future, in the hope, in the promise
of the future; it moves through desire. Desire needs time, desire
cannot exist if there is no time. If suddenly you come to a moment
where you realize that time has disappeared, that now there is no
time, no tomorrow, what will happen to your desire? It cannot
move, it disappears with time.

Basically time is not a physical phenomenon, it is psychological.
Time is not there outside you, it is the very functioning of your
mind that creates time. A Jesus lives without time, you live in
time. Hence, all the Buddhas—*Jesus is a Buddha*, an Enlightened
person—have been emphasizing, "Be desireless! Then suddenly
the gates of Heaven are open for you." But to be desireless you
have to be here and now, because then there is no bridge to move
into the future; then there is no bridge to move anywhere. Desire
is the bridge.

Mind needs time, mind cannot exist without time. The more
time you have, the more ground mind has to play, to fool around.
Then it can make many, many desires and dreams and live in those
desires and dreams. Priests have always been talking as if Heaven
were in the future, because only the future can be understood by

the mind, and only because of that future can you be exploited—
and you also feel at ease.

I have heard that in one church the minister was praising the
Kingdom of God and he said, "There are streets of gold and fields
of emeralds!" And he praised as much as he could and then he
asked, invited: "Who would like to go there?" All the hands were
raised except one old man's. He couldn't believe it, the minister.
Why has this old man not raised his hand? He should be the first
because he is just nearing death. Then he condemned and painted
a picture of Hell, with all its ugliness, torture, pain, suffering, the
fire. Again he challenged: "Now, who would like to go to the
Kingdom of God, to Heaven?" All hands were raised—but that
old man was still sitting without raising his hand. The minister
was puzzled. He asked that old man, "Don't you hear me? Are
you deaf? You would not like to go to the Kingdom of God,
to Heaven?"

The man said, "Eventually, yes. But the way you are carrying on,
it seems you want to carry a load right now. Eventually yes, but
right now, no!"

If you are told, "The Kingdom of God is here and now," you are
not ready. Many are the desires to be fulfilled before you can leave;
many many things have to be done before you would think of
entering the Kingdom of God. You are still dreaming and not
ready to be awake, you need time. The priest appeals to you,
but not a Buddha, not a Jesus, because Jesus talks in terms of
no-time. He makes an uneasy friend. To live with Jesus is to live
in constant discomfort. He doesn't allow you the convenience of
dreaming, he doesn't allow you time, future—he says that there
is no tomorrow.

Tomorrow helps in another way: as you are, right now, you
don't accept yourself, you know you are not worthy. You know
that as you are, even you yourself cannot accept yourself. How
is God going to accept you? No, it is impossible! You cannot
conceive of it. You have condemned yourself. You are so guilty
that how can God accept you? It is impossible. Right now, if the
Kingdom opens, if the door invites you, you will not be able to
have that much courage to enter. You need a little time to
transform yourself, you need a little time to be good, you need

a little time to be a saintly man. You need a little time to do many things so that your being becomes acceptable, so that even God can love you. Many desires are there—they need time. And many 'shoulds' are waiting—they need time.

The whole morality of the world—forms differ, but the essential base is the same—has been condemning you: you are wrong, something has to be done, you have to be put right, you have to be polished, you have to be made worthy. So if somebody says, "The door is open right now," you feel uncomfortable. Then you cannot enter. But if he says, "It is in the future," then there is time enough. You are at ease, you can work it out, you will polish yourself. You can create an image, an ideal, and you will follow that ideal so some day or other you will become a saint. And this is the trick of the mind: if you can postpone, the mind remains the same; to remain the same, the mind wants to postpone. Not to change, ideals are needed; not to take the jump, time is needed so that you can postpone.

Postponing is the base of your continuity as you are. If this house is on fire you will not postpone, you will simply jump out. You will not even ask, "Where is the door? Where are the steps? From where to go?" You will not seek a teacher, a guide—you will simply jump out. *Anywhere* will be the door! Wherever you are, from *there* the journey starts out. And you will not say, "Am I really worthy to be saved? Am I *worthwhile*?" No! All these questions will not arise.

Philosophy is for luxurious moments when you can ask questions and get answers and go on postponing. But when there is danger you put aside all philosophy. Have you observed, whenever you are in danger you put aside your mind? You don't think at all, there is not enough time to think—the house is on fire, you jump! And when you are out, then you can sit under a tree and think again about what has happened. But in the moment when danger is there, when death is there, time is no more. You simply have to *act*, there is *no* gap to think; you have to act, only *action* can save you.

Time is postponement, and you would like to postpone for millions of reasons. One is: many things are yet unfulfilled—you have not tasted this world. You have been in this world millions of times, you have tasted it in millions of ways, but still the hunger remains, the thirst is there. Not because there was not enough time. For the whole past you have been here—and the whole past means eternity, it is beginningless—since eternity you have been here, acting in millions of ways, fulfilling millions of desires, and yet you are still hungry and thirsty. You think more time is needed? More than enough you have had already! Not more time, but under-standing, awareness is needed that the very nature of desire is to remain unfulfilled.

However much time is given, even many eternities, the desire will remain unfulfilled. It is the very *nature* of desire that it remains unfulfilled. It will arise again and again, and the more you try to fulfill it, the more it will arise; you are simply feeding the desire when you think you are fulfilling it. You move into sex, you think you are fulfilling it—you are simply feeding the desire. Tomorrow it will come back even more greedy, even more full of lust, with even more expectations. You feed it again, tomorrow it will knock at your door again, with more madness, with more hope—and every day it will grow. As you experience it, you feel more and more hungry. You are feeding it, the fulfillment is not there.

And this is so with every desire. Look at ordinary desires, very ordinary ones: you take food, the hunger disappears, but it disappears only to come back again. Can hunger disappear forever through food? Is there any possibility that just by taking food, hunger will disappear forever? You are thirsty, you drink water—do you think the thirst is going to disappear forever? No, that is not the *nature* of desire. And these are ordinary desires that you can understand. They are repetitive, and the more you repeat, the more you are hypnotized, because repetition is hypnosis: you did it yesterday, you are doing it today, you are hoping to do it tomorrow; you are repeating the desire. And the more you repeat it, the more you get into it.

For millions of lives you have desired in *many* ways, and you are born in that particular way that you desire. And you fulfill it: a man who wants to have sex like a dog will be born like a dog; a man who is greedy like a pig will be born like a pig, so that he can fulfill his desire. You have been born in every possible way, because for eternity you have existed—like a tree, like a bird, like an animal.... This is what Hindus call *yonis*. They say you have been born through millions of wombs, your desire has taken many forms, and you have tried through every possible dimension.

Nothing has happened up to now, nothing is ever going to happen, because the very nature of desire is to remain unfulfilled. If you understand this then the future is not needed—then you can remain here and now. And when the future drops, desire drops.

Try to understand from another direction: you have tried in every way to transform yourself—you don't remember your past lives, but you know this life—you have done everything to transform yourself. Are you even a little bit transformed? Even a little bit, I say? Are you even a little bit transformed? Or do you simply remain the old—a little polished here, a little polished there, a little modified here or there—but is there really any change? Has any mutation happened to you? And if it has not happened up to now, what reason is there to think it is going to happen in the future? And if you go on living the same way you have lived, postponing, then it is not going to happen ever. Because postponing is a trick of the mind *not* to allow transformation to happen.

This is the deepest trick, and one has to understand it. Why do you postpone for tomorrow? Because you don't want to do it now, right now. You play a logical game: you say, "Right now it is difficult, but tomorrow it will be simple." But every tomorrow comes as today, and when tomorrow comes again it will be today and you will say, "Right now it is difficult, but tomorrow I will do it!" This is the way of the mind to feel at ease—and tomorrow never comes.

Postponing is not the way of transformation. Up to now you have been postponing, been postponing again and again. Each moment you have been postponing, and that is why you have remained the same. Understand this: transformation is *this* moment, because it needs no effort, it is an awakening. It is not a question of modification, it is not a question of doing something with yourself. As you are, you are perfect; as you are, you are Divine; as you are, you lack nothing at all—simply awakening is needed. Just come out of your dreaming and your sleep, just open your eyes and see the fact, and the fact transforms: suddenly, you are no more the past!

When you drop the future, the past is dropped immediately. This is one of the fundamental laws of life: if you can drop the future, the past drops immediately because it cannot remain there. It is just like making a bridge on a river. The bridge needs two banks to exist. If one bank disappears, the other bank alone cannot support the bridge—the bridge falls, everything disappears. The past and the future are the two banks, and between these two you have made a bridge of desire. You are always going somewhere, *always* going somewhere. If you are not reaching, then the mind says, "Move fast!"

This is why the whole modern trend is for speed. The mind says, "You are not reaching because your speed is not great enough. The goal is just there, you can see it is attainable tomorrow, or the day after tomorrow at the most; the goal is there, you can see it on the horizon. Your speed is not great enough—move fast, run! Create new mechanisms to help speed and you will reach."

We have reached the moon because of this logic—and we have not achieved any goal. Speed goes on becoming faster and faster and faster; sooner or later we will be moving with the speed of light, right now we are moving with the speed of sound. The more speed, the more lost you will be, because then it will be very difficult to come back home. Right now, you cannot go very far away; the more speed, the more difficult to come home.

This is why self-knowledge has become almost impossible in this age, the age of speed. Buddha realized himself easily, Jesus realized himself easily, because they lived in the age of no speed—they simply walked. The bullock cart was the fastest thing possible, and you can walk faster than a bullock cart; they walked on the earth. We are flying in the skies, we have penetrated space, and the faster we move, the more difficult it becomes to come back home.

I have heard, once it happened: Two beggars found a motorcycle on the street—somebody had forgotten to take the key with him. The motorcycle was there with a side-car, so one tramp jumped on the motorcycle, the other in the side-car, and they sped away bound for the next town. After fifteen minutes the man who was driving looked at his friend. The friend's face was absolutely red, as if he had gone mad, or as if he were dying. He asked, "What is the matter?" The other said, "Slow down a little, because this thing has no bottom, and I have been running all the way!"

This thing desire has no bottom. You are dying because you have been running all the way, and faster and faster and faster and this thing has no bottom. Desire has no bottom, that is why it cannot be fulfilled. If you try to fill a pot with water and it has no bottom, when will you be able to fill it? It is impossible! Why are you not able to fill this bottomless pot of desire? You have never looked to see whether it has a bottom or not—you simply jumped. And you have been running so fast that there is no gap to stop and have a look to see what is happening.

All the priests exploited this. But Jesus is not a priest—you cannot find a man more anti-priest than Jesus. A real religious man is never a priest, he cannot be, because the priest is exploiting your weaknesses. A real religious man, a Master, wants to make you stronger. And a priest is just a cunning man who knows what your weakness is. The weakness is to look to the future, to postpone: somewhere, eventually, you will enter into the Kingdom of God— but not right now. Many other more important things have to be done, many more important desires have to be fulfilled. God is always the last item on your list, and the list is infinite. He is not going to get any chance. He is the last item.

Now look at these words of Jesus.

"If those who lead you say to you: 'See, the Kingdom is in heaven,'" not here, somewhere high in the skies, somewhere far away; the Kingdom of God is somewhere distant, very far away, *"then the birds of Heaven will precede you."* They will reach before you, then you will be at a loss. Jesus is joking, he is saying: "Then don't hope, because the birds of Heaven will reach before you!"

"If they say to you: 'It is in the sea,' then the fish will precede you." And they will reach before you, you will miss.

About whom is Jesus talking? He is talking about the priests. The priests are the enemies of religion, but they have become the managers. They manage everywhere, and then they don't allow a Jesus-like person to enter their temples.

There is a beautiful story in Dostoyevsky's *Brothers Karamazov*. After eighteen hundred years Jesus thought: "Now I must go and visit the earth again, because after eighteen hundred years of

Christianity, now the earth may be ready to receive me. Now, they will not reject me as they did before, because when I went there before there was not a single Christian, I was a stranger. Now, half the earth is Christian; millions of churches and priests continuously preaching Jesus' word. Now I am going to be received, welcomed; all the doors will be open to me. Now is the time! I should not have gone before—that was not the right time."

He came again, on a Sunday morning, of course, because it is difficult to find who is a Christian or not if you come on other weekdays. It is impossible, everybody is the same! Only on Sunday can you distinguish who is a Christian, because religion is a Sunday affair. It is not concerned with life, it is just a ritual to be done, a formality to be fulfilled—without any heart in it. And he reached his village, where he had come eighteen hundred years before: Bethlehem. He stood in the market place, a little apprehensive because people looked at him and nobody recognized him, and they were coming in and going out of the church. And then a few people gathered around him and they started telling him, "You look just like Jesus—you have done a good act, you are a good actor!"

Jesus said, "I am not an actor. I am the real Jesus".

So they started laughing and they said, "If you are the real Jesus, then escape before the priest comes out. Otherwise you are *bound* to get into trouble." Then small urchins started throwing stones and people started laughing: "The real Jesus has come, the King of the Jews! This is the man they crucified—he is resurrected!"

And they were joking and laughing, and Jesus felt very much, because these were *his* people: they were no longer Jews, they were Christians; they followed him, and even they could not recognize him. But he waited, hoping, "At least my priest will recognize me. These may be foolish people, ignorant—but my priest *knows.*"

And then came the priest. People stopped laughing, just out of respect for the priest. They made way for him, the crowd allowed him to go in, they bowed down in deep respect. Jesus laughed in his heart: "They have not bowed down to me, they have not given me any respect, but they respect the priest. At least that is a good sign, because he is *my* priest. Through him they will recognize me.

They recognize me through him, not directly, because they are blind and they cannot see."

And then the priest looked at him and said, "Come down, you ruffian! What do you think you are doing? Insulting our God?"

Jesus said, "Can't you recognize me?"

The priest collared him and said, "I recognize you well. Come and follow me." He took him into the church and locked him into a cell. Jesus was very puzzled: "What is going to happen? Are my own people going to crucify me again?"

And then in the night, the priest came with a small candle in his hand and unlocked the door. He locked the door from the inside, bowed down, touched Jesus' feet and said, "I recognize you well! But not in the market place, not before the worshippers, because you are an old troublemaker. Somehow we have managed everything well, but you will disturb things. Now everything is smooth, Christianity is established: half the earth we have converted, the other half sooner or later will be converted. You just wait there, you need not come here! And we are doing so well—you could not convert a single man when you were here—we have managed so well, you should be thankful to us.

"And we can recognize you when there is nobody, but we cannot recognize you before others because you are anti-priest, anti-church, you are anti-establishment. And if you insist, then we will have to crucify you again. We can worship you when you are not present because that doesn't disturb anybody. Everything is smooth, moving well—look how we have managed! Half the earth converted, millions of churches and priests preaching your word. You should be satisfied. So escape immediately from here, and don't come again. Whatsoever you want to do, we are the agents here and you can do it through us. Directly, you cannot be allowed to move among the masses. You are dangerous!"

This priest is stating one of the basic truths: that the priest cannot be religious. He may be a priest of Buddha but he is against Buddha. He works for him, or appears to; he quotes his words, or appears to. But if Buddha comes he will stand between you and the Buddha and won't allow you in, because a Buddha, a Jesus, is always rebellious, he is never conformist. He can create a revolution, he cannot create an establishment.

When Jesus says: "If those who lead you say to you..." he is indicating towards the priests "...'See, the Kingdom is in heaven,' then the birds of Heaven will precede you. If they say to you: 'It is in the sea,' then the fish will precede you." And the priests always say it is somewhere else.

India is the oldest land of the priests. Nowhere has such a priesthood come into existence as in India—it became a caste, *Brahmins*, they are the priests. They secluded themselves totally from the society, they made everything secret, their language was not allowed to be known by everyone. Not everyone was educated in their ways, because when people are educated and they can read the scriptures, it is difficult to hide the truth from them. Only the priest was allowed into the innermost shrine of knowledge— nobody else.

These *Brahmins* ruled this country for thousands of years. First they were saying that God was in the Himalayas, because the Himalayas were unapproachable. But, by and by, people approached the Himalayas and they found no God there. So the *Brahmins* said, "These are not the Himalayas we were talking about, these are just a copy of the real Himalayas which exist in Heaven. These are just a reflection—you will not find God in the reflection. The real *Kailash*, the real Himalayas, is in the other world." Then their gods moved to the planets, to the moon, to the sun.

When man reached the moon for the first time, Hindus were very much disturbed, Jains were very much disturbed. The West does not know how much they were disturbed, because the West does not know how much was invested in the moon. In India there was much disturbance.

There is a priest, a very learned one, who has been trying to prove that the whole thing, this journey to the moon by man, was false. Why? Such a simple fact, it has happened! Why is he denying it? He has made a big institute. Many have donated *lakhs* (hundreds of thousands) of *rupees* to the institute to prove that this is sheer myth that man has reached the moon, to prove that nobody has reached the moon. Why? Because they have much investment there. If man has reached the moon and God is not there, then they must again shift His residence to somewhere else. And these scientists are going to reach everywhere. Now you cannot allow God to stay anywhere for a long period—wherever you say God is, man is going to reach there. Heaven was unapproachable, the sea was unapproachable. There are primitive religions which say that God lives in the sea, under the sea, and there are religions which say God lives in Heaven. But one thing is certain for the priest: *that God doesn't live here,* because if He lives here, then it is very difficult—then what need is there of a priest?

A priest is needed as a broker in between. He is an agent, a mediator. If God exists here, then you can encounter Him directly— why is the priest needed? The priest is needed because God is so distant, His voice cannot penetrate you directly. He gives His message to the priest, and then the priest interprets it for you. And through this interpretation he becomes powerful: he knows the keys, you are ignorant; he will lead you, he is the master, the *guru*—you are to be his followers.

The most cunning profession on the earth is that of the priest. Why the most cunning? Because he is exploiting a very innocent heart. A man who is seeking God, a man who is seeking purity, a man who is seeking Truth—that man he is exploiting. If you exploit a man who is seeking money, there is not much difference between you and him because he is also seeking money; there is not much difference. But if you exploit a man who was seeking Truth, this is cunning—the most cunning thing possible, the most evil thing possible. Priests should think and say and prove whether they are really the representatives of God, or not really representatives of God. If they are representatives of anything, they are representatives of the Devil. But they have taken over, they have become the managers.

Jesus said: "If those who lead you say to you: 'See, the Kingdom is in Heaven,' don't listen to them, otherwise you will miss that Kingdom forever and forever."

"But the Kingdom is within you..." it is not anywhere else, it is exactly where you are this moment *"...and it is without you."* It is within you and it is without you. It is within you like a center, it is without you like a circumference.

What is Jesus saying? Within plus without is the whole world, within plus without is the whole universe—nothing is left. Jesus is saying, "God is *this* universe, this whole existence. As it is, it is Divine. God has dissolved himself into His creation." He is not like a painter who paints, and then remains separate. He is like a dancer who dances, and becomes one with the dance—you cannot separate the dancer and the dance. You can separate a painter from the painting, you can separate poetry from the poet, but you cannot separate a dancer from the dance. That is why Hindus call their *Shiva, Nataraj,* the greatest dancer: because there is no separation, he is in the dance.

If you can understand the dance, you can understand the dancer; if you can catch hold of the dance, you have caught hold of the dancer. If you can love *this* world, you have loved Him. If you penetrate even into a flower, you will find Him. He is hidden here— and He is not hidden because He tries to hide Himself; He is hidden because you are not open. Otherwise, He is an open secret. He is everywhere, all around, within and without. The Kingdom is within you, it is without *you.*

"If you will know yourselves, then you will be known and you will know that you are the sons of the Living Father. But if you do not know yourselves, then you are in poverty and you are poverty."

Listen! The Kingdom is within you! Then all temples become useless, because you are the temple. Then you are the church! Then the Vatican becomes useless, then Rome is just a burden. Then there is no need for a Mecca and Medina, no need for a Girnar and Kashi. *You are the temple,* the live temple of God! He is within you. Then what is the need of a priest, a mediator? Then the whole profession loses meaning.

He exists in you, as you are. He has always been existing in you, as you are.

Somebody asked Rinzai, "I would like to be a Buddha myself. What to do?" Rinzai said, "If you seek, you will miss—because you are already the Buddha."

It is absurd: Buddha seeking, Buddha making efforts to become a Buddha! You cannot find God because He is not somewhere else, He is within you. And there you never look because all the priests say, "Look! There in heaven, far away He exists. Long is the journey, so the priest will be needed to help you."

Jesus cuts away the very ground of all churches, temples, priests, mediators. He says, "He is within you." But he also says a very rare and beautiful thing, he also says, "and He is without you."

There are three types of religions: one which says, "God is without." Hindus, Mohammedans, their insistence is that God is without. Then there is another type of religion which says, "God is within." Jains, Buddhists, they say you are God but they never say God is without, no. Jesus says, "God is within and without." This is the greatest synthesis, the highest synthesis possible. He is not choosing an extreme.

One extreme is: God is without. That is why Mohammedans are very much against you if you say, "I am God." They will kill you because this is one of the most evil assertions; it is *kufra*, blasphemy. Hence, they killed Mansoor, because in his ecstasy he danced and asserted, *"Anal Hak, Aham Brahmasmi,* I am God." This is blasphemy; a Mohammedan cannot tolerate it because God is without. At the most, you can come nearer and nearer to Him, but you can never become Him. How can a creature become the Creator? The creature remains a creature, and the Creator remains the Creator. They think this is disrespectful if you assert, "I am God." That means a creature, a slave, a created thing is asserting, "I am the Creator." This is blasphemy, it is irreligious.

Then against this pole there is Jainism. They say that God is within; your soul is the supreme God and there is no other God. They have moved to the other extreme, so they don't worship any God; worship has lost meaning for them, they cannot pray. Whom to pray to? And prayer is such a beautiful thing, but it has become meaningless.

Look at a Mohammedan in prayer. He is beautiful. He can pray because God is there. There is nothing like a Mohammedan praying. If you want to see prayer see a Mohammedan pray: he looks so innocent, so completely surrendered—but he is dangerous. If you assert that you are God, he will kill you, this man who was praying. Jains cannot pray, they cannot worship; for them the dimension of prayer and worship has simply disappeared. They can only meditate. Meditation is allowed because God is within; you just have to close your eyes and meditate.

Jesus reaches the peak of the synthesis. Here he asserts one of the greatest truths: that God is within and without. Prayer is possible, meditation is also possible; you can sing in ecstasy about the without, you can be silent in ecstasy about the within—He is everywhere. No need to drop prayer, no need to drop meditation. Nothing like meditation exists in the Mohammedan tradition; it cannot exist, only prayer is possible. Nothing exists in Jainism like prayer, only meditation exists. Both have moved to extremes.

Jesus remains balanced. He says: "God, the Kingdom of God, is within you and it is without you."

"If you will know yourselves, then you will be known."

This is the synthesis. If you know yourself, Jains will say you have known all. Finished ! There is nowhere further to move. Mohammedans cannot say you can know yourself; they can say you can know God and be filled with His grace. There is no possibility of self-knowledge, because self-knowledge will make you God. Only God knows Himself, not a creature. A man can know God, that is all. He can exist in His glory, he can be filled with His grace, His light; he can allow himself to move and float with the Divine force, but no self-knowledge is possible. Jains say only self-knowledge is possible; if you know yourself, you have known all that is to be known, nothing remains. But Jesus says: "If you will know yourselves, then you will be known."

This is very subtle. What does he mean when he says, "...then you will be known"? If you know yourself, the whole existence will know *you;* in your knowledge, the whole existence will look at you. Not only will you be looking at existence, the whole existence will also *respond,* because God is within and without.

When somebody comes to know himself, it is not only self-knowledge—the whole existence knows you. In your self-knowledge, you are known. God looks at you from every flower, every leaf, every rock—you don't feel you are alone in your self-knowledge. Really, until you know yourself, you are alone. When you know yourself, the whole existence knows you. Your knowledge is not a solitary act, it is not a solo thing, it is a symphony. When you know, everything knows you; when you recognize yourself, everything recognizes you —even this tree will be different, even this rock will be different, even a bird will react differently. Why? Because the same exists within and without.

One consciousness exists within and without. When you know yourself, the whole existence recognizes you, celebrates. And it should be so, because you are part of existence. The whole existence *must* celebrate your Ultimate Knowledge, because a part has become a knower, a part has become a Buddha, a part has become a Christ; through that part, the whole existence has reached a peak, a crescendo. The whole existence will be happy, the whole existence will flower and bloom in a different way. You will be recognized, you will be known!

You will not be alone in your self-knowledge—it is going to be a celebration of the Whole. This is the most beautiful thing Jesus asserted: existence celebrating your self-knowledge; the Whole blissful because one part has bloomed, reached its fulfillment.

"If you will know yourselves, then you will be known."

There is a deep tendency to be known, deeper than that for self-knowledge. You want to be known, a deep desire is there that everybody should know you. It may be moving in a wrong direction, you may be trying to get the attention of people through wrong ways, but deep down the desire has a seed, a very meaningful seed. It says that you will not be fulfilled unless the whole existence recognizes you, is happy with you.

You have a need to love, and you have a need to be loved. You have a need to know yourself, and you have a need to be known. A response is needed, otherwise the whole existence is dead; otherwise you alone have come to know, and the whole existence remains silent as if nothing has happened. A man has become a Christ and the whole existence remains unaware, inattentive, not bothering at all, not happy in any way, as if nothing has happened. How can this be so? The whole existence *must* recognize, because we are not strangers to this existence. This existence is a family, this existence exists as an interrelated phenomenon. One is Enlightened and his light fills all hearts, knowingly, unknowingly; everywhere there will be rejoicing, celebration.

This is why Jesus says:

"If you will know yourselves, then you will be known and you will know that you are the sons of the Living Father."

What have Christians been saying? Just the opposite. They say,

"Jesus Christ is the only begotten son of God." Their whole dogma moves around this thing "the only," because if all are the sons, then what is the speciality in Jesus? Then how is he unique? Then why should he be worshipped? Just to make Jesus special, and they have forgotten that they are going against Jesus.

Jesus says, "...and you will know that you are the sons of the Living Father."

Two things—one: everything that exists in this universe is son to the Whole, it has to be so. You are born in it, through it. The whole existence has been fathering you—or it would be even better if we could say, is mothering you. It would have been better to use the word 'mother' rather than 'father', but it was difficult because Jews have remained male chauvinists. It was difficult to say 'mother'.

There are male chauvinist countries, races: Germans call their country 'fatherland'—the only country which is known as 'fatherland'; every other country calls itself 'the motherland'. These Germans are dangerous people—why 'fatherland'? Man and his ego. Why should God be the father? Why should God not be the mother? Why should He be 'he' and not 'she'? Mother seems to be more relevant, because the father does not take much part in the creation of the son. At the most, he just triggers the thing, nothing else. And a father is disposable.

Even an ordinary injection can do; the work of the father can be done by a syringe, he is disposable. The whole creation comes through the mother: she carries the child for nine months; her blood, her whole being, moves into the child. You exist in the universe as if you exist in a womb.

There are people who have used 'mother' for God. They are more right, but just 'more right.' To be absolutely right is impossible because then God will be both father and mother. He cannot be male, He cannot be female, because there is no one who can trigger the thing. He is both: *Ardhanarishwar*, half-male, half-female; He is both, he and she.

But it depends. When Jesus was there, it would have been very difficult for him to say 'God the mother', because nobody would have understood. His audience was Jewish, and they believed in a very ferocious father God, very revengeful—you went against Him, and He would take revenge. A mother can never be revengeful, she is always forgiving, she is always understanding. A mother never insists on being obeyed, a father insists on being obeyed. The Ten Commandments cannot come from a mother, they can come only from a father. Commandments—the very word is ugly, as if he is a general and existence is something like a military camp—commandments! Then you disobey at your own responsibility and risk.

Jesus used the current language, but I know that he would have preferred 'mother'. A mother is more than a father: a mother exists at the center, a father at the periphery—but God is both. Remember this: I also use the word 'he' for Him, but always remember that whenever I use 'he' it is just for convenience; He is both, he and she.

"And...you are the sons of the Living Father."

Everybody is a son. This is not as logicians, sociologists, and psychologists will think—this is not anthropomorphism. It seems, appears, that to think of God as a father or a mother and to think about yourself as a son, you are projecting human relationships onto the cosmic, you are making the whole cosmic phenomenon a family affair; you are thinking in human terms. This is a condemnation.

Sociologists, psychologists, who say that this is anthropocentrism —that man thinks of himself as if he is in the center, and projects his own terms, feelings about everything—whenever they say this is anthropocentric, they are saying this is wrong. But they have not understood: it appears anthropocentric, it *has* to appear so, because whatsoever man says is *bound* to be human. Even an objective truth is going to be coloured by the person who asserts it. Even objectivity cannot be without the subjective; the subjective goes and colours it.

Even scientific truths are not objective: the man who discovered them has entered into them. There is no possibility of coming to the objective truth, because the knower will almost always colour it. All knowledge is personal. And whenever man says something, because man says it, it is going to be human. And no need to be apologetic about it—it is beautiful.

When Jesus says that we are all sons of God, this is just a symbol, a simile. What does he mean? He means that between the Creator and the created, the relationship is not mechanical, it is organic. The relationship is not just like a mechanic creating a machine—he is not a father because he remains aloof, out of it, detached. *This* is the meaning: God cannot be detached from you. He is just like your father, attached to you, moving through you, working through you, caring for you, loving you, searching for you, in every way creating a blissful world around you so that you can reach fulfillment.

When Jesus says, "God is the Father," he means all these things: that the universe cares about you, it helps you. Not only are you in search of God, God is also in search of you. The universe is not dead and detached, it responds with a loving heart. If you cry, it cries with you. If you laugh, it laughs with you. If you are in pain, the existence feels the pain. If you are happy, the whole existence feels happy with you. Between you and the existence there is a deep relationship. This is the emphasis: the relationship of a father to a son.

Even if the father dies, he hopes to live through the son; he will be somewhere in the son, the son has become just a new version of the father. That is the meaning: the son is just a rebirth of the father. That is why Jesus says again and again, "I and my Father are one." He means the son represents the Father—he is the Father. They are joined together; they are not two, they are one, the relationship is organic. And you need not feel alone.

Now the whole world feels an aloneness. Everybody feels a stranger, and everybody is in difficulty. And people come to me and they ask, "How to relate?" What has happened? This is a very new question—nobody ever asked two hundred years ago, "How to relate?" Now everybody asks, "How to relate?" Relationship has become very difficult. It is a logical consequence: if you cannot relate to the Whole, you cannot relate to anybody; if you can relate to the Whole, then you can relate to anybody. You cannot relate to your father if you cannot relate to the universe; impossible, because that is the source of all. When religion disappeared, relationship disappeared.

A country which has become irreligious will always feel difficulties in relationship. You cannot relate to your wife, to your brother, to your sister, to your son, to your father, to your mother—impossible! Relationship is impossible because the base of all relationship has disappeared. You have denied, you have said, "God is no more, God is dead." Then the whole universe is alien, and you feel alienation, you feel cut off, unrelated; then you have no roots in it, and you feel the universe is not caring about you.

The universe of the scientist and the universe of a religious man like Jesus are totally different. The universe for the scientist is just accidental: there exists no relationship between you and the universe; it is uncaring, it does not bother about you. You are just accidental; if you were not there, existence would not have felt your absence a little bit; if you are there, your presence is not known to the universe. If you disappear, the universe is not going to shed tears for you.

The universe of the scientist is dead. Whenever you say, "God is dead," the universe is dead. And if you live in a dead universe, how can you relate? Then you live among things. Everything will be accidental, just arbitrary. You have to make some arrangements, but there is no organic unity. You exist alone, and then you carry the whole burden. It is just like a small, lost child: he was holding his father's hand, now he has lost the hand and he cries and weeps—and there is nobody to hear.

Just this is the situation of man: a small child who was holding the hand of his father is now lost in the wood. With the hand of the father in his hand, he walked like an emperor, unafraid. There was no fear because father was there; it was his responsibility, the child was not responsible for anything. Whatsoever was needed would be done, he was not to worry about himself. He walked, he looked at the butterflies, at the flowers, at the skies, he enjoyed everything. Life was blissful. Suddenly, he becomes aware that the hand is not there—he has lost his father. Now there are no butterflies, no flowers. Everything has become stony, dead, and everything is alien and foreign, inimical. Now from every shadow of every tree there is danger; all around, he is afraid of death. From any corner, any moment, death will jump and kill him.

Just a moment before everything was alive, friendly, a rapport was there between the child and the whole universe. Why? Because the hand of the father was there. Through the father, the universe was friendly, there was a relationship. Father disappeared, now relationship has disappeared. Now he is crying, now he is weeping, now he is in deep anxiety, anguish. This is the situation of the modern man, because you have become incapable of looking at the universe as a father or a mother. No wonder that everybody is neurotic ! This child will become neurotic, this child will become abnormal. This child will always carry a wound in his chest, and that wound will disturb all his relationships. He cannot feel at home anywhere now.

Look at your hand. You can't feel a cosmic hand in it? Then you will be in difficulty. This is what Jesus says: "God is the Father. This whole universe cares about you." Otherwise why should you be here? Why should you be allowed to exist? This whole universe cares about you. It has brought you up to this point of consciousness, it wants to carry you to the ultimate peak, to the final peak of Enlightenment, it helps you in every way. Even if you go astray it will follow you. Feel the hand in your hand, and suddenly the total perspective changes.

And Jesus says, *"Everybody* is the son"— not only Jesus alone. But Christianity cannot exist if everybody is the son because then there is nothing unique in Jesus. This attitude is false. Everybody is the son, and still Jesus is unique, because he has recognized it and you are still in search.

The uniqueness is not in the nature of being, the uniqueness exists in the nature of recognition. Jesus *knows* this and you don't know. Hindus have always said that the difference between one who is Enlightened and one who is ignorant, is not in being but only in knowing. It is just like when somebody is asleep and you are awake: being is the same, but one who is asleep dreams and you are not dreaming. Shake him, make him awake, and he is as awake as you are—his dreams have disappeared. Only a shaking is needed. Jesus is awake and you are fast asleep, that is the distinction. In this respect he is unique, but not in being. He himself says, "You are the sons of the Living Father."

And the second insistence is on "the Living Father," because ordinarily a father is going to die. The physical part of the father will die, the biological part of the father will die but the cosmic Whole is always alive, it never dies—it is eternity.

Just a few decades ago Nietzsche declared, "God is dead !" That is impossible because the universe cannot die, and God is not a person. If He were a person, He could die—persons have to die.

God is not a form—forms have to die; God has no body—bodies have to die. God is all. In God we are born and we die. We take form and the form disappears, but the Whole remains. The Whole cannot die, the Whole is life itself. So you are not living in a dead universe, but in an alive God who is a father, a mother; the relationship is deep and organic. You are not uncared for, somebody goes on looking after you.

This feeling gives you roots, then you don't feel a stranger; then you are *not* an outsider, you are an insider. This is your home.

"But if you do not know yourselves, then you are in poverty..."

This is the only poverty: ignorance of oneself—there is no other poverty. You may not have riches, you may not have great palaces, you may not have empires, but those are not real riches. Only one thing is real wealth and that is self-knowledge, because it cannot be destroyed.

And Jesus says: *"But if you do not know yourselves, then you are in poverty,"* and not only that, *"you are poverty."*

You are poor. There is only one poverty: when you don't know yourself. Why is it poverty? Because you are emperors, sons of a Living God! The greatest that is possible has happened to you! And you are unaware of it, and you go on begging.

All desires are begging. It is said that if wishes were horses, beggars would be the riders. But all desires *are* horses, and beggars are riders—you are all riders. Look at your horses! They are your desires: begging, demanding, asking—and you have all within you but you never look within. Once you look, riches will be revealed, eternal, in abundance, you cannot exhaust them. And once you look within, the whole existence recognizes your emperorship, the whole existence recognizes who you are: you are the son of the Whole. Then all begging disappears, you become rich for the first time.

"But if you do not know yourselves, then you are in poverty and you are poverty."

I have heard a story: Once it happened, a great Emperor was very much annoyed by his son and his ways and his styles of life. He was the only son, but he annoyed his father so much that the son was expelled from the kingdom. He was the son of a great

Emperor so he knew nothing, he was not skilled in anything—emperors are not skilled in anything. He did not know how to do anything, he had not learnt; everything had always been done for him, he never knew that you have to do things on your own. But he was a lover of music. That was the only thing he could do, because he had learnt it as a hobby. He played on his sitar, that was the only thing he knew.

So he started begging. He would play on his sitar and beg. If emperors lose their empires they cannot do anything except beg. This is something beautiful, it shows that deep down emperors are beggars. Just because of the empire you cannot see their beggary. If the empire is taken away, they are beggars, they cannot do anything else. For ten years continuously he was begging. He completely forgot that he was the son of a great Emperor. Ten years is too long to remember. And when you are a beggar every day from the morning to the evening, how can you remember that you are the son of a great Emperor?

He became a beggar and he forgot himself completely, even the memory went. And these memories are bad, nightmare-like, you want to forget them, because through them much misery comes in the mind. Comparison comes: "I am the son of a great Emperor—and begging!" Then begging becomes too painful. So he simply dropped the idea, he simply forgot, he became identified with the begging.

After ten years, the father started feeling for the son. He was not exactly right, the son, his ways were different, but he was the only son. And now the father was getting old and any day he would die. And the son was his heir, he had to be brought back. So his vizier went in search.

The vizier arrived. Even if the son had completely forgotten that he was the son of an Emperor, even if he had completely identified with being a beggar, still something had remained because it was not part of his memory, it was part of his being. The way he walked, even the way he begged, was just like an emperor. He would beg, but as if he were obliging you; the way he would look was as if he had obliged you by begging. The way he walked was kingly, his clothes were rotten, but still they were the same clothes that he had used as a prince. He was dirty, unclean, but you could see that he had a beautiful face hidden under that dirt. And his eyes: even if he was a beggar, his eyes were still of that same ego, the same pride. Mentally, consciously he had forgotten, but unconsciously he was still the King, the heir of a great Emperor.

The vizier recognized him. The moment when he recognized him, he was begging. Under a tree a few people were playing cards, and he was begging there. It was a summer afternoon, very hot, and he had no shoes, he was perspiring, and he was begging for a few *paise*, saying, "Give me something—I have been hungry for two days." The vizier recognized him, and the chariot in which the vizier had come stopped. The vizier came down, he touched the feet of the son, and the son looked at him and he said, "What is the matter?"

The vizier said, "Your father the Emperor has called you back. He has forgiven you." In an *instant* the beggar disappeared. Nothing was to be done—in an *instant*, the recognition that, "My father has called me back, I am forgiven!" and the beggar disappeared. The clothes were the same, the man was still dirty, but everything changed: there was glory, a light, an aura around him.

He gave orders to the vizier, begging disappeared. He said, "Go into the market, purchase shoes and clothes for me and arrange a good bath." He went up into the chariot and he said, "Take me to the best hotel in the town!" And the vizier had to follow the chariot on foot.

This is a Sufi story. This is your situation also: once you are recognized by the father, by God, your begging disappears—suddenly, in an instant! Nothing is to be done because you have always been the same. Only the identity had gone wrong, only in the superficial part of the mind you had become something else. Deep down you have remained sons of God.

But this will happen only if you know yourself. Then the whole universe knows you, recognizes you. And Jesus says, "But if you do not know yourselves, then you are in poverty and you are poverty."

Fourteenth Discourse

3rd September 1974, Poona, India

THE FOURTEENTH SAYING

Jesus said:
Blessed is the man who has suffered,
he has found the Life.

Jesus said:
Look upon the Living One as long as you live,
lest you die and seek to see Him
and be unable to see.

They saw a Samaritan
carrying a lamb on his way to Judea.

He said to his disciples:
Why does this man carry the lamb with him?

They said to him:
In order that he may kill it and eat it.

He said to them:
As long as it is alive he will not eat it,
but only if he has killed it
and it has become a corpse.

They said:
Otherwise he will not be able to do it.

He said to them:
You yourselves, seek a place for yourselves in repose
lest you become a corpse and be eaten.

Jesus said:
Two will rest on a bed:
the one will die,
the one will live.

From the most ancient days, man has asked again and again why there is suffering in life. If God is the Father then why is there so much suffering? If God is love and God is compassion, then why does existence suffer? And there has not been a satisfactory answer to it. But if you understand Jesus you will understand the answer. Man suffers because there is no other way to mature, to grow. Man suffers because only through suffering can he become more aware. And awareness is the key.

Observe your own life: whenever you are comfortable, at ease, happy, awareness is lost. Then you live in a sort of sleep, then you live as if hypnotized, you live as if in a sleep-walk; you move and do things—but somnambulistically. That is why whenever there is no suffering, religion disappears from your life. Then you never go to the temple, it carries no sense for you; then you don't pray to God, because why? There seems to be no reason.

Whenever there is suffering you move towards the temple, your eyes move towards God, your heart moves towards prayer. There is something hidden in suffering which makes you more aware who you are, why you are, where you are going. In a moment of suffering your awareness is intense.

Nothing can be meaningless in this world. It is a cosmos, it is not a chaos. You may not be able to understand—that is another thing—because you know only fragments, you don't know the whole. Your experience of life is just as if you have only one tattered page of a novel: you read it but it makes no sense because it is just a small fragment, you don't know the whole story. Once you know the whole story, then this page will become comprehensible, then this page becomes coherent, meaningful.

What is meaning? Meaning means to know the fragment in relation to the whole; meaning is a relationship of the fragment to the whole. A madman talking on the street is meaningless. Why? Because you cannot relate his talk to anything, his talk is a fragment. But he is not talking to anybody, there is no need, there is nobody there to talk to. His talk is fragmentary, it is not part of a bigger whole, that is why it is incoherent. The same words may be used by another man—exactly the same words—but he is talking to somebody, then it is meaningful. Why? The words are the same, the sentences the same, the gestures the same, and one man you say was mad and the other man is not mad—why? Because there is somebody to listen; the fragment is not fragmentary, it has become part of a bigger whole—it carries meaning.

Cut a piece out of a Picasso painting: it is meaningless, it is just a fragment and a fragment is dead. Put it back into the painting and suddenly the meaning appears. It has become coherent because now it has become part of the whole. Only when you are part of the whole are you meaningful. And if the modern man seems to feel continuously that he has become meaningless, it is because God has been denied—or forgotten.

Without God, man can never be meaningful, because God means the Whole and man is just a fragment. You are just a line of poetry—alone, you are just gibberish. With the whole poem significance appears, because significance lies in relationship to the whole. And remember this.

I am reminded of a dream of Bertrand Russell. He was an atheist, he never believed in God, he could never see any wider meaning that could comprehend the Whole. He relates one dream: one night, he heard somebody knocking on the door in his sleep. So in the dream, he went to open the door, and he saw old God standing there. He couldn't believe his eyes because he could never believe in God—even in his dream he could remember that, "I don't believe in God." But the Old Man looked so forgotten by everybody, abandoned by everybody; His clothes were tattered, dirt had gathered on His face and body; He looked so out-of-date—almost like a faded painting in which you could not see clearly what was happening—Russell felt much pity for Him. Just to cheer Him up he said, "Come in!" He slapped His back like a friend and said, "Cheer up!" And then suddenly he awoke and the dream disappeared.

This is the state of the modern man, the modern mind: God is out-of-date. You are either against Him, or at the most, you pity Him. Through pity you may try to cheer Him up, but He is no longer a meaningful thing for you—just an out-of-date painting, faded, useless, junk from the past. Either He is dead or deadly sick, on His death-bed. But if the Whole is dead, how can the fragment be meaningful? If the Whole is out-of-date, how can the part be new, fresh and young? If the whole tree is dead, then any leaf of the tree, if it thinks it is alive is simply stupid. It may take a little more time for the leaf to die, but if the tree is dead the leaf has to die—it is already dying.

If God is dead, then man cannot live. And he is deadly sick, because without the Whole the fragment has no meaning. But whenever you are happy—glimpses of happiness, not in fact happiness— whenever you are just comfortable, at ease, when nothing disturbs you, then you think you are the Whole. And this is fallacious. When you are in suffering, suddenly you become aware that you are not the Whole. When you suffer, you suddenly become aware that you are *not* as you should be, something is wrong, the shoe pinches. Something *is* wrong and some transformation is needed. Hence the value of suffering.

Suffering gives you awareness: suffering gives you the feeling that you have to mutate, you have to become new, you have to be re- born. As you are, you are in suffering, so something has to be done.

"Jesus said: Blessed is the man who has suffered, he has found the Life."

Looks absurd and paradoxical! He says, "Blessed is the man that has suffered..." We always call that man blessed who has never suffered. But have you seen any man who has never suffered? If you ever see such a man, you will find him absolutely juvenile, childish, without any growth, without any depth, without any aware- ness—he will be an idiot. And you can never say that he is blessed.

Only one who has never tried to live, who has been avoiding life can remain without suffering. That is why in very very rich families, only idiots are born, because they are protected so much. And when you protect somebody so much, it is not protection against death, it is protection against life. But this is the problem: if you want to protect somebody against death, you have to protect him against life, because life leads to death. So don't live if you are afraid to die—this is simple logic—don't be alive if you are afraid to die, then cut all the dimensions where life exists. Then you can simply vegetate.

Jesus cannot call a vegetative life blessed, nobody can say that a vegetative life is blessed. That is the greatest misfortune that can happen to a man, because he will never grow in awareness and maturity; he will not have higher layers of consciousness either, because those higher layers come into existence only when they are challenged. Suffering is a challenge; when you suffer you are challenged, when there is a problem you are challenged. When you encounter the problem, only then do you grow. More insecurity, more growth; more security, less growth. If everything is secure around you, you are already in your grave, you are no longer alive. Life exists in danger, life always exists in the possibility of going astray. But one who goes astray can come back, one who fails can succeed.

Napoleon was defeated. He wrote in his diary a beautiful sentence —sometimes madmen also observe beautifully—he said, "Only a fight is lost, only a battle is lost—not the war." But if you want to win the war, you will have to lose many battles. If you are afraid to lose a battle, you will never enter into the war, then there is no possibility.

Whenever you fail in something, it is not the ultimate failure, you can transcend it. Next time you need not do it again, next time you need not commit the same error and the same mistake, next time there is no need to move in the suffering. A man who is wise suffers as much as a man who is not wise, but in a different way each time. A wise man commits as many mistakes—even more than a stupid man—but he never commits the same mistake twice. That is the only difference: the quantity may be more, but the quality is different. An idiot may not commit many mistakes, he may not commit mistakes at all, because he is never going to do anything. You only commit a mistake when you do something.

You can go astray if you seek and search. If you walk on the path, if you are simply sitting at home, how can you go astray? If you don't do anything you will never commit a mistake, you will be a mistakeless man, but you will never move; by and by, you will simply rot, vegetate and die. Never be afraid of making mistakes, simply remember that there is no need to make the same mistake twice. Why do you make the same mistake twice? Because the first time you made it, you didn't learn anything from it. That is why you have to make mistakes again and again and again. And people go on making the same mistakes, repeating them their whole lives; they move in a circle. That is why Hindus have called this world *sansar*.

Sansar means the wheel: you simply repeat the same mistakes again and again and again. Situations may differ but the mistake remains the same, of the same quality. What does it show? It shows that you are not alert, otherwise why commit the same mistake again? Commit another because then you will learn. Nobody learns without mistakes. Whenever you commit a mistake you have to suffer. Nobody learns without suffering. Hindus have said that you have to be born again and again because you have not yet grown.

Only a grown-up person goes beyond this world. Those who have not grown, they have to fall back in the pit, they have to learn. And every learning is the hard way, there is no shortcut. That hard way is suffering. Don't protect yourself against suffering, rather on the contrary, move into suffering as fully aware as possible. Take the challenge, encounter it! You will grow through it. Try to transcend it, go beyond it. Don't be afraid—once you become afraid you are already dying. That is why Jesus says, "Blessed is the man who has suffered, he has found the Life." And he who suffers becomes more alert, and alertness is the key to the temple of life. The more alert you are, the more aware.

What is the difference between you and the trees? The trees are beautiful, but they are not higher than you because they remain unconscious. A stone, a rock is even below the level of the trees, more unconscious. A stone also suffers, but it is not aware; a tree also suffers, but not consciously—and if you also suffer without consciousness, then what is the difference? Then you are just a moving tree.

Deep down, the basic thing that makes you human has not happened yet. Consciousness makes you human. And this is the beauty of it: that whenever you are conscious, suffering disappears. Suffering brings in consciousness, but if you move more and more in consciousness, suffering disappears. This law has to be understood: if your head is hurting, it brings consciousness, you become aware of your head; otherwise nobody is aware of their head. You become aware of the body only when something is wrong.

In Sanskrit, they have a beautiful word for suffering. They call it *vedana*, and *vedana* has two meanings: one, suffering; the other, knowledge. *Vedana* comes from the same root as *veda*. *Veda* means the source of knowledge. Those who coined this word *vedana* came to know a fact, that suffering *is* knowledge. Hence they used the same root word for both.

If you suffer, immediately you become aware. The stomach comes into existence only with a stomach-ache. Before, it may have been there but it was not in your consciousness. That is why medical science, particularly *Ayurveda*, defines health as bodilessness: if you don't know the body, you are healthy; if you know the body, something is wrong, because knowing exists only when something goes wrong. If you are a driver, a slight noise in the engine and you become aware, otherwise everything was humming, everything was monotonous, everything was okay. A small noise somewhere in the engine, in the other parts of the car, and you become aware that something has gone wrong. Only when something goes wrong do you become aware.

And if you become *really* aware, you don't become involved in the wrong, rather on the contrary, you grow in your awareness more and more. Then a second phenomenon happens: in your awareness you come to know that the disease is there, the discomfort is there, the suffering is there—but that is *not* in you, that is just around you, on the circumference. In the center there is awareness, on the circumference there is suffering, as if suffering belongs to somebody else, you are not identified. Then a headache is there, but it is not painful to *you;* it is painful to the body and you are simply aware. The body becomes the object and you become the subject—there is a gap.

In awareness all bridges are broken, the gap is immediately present there. You can see that the body suffers, but the identification is broken. Suffering brings in awareness, awareness breaks the identification—and that is the key to life.

"Blessed is the man who has suffered, he has found the Life."

Jesus on the cross is just a symbol of the final suffering, the absolute suffering, of the peak of suffering. When Jesus was on the cross, at the last moment he wavered a little. The suffering was too much. It was no ordinary suffering, not ordinary bodily pain, it was anguish—not only physical, but deep psychological anguish. And the anguish was this: that suddenly he started feeling, "Am I abandoned by God? Why should this happen to me? I have not done anything wrong. Why should I be crucified? Why this pain? Why this crucifixion? Why this anguish to *me*?" And he asked God, "Why?" He questioned.

It must have been a very deep moment of anguish, when all the foundations are shaken and even your faith is shaken. The pain was so much—the humiliation of the whole thing! The same people for whom he had lived, for whom he had worked, whom he had served, to whom he had been a healer—they were murdering him, and for no reason at all. He asked God, *"Why? Why is this happening to me?"* Then suddenly he realized why, because he became very much aware; at the moment of crucifixion he came to the perfect awareness.

I always say that before that moment he was Jesus, after that moment he became Christ. At that moment the total transformation happened. Before it he was coming nearer, nearer, nearer, coming closer and closer and closer, but the last jump happened in that moment: Jesus disappeared and there was Christ—suddenly a transmutation.

What happened? He said, "Why this suffering to me? Have you forsaken me? Am I abandoned?" And immediately after this anguish he said, "No! Thy will should be done." He accepted it. The *why* was a rejection, because questioning means doubt. Immediately he understood and he said, "I accept, and I understand. Thy will should be done, not mine, because my will is going to be wrong." Then he relaxed, then there was a let-go, the final surrender. At the moment of death, he accepted death also. In that acceptance, he became Life Eternal—the key was found. That is why he says, "Blessed is the man who has suffered, he has found the Life."

Whenever you suffer, next time don't complain, don't create anguish out of it. Rather, watch it, feel it, see it, look at it from all possible angles. Make it a meditation and see what happens: the energy that was moving into the disease, the energy that was creating suffering, is transformed, the quality changes. The same energy becomes your awareness because there are not two energies in you, the energy is one. You can make it sex, you can transform it and make it into love; you can transform it still higher and make it into prayer, and you can transform it still higher and make it into aware-ness—the energy is the same.

When you suffer you are dissipating energy, in your anguish you are dissipating energy, the energy is leaking out. Whenever there is suffering, shake yourself. Close your eyes and look at the suffering. Whatsoever it is—mental, physical, existential—whatsoever it is, look at it, make it a meditation. Look at it as if it is an object.

When you look at your suffering as an object, you are separate, you are no longer identified with it, the bridge is broken. And then the energy which was going to move into suffering will not move, because the bridge is no longer there. The bridge is identification: you feel you are the body, then the energy moves into the body. Wherever you feel any identification, your energy moves there.

You may not have known this, but you can try a simple experi-ment: if you love a woman, just sit by her side and feel identified, as if you are the woman, the beloved; and let the woman feel that she is you, the lover. Just wait and feel identified. Suddenly you will both have a shock of energy. You will both feel that some energy has moved from the other to you. Lovers have felt as if an energy jumps just like an electric shock and reaches the other. Whenever you are identified with something there is a bridge, and the energy can move through that bridge.

When a mother is feeding her child, she is not only giving milk as was always thought. Now biologists have stumbled upon a deeper fact, and they say she is feeding energy—milk is just the physical

part. And they have done many experiments: a child is raised, food
s given—as perfect as possible, whatsoever medical science has
found. Everything is given, but the child is not loved, not cuddled;
he mother does not touch him. The milk is given through mechanical devices, injections are given, vitamins are given—everything is
perfect. But the child stops growing, he starts shrinking, as if life
starts moving away from him. What is happening? Because whatsoever the mother was giving is being given.

It happened in Germany that during the war, many small orphan
babies were put into a hospital. Within weeks they were all almost
dying. Half of them died, but every care was taken. Scientifically
hey were absolutely right, doing whatsoever was needed. But why
were these children dying? Then one psycho-analyst observed that
hey needed some cuddling, somebody to hug them, somebody to
make them feel significant. Food is not food enough. Jesus says,
"Man cannot live by bread alone." Some inner food, some invisible
food is needed. So the psycho-analyst made a rule that whosoever
came into the room—a nurse, a doctor, a servant—had to give at
least five minutes in the room to hug and play with the children.
And suddenly they were not dying, they started growing. And since
then many experiments have been done.

When a mother hugs a child, energy is flowing. That energy is
invisible—we have called it love, warmth. Something is jumping
from the mother to the child, and not only from the mother to the
child, from the child to the mother also. That is why a woman is
never so beautiful as when she becomes a mother. Before, something
is lacking, she is not complete, the circle is broken. Whenever a
woman becomes a mother, the circle is complete. A grace comes to
her as if from some unknown source. So not only is she feeding the
child, the child is also feeding the mother. They are happy 'into'
each other.

And there is no other relationship which is so close. Even lovers
are not so close, because the child comes from the mother, from
her very blood, her flesh and bones; the child is just an extension of
her being. Never again will this happen, because nobody can be so
close. A lover can be near your heart, but the child has lived
inside the heart. The mother's heart has been beating, and that was
the heartbeat of the child, he had no other heart; the mother's blood

circulated in him, he had no independence, he was just *part* of her
For nine months he remained as part of the mother, organically
joined, one. The mother's life was his life, the mother's death would
have been his death. Even afterwards it goes on: a transfer of
energy, a communication of energy exists.

Whenever there is suffering, become aware; then the bridge is
broken, then there is no transfer of energy to suffering. And by and
by suffering shrinks, because the suffering is your child. You have
given birth to it, you are the cause, and then you feed it, you water
it, and then it grows and then you suffer more. Then you complain
then you are miserable, then your whole attention become identified
with the suffering.

I have heard, once it happened: Two old women met in a market
One asked the other how she was feeling, because she was always
feeling ill. There are women who always feel ill. Something has gone
wrong; it is not illness, it is something deeper, a neurosis, because
they cannot feel at ease if they are not ill; illness has become part
of their ego. She asked, "How are you feeling?"

The woman who was always ill or talking about illness, started
She said, "Very bad—never has it been so bad. The arthritis is
acting up, I have a severe headache, and the stomach-ache is terrible
and my legs hurt...." and on and on she went.

The other said, "Then go and see a doctor."

The first woman said, "Yes, yes I will go when I feel a little
better."

But this is happening: you will go to the doctor when you feel
a little better. But nobody goes—when one feels a little better there
is no need. Go to the doctor when you are suffering, pray when
there is suffering, meditate when there is suffering. Don't say, "I will
meditate when I feel a little better." That won't help—you won't
meditate and you will have missed a blissful moment, a moment of
suffering. Meditate, become alert and aware. Don't miss the opportunity, it is a blessing!

Use all your suffering for meditation and soon you will come to
know that the suffering disappears, because the energy starts moving
inwards. It is not moving to the periphery, to the suffering, you are
not feeding your suffering. It looks illogical, but this is the whole
conclusion of all the mystics of the world: that you feed your

suffering and you enjoy it in a subtle way, you don't want to be well—there must be some investment in it.

Buddhas, Jesus', Zarathustras have been talking in vain, you don't listen to them. They say there is a possibility of ultimate bliss. You listen to them and say, "Okay, I will see some time, when I feel better." But whenever you are happy what is the need? That is why Buddha goes on insisting: "The whole of life is suffering, *dukkha*—don't wait! There is going to be no happiness in the life that you are living. Be awake, watch. It is anguish itself that you call your life." People think that he must have been a pessimist. He was not, he was just emphasizing. And you have become so much attached to your suffering that you don't know it.

What is the investment? From the very beginning, from the very childhood, one thing almost always goes wrong, and that is that whenever a child is ill he is paid more attention. This creates a wrong association: the mother loves him more, the father takes care of him more; the whole family puts him in the center, he becomes the most important person. Nobody bothers about a child otherwise—if he is well and okay, it's as if he is not. When he is ill, he becomes dictatorial, he dictates his terms. Once this trick is learnt, that whenever you are ill you become in some way special, then everybody has to pay attention, because if they are not paying attention you can make them feel guilty. And nobody can say anything to you, because nobody can say that you are responsible for your illness.

If the child is doing something wrong you can say, "You are responsible." But if he is ill you cannot say anything, because illness is not in any way concerned with him—what can he do? But you don't know the facts: ninety percent of illnesses are self-created, generated by yourself to attract attention, affection, significance. And a child learns the trick very easily, because the basic problem for the child is that he is helpless. The basic problem he feels continuously is that he is powerless and everybody is powerful. But when he is ill he becomes powerful and everybody is powerless. He comes to understand it.

A child is very sensitive about knowing things. He comes to know that "Even father is nothing, mother is nothing— nobody is anything before me when I am ill." Then illness is getting something very meaningful, it becomes an investment. Whenever he feels neglected in life, whenever he feels, "I am helpless," he will get into illness, he will create it. And this is the problem, a deep problem: because what can you do? When a child is ill everybody *has* to pay attention.

But now psychologists suggest that whenever a child is ill, take care of him, but don't pay much attention to him. He should be taken care of medically, but not psychologically. Don't create any association in his mind that illness pays, otherwise his whole life, whenever he feels something is wrong, he will be ill. Then his wife cannot say anything, then nobody can blame him, because he is ill. And everybody has to pity him and give affection.

Ninety percent of suffering exists because you have associated something which looks good to you with suffering. Drop this association! Nobody else can do it for you. Drop that association completely, cut that association completely! Suffering is simply wasting your energy. Don't get involved in it, don't think that it pays. There is only one way in which suffering can pay, and that is with awareness. Become aware.

Remember how to drop that association: one, never talk about your suffering. Suffer it, but don't talk about it. Why do you talk about it? Why do people go on talking and boring others about their suffering? Who is interested? But just not to offend you, if you start talking about illnesses and anguish, others have to tolerate it—but they start escaping, they start wanting somehow to get rid of you. Nobody wants to hear, because everybody has too much suffering of his own. Who bothers about your suffering? Don't talk about it, because talking creates associations.

Don't complain, because then you are asking for affection, pity, compassion, love. Don't ask, don't sell your suffering—bring back your investment. Suffer privately, don't make it public—then it becomes a *tapascharya*, it becomes an austerity, one of the best. But look at your saints: if they do *tapascharya*, austerities, they make it very public. And I am saying make your suffering private, then it becomes *tapa*, austerity. They make it public, they announce that they are going on a long fast—everybody must know.

These are children gone mad, these are childish people. They have invested more than you: they depend on their suffering, their prestige depends on their suffering—how long they can fast, how long they can attract the attention of the whole country or of the whole of the world. They are very tricky, they are using suffering to exploit others. But this is what everybody is doing, only they are doing it to its climax. Don't do it, don't try to be a martyr, it is futile. Don't be an exhibitionist.

Suffer privately, suffer so privately that nobody ever becomes aware that you are suffering. And then meditate on it: don't throw it out, accumulate it within and then close your eyes and meditate on it. Then the bridge will be broken. This is the technique for suffering, use suffering as a method.

This is what Jesus means when he says: "Blessed is the man who has suffered, he has found the Life." Suffering belongs to the realm of death, awareness belongs to the realm of life. Break the bridge and you will know that something in you, around you is going to die—it belongs to death; and something in you, your awareness, is not going to die, it is deathless, it belongs to life. That is why suffering can give you the key towards life.

"Jesus said: Look upon the Living One as long as you live, lest you die and seek to see Him and be unable to see."

These are techniques: "Look upon the Living One..." In you there is one who is a Living One and one who is already dead. In you two worlds meet, the world of matter and the world of spirit—you exist on the boundary. In you two realms meet, the realm of death and the realm of life—you exist in between. If you pay too much attention to that which belongs to death, you will always remain afraid, suffering, fearful. If you pay attention to your center, which belongs to life, to eternal life, to immortality, fear will disappear.

Jesus says: "Look upon the Living One as long as you live..." Don't miss, because at the moment of death it will be very very difficult to look upon the Living One.

If for your whole life you have been attentive to the realm of death—the realm of things, the realm of matter and the world— if you have been attentive only to the realm of death, it will be difficult, almost impossible, to look at the realm of life when you are dead or when you are dying. How can you suddenly turn your back, how can you suddenly turn your head? It will be impossible,

you will be paralyzed. Your whole life you have been looking
outward, your neck will be paralyzed, you cannot turn back. It
needs a continuous movement towards the world of the deathless.

While you live, "Look upon the Living One as long as you
live..."

Whenever you have a moment of silence, close your eyes and
look within so that your neck remains flexible, otherwise, at the
moment of death you will be paralyzed. You would like to see
the eternal life, but you will not be able to because you cannot
turn back.

"...lest you die and seek to see Him and be unable to see."

And He is there within you, but you become fixed, you become
obsessed. Obsession with the outside has to be broken. No need to
escape to the forests, that will not help, but in twenty-four hours
you have enough moments to look within. Don't miss them! Whenever you find time, just close your eyes, even for a single moment,
and look within towards the Living One. It is there, just a little
practice is needed to see and become attuned to the inner darkness.
It is dark right now because you are attuned to the outer light.
When you become attuned to the inner light you will see it is a
diffused light, not dark; a very silent, a very consoling, soothing
light, but not an intense light—it is a twilight.

It is just like when the sun has not come up, and the night is
almost gone. That is what Hindus have called *Brahma Muhurta*.
Why do they call it *Brahma Muhurta*, the moment of God? They
call it that because of this inner thing: when you are turning in,
the outer light has gone and the inner darkness has not yet left,
because one has to become attuned, only then will it leave. There
is a twilight, *sandhyakal,* a moment when there is no light and no
darkness. This they call *Brahma Muhurta,* the moment of the
Divine. Become attuned, look, wait, watch. Soon your eyes will
become accustomed and you will be able to see.

There is no intense light, just diffused light, because it is not
generated by a sun. It is just your natural light, not generated by
anything else. It is your own light, your own inner aura—it is
there. Whenever you can find time, don't waste it. And then you
will find moments enough: just going to sleep, look in; the day is

over, the world of death is no more, you are going to retire—look within. In the morning, when you first become aware that sleep has left, there is no need to jump out of bed and into the world. Wait a little, close your eyes, look within: it is silent. The whole night's rest helps, you are not so tense, it will be easier to move within.

That is why all the religions insist on prayer when you go to sleep, and prayer when you come back from the world of sleep. These moments are very good: in the evening you are tired of the world, you are fed up with the world, you are ready to look to something else. In the morning you have rested and the rest helps, you can look towards the inner. This is what Jesus says: "Look upon the Living One as long as you live, lest you die and seek to see Him and be unable to see." And He will be there, but you will be unable to see Him just because of a wrong practice your whole life.

"They saw a Samaritan carrying a lamb on his way to Judea. He said to his disciples: Why does this man carry the lamb with him?

They said to him: In order that he may kill it and eat it.

He said to them: As long as it is alive he will not eat it, but only if he has killed it and it has become a corpse.

They said: Otherwise he will not be able to do it.

He said to them: You yourselves seek a place for yourselves in repose lest you become a corpse and be eaten."

Your body is going to become food for worms, for birds. Your body *is* food, it is nothing else, it cannot be anything else—your body comes out of food. That is why if you don't eat, your body will start disappearing. If you go on a fast, two pounds of the body will disappear every day. Where is that body going? Every day you have to fill it with food—it is a by-product of food. So when you die, what will happen to your body? The world will use it as a food: the worms of the earth will eat you, or the birds of the sky will eat you. It just gives you a fear, you become apprehensive that, "I will be eaten." Because of this, all the world over, people have created ways in order not to be eaten. But they are foolish!

Hindus burn the dead body just to avoid one thing, just that you should not be eaten. Mohammedans put the dead body inside a casket and put it into a grave just to protect it. Christians do the same. Only Zoroastrians have not done that: they leave the body to become a food. They are the most natural about it, and the most scientific too, because you should not destroy food. You have been eating birds, animals, fruits, your whole life, and now you have accumulated a two hundred pound body and you destroy it, burn it. This is not good, you are not grateful to the world. You should return it back to the world of food—it is a food!

And why do you think that burning is better, throwing it into a fire is better than letting it be eaten by a worm or by a bird or by an animal. Why? Because there too fire is burning—in the stomach of the bird, in the stomach of the lion—and that fire will dissolve your body. But that is natural fire and at least it will fulfill some hunger somewhere.

Only Parsees have remained natural about it, but even they have become wavering now because everybody says, "That is wrong—leaving your father, your mother. What type of people are you? You are very cruel!" But throwing a corpse in fire is not cruel? Or burying it deep down in the earth is not cruel? They are more ecological, they are completing the circle. Hindus and Mohammedans and Christians are less ecological, they are breaking the circle and this is not good.

Jesus says: "If you don't realize the Inner One, the Living One, the Conscious One, then you are just going to be eaten, that's all." Your whole life has been futile: eating your whole life, working to eat, and then being eaten—this is the whole story. "A tale told by an idiot, full of sound and fury, signifying nothing." The whole life a struggle to eat, and then being eaten. What is the meaning of it?

Jesus says, "Before you are dead, before you are eaten, realize that which is not food in you, which is not created by food in you." Then you will have to understand one more thing.

All the religions have tried fasting. Why? Because when you fast awareness grows intense, because it is not part of food. Really, food destroys awareness, and when you don't eat you become more aware because food gives a sort of sleep, it is an intoxicant. So if you eat too much you immediately feel sleepy, it is alcoholic; whenever you eat you have to go to sleep. If you ever fast, you will find it is difficult to sleep that night. You think it is because of hunger? No, it is because without food, more awareness happens.

And if you go on a long fast, after the third, fourth or fifth day, hunger disappears, because the body insists for three, four, five days—the body has not got a very long memory—it insists on the old habit for a few days, and then if you don't listen the body makes its arrangement in a different way. The body has a double arrangement, it is needed as a security measure. Every day you have to eat to give the body its daily quota. If you don't give it food for five, seven days, then the body has an emergency measure: the accumulated flesh in the body, the accumulated fat—it accumulates.

Every ordinary, healthy person accumulates enough fat for at least three months; that is a reservoir. When the body thinks that you are not going to give food, the body starts eating its own reservoir. When the body starts eating its own reservoir, then the consciousness is not involved at all in it. You need not go and earn and work, and get tired and then give the body food. And when you give it food, to absorb the food, to digest it, your whole energy is needed. That is why immediately you eat food, your head feels sleepy: because the energy that was working as consciousness is required in the stomach to work as a digestive force; it immediately moves.

So people who eat too much cannot meditate well, impossible! They can sleep well, but they cannot be aware, they cannot be very conscious. They are food and nothing more—and they will be eaten; their whole life is a food-circle. All the religions became aware that if you fast, awareness increases, because the energy is released when there is nothing to digest. Nothing to be taken in and thrown out; all work stops. The work at the factory of the body is not there, the factory is locked. Then the whole energy that you have got becomes awareness. That is why it is difficult to sleep when you are on a fast.

And if you have been on a fast for at least twenty, thirty days, forty days, you will have a new type of sleep: your body will sleep and you will remain alert. That is what Krishna said to Arjuna, "When everybody is asleep, a yogi remains awake." That is what Buddha said, "Even while I am asleep, I am not asleep—only the

body sleeps." That is why when Mahavir slept, he never moved in
his sleep—not even a single movement. He never changed sides
because he remained alert. And he said, "Changing sides won't be
good; some insect may have crawled underneath"—because he used
to sleep on the floor or under a tree—"and if I move in the dark,
and change my side, there may be some violence—unknowingly,
but still. And if I can avoid it...." So he remained perfectly in
one posture the whole night, he remained exactly as he was when
he went to sleep, not even moving his hand. This can be done only
if you are perfectly aware in sleep, otherwise you will not know
when you have moved.

If you become aware, then you become aware of a different
dimension within you. The visible belongs to death, the invisible
belongs to the deathless.

Jesus says: "You yourselves, seek a place for yourselves in
repose..." Seek a state of silence, repose, tranquillity, balance,
where you can become aware of the Living One "...lest you
become a corpse and be eaten."

*"Jesus said: Two will rest on a bed: the one will die, the one
will live."*

Exactly the same words are in the Upanishads. They say that
there are two birds on a tree, one sitting on a lower branch,
another sitting on a higher branch. The bird on the lower branch
thinks, gets worried, desires, demands, accumulates, fights, com-
petes; it remains in anguish, tension, jumps from this branch to
that, always moving, never in repose. The other bird, who is sitting
on a higher branch, is in repose. He is so silent, as if he is not.
He has no desires, no dreams happen to him. He has no needs to
fulfill, as if everything is fulfilled, as if he has attained, nowhere to
go. He simply sits, enjoying himself, and he watches the bird who
is on the lower branch.

These are the two dimensions in you. You are the tree. And the
lower is always disturbed. The lower is your body and the bodily
needs and the bodily desires. On the higher branch, at the top
of the tree, sits the other bird who is a witness, who simply looks
down at this foolish bird jumping, moving in anguish, anxiety,

anger, sex—everything happens to it. This other bird is simply a witness, he simply looks on and on, he is just a spectator. And if you forget yourself completely into it then you become one. You are the tree.

Jesus says the same thing with a different symbol: "Two will rest on a bed..." You are the bed. "Two will rest on a bed: the one will die, the one will live." You are the bed, two are there: "...the one will die, the one will live." Now the whole question is to whom the attention should be paid. Towards whom should you move, towards whom should your whole energy flow? Who should become your goal?

Ordinarily, that one who is going to die is your goal. That is why you are always in anxiety, because you are building a house on sands. It is going to fall—even before it is built it will fall and become a ruin. You are always trembling because you are making your signature on water—before you have completed it, it is gone. Your anxiety is because you are concerned with the realm of death and you have not looked towards life. And on each bed two are sleeping—the other is just a witness.

Pay more attention to it, turn towards it more and more—that is what conversion means. Conversion doesn't mean a Hindu becoming a Christian, or a Christian becoming a Hindu. This is foolishness, you simply change labels. Nothing is changed because the inner man remains the same, the old pattern. Conversion means the movement of attention from the death realm to the life realm. It is an about-turn: looking at the witness, becoming one with the witness, losing yourself into the witness, into awareness, and then you know that which is going to die will die. It makes no trouble, no problem —because you know you are not going to die, there is no fear.

"Jesus said: Two will rest on a bed: the one will die, the one will live."

And it is up to you. If you want to remain in trouble, never pay attention to the Inner One; if you want to remain always in anguish then remain on the periphery, don't look within. But if you want repose, a peaceful eternity, truth, the doors of Heaven open for you, then look within. It is difficult—it is difficult because it is very subtle. Where the invisible and the visible meet, where matter and spirit meet, it is very subtle. You can see matter, you cannot see spirit, it cannot be seen. You can see where the visible ends, you cannot see the invisible, it cannot be seen.

Then what is to be done? Just remain at the boundary of the visible, and don't look at the visible, look in the opposite direction. Gradually the invisible can be felt. It is a feeling, it is not an understanding; you cannot see it, you can only feel it. It is just like a breeze: it comes, you feel it, but you cannot see it. It is just like the sky: it is there, but you cannot say *where,* you cannot pin-point it, you cannot touch it. It is always there, *you are in it,* but you cannot touch it.

Remain at the boundary of the visible looking in the opposite direction. This is what all meditation is about. Whenever you can find a peaceful moment, close your eyes, leave the body behind and the bodily affairs and the world of death; the market, the office, the wife, the children—leave them all. The first time you will not feel anything inside. Hume has said: "Many people have talked about going in and looking there. Whenever I look, I find nothing—just thoughts, desires, dreams, floating here and there— just a chaos." You will also feel the same. And if you conclude that there is nothing worthwhile in going again and again to see this chaos, then you will miss.

In the beginning you will see this, because your eyes can only see this—they need a tuning. Just remain there looking at the floating dreams. They float like clouds in the sky, but between two clouds, sometimes you will see the blueness; between two dreams, two thoughts, sometimes there will be a glimpse of the sky behind. Just don't be in a hurry. That is why they say that if you hurry you will miss.

There is one Zen saying which says, "Hurry slowly." That is right! Hurry, that is right, because you are going to die—in that sense hurry. But inside, if you are in too much of a hurry you will miss, because you will conclude too soon, before your eyes have become attuned. Don't conclude too soon.

Hurry slowly. Just wait! Go there and sit and wait. By and by, a new world of the invisible becomes clear, comes to you. You become attuned to it, then you can hear the harmony, the melody, the silence starts its own music. It is always there, but it is so silent that very trained ears are needed. It is not like a noise, it is like silence. The sound within is like silence, the form within is like formlessness. There is no time and no space within, and all that you know is either in space or in time. Things are in space, events are in time, and now physicists say these two things are not two; even time is just a fourth dimension of space.

You know only time and space, the world of things and events. You don't know the world of the witnessing self. It is beyond both, it is not confined to any space and it is not confined to any time. There is duration without time, there is space but without any height, length, breadth—it is a totally different world. You will need to become attuned to it, so don't be impatient—impatience is the greatest barrier. I have come to feel that when people start working towards the Inner One, impatience is the greatest barrier. Infinite patience is needed. It can happen the next moment, but infinite patience is needed.

If you are impatient it may not happen for lives, because the very impatience will not allow you the repose that Jesus talks about, the tranquillity. Even if you are expecting something, that will be a disturbance. If you are thinking something is going to happen, something extraordinary, then nothing will happen. If you are waiting, expecting that some Enlightenment is going to happen, you will miss it. Don't expect! All expectations belong to the world of death, the dimension of time and space.

No goal belongs to the inner. There is no way to it except by waiting, infinite patience. Jesus has said: "Watch and be patient." And one day, suddenly you are illumined. One day, when the right tuning happens, when you are ready, suddenly you are illumined. All darkness disappears, you are filled with life, eternal life, which never dies.

Fifteenth Discourse

4th September 1974, Poona, India

THE FIFTEENTH SAYING

Jesus said:
I am the Light that is above them all,
I am the All,
and the All came from me
and the All attained to me.

Cleave a piece of wood
and I am there;
lift up the stone
and you will find me there.

Jesus was trained in one of the oldest secret schools. The school was called Essenes. The teaching of the Essenes is pure Vedanta. That is why Christians don't have a record of what happened to Jesus before his thirtieth year. They have a little record of his childhood, and they have a record after his thirtieth year up to the thirty-third, when he was crucified. They know a few things, but a phenomenon like Jesus is not an accident; it is a long preparation, it cannot happen just any moment.

Jesus was continuously being prepared during these thirty years. He was first sent to Egypt and then he came to India. In Egypt he learned one of the oldest traditions of secret methods, then in India he came to know about the teachings of Buddha, the Vedas, the Upanishads, and he passed through a long preparation. Those days are not known because Jesus worked in these schools as an unknown disciple. And Christians have knowingly dropped those records, because they would not like the son of God to also be a disciple of somebody else. They would not like the very idea that he was prepared, taught, trained—that looks humiliating. They think the son of God comes absolutely ready. Nobody comes absolutely ready. If somebody is absolutely ready he cannot come.

In this world, you always enter as imperfect. Perfection simply disappears from this world. Perfection is not of this world, cannot be—it is against the very law. Once somebody is perfect, his whole life enters into a vertical dimension. This has to be understood: you progress on a horizontal plane, from A to B, from B to C and D, and so on up to Z; horizontal, in a line, from past to present, from present to future. This is the way of the imperfect soul, just like water flowing in a river from the hills and plains to the sea—in a line, horizontal, always maintaining its own level.

Perfection moves in vertical lines, not horizontally. From A it doesn't go to B, from A it goes higher than A, then higher, still higher. On the horizontal line, for those who live on the horizontal line, perfection simply disappears. It is not there because they can look in the future or in the past. They can look back, but the perfect man is not there; they can look ahead, but he is not there; they can look here, he is not there—because a new line of vertical progression has started. He is going higher and higher and higher. He moves in eternity not in time.

Eternity is vertical, that is why it is eternal now—there is no future to it. If you move in a line there is future: if you move from A to B, the B is in the future; when B becomes the present, A has gone into the past and C is in the future. You are always between past and future, your present moment is just a passing phase: the B is turning into C, the D is turning into E; everything is moving into the past. And your present is just a cut line, just a small fragment. By the time you become aware of it, it has moved into the past. A soul which becomes perfect moves in a different dimension altogether: from A to A_1 to A_2 to A_3—and this is eternity, it lives in the eternal now. That is why it disappears from this world.

To enter into this world you have to be imperfect. It is said in old scriptures that whenever a man comes near perfection—many times it has happened—he will leave something imperfect in order to come back. It is said of Ramkrishna that he was addicted to food, just obsessed. Virtually the whole day he was thinking of food. He would be talking to his disciples and just whenever he got a chance he would go into the kitchen to ask his wife, "What is new? What new thing are you preparing today?" Even his wife felt very embarrassed many times, and she would say, "Paramahansa Deva, this doesn't suit you." And he would laugh.

One day his wife persisted, saying, "Even your disciples laugh about it and they say, "What type of liberated man is Paramahansa?'" He was so addicted to food that whenever Sharada, his wife, brought food, he would immediately stand to look in the *thali* and see what she had brought. He would forget everything about Vedanta, the *Brahma*, and sometimes it was very embarrassing because people were there, and they never thought, they could never conceive, that a liberated man could be addicted to food.

So one day his wife persisted, "Why do you do this? There must be some reason."

Ramkrishna said, "The day I don't do it, then you can count three more days that I will be alive here. The day I stop, that will be the signal that I will be here only three more days."

His wife laughed, the disciples laughed. They said, "This is no explanation!" They couldn't follow what he meant.

But it happened the same way. One day his wife came in and he was lying on his bed resting. He turned aside—usually he would have jumped out of the bed to see. And his wife remembered that he had said that he would live only three more days the day he showed his indifference towards food. She couldn't hold the *thali;* the *thali* dropped down and she started crying. Ramkrishna said, "But you all wanted it to be so. Now, don't get worried about it. I am here for three more days." And the third day he died. Before dying he said that he was clinging to food just as a part of something imperfect in him, so that he could be here and serve you.

Many Masters have done that. The moment they feel that something is going to become completely perfect in them, they will cling to some imperfection, just to be here. Otherwise this bank is not for them. If all the fetters are broken then their boat sails towards the other bank, then it cannot remain here. They will keep one fetter: they will keep some relationship, they will choose some weakness in themselves, and they will not allow it to disappear. The circle will not be complete, a gap will remain. Through that gap they can remain here. That is why Hindus, Buddhists, Jains, who know very deeply because they have known many Masters, know well that perfection is not of this world. The moment the circle is complete it disappears from your eyes. You cannot see, it is not then on the line of your vision, it has gone above you— there you cannot penetrate.

But to say that Jesus was perfect when he was born, to emphasize this fact, Christians have dropped all the records. But Jesus was as much a seeker as you, he was as much a mustard seed as you are. He became a tree, and a great tree, and millions of birds of Heaven took shelter in him—but he was also a mustard seed. Remember that even a Mahavir, a Buddha, a Krishna, they are all born imperfect, because birth belongs to imperfection. There is no birth for the perfect; when you are perfect then there is no transmigration.

This training of Jesus—moving into Egypt and India, learning from Egyptian secret societies, then Buddhist schools, then Hindu Vedanta—made him a stranger to the Jews. Why did he become so much of a stranger to the Jews? Why couldn't the Jews absorb him? Why couldn't they forgive him?—they have not forgiven him yet. What was the reason? He was bringing something alien, something foreign, he introduced some secret which didn't belong to the race. That is why the crucifixion happened.

Hindus tolerated Buddha because whatsoever he was saying, it was not alien. He may contradict Hinduism, but he can contradict only the superficial Hinduism. Even in his contradiction he proves the deeper Hinduism right. He may say that the establishment has gone wrong, he may say that the organization has gone wrong, he may say that all the followers have gone wrong, but he cannot say that Hindus are basically wrong. Whatsover he says, Hindus can understand it, it is not foreign, it is not alien. Whatsoever Mahavir said, Hindus simply tolerated it. He may be a revolutionary, but he remains a Hindu; Buddha may be a revolutionary, but he remains a Hindu; he may be a rebel son, but he belongs to Hindus— nothing much to worry about.

But Jesus is not only a revolutionary, he doesn't belong either. How has it happened that he doesn't belong to the Jews? Christians have no answer for it. From where did he bring this alien teaching? From Egypt and from India.

India has been the source of all religions. India has been the basic source of even those religions which are against Hinduism. Why has it happened that India has been the basic source of all religions? India is the oldest civilization, and the whole mind of India has been working and working and working in the dimension of religion. It has come upon all the secrets of religion—no secret is unknown. In fact, for thousands of years you have not been able to teach any secret to India about religion, because they know all. They have discovered all, they have completed the whole journey in a way. So all that is beautiful in religion, wherever it is, you can be certain that somehow it comes from the source, just as the Greek mind is the source of science. The whole scientific development comes from the Greek mind, the logical mind, the Aristotelean mind, and all mysticism comes from India. And only two types of mind exist in the world: one is Greek, the other is Indian.

If you are basically a Greek mind, it is impossible to understand India at all because it looks absurd. Whatsoever they say looks unproven, whatever statements they make look meaningless. Aristotle will be an absolute foreigner in India because he believes in definitions, clear-cut demarcations, distinctions. And he believes in the law of contradiction, that two contradictory things cannot be together: A cannot be A and not A simultaneously, that is impossible; a man cannot be alive and dead simultaneously, that is impossible. Apparently he is right.

Hindus believe in contradiction. They say man is alive and dead, both simultaneously, because life and death are not two things, you cannot demarcate them. The Greek mind is mathematical, the Hindu mind is mystical. All mysticism comes from India; just as the sun rises in the East, all mysticism rises in the East—and India is the heart. For this *sutra* to be understood you have to go to the Upanishads, the roots are there. You cannot find anything in the Old Testament or in other Jewish records from where this saying can come. That is why the Jews could not believe what Jesus was saying.

Jesus says again and again: "I have come not to contradict the old scriptures, but to fulfill them." But what scriptures, which scriptures? That he never says. If he has come to fulfill the Old Testament then his statement is wrong, because he almost always contradicts the Old Testament. The Old Testament depends on revenge—the Father, the God, is very revengeful. Fear is the base of the Old Testament and its religion: you should be God-fearing. And Jesus says, "God is love." You cannot fear love, and if there is love there cannot be any fear. And if you have fear how can you love? Fear is poison to love, fear is death to love. How can you love a person if you are afraid? Fear can create hate, but fear cannot create love.

So a religious man in the Old Testament is God-fearing, and in the New Testament a religious man is God-loving. And love and fear are totally different dimensions. Jesus has said: "It is said that if somebody harms one of your eyes, pull out both his eyes. But I tell you, if somebody hits you on one cheek, give him your other cheek also." This is absolutely non-Jewish, it was not there in the tradition. So when Jesus says, "I have come to fulfill the scriptures," which scriptures does he mean? If he had been in India and he had said, "I have come to fulfill the scriptures," we would have understood, because the Upanishads are the scriptures he has come to fulfill; Dhammapada Buddha's sayings, are the scriptures he has come to fulfill—they depend on love, compassion.

But Jewish scriptures are not at all concerned with compassion and love, they are concerned with fear, guilt. That is why whatsoever Jesus said, Jews understood well that, "He has not come to fulfill *our* scriptures." You cannot find a saying like this in the Old Testament:

"I am the Light that is above them all, I am the All, and the All came from me and the All attained to me.
Cleave a piece of wood and I am there: lift up the stone and you will find me there."

You can find thousands of sayings like this in the Upanishads, in the Gita, in Buddha, but you cannot find a *single* parallel in the Old Testament. So which scriptures has he come to fulfill? He has come to fulfill some other scriptures, some other traditions. This saying is absolutely Vedanta, so try to understand first the standpoint of Vedanta, then you will be able to understand this saying.

Jesus was born as a Jew, lived as a Jew, died as a Jew, but this was only as far as his body was concerned. Otherwise Jesus was a pure Hindu. And you cannot find a purer Hindu than Jesus, because the base of Upanishadic religion is his base. He created the whole structure on that base, so try to understand what that base is.

Jews say, "God is the Creator and this universe is the created, and the created can never become the Creator. How can a painting become the painter? How can a poem become the poet? Impossible! And if the poem tries to become the poet, the poem has gone mad; and if the painting tries to prove and assert and claim that 'I am the painter' then the painting has gone wrong. Man is the creature and God is the Creator. And this distance can never completely go, this space will remain. You can come closer and closer and closer to God, but you can never become God." This is the base of Jewish thought. And Mohammedans learned this from Jews. Mohammedans are more Jewish than Jesus; as far as the thinking, the way of thought is concerned, Mohammed is nearer to Moses than Jesus. Mohammed did not learn much from Hindus.

But Vedanta says, "God is the creation, there is no distinction between God and the creation. He has not created the universe like a poet creates a poem, the relationship is just like a dancer and the dance, they remain one: if the dancer stops, the dance disappears; and if the dance disappears, the person is no more a dancer. The universe is not separate, it is one. The universe was not created in time and finished, it is created each moment; it is being created each moment because it is God's own Being. Just as you move, you sing, you love, so God creates—*every moment* He is creating. And the creation is never separate, it is His movement, His dance." That is why the Upanishads can say, *"Aham Brahmasmi"*. The Upanishads can say, the seers who have come to know this secret can say, "I am God." And nobody thinks this is blasphemy—this is a truth.

Jews can never say, "I am God"—this is blasphemy, nothing can be worse than this assertion. You trying to be God? A creature trying to be God? A slave trying to assert that he is the master? This is egoism! What is pure religion in Vedanta is egoism for Jews and Mohammedans. Vedanta says this is not ego, because this feeling that "I am God" happens only when the 'I' has disappeared completely. When you are no more there, when the house is vacant and the boat is empty, then suddenly you become aware that you are the All. If *you* are there, how can you think that you are the All? If you are there then you have a boundary, a personality—then your assertion is false. When 'I' disappears, when there is egolessness, only then can you feel you are the All. Jesus' assertion comes from the Upanishads.

The first thing to be remembered: the creation and the Creator are not two, they are one.

Second thing to remember: ordinary mathematics says that the part is never equivalent to the whole, the part can never be the whole. In mechanisms it is so: take a part of your car—the part cannot be the car, it is so obvious; you cut your hand—your hand is not you. A part cannot be the whole, this is ordinary logic. And if the world is a mechanical thing, then it is true.

But Vedanta says that existence is organic, not mechanical. With organic unity a different type of mathematics becomes applicable: the part is the whole. That is why they could say, "I am God— because I am just a part, God is the All." But how can the part be the whole? This is the greatest absurdity! If there is a mechanical relationship between me and existence, then this is not possible. But if there is an organic unity, then this is possible. And there is organic unity.

You exist not as a separate unit complete unto yourself. No! You exist not as an island, you exist as a wave of the ocean, an organic unity, you are one: the ocean goes on moving and 'waving' in you— you cannot exist without the ocean. And if you understand deeply, the ocean cannot exist without you either; you are totally joined together. You can say that in every wave the ocean is there, and you can say the ocean is nothing but the totality of all the waves. So a wave is not separate: you cannot take a wave away from the ocean, you cannot bring it home to show to your children that, "I have gone to the ocean and I have brought a wave"; you cannot bring the wave. You can bring the water, but that will not be a wave— that will not be alive.

Look at the ocean when the waves are there: they are alive because the ocean is their *life*. When they are jumping hundreds of feet, reaching towards the sky, the ocean is reaching through them. You may not see the ocean, you may just see the wave, but you cannot separate the wave from the ocean—they are organically one.

Vedanta says that the created is organically one with the Creator, the world cannot exist without God. This can be understood by Jews and Mohammedans also. But Hindus say something else too, the second part: they say that God cannot exist without the world.

That is blasphemy for Jews. What are you saying? That God cannot exist without the world? Yes—He cannot exist, it is impossible for Him to exist. If He is a Creator, if creativity is His quality, how can He exist without the universe? When there is nothing created, how can He be a Creator? The world depends on Him, He depends on the world; it is an interdependence. The world is not independent of Him, and neither is He independent of the world. There is a deep love relationship: they depend on each other, they fulfill each other, they are one. The fulfillment is so total that you cannot separate and divide them.

So a seer, one who has come to know, can declare: "*Aham Brahmasmi, Anal Hak,* I am God." And when he says this, he is simply saying, "I and this existence are not two." He is simply saying, "You will find me anywhere you go, wherever you go you will find me. The form may be different, but I will be there." This is what Jesus is saying: "Cleave a piece of wood and I am there..." How can Jesus be there if you cleave a piece of wood? You cannot find the form, you will not find the son of Mary and Joseph there, you will not find this carpenter boy there if you cleave wood. Then what will you find? Being you will find—and he is saying, "I am Being. My form will change, but not I."

"Cleave a piece of wood and I am there; lift up the stone and you will find me there."

This is pure Vedanta—an organic unity. That's why Hindus are the only ones in the world who don't bother much about temples, they can make anywhere their temple. Just under a tree they will put a stone—any stone, not even carved—and they will paint it red and God is there, they can worship. Any tree is enough, any river, any mountain, anything will do because: "Cleave a piece of wood and I am there; lift up the stone and you will find me there." So why bother?

Hindus alone dispose of their gods. They make a god for two or three weeks, they worship it, and when the worship is over they go to the ocean and dispose of the god. You cannot think of a Mohammedan disposing of a god, you cannot think of a Jew disposing of a god. What are you doing? Disposing of a god in the ocean? Are you a heretic? Have you gone mad? Only Hindus can do this, because they say the ocean is also God. And why carry a god too long? When the function is finished, dispose of it, because He is everywhere, all over. And we can make Him again, any moment—any stone will do. Being, not the form of Jesus, you will find everywhere. And that 'beingness' is the point to be understood: that 'beingness' is God.

When a tree flowers it is God flowering, when a seed sprouts it is God sprouting, when a river flows it is God flowing. God is not a person. If God is a person then there is a problem—and Jews had the idea that God is a person. God is a 'no-person': He is pure being, He is existence itself, He exists in all, but you cannot find Him anywhere in particular. He has no abode, you cannot go and knock; He has no address, you cannot write a letter to Him. In a way He is nowhere, because He is everywhere. You cannot pinpoint Him; you cannot say, "Here is God," because that will be wrong. Only something which has a form, which has a distinction from other things, can be pinpointed. How can you pinpoint something which has no form, which is in all, spread all over?

But Jews had a conception of a very personalized God. And whenever there is personality there is ego. The Jewish God is very egoistic—very, very egoistic. You disobey Him and you will suffer for eternity in Hell. It is very serious: God becomes a dictatorial force and the whole existence becomes a slavery. Then freedom is not for you; freedom is God's nature, not yours. Slavery is going to be your discipline.

Jesus is saying absolutely the contrary, that God is not a person, God is energy, the very life-force, what Bergson has called the *élan vital*—it is existence as such. And wherever something exists, God exists, because nothing else can exist. This was the difficulty, why he could not be understood—and he had to be crucified. Even if he was saying, "I am the son of God," it was possible for the Jews to forgive him, but basically he was asserting more. As his disciples became attuned to him, he went even further.

In this *sutra* he says: *"I am the Light that is above them all..."* He is not saying that he is the son, here he is saying that he is the Father: *"I am the Light that is above them all, I am the All..."* Here he is saying, "I am God, not the son."

"...and the All came from me and the All attained to me.

Cleave a piece of wood and I am there; lift up the stone and you will find me there."

In this *sutra* he asserts, "I am God, not the son of God." Even a son can be forgiven because a distinction remains: the father remains the source, the son is just a product. They may be in deep intimacy, but a son remains a son, a father remains a father. The distinction can be maintained, and the son has to obey the father; a relationship exists. It is not the relationship of a slave to his master, but of a son to his father—more intimate but still a relationship; they remain two.

This *sutra* is not recorded in the Bible—cannot be recorded. He must have asserted it only to his disciples, because now those who had been in deep intimacy with him would be able to understand. This cannot be told in a market place. There he was saying, "I am the son of God." With his disciples he says, "I am God, not the son. I am the source of all, I am the *alpha* and the *omega*. Everything comes from me and everything attains to me."

This is pure Vedanta. You cannot find assertions like this anywhere else, you will have to go to the Gita and the Upanishads. This is what Krishna says to Arjuna: "I am the All, the source of everything. Everything comes from me and everything dissolves in me. Throw your ego and come to my feet." This sounds as if it is Krishna speaking.

There is a tradition, a beautiful tradition—I don't know how much it can be proved, but it is beautiful, needs no proof—there is a tradition that the word 'Christ' is just a form of the word 'Krishna'. It is possible: in Bengali, Krishna is still called Kristo, because 'Krishna' is not the name of the person, 'Krishna' is his absolute achievement, just like 'Buddha'. 'Buddha' is not the name, it is the absolute achievement when one becomes Enlightened. The word 'Buddha' means one who has awakened. What does 'Krishna' mean? The word means one who has become the center of the world. 'Krishna' means the magnetic center, one who attracts, who is now the center of the whole existence. 'Christ' has the same meaning. Mary named her son Jesus. 'Christ' was added to Jesus when he became the center of the world. In this assertion he is saying, "I am the center, the All. Everything comes from me, everything goes back to me. If you go away from me, then you have to attain to me." It is possible that 'Christ' is just a form of 'Krishna'. It is significant because Krishna's assertions in the Gita and Jesus' assertions like these, are exactly the same.

The third thing to be understood about Vedanta is that Vedanta accepts you as you are, because rejection will mean rejection of God Himself. Rejection means that something has to be done: as you are, you are wrong, something has to be cut, something has to be thrown. As you are, you are not accepted, you are not welcome. You will have to change yourself, only then will you be welcome.

Vedanta says that as you are, you are welcome. Nothing is to be done—the very concept of doing has been the cause of your misery. The very concept of doing, that something has to be done, has been the very cause of your misery, because whatsoever you do will lead you into the world. That is why Hindus say it is because of karma— karma means doing—you are in the world. Karma does not mean doing bad, karma simply means doing. Because you have been paying too much attention to doing this or that, you are in the world.

Don't pay much attention to the doing, pay much attention to the being. Don't think of what is to be done, just think of who you are. Vedanta is amoralistic; it doesn't bother about morality and immorality. It has no Ten Commandments, it does not give you any orders, it does not talk in terms of 'ought'. It says that as you are, you are welcome—as you are, you are good, beautiful, true. The problem is not that others reject you, the problem is that you reject yourself. And if you reject yourself, you are in a vicious circle. Then you will try to improve, and nothing can be improved because you are God Himself. Then you will be in misery, because it is impossible to improve you.

As you are, you are Divine. How can the Divine be improved? And if you try to improve the Divine, then you will move from one life to another, improving, improving, and never will any improvement happen, you will remain the same. It is just like jogging on the same spot: you think you are running fast because you are perspiring and breathing so hard, and doing such great work; you think you are running fast, reaching somewhere—and you are standing on your spot jogging.

Your whole life is jogging. You are not going anywhere because there is nowhere to go; you are not improving because it is impossible to improve. The Ultimate which is within you cannot be improved—there is no 'further' to it, there is no 'better' to it. This is what Vedanta says: Vedanta says that you are Divine. This has to be realized, not worked out; you simply have to look within and realize who you are. The problem is not that you are bad, the problem is that you don't look at yourself; the problem is of knowledge, not of being. The problem is of a right perspective from where you can see yourself.

It is just as if a diamond is taught how to become a valuable stone. And if the diamond gets the idea and it starts trying to become a valuable stone, just this idea will become the barrier. All the efforts the diamond can make are going to be futile, because it is already the most precious stone. When the diamond comes to understand the futility of its effort, it will drop all effort and become aware of who it is. Then the problem will be solved.

I have heard: Once a man rushed into the office of a psychiatrist and said, "Doctor, now you have to help me—it has gone beyond my limits! My memory is lapsing. I cannot even remember what happened yesterday. I cannot even remember what I said this morning. Help me, I am going crazy!"

The psychiatrist asked, "When did this problem start? When did you become aware of this problem?"

The man looked puzzled and said, "What problem?" because he had forgotten.

That is the problem: you have forgotten yourself. That is the problem.

Whatsoever you do will create *karma,* and *karma* is a cycle, a wheel: one *karma* leads to another—A to B, B to C—you move from one part of the wheel to another. It is a wheel and it goes on moving, it goes on moving. *Karma* can never lead you to liberation because you are already liberated. This is the most difficult thing to follow: that you are already liberated.

People come to me and I have to tell them to do this and that, because they will not understand that they are already liberated. I have to tell them to do this and that just in order to exhaust them, just in order that one day they become so exhausted with the effort that they will come to me and say, "I don't want to do anything." Only then can I say there is no need to do anything. But you needed much when you came in the beginning, you needed to do much. And if I say there is nothing to do, you will go and move to somebody else who can say that there is something to do.

Nothing is to be done. Absolutely as you are, you are already Divine. This is Vedanta. It is not a morality, it is pure religion. And that is why there are not many Vedantists in the world— cannot be. That is why Vedanta cannot become a world religion like Christianity or Islam. Impossible! Because you have a deep need to do something. And if somebody says, "Nothing is to be done, it is already the case that you are Brahma, you are Divine," you will not listen to him. He is talking nonsense, because you don't accept yourself, you reject yourself. You have to reach a goal.

Why has this thing happened in the mind of man? It has happened because of his childhood. And everybody passes through almost the same childhood, only trivial things differ. Otherwise, childhood has one basic element and that element creates the whole problem. The element is that no child is accepted as he is. A child is born—you were a child—and immediately the society, the parents, mother, father, brothers, people all around you, start to change you, to make you more beautiful, to make you more moral, to make you better. As you are, you are wrong, something has to be done, only then can you be accepted.

And the child by and by starts to feel that he is not accepted. If he does a good thing, then he is accepted; if he does something wrong, then he is rejected. If he follows, obeys, he is accepted; if he disobeys, nobody loves him, he is hated, and everybody becomes angry. One thing he learns: that doing is the question, not being. Do the right thing and everybody will love you, do the wrong thing and everybody will reject you and hate you, be angry and be against you. *You* are not the point. Do something right and the world is welcoming, do something wrong and every door is closed. And if even father's and mother's door is closed, if even those who love him can't see the being of the child, what to say about this strange world?

The child learns one thing: that to exist in this world it is basic that you should behave, you should always do the right thing, never do the wrong thing. This creates a deep rejection about himself because those wrong things go on coming up—just by saying that something is wrong, it is not dropped, it goes on coming. Then the child starts feeling guilty about himself, he rejects himself. He says, "I am no good. I am a bad child, a bad boy, a bad girl." And the problem is that things which we call wrong are natural, so the child cannot throw them, they have to persist.

Every boy, every girl, starts playing with his or her sex organs. It is enjoyable, it gives a soothing feeling, the whole body feels blissful. And the moment the child touches his sex organ, everybody stops him immediately—everybody feels embarrassed. The father, the mother, will stop him, they may even bind his or her hands so he cannot touch them. Now the child feels in a very deep riddle. What to do? He likes the feeling that comes from the touch, he enjoys the feeling, he feels it is beautiful, but if he is to follow that feeling, then everybody rejects him. He is a bad child and they punish him. And they are powerful, so what to do?

"And such a wrong thing is happening to me!" The child thinks, "It may be that only I am doing this wrong thing, nobody else is doing that wrong thing." And he cannot know about others so he feels guilty: "The whole world is good, only I am guilty." This is a deep problem.

The child doesn't feel like eating, because he knows more about his hunger than you. But you follow a medical routine because the doctor says that after every three hours the child has to be fed. It is written in the books, and you have read the books and you are an enlightened parent, so after three hours, with the alarm, you have to feed him. Look at children when they are forcibly fed: they reject it, they are not opening their mouths, the milk is flowing down—they are rejecting everything. They will not even swallow because they know their hunger. They don't live by the routine, by the clock, they don't know what your medical science says. They are not hungry, that's all—and you are forcing food. And when they are hungry and they are crying, you will not give them food because this is not the right time. Who is to decide? The child or you?

If you decide then you will create a guilt feeling in the child because he will think something is wrong: "When I should feel hungry, I don't. When I should not feel hungry, I do." St. Augustine has said, "God forgive me, because whatsoever is good I never do, and whatsoever is wrong I always do." But this is every child's prayer. You decide, then guilt is created: the child is not feeling like going to the toilet and you force him. Toilet-training is such a guilt-creating thing—you cannot conceive of what you are doing.

If the child is not feeling like it, how can he go? Try yourself—if you are not feeling like it, what can you do? And when the child is not feeling like it, you force him, you persuade him, you coax him, you bribe him, you try every method possible. You are creating guilt that something is wrong with him, something is bad.

The child feels guilty and he cannot do anything about it. He does not know how to, because the body is not voluntary, it is a non-voluntary phenomenon. The child doesn't feel like going to sleep, he is feeling perfectly alive, and he wants to run around the house or in the garden, and you say, "Go to sleep." What can you do if you are not feeling sleepy and somebody says, "Go to sleep"? You can close your eyes—but when the father is gone, the mother is gone, the child is simply left in an abyss. What to do? How to follow the order? How to be a good boy or a good girl?

Sin is created and by and by the small child is poisoned. He becomes aware that, "I am not good. Everything is wrong—whatsoever I do is wrong." If he plays he is wrong because he is creating noise, he is disturbing you. If he sits silently in a corner, something is wrong: "Are you ill?" He is always wrong only because he is helpless, nothing else, and you are powerful. He is continuously confused, he cannot sort out what to do and what not to do. And by and by he rejects all that is bad and he forces all that is thought good. He becomes a mask, and deep down in the unconscious all the wounds are carried his whole life.

That is why if I say, "As you are, you are God," you cannot believe it. You are not even good—how can you be God? God means the ultimate good. You are not even ordinarily good—how can you be God? You will not listen to me, you will go to some teacher who will condemn you, who will say you are guilty, you are a great sinner. Then you will be at ease: he is right because this is what you also feel. That is why you worship those people who can condemn you, who can look at you as if you are worms, ugly, dirty. If you see a great following around a saint, a so-called saint, you always find this reason: he is going to condemn everybody. He will say, "You are sinners, and if you don't listen to me you are going to be thrown into Hell." He feels absolutely right because this is your feeling, he agrees with you. So whenever he condemns you, you feel good. What absurdity! What nonsense! And you feel uneasy if somebody says, "You are good and I accept you—whatsoever you are, as you are. The Divine has chosen *this* way to be, in you the Divine has chosen *this way* to be, this is how the Divine exists in you—and I accept it, I don't reject any part. I accept your sex, your anger, I accept your hatred, your jealousy. I accept you in your totality, because through this acceptance, when you are total, the One will happen—and that One immediately transcends all jealousies, all anger, all sex, all greed. Nobody can transform greed—one has to become One, then there is transformation."

That is why Jesus could not be forgiven, because Jews are the greatest guilt-creators. The whole world has done that, but with no comparison to Jews. The whole world exists, according to Jews, because Adam and Eve committed the original sin. You are born out of Adam and Eve and their sin, man is born in sin—sin remains as the central concept. How can they accept that you are God? You can be close to God if you repent, if you change yourself, if you become good. Then God the Father will accept you. Otherwise, as you are you cannot be accepted, you have to be thrown away and away and away from God.

And what was the sin of Adam and Eve? Their disobedience. But why should God be so obsessed with obedience? Because every father is, and your God is nothing but a cosmic father. Why should God be so obsessed with obedience? Couldn't He take a little joke? Couldn't He be a little playful with His children, who were enjoying themselves? Couldn't He take it a little less seriously? And what had they done? Just eaten one apple from a tree which God had forbidden. God seems to be very egoistic because ego is always obsessed with obedience: "Follow me, I am the rule. If you disobey you hurt my ego." But God cannot have an ego, He cannot insist on obedience. This must be the priest, not God, who has created the whole story.

And then you feel guilty: you are born in sin, you are already a sinner when you are born; from your very birth you are a sinner. All that is left to you is to polish yourself, cut yourself here and there and make yourself acceptable.

Vedanta says you are not a sinner—you may be ignorant but you are not a sinner. This is a totally different attitude: God is not against you—you may be against God—and He is not taking any revenge on you. If you are ignorant you are creating your own trouble. This is a totally different attitude: if you are in ignorance you create your own trouble. If you ask Hindus, they will say you may have got into trouble because you ate the fruit of the tree of ignorance, not of knowledge. Man can be ignorant—he is, because he is not aware of himself, of who he is—and then everything goes wrong. But this is not a sin.

So religion means gaining more light, more knowledge, more awareness, not more morality, not more virtue. Virtue will be a by-product. When you are aware, virtue will happen, it will follow like a shadow. When you are unaware, sin will follow because ignorance cannot do anything else, it can only commit mistakes.

Sin is like a mistake. It is just like somebody adding two to two and concluding five—but this is not a sin! If somebody thinks that two plus two makes five, will you think that now he is to be thrown into Hell for eternity? It is a mistake, an error, but it is not a sin. He has to be taught, he has to be given a right perspective of things—he may not know mathematics, that's all.

Vedanta says you are simply unaware, ignorant of yourself. If you become aware, you are God Himself. There is no God except you, other than you. But this is not an egoistic assertion, because this can happen only when the 'I', the center, has disappeared and you have become the All.

"Jesus said: I am the Light that is above them all, I am the All, and the All came from me and the All attained to me.

Cleave a piece of wood and I am there: lift up the stone and you will find me there."

This is one of the greatest poetic assertions. And I would like to say to you that a man like Jesus is more like a poet than like a philosopher or a theologian or a mathematician. He is more like a poet, and if you miss his poetry you miss his message completely. If a poet says something, you can forgive him because you say, "It is mere poetry." But if a saint asserts something, you take it very seriously because much is at stake.

Jesus is a poet, a poet of the Ultimate. And all those who have reached the Ultimate are poets. The language of mathematics is very narrow, it cannot say much. It is very exact, that is why it is very narrow. Poetry is inexact, vague, that is why much can be said through it. But with a poet you have to remember this: that he is talking about mysteries.

Hindus have never killed *any* Enlightened person. Why has it never happened? Because they thought that whatsoever they are saying, whatsoever they assert, is a poetic way to say a thing; you need not analyze it, otherwise it will be stupid. For example, if you go to Jesus and say, "Okay, if you say you are the Light that is above them all, if you say you are the All, if you say, 'The All came from me and the All attained to me,' then show us, prove it. Tell the sun to go off, or create another moon tonight, then we will believe you"—then you are stupid. You have not followed it, because it is a poetic assertion, it is not a scientific statement.

Because of this, Christians have continuously been trying to prove that he did miracles: that he created bread out of stone, he revived a dead man, he did this and that, he opened the eyes of those who were blind, he touched the lepers and they were healed. Why so much insistence on miracles? Because we have never paid any attention to Buddha as a miracle-maker, nobody ever bothered whether this man could do any miracle or not. But why so much insistence about Jesus? If somebody proves that he did not do the miracles, then the whole point will be lost—then Christianity will disappear.

Christianity depends, not on Jesus, but on Jesus' miracles. If some day it is proved that he never raised a man from death, that he never cured a blind man, he never healed a leper, then Christianity will immediately disappear. There will be no Church, no Pope, everything will go—because they don't depend on Jesus directly, they depend on the miracles. Miracles prove that he is the son of God.

No miracle can prove anything. Miracles really prove the ignorance of those who are impressed by miracles, nothing else. As far as I know, Jesus never did anything of this sort. He was not so stupid as to do miracles to convince you. Miracles happened around him of *far* greater significance than you can think. Yes, blind people started seeing, but this is not concerned with the physical eye, it is concerned with a deeper spiritual blindness. Yes, dead people were revived, but this is not concerned with corpses; it is concerned with you who just think you are alive and are not. He made many dead people alive, he brought them to life from their corpselike existence. And this is a greater miracle, because the other miracle will be done by medical science any day now. And the day is not far off—it has already been done.

In Soviet Russia in the Second World War, they revived six men from death. They succeeded—two or three of them are still alive. This will be done by medical science any day now, this is nothing. And once medical science is able to do it, what will you do with your Christ the miracle-maker? Then he may have been a very good doctor, a scientist, but not an Enlightened man.

Eyes can be cured, they will be cured. The body is not the point, the body should not be the concern really. Jesus did miracles, but those miracles were spiritual, they were concerned with your inner being. You are blind because you cannot see yourself. What type of eyes do you have? A person who cannot see himself, what type of eyes does he have?

Jesus made you see, he looked into the inner world, he gave you eyes, right—but not these eyes that look into the world. This has to be understood. He never made any bread out of any stone, because this is foolish. But followers look for miracles, because they cannot see Enlightenment, they cannot see Christhood, a Krishna is invisible to them—they can only see a stone turning into bread. They can only believe in this world, and if something is done in matter then it becomes a proof to them. That is why they follow magicians rather than Enlightened persons, they follow people who can do tricks. And all tricks are useless, they prove nothing except your ignorance, and they prove that the other man is cunning and exploiting you.

Jesus was not cunning, you cannot find such an innocent man. He was not cunning, he could not have been a miracle-maker, he was not a magician and he was not interested in exploiting your ignorance. And think, if he had really done these things—turned stones into bread, turned water into wine....

I have heard about one woman who was carrying whisky in a

bag and was entering into another country. At the border she was stopped and asked what she was carrying. She said, "Holy water."

But the man on the check-post was suspicious, so he said, "I would like to look, because these people who carry holy water are always suspicious. Water is enough! Why 'holy'?" So he looked, and it was whisky. So he said, "What!"

And the woman said, "Lord! See the miracle again!"

Jesus turned water into whisky? He revived dead persons? Lazarus came out of his grave? Eyes were given? People who could not walk, walked; who could not see, could see again; who could not hear, started hearing? If these miracles really happened, then the Jews themselves would have believed that this was the man of God, because Jews are as materialistic as anybody. If these things had really happened, then the Jews would have become mad after this man—they are even more materialistic than any other race—but they didn't pay any attention.

It is impossible not to follow a man who is doing such things, because everybody is ill, and everybody is afraid of death, and everybody is in trouble, and this man is the right person: even if you die he will revive you again, if you are ill he will heal you, if you are poor, stones can become notes—anything is possible with this man. The whole Jewish race would have followed this man, but they didn't follow him, and he was crucified.

What is the reason? The reason is that miracles did happen, but they were not visible things. Only those who were near could feel those miracles. They *did* happen: Lazarus *was* dead—just as you are dead. If I make you alive, that will be something between me and you, nobody else will be aware of it. It will not be announced from the radio and the T.V. Nobody else will be aware of it if I revive you in your inner world, this will be a matter between me and you. And you cannot prove it to anybody because it is invisible. That is why miracles happened, but Jesus' disciples could not prove them, they were such invisible phenomena. They looked within, but how can you prove that you have looked? No photograph can be taken, nobody else can be a witness to it.

They started going around and telling people, "We have seen miracles: those who cannot see have seen, those who were dead have become alive!" This created the trouble, and Jews started asking, "Show us! And if this man is really the son of God, and if he can do such miracles then let us crucify him and see what happens. If he can revive others, he can resurrect himself—we will give him a crucifixion and he will not die. If he knows the secret of immortality, if he is such a healer, then we will make wounds in his body, and we will see whether blood comes out of them or not."

It is because of these disciples' foolishness, because they started talking about miracles which are inner things, that Jesus became a focal point for the whole country: he looked false, he was not the real, authentic Messiah. Then people were waiting for some miracle to happen. Nothing happened—he died just like the other two criminals; *just* like the other two, simply the same—an ordinary human being. Nothing of God happened, no light descended from Heaven; neither was the earth shaken, nor was there an earthquake, nor was God angry and rolling in the sky. Nothing! The son was crucified, and God remained absolutely silent.

That is why Jews have not recorded anything of Jesus: this man was a false man because he couldn't prove himself at the crucifixion. The crucifixion was the test, there it was to be proved whether he was a man of God or not. But those who could see, they saw a great miracle there also. Christians have missed that, and the Jews missed the first miracle, because they were waiting for something *outside* to happen. It never happened and they forgot this man—he was an impostor.

Christians missed the inner thing that happened at the crucifixion. Only a few can see it. Those who have seen themselves can see what happened at the crucifixion: this man accepted—that was the miracle. This man suffered and accepted, this man suffered and still remained filled with love—that was the miracle. Those who were killing him, murdering him, he could pray even for them—that is the miracle, the greatest miracle that ever happened on earth.

The last words of Jesus were: "God, forgive them because they don't know what they are doing. Don't punish them, because they are ignorant." This is the greatest miracle, at the crucifixion: the whole body is suffering, and he is dying—yet still filled with love. Anger would have been absolutely okay. If he had cried and cursed and said, "God, look what they are doing to your son. Kill them all!"—that would have been ordinary, human. This is Divine. At the crucifixion he proved that he was the son of God, because compassion remained pure.

You could not poison his compassion, you could not destroy his prayer, you could not destroy his heart. Whatsoever you did, he accepted you. He would not reject you—even in that moment of suffering and misery he would not reject you. He said, "Forgive them, because they don't know what they are doing."

Miracles did happen but they were not miracles which the eyes can see, they were those which only the heart can feel. He was not a magician. If he had been a magician, and really tried to turn stone into bread, and tried to heal lepers into whole bodies, he would not be worth much, I would not bother about him at all. The whole thing is useless then.

But try to understand: as there is an inner blindness, there is an inner leprosy. You are so ugly and you have done this ugliness to yourself: so guilt-ridden, fear-filled, jealous, anxious—this is the leprosy. It is eating your inner world like a worm; you are a wound inside. He healed, but that is a private thing. It happens between a Master and the disciple. Nobody else becomes aware of it, even the disciple becomes aware only later on. The Master becomes aware in the beginning that the wound is healed. It takes time for the disciple to become aware that the wound is healed. Ordinarily, for many many days, he continues in the old idea that the wound is there—but nobody else can see it.

Jesus says, "I am the All." You are also the All—Jesus is simply saying that which should be known to everybody, which should be felt by everybody. You are the All, you are the source of the All, and the All is moving towards you. Jesus is just a representative of you. He is not saying anything about himself, he is saying something about you. You are the mustard seed, he has become the blooming tree—he is making an assertion about you. He is saying, "I am the All." What does he mean? He says you also can become the All. You are already the All, but you are not aware of it.

Your misery is that you cannot remember who you are. Self-remembering is needed, nothing else is to be done. You have to become more conscious, more conscious. You have to raise your consciousness to a peak from where you can see. At that moment you become illuminated; no corner remains dark, your whole being becomes aflame. Then you will understand Jesus, then you will understand Buddha, then you will understand Krishna, or then you will understand me, because the whole effort is to make you aware of who you are.

Remember these words. Let them vibrate into your heart again and again, because through these words your seed will undergo a shaking:

"Jesus said: I am the Light that is above them all, I am the All, and the All came from me and the All attained to me.

Cleave a piece of wood and I am there; lift up the stone and you will find me there."

Sixteenth Discourse

5th September 1974, Poona, India

THE SIXTEENTH SAYING

Jesus said :
Whoever is near to me
is near to the fire,
and whoever is far from me
is far from the Kingdom.

Jesus said :
Come to me,
for easy is my yoke
and my lordship is gentle.

Jesus said :
Whoever drinks from my mouth
shall become as I am
and I myself will become he,
and the hidden things
shall be revealed to him.

Man is born a slave, and remains a slave all his life—a slave of desires, lust, a slave of the body, or of the mind, but all the same, slavery continues. From the moment you are born to the moment you die, it is a long struggle against slavery. And religion consists of being free. Religion is freedom, freedom from all slavery. But man goes on playing with himself, goes on fooling himself, because that is easy.

To be completely free is very difficult. It will need a crystallization within you, it will need a center. And right now there is no center in you, you are not a crystallized being—you are just a chaos. You may be like an assembly, but you are not like an individual. Sometimes one desire overpowers you and then that becomes the chairman of the assembly. Only a few minutes later the chairman is gone, or thrown, then another desire overtakes you. And you get identified with each desire; you say, "I am this."

When sex is in the chair, you become the sex; when anger is in the chair, you become the anger; when love is in the chair, you become the love. And you never remember the fact that you cannot be this or that—sex, anger, love. No! You cannot be, but you get identified with the chair, whatsoever is powerful at a particular moment, you move with it. And this chairman goes on changing, because whenever a desire is fulfilled, temporarily, it is thrown out of the chair. Then another, which is next to it, thirsty, hungry, demanding, becomes the chairman. And you get identified with every desire, with every slavery.

This identification is the root cause of all slavery, and unless this identification disappears, you will never be free. Freedom means the disappearance of identification with the body, mind, heart, whatsoever you call it. This is the basic fact to be understood: that man is a slave, born a slave, born crying and howling for some desires to be fulfilled. The first thing a child is going to do when he is born is to cry. And that remains your whole life—crying for this or that. The child cries for milk; you may be crying for a palace, or for a car, or for something else, but the crying continues. It stops only when you are dead.

Your whole life is a long cry—that is why there is so much suffering. Religion gives you the keys to make you free, but you being a slave, and the life of slavery being convenient, comfortable, you create mock religions which don't give you any freedom, which simply give you new types of slavery. Christianity, Hinduism, Buddhism, or Islam, as they are, organized, established, they are new sorts of imprisonments.

Jesus is freedom, Mohammed is freedom, Krishna is freedom, Buddha is freedom, but not Buddhism, not Mohammedanism, not Christianity, not Hinduism—they are mock. So a new slavery is born: not only are you a slave to your desires, your thoughts, your feelings, your instincts, you also become slaves to the priests. More slavery happens out of your mock religions, and nothing changes in you.

I have heard, once it happened: Mulla Nasrudin was very much hounded by his creditors. He had taken much money from many people, and there was no way to get rid of them. So he asked his lawyer, and as lawyers do, he suggested, "Do one thing, Nasrudin, because there is no way out: make arrangements for a mock funeral with you in the casket. Let the whole town know that you are dead, and then escape from this town. All your creditors will know then that you are dead, and they won't bother."

It looked workable, it appealed to him. Nasrudin arranged a mock funeral. He was in the casket, the whole town gathered to say goodbye to him. The first creditor very sadly said goodbye, then the second, the third, the fourth, the fifth. . . . But the ninth creditor pulled out a gun and hollered and said, "Nasrudin, I know you are dead, but still I will shoot you, just to have a little satisfaction." Nasrudin jumped out of the casket and said, "Hold on! You, I will pay!"

You cannot play with death, you cannot be mock about death, you cannot fool death. How can you be alive in a false way if you cannot even die in a false way? If you cannot die in a false way, it is almost impossible to live in a false way. You create more misery around you, nothing is solved through it; everything becomes more and more a riddle.

The more you try to solve, the more insanity is created, because within your heart you know that it is false. You go to the temple. Have you ever really gone to the temple? It is a mock religion, just to show to others that you are religious. But is this going to help? Then this temple also becomes a slavery—ritual *is* slavery. Then this priest also exploits you because he knows your weakness.

With religion we have played the greatest game, and the game is that we have moulded fetters out of freedom. That is why a man like Jesus or Krishna is dangerous: he is not going to give you a mock life, he will give you the real thing.

That is why Jesus says:

"Whoever is near to me is near to the fire..."

What fire does he mean? The fire in which you will not remain. You will have to disappear completely. This crowd that you are cannot be allowed to remain, because this has been your misery, and this is your misery and anguish. This crowd has to disappear, disappear in a crystallized center.

Fire is an alchemical term; anything that needs to be crystallized will have to pass through fire. If you want to make something out of gold, the gold will have to pass through fire. First it will have to become liquid, then it will be purified—it will be pure gold— and then you can mould it into anything else. But it will have to pass through fire. And the same is going to happen to a disciple: the Master is a fire, and you have to become completely liquid so that all that was wrong is burnt, and all that was right has become liquid and one. Then you will crystallize.

First a Master is a fire, and then infinite coolness happens through him. But the beginning is fiery, and that creates fear. It is easy to approach a priest—he is as false as you. There is no danger, you know it well. It is easy to pass through a ritual, you know it is mock. But to come to Jesus is difficult: you are coming near a fire; the nearer you come, the more you will feel burnt. When a disciple comes really close—that is what a disciple does: gathers courage, and comes nearer and nearer, and allows the fire to work—he passes through a furnace. Jesus is a furnace.

But when he comes out of it, the disciple is totally different: the crowd has gone, now he is a different, totally different metal. The baser metal has changed into the higher, the iron has become gold—it has been a transformation. When I say it has been a transformation, I mean it is discontinuous with the past. If there is a continuity, there is no mutation, only modification. That is what you have been doing.

You go on modifying yourself a little bit here and there. It is a patch-work, but a patch-work is never revolution. And a patch-work is not going to help you ultimately; a patch work is a patch-work—you are never transformed. Somewhere you change a little, but the totality remains the same. And the totality is so powerful, that the new that you have made will not remain new for long. Sooner or later the totality will absorb it, and it will be old. You go on improving yourself, but no improvement can lead you to religion. Religion is not an improvement. Whom are you improving? You are the illness, *you* are the disease, and you are improving a disease. You may polish it, you may paint it, you may give it a mask—ever the ugliness may not look so ugly—but the illness remains.

A transformation is a discontinuity with the past, it is not a patch-work; you completely dissolve, and something new happens. That is what Jesus says: a new birth, a resurrection. The old is gone and the new has come in. *And the new is not out of the old,* it is totally new—that is why it is a birth; it is not just the old, continuous, modified. No! The old is no more, and something has happened which was never there before. There is a gap: the old drops and the new comes, and there is no causal link. This is very difficult to understand, because the scientific training of the mind has given us an obsession with causality.

We think everything is caused—so even a Buddha is caused, a Jesus is caused, he is out of the past. No! If you think Buddha is out of the past you have missed the whole thing. The past is no more, Buddha is absolutely new—this man never existed before; Gautam Siddhartha was there, but this man Buddha was never there. The old has gone into nothingness, and the new has come out of nothingness. The new is not born out of the old, the new has come in the place of the old because the old is no more, and the old place is vacant, empty. The new has come from the unknown. The old has disappeared from the known, and the new, finding a place, an emptiness in the heart, has entered.

It is just like when your room is dark: it is closed, all the windows and doors are closed, it is as dark as if it were night. And then you open the window or the door. Suddenly the darkness has disappeared, now it is light, the sun has entered. What will you say? Will you say that the sun, this light, is caused by the darkness that was there? The darkness has changed into light? No! The darkness has simply disappeared from the room and light has entered. This light is not in any way related to the darkness, it is not caused by the darkness, it is totally new. It was waiting outside the gate, the doors opened and it entered—just an opening was needed.

Whenever you meditate you are creating an opening; when you pray you are creating an opening. The old, the darkness, will disappear and the light will be there. And this light is no longer related to the past, just like darkness is not related to the light. They are discontinuous, they are different dimensions, they are different existences. Try to understand this, because this is the miracle that religion has always been insisting on. Science cannot understand it because science thinks in terms of modification, change, continuity. Religion thinks in terms of discontinuity, transformation, mutation.

You are not going to become a Jesus or a Buddha—*you* are the barrier. You have to be burnt completely, you have to be finished completely. When Jesus descends into you, you will not be there. You will feel as if your past was just a dream that you dreamt, it was never you; the identity is broken.

Hence, Jesus is like a fire. If you come near a Jesus, be ready to die, because Jesus cannot mean anything other than death to you. And rebirth is possible only if you die. If you are afraid to die, escape from a man like Jesus. Don't go near him—he is dangerous, he is like an abyss: you will feel dizzy and fall into him.

"Jesus said: Whoever is near to me, is near to the fire..." near to death, near to dying; the old disappearing, the baser metal dissolving. And immediately he says another thing. If you can tolerate the heat, the fire of a Jesus or Buddha or Krishna, then the second thing will immediately become possible for you.

"Whoever is near to me is near to the fire, and whoever is far from me is far from the Kingdom."

If you can pass through the fire of Jesus, if the disciple can pass through the fire of the Master, immediately a new world opens before him: the Kingdom of God, the Kingdom of immortality, the deathless, real Life.

So Jesus says: "Whoever is near to me is near a fire, and whoever is far away from me is far away from the Kingdom." If you escape from Jesus, you are also escaping from the Ultimate Kingdom that can be yours. That is the problem: the attraction and repulsion with a Master. Sometimes you feel like coming near, whenever the Kingdom attracts you—but when you come near you feel the fire, then you try to escape.

Once you are near an Enlightened man, this will remain a problem for you your whole life: to come near, then how to escape. Whenever you are far away, you will again think of how to come near him, because whenever you are distant the fire disappears. So, the Kingdom again, because that Kingdom has to be achieved, that is the fulfillment. Without it you will remain unfulfilled; without it you will remain a barren womb, without giving birth to anything; without it you will remain futile, meaningless; without it your whole life will be just a nightmare, leading nowhere—running so fast and reaching nowhere. Immediately you start feeling how to bloom and how to flower.

That can happen only near a Master, one who has flowered already. Only there will your seeds become uneasy, uncomfortable, in their dead cells. They will start fighting with the cells, and they will break down the cells and come out of the earth to reach to the sun. But that can happen only if you are ready to go through the fire. This is the problem for the disciple: when he comes to the Master, immediately his whole mind-body thinks of escaping.

He finds all sorts of rationalizations to escape; inside he argues continuously how to escape this man, this man seems to be dangerous. When he escapes he starts feeling the desire again.

One has to decide. Decision is final because you cannot go back. Once you are in the fire you cannot go back. Once you are *really* intimate with Jesus, then there is no going back. A point of no return has come, because even when you are passing through the fire you can have glimpses of the Kingdom. Then the fire is not fire, then you are happy and blessed. Then you are grateful to this man because he has become a fire for you. And now the glimpses are not far away, the Kingdom is near.

Once you have had one glimpse of the Kingdom, then all fire ceases to be fire. It becomes so soothing that you have never known anything in life as soothing as it is. But if you escape just at the boundary before jumping into the furnace, you will be in constant trouble—and you have been.

You are not new on this earth, nobody is new; you are as old as this earth, even older than this earth, because you have been to other earths also. You are as old as this universe. You have always existed, because all that is in existence remains in existence—there is no way to go out. You are an integral part of this existence, you have always been here. You have been near many Buddhas, you have been near many Jesuses and Mohammeds. And this problem has always been the trouble.

You were attracted when you heard. When you were very, very far away, they became magnetic forces. Then you came nearer, and the nearer you came, the more fearful you became, because the fire was there. You decided to escape—that is why you are still wandering. But some day, one has to decide to go through the fire because there is no other way. And then you console yourself with false masters who are not fires: then you go to the priest, then you go to the temple and the mosque and the church; then you do rituals, all sorts of mock things, just to escape Jesus and Krishna, because with them the real happens—and the real happens only through fire.

You have to be purified, you have to be really completely dissolved so there comes an emptiness. And in that emptiness, the ray of Creation, God's ray, enters, and then you are fulfilled. Then there is no misery, no *dukkha*, then there is no anguish. Then you remain in the bliss eternal, then the ecstasy is there. Not that it happens through something—then it is your nature, your very being. If ecstasy happens through something, it cannot be eternal, because that something can be lost; if it is caused by something outside, then it cannot remain forever, it can be only momentary.

Ecstasy and bliss can remain permanently with you, eternally with you, non-temporally with you, only when you have come to realize them as your *being*—then nobody can take them. But that being needs a crystallization, needs a purification, it needs an alchemical transformation. The old *must* go for the new to come, the past *must* die for the future to be born. And this is the decision a disciple has to take.

"Whoever is near to me is near to the fire, and whoever is far from me is far from the Kingdom."

Remember that wherever you feel fire, decide—this is the place to go and jump. Wherever you feel only consolations, escape from there—priests may be there but not a Master. They always console you and that is why they appeal to you.

You come to the priest to be consoled, because life is such a misery. The priest is therapeutic, he is a consoler. He listens to you and he says to you, "Don't be afraid. Just pray and God will do everything." He says to you, "Don't be afraid, God is compassionate. Your sins will be forgiven." If you are afraid of death, he says, "Don't be afraid, the soul is eternal, there is no death to it." If you feel too guilty, he gives you means and ways to feel guilt-free. He says, "Donate some money to the temple, donate some money to the church. Donation is good, because that is how you negate your sins, through donation. Do something good: make a hospital, a school, go and serve the masses, the poor, the downtrodden, the ill."

These are the ways to console you, but there is no transformation in it. You may leave your shop, your office, and become a social worker; you may go to the primitives and serve them, but you remain the same, the old continues. You may not exploit, you may start serving, but the old is there—it is a continuity.

You were greedy and you accumulated wealth. Now you donate, but you remain the same. You may have become fed up with greed, now it has become donation; first you were snatching from others, now you are giving—but you remain the same, the inner being has not come to any transformation. People will appreciate you, the society will say, "Now you have changed," but this is no change. This is just throwing away guilt, because you have become guilty of too much exploitation.

Donation becomes a release, it gives you a feeling that you are good, but this is only a feeling. Because you have been bad you are just trying to balance the account; but you remain the same, the same cunning mind, thinking in terms of mathematics, balancing, calculation. What change has happened in you? The money was important before, the money is still important now. It was important, that is why you accumulated it; it is important, that is why you donate it.

Before, you felt you were doing a very good, successful job of it, accumulating, because it was the most significant thing—you were money-obsessed. Still you are money-obsessed: still you are giving, and you think that you are serving people by giving them money, but money remains meaningful. It has changed: from positive, the greed has become negative. But you have not changed, you remain the same—first it was positive, now it is negative.

You were in sex, you lived a life of sex. Now you have become a *brahmachari*, a celibate; you are fed up with women and men, you are finished with all that. But are you really finished? It has become negative. Always remember that when the positive becomes negative, it gives you a false feeling that you have changed. It is just like a man standing on his head: the man remains the same. First he was standing on his feet—that was more natural, sex is more natural—now he is standing on his head, he is doing *shirshasan*, now he thinks he has changed. But how, just by standing on your head, can you be changed? You can become a celibate but you remain the same, nothing changes.

It happened: One of Mulla Nasrudin's friends, Abdullah, was going on a *haj*, a religious pilgrimage, to Mecca. He was an old man and he had just married a young girl. The young girl was very beautiful. Of course, he was going on a *haj*, but he was very worried about his wife. There was every possibility she might not be faithful to him. What to do? So he purchased a chastity belt and locked up his wife. But where to keep this key? To carry it with himself on the *haj* would not look good, because this would be a burden on his conscience, that he didn't believe his wife, didn't trust her. And constantly the key would make him remember his wife and the possibility of her being unfaithful. So he thought, and he went to Mulla Nasrudin, his friend.

Nasrudin was an old man now, almost ninety-nine, and everybody knew that he was finished with women. And when people are finished, fed up with women, they start talking of *brahmacharya*. He was always talking about *brahmacharya*, and condemning people who were still young, and he used to say, "You are wasting your life. This is useless, a wastage of energy and nothing else, and it leads nowhere."

His friend, this Abdullah, came to him and said, "Nasrudin, I am in trouble. My wife is young and it is difficult to trust her, so I got a chastity belt and I have locked my wife into the chastity belt. Now where to keep this key? You are always in favour of *brahmacharya*, and you are my most trusted friend, my best friend, so you keep this key. Within three months I will be back."

Nasrudin said, "I feel very grateful to you that you thought about me in this moment of trouble. And I assure you that the key could not be in better hands. Your wife will be safe."

Abdullah left, easy in his heart now. There was no danger: the man was ninety-nine, one thing; then he was always in favour of *brahmacharya*, and for almost twenty years he had been preaching celibacy. Happy that things had worked out well, he left. But just one hour or so later, he heard a donkey galloping fast behind, coming towards him. When the donkey came near he saw Mulla Nasrudin was on it, tired from the hard ride, perspiring. And he said, "Abdullah! Abdullah, you gave me the wrong key!"

This is going to happen to the negative mind, it always happens. If you can change from the positive to the negative, you can change from the negative to the positive. These are two poles of the same mind. So you may be surprised that *brahmacharis,* celibates, monks, they are constantly thinking of sex, constantly condemning, constantly thinking about it. Both can be dropped, but you cannot do the impossible, choosing one and denying the other. Whosoever denies, affirms; whosoever suppresses, feeds.

You can throw the whole thing out, that is possible, but then you are neither a *brahmachari* nor one who indulges, you simply escape from both, you are neither. Then you are neither male nor female. That is what Jesus means when he says, "Eunuchs of God": when both the polarities have been thrown out. Otherwise, you can retain one polarity: from greed you can move to donations, charity, but the miserliness remains the same. I have seen misers, many types of misers. Basically the types are two: the negative and the positive. The positive miser accumulates money, the society is against him; the negative miser donates, the society is for him— but the miser is the same.

Mulla Nasrudin died, and after just six months, his wife was dying. And they were the most miserly couple in the valley. His wife called a neighbour, a woman, and told her, "Listen to me, Rehamatullah, you have to bury me in my black silk dress. But the material is costly and the dress is almost new, so do one thing. Nobody will see it because I will be lying in the casket on my back. So cut the back portion of the dress and make a dress out of it for yourself."

The woman could not believe it. First she could not believe that Mulla Nasrudin's wife was becoming so charitable, and then she could not believe what nonsense she was saying.

Nasrudin's wife said, "I would be very happy to give you some gift before I leave, and this is my gift. And I hate to destroy this material, it is so costly and so beautiful and so new. So just cut the back part of the dress. Nobody will see."

But the neighbour said, "Here we may not see, but there on them golden stairs, when you and Mulla Nasrudin walk and enter, on them golden stairs, then the angels will laugh."

Nasrudin's wife started laughing. She said, "Don't worry. They will not look at me, because I have buried Nasrudin without his pants!"

A man of greed remains a man of greed, a man of anger remains a man of anger, a man of sex remains a man of sex; just by moving to the opposite pole makes no change, remember this. So you can move to the mock religion easily, because the mock religion always emphasizes the other pole. If you are angry then the mock religion says, "Have compassion, love thy neighbour as thyself. Be friendly, don't be angry—and this will pay!" If you are greedy the mock religion says, "Have control of your greed, because this will pay in the other world." The appeal is again based on the greed, because this is going to pay. So donate, be charitable! If you pay one *rupee* here, if you give one *rupee* here in this world, one million you will get in the other. This is what mock religion is doing: it simply helps you to move to the opposite pole, it is easy.

Mind always likes to move to the opposite pole, because mind always gets fed up with one thing. And the opposite gives the taste again, gives you the possibility to move again. One man who is eating too much gets fed up. The taste is lost, the body hungers no more, he cannot enjoy food, so he starts thinking about fasting. Not that he is changing—fasting will give him the taste again, the body will hunger again. Fasting is always good for those who are obsessed with food. Fast for two days and the hunger comes back, then you can be a glutton again.

Whenever you make love to a woman or a man, the body is satisfied—of course, only for twenty-four hours, but the body is satisfied, you feel fed up. After making love, every man, every woman, thinks of dropping this whole nonsense, it looks so absurd. The peak has gone, now the valley has come and you think that you are deciding something—then you are wrong, you are not deciding anything. Within twenty-four hours, the body will again accumulate energy, and within twenty-four hours the taste will be back again and you will have to break your fast. A twenty-four hour fast is needed for sex, and as you grow older, more time will be needed to break the fast. But when the energy is again full, you are again sexual.

Look at this polarity. Mock religion and real religion have this significant distinction: mock religion helps you to move to the opposite pole, which is not a transformation; real religion simply helps you to burn both the polarities completely. That is why real religion is real fire. Says Jesus: "Whoever is near to me is near to the fire, and whoever is far from me is far from the Kingdom." And when desire, positive and negative, both disappear, the Kingdom is there. The Kingdom is not very far away, it is always there within you. Only because of the desires, you cannot look at it; obsessed with desires, you cannot look at it.

When your eyes are not filled with desire, this way or that way, when you are not moving in sex or against sex, when you are not obsessed with food or obsessed with fasting, when you are simply without desires, then your eyes have no smoke, they are clear, they can see, they have a clarity. In that clarity the Kingdom is there. The Kingdom has always existed within you, but your eyes are filled, overfilled with desires. And desires bring frustrations, tears: desires create hope, dreams. Your eyes are completely filled, that's why there is no clarity. Eyes not filled with desire, dreams, hope, frustration, simply empty—you have the first glimpse.

Near a Jesus, near an Enlightened man, you have to pass through a fire. That fire will burn all your desires—negative and positive both; of this world and that, both. It will burn all your hopes, because through hope, desire lives. In fact, it will burn all your future and past, it will leave you simply here and now; no more past, no more future, no more to look at. Suddenly the energy turns within, there is a conversion, a transformation. Nowhere to look outside: past is useless; death, the future has not yet come— where to go? You have to go within, energy has to move; finding no passage outside, the whole energy turns within. The Kingdom of God is there.

"Jesus said: Come to me, for easy is my yoke and my lordship is gentle."

This has to be understood very, very deeply and remembered, because this is going to help you.

Whenever you come to a man like Jesus, the problem arises in the mind: "Why surrender to this man? This looks like slavery." And then the whole thing looks very contradictory because Jesus goes on saying, "I am here to liberate you, I am here to give you total freedom," and then he demands surrender. Looks contradictory: "Why surrender? Why should I surrender to another man?" And he says, "I am going to give you total liberation." This looks contradictory. "Then he should give it to me right now. Why should I surrender to anybody? Why should I make him a lord? Why should the *guru*, why should the Master, be the lord of my soul and of my being? Why should I surrender?"

Jesus says: "Come to me, for easy is my yoke and my lordship is gentle."

He says, "Yes, I know this is how you will feel, that this too is a sort of slavery." Unless Jesus liberates you, how can you feel that this is really liberation?

You have known only slavery. Everywhere you have moved, you have known slavery. In the name of love, you have known slavery. And love promised that it would be a liberation, but it has not been. Look at any wife, any husband—it has been a slavery, and the yoke has been very hard. You moved in the world in search of freedom, and everywhere you have created prisons, whatsoever you did. In the name of liberty there are all sorts of slaveries: the nation is a slavery, the race is a slavery, religion is a slavery, love—so-called love—is a slavery. And everybody is burdened with too many slaveries. Then comes Jesus and he also wants surrender.

Of course your mind says, "This is again going to be a slavery." Jesus does not deny it, because at this moment, at this state of mind, you cannot understand what liberation is. So he says, "Come to me, for easy is my yoke..." That is all he promises you. He does not say, "I will give you freedom right now." That may happen, but right now he gives only one promise, he says, "...easy is my yoke and my lordship is gentle."

In life, hard is your yoke, and in life, all around you, there are lords dominating and dictating to you. And they are dangerous, ferocious; they are like lions jumping on you and murdering you. Jesus says, "At this moment, only this much can be said which will be understood by you: my yoke is not hard, it is not heavy." And when you think, "Why surrender?" then you are not choosing freedom. You are simply choosing your old slavery in the name of freedom, because your mind itself is a slavery, your desires are slaveries. And you cannot move beyond them without some help that comes from the outside.

You have remained in the prison so long that you think it is your home. And the prison is so heavily guarded that you cannot get out of it unless somebody who is outside the prison helps you, unless there is somebody who has got out of the prison and knows the way to get out of it.

A Master only means this much: that he was also in the prison, the same prison in which you are, but somehow he has escaped; he found a door, he found a lock and key, some method, and he has escaped—now he can be helpful. If you are all asleep, you cannot get out of the sleep. Something from the outside is needed, even an alarm may be helpful, still it is something from the outside. But you can deceive yourself with an alarm, because you can dream that there is a temple and the temple bell is ringing; you can create a dream and go on sleeping. Somebody—not a mechanical device but somebody alive—a Master is needed, who is awake, who will not allow your sleep to create new dreams, who will go on shaking you.

Jesus says: "Ultimately, freedom will happen to you, but right now I can promise only this much, that my yoke is not hard, it is easy, and my lordship is gentle." And you have chosen such hard lordships, all around you.

It happened: A very meek man entered an office, thin-looking, ill-looking, very humble. He said, "I have come to know that you need a night-watchman."

The manager looked at him dubiously and said, "Yes, we need a night-watchman, but we need a person who is continuously uneasy, and particularly at night. We need a person who never believes anybody, who is a skeptic, a born skeptic: whatsoever you do, he will never trust you. And he must be a person who is always searching for trouble, and who is always listening to what is happening all around; who is almost a neurotic, and once roused, becomes a fiend incarnate."

That meek and humble man stood up and said, "Then I will send my wife."

This is how a husband feels about a wife, and this is how a wife feels about a husband—the lordship is really heavy. But this is how, if you become aware, your every desire is heavy, and goads you continuously towards futile goals. If you don't go there is trouble; if you go there is frustration. Each desire is a master and millions are the desires. So you are a mass, you are a slave to millions of masters. It is hard, and every desire is goading you towards a goal of its own, not worried about you. And if you don't go, there is trouble; the desire is not going to leave you so easily because it is a question of lordship. And if you go, there is going to be frustration, because that goal may have been the desire's goal, but it was never your goal. And you don't know what your goal is, because you don't know who you are.

Surrender means choosing one Master as the lord, against these millions of masters of desires and instincts. The lordship is gentle, it is gentle for many reasons: basically because one is the master. It is always good to have one master. Even if you have two masters you will know trouble, and if the masters are millions, you will be in constant confusion. Millions of orders will be received, and in every direction you will be pulled; you will become a chaos. That is how madness happens, because you cannot see what to do. Whom to follow and whom not to follow? Your greed says, "Just go on accumulating money." Your sex says, "Go on indulging in sex." But then there is a problem because there is conflict.

If you indulge too much in sex you cannot accumulate money. Misers are always anti-sexual, they have to be, because the same energy has to be converted into accumulating money. Misers are not lovers, they are very anti-sexual. And people who indulge in sex can never accumulate money, difficult. Even if their forefathers did, they will throw it away, they will find ways to throw it away.

One desire says, "Accumulate money, because money means security. Who is going to help you in your old age? Have a bank balance, that is protection." And then sex says, "But life is going, why think about old age? Your youth is being wasted, go and indulge before the moment is gone and energy is lost. Use it, enjoy it!" Sex says, "Be here and now, this moment, indulge!" And greed says, "Don't think of this moment, think of the long-range goal." There is conflict, and this is not only between two desires— every desire is in conflict with others. Anger says, "Kill immediately, murder this man!" But your own fear says, "Don't do this, because if you kill others, others will kill you. Be polite, smile. You are a good man, you are not a murderer, you are not a criminal." So what to do? So many masters, and only one is the slave.

It is good if you choose one Master. At least a million voices dissolve, only Jesus has to be followed, and you can throw all the responsibility on him. And he says: "Easy is my yoke..." Why is it easy? Because even if he asks you to surrender, he is asking you to surrender only so that you become free of your other masters. Once you are free of your desires he will throw this yoke also. This is just an interim arrangement, just a passage. Once you have thrown all the desires, then this surrender is not needed. The Master himself will say, "Now drop this surrender also, because you have become Enlightened in your own light, in your own right."

"Jesus said: Come to me, for easy is my yoke and my lordship is gentle.

Jesus said: Whoever drinks from my mouth shall become as I am and I myself will become he, and the hidden things shall be revealed to him."

The surrender is a passage for the disciple to become a Master himself. And if you totally surrender, in that very moment you have become one with the Master, because then there is no conflict. Then there is no ego, the 'ego-trip' is finished, you have dropped out of it. And when you are not, that is what the surrender means: when you say, "I am not, you are, and lead me wheresoever.... I am not going to decide, you decide. I will simply follow like a shadow, I will be blind in my trust. Even if you say, 'Jump and die!' I will jump and die. There will be no more *no* coming from me; my *yes* is final and total and absolute." This absolute *yes* is surrender.

What does it mean? It means now the ego cannot persist in you, there is no meaning to it and there is no feeding it. If this can be done, then even in a single instant, when you are not, the doors are open and Jesus has entered you, the light of the Buddha has penetrated you.

Why are you afraid of surrendering? Because the doors will be open, you will become vulnerable. You are afraid of the outside world; you have lived in your dark room, closed, for so long that you have become attuned to it, you have become one with the darkness. You are afraid of the light. When you open the door you may not be able to see the light at all. It may dazzle you so much that you may close your eyes. The fear is that if you surrender then you enter on an unknown path. And the mind is always afraid of the unknown. And the unknown is God, the unknown is Jesus! He is just a messenger of the unknown, just a ray from the sun. The sun may be very very far off, but the ray has knocked at your door. Surrender means to open the door.

"Whoever drinks from my mouth..."

This is very symbolic and very meaningful. Lovers drink from each others' mouths. That is what a kiss is: a deep kiss is drinking the wine of the body from each others' mouths. It is one of the most intoxicating things, no alcohol can compete with it. But the same phenomenon exists on the spiritual level also: a disciple drinks from the Master's mouth. It is not a bodily phenomenon, it is at the deepest core, where the disciple meets the Master's being, where they embrace each other, where they kiss each other. This is what Jesus means:

"Whoever drinks from my mouth shall become as I am and I myself will become he, and the hidden things shall be revealed to him."

Jesus has used the symbolic terms of drinking and eating very much. He says, "Eat me, drink me, absorb me completely in you." That is what the meaning of eating and drinking is: let me move within you, digest me so completely that I become part of your being—and then there is no disciple and no Master, the distinction is there no more. Then there is no lord and no slave, then the disciple has become the Master. Then I am you, then Jesus is you. Then he has become you, you have become him; then the distinction is there no more. The distinction has never been there from the side of Jesus, it has been from your side.

Surrender means that you also dissolve that distinction, you are ready to meet. It is just like lovers: even in ordinary physical love you have to surrender your ego—maybe for a moment, but you have to do it; maybe just for a moment, but you have to become one with the lover, the beloved. For one moment your bodies are not two, they have become one whole, one circle. For a moment your bodies meet and mingle into each other, fuse into each other, they are not two separate existences. After a moment they will be separate existences, because bodies cannot meet eternally, but souls can meet eternally. Bodies are solid, they can come closer and closer, but there is no merging really.

Souls are not physical, they are not solid. They are just like the light when you burn a candle in your room: the room is filled with light; you burn another candle in the room, the room is filled with more light. Can you make any distinction between where the light of the first candle ends and the light of the second candle starts? No, there is no distinction; lights meet and mingle and become one. The spiritual is just like light.

When the disciple allows the Master to penetrate, it is just like a sexual penetration on a higher level: the disciple has become the feminine part. That is why surrender, because a woman is at her peak when she surrenders, she is in love when she surrenders. She is not aggressive, she is a passive pole. And a man is aggressive. He has to reach and penetrate, only then is the meeting possible. The disciple has to become just like the feminine: passive, allowing, not creating any hindrances, surrendered. The Master has to be like a male phenomenon. That is why you can understand the phenomenon that there have been very few female Masters. It is almost impossible, rarely it has happened, and whenever it has happened— one, two, three cases in the whole history of man—those women were not woman-like at all.

It happened once in Kashmir: there was a woman, her name was Lalli. And in Kashmir, they have a proverb that Kashmir knows only two names, Allah and Lalli. She was a rare woman, but you cannot conceive...she was not a woman at all: she lived naked, her whole life she moved naked. A woman hides, a woman is shy, a woman is passive—she was very aggressive, she was just a male mind in a feminine body. She had disciples, but it has happened only rarely, very rarely.

Women Masters are rare because it is impossible, but women disciples number four times more than men disciples, the ratio is four to one. Mahavir had fifty thousand monks; forty thousand were women, nuns, and ten thousand male monks. And you cannot compare feminine disciples, impossible. A man can never become so surrendering, because his whole mind, the type, is aggressive. The feminine mind can easily surrender, surrender comes easy— it is her very being. So you cannot find better disciples than feminine minds, you cannot find better Masters than male minds. But this should be so, because on *every* level the polarity remains.

On the physical level you meet a lover; the woman surrenders, she never takes the initiative. And whenever a woman takes the initiative she is not womanly, and no man will love her. If a woman comes and proposes, you will simply be put off. She waits, she may be thinking and dreaming, but she will wait. The proposal must come from the man, he should take the initiative, he is the one to be aggressive. And she will behave in such a way that she seems absolutely innocent, does not know what you are talking about—but she has been planning and planning, and waiting and waiting for when you will come and propose.

Mulla Nasrudin and his wife were sitting on a park bench hidden behind a row of palms. And suddenly a young couple came on the other side of the palms. The young man immediately started to talk in a very romantic way, in a very poetic way. And Mulla Nasrudin's wife became fidgety, uneasy. She said, whispered in Nasrudin's ear, "It seems that young man is not aware that we are here. So you whistle, to make them aware. And the young man seems so much in love, that I feel that he is just about to propose."

Nasrudin said, "Why should I whistle? Nobody ever made me alert, nobody whistled when I was proposing."

A woman is waiting, she is a womb. Her body, her being is a patience, passivity. And the same happens at the higher level of spirituality: there also she is a waiting. And a disciple has to become like a woman. He has to fall in deep love with the Master, and then there will be a meeting, a merging of higher spiritual beings. And that merging is just like a sexual penetration again— more existential, absolutely non-bodily. And from that meeting the disciple is born again; he becomes pregnant from that meeting, pregnant with himself. Now he carries his own new being in his womb. The whole apprenticeship, the time when he is near the Master, is the time to carry the pregnancy. It can be done only in deep trust; if you doubt, it is impossible, because then you will defend, then you will make an armour around yourself, then you will try to protect yourself.

"Jesus said: Whoever drinks from my mouth shall become as I am and I myself will become he, and the hidden things shall be revealed to him."

Once surrender has happened completely, the Master becomes the door for you. Then a different world of light, life and bliss opens—satchitananda Hindus have called it. The true existence, the true consciousness, and the true bliss, *satchitananda,* becomes possible for you. The Master becomes the door, and once you have attained this you are Enlightened. You can help others now to pass through your fire. Now you can help others to have a glimpse of the Absolute, or to reach the Ultimate and be dissolved in it.

But before you can become a Master, you have to be totally a disciple. Before you can teach, you have to learn, and before you can help, you *have* to be helped. You have to allow somebody to help you deeply. And that deep help is possible only when you are not there, because you are the disturbance, you are the hindrance. You continuously create barriers for your own growth in fear of the unknown. You cling to the known and then there can be no meeting, because the Master is one who is unknown. You remain in the world of the known, the past—the Master is the unknown. And a meeting of two points is possible: the unknown meeting the known. The known will dissolve, the known will burn, the known will be found no more, just like when the sun enters the darkness, it dissolves, disappears.

Be a darkness before a Master, humble, knowing your ignorance well, ready to surrender and wait—then Jesus can transform you, Buddha can transform you. In fact, Jesus and Buddha are just catalytic agents. Your surrender transforms you, they are just excuses. If you can surrender even without a Buddha, without a Jesus around you; if you can surrender to the cosmos, the same will happen. It will be difficult for you to surrender then, because there will be no object to surrender to. It will be more difficult— that is why Buddha, Jesus, they are just excuses.

And then I would like to tell you of one very strange phenomenon that sometimes happens: even surrendering to a wrong master, sometimes you become Enlightened—the master himself is not Enlightened. It has happened, it can happen again, because the basic thing is to surrender. The transformation comes through surrendering, the Master is just an object. Right or wrong does not make much difference.

When *you* surrender, the door opens. So don't bother much where to surrender, simply think about more and more surrendering. That is why even before a stone statue it can happen, or before a tree it can happen. It happened before the Bodhi Tree—that is why Buddhists have been preserving that tree for so long, because it happened before the tree itself. Just the feeling that Buddha attained under this tree, and you surrender to the tree.

Surrender is the thing, everything else is just a help towards it. If you can find a right Master, so far so good; if you cannot find one, don't bother much. Surrender anywhere you like, but let the surrender be total. If the surrender is partial, even a Jesus or Buddha cannot help you. If the surrender is total, then even if they are not there, any ordinary man can also be helpful to you.

This emphasis has to be remembered, otherwise the mind goes on playing tricks. It thinks, "How should I be certain that this Master is right? Unless I am certain, how can I surrender?" And you cannot be certain before you surrender, there is no way to be certain. If you want to be certain about the taste of the food, then the taste of the pudding is in its eating. How can you be certain without eating it? There is no way.

You have to eat Jesus, you have to drink Jesus—that is the only way. You will be transformed because you believed, because you trusted, and surrendered, and then many hidden dimensions will be open to you. The life that you see is not all; it is such a minute part, atomic part of the Whole. The pleasures that you have known are just rubbish. Not even a single ray exists in them of the bliss that is possible, that is your birthright.

All that you have accumulated is junk—if you can come to know the real treasure that is hidden within you. All your life is a begging, and the Emperor waits just within your heart—this is what Jesus calls the Kingdom. Don't be a beggar, you can be kings! But then one has to dare. A beggar need not dare, but to become a king one has to dare and pass through transformations. Surrender is the gate.

I will repeat the words:

"Jesus said: Whoever is near to me is near to the fire, and whoever is far from me is far from the Kingdom.

Jesus said: Come to me, for easy is my yoke and my lordship is gentle.

Jesus said: Whoever drinks from my mouth shall become as I am and I myself shall become he, and the hidden things shall be revealed to him."

Seventeenth Discourse

6th September 1974, Poona, India

THE SEVENTEENTH SAYING

Jesus said:
Blessed are the solitary and elect,
for you shall find the Kingdom;
because you come from it
and you shall go there again.

Jesus said:
If they say to you:
'From where have you originated?'
say to them:
'We have come from the Light,
where the Light originated through itself.'

If they ask you:
'What is the sign of your Father in you?'
say to them:
'It is a movement and a rest.'

The deepest urge in man is to be totally free. Freedom, *moksha*, is the goal. Jesus calls it the Kingdom of God: to be like kings, just symbolically, so that there is no fetter to your existence, no bondage, no boundary—you exist as infinity, nowhere do you clash with anybody else, as if you are alone.

Freedom and aloneness are two aspects of the same thing. That is why Mahavir called his concept of *moksha, kaivalya. Kaivalya* means to be absolutely alone, as if nobody else exists. When you are absolutely alone, who will become a bondage to you? When nothing else is there, who will be the other? That is why those who are in search of freedom will have to find their solitariness; they will have to find a way, means, method to reach their aloneness.

Man is born as part of the world, as a member of a society, of a family, as part of others. He is brought up not as a solitary being, he is brought up as a social being. All training, education, culture, consists of how to make a child a fitting part of the society, how to make him fit with others. This is what psychologists call adjustment. And whenever somebody is a solitary he looks maladjusted.

Society exists as a network, a pattern of many persons, a crowd. There you can have a little freedom—at the cost of much. If you follow the society, if you become an obedient part to others, they will lease you a little world of freedom. If you become a slave, freedom is given to you. But it is a given freedom, it can be taken back any moment. And it is at a very great cost: it is an adjustment with others, so boundaries are bound to be there.

In society, in a social existence, nobody can be absolutely free. The very existence of the other will create trouble. Sartre says, "The other is the hell," and he is right to a very great extent because the other creates tensions in you; you are worried because of the other. There *is* going to be a clash because the other is in search of absolute freedom, you are also in search of absolute freedom—everybody needs absolute freedom—and absolute freedom can exist only for one.

Even your so-called kings are not absolutely free, cannot be. They may have an appearance of freedom but that is false: they have to be protected, they depend on others—their freedom is just a façade. But still, because of this urge to be absolutely free, one wants to become a king, an emperor. The emperor gives a false feeling that he is free. One wants to become very rich, because riches also give a false feeling that you are free. How can a poor man be free? His needs will be the bondage because he cannot fulfill his needs. Everywhere he moves comes the wall which he cannot cross.

Hence the desire for riches. Deep down is the desire to be absolutely free, and all desires are created by it. But if you move in false directions, you can go on moving but you will never reach the goal, because from the very beginning the direction has become wrong—you missed the first step.

In old Hebrew, the word 'sin' is very beautiful. It means one who has missed the mark, there is no sense of guilt in it really. Sin means one who has missed the mark, gone astray, and religion means to come back to the right path so you don't miss the goal. The goal is absolute freedom, religion is just a means towards it. That is why you have to understand that religion exists as an antisocial force: its very nature is antisocial, because in society absolute freedom is not possible.

Psychology is in the service of the society. The psychiatrist goes on trying in every way to make you adjusted again to the society; he is in the service of the society. Politics, of course, is in the service of the society. It gives you a little freedom so that you can be made a slave. That freedom is just a bribery—it can be taken back any moment. If you think that you are really free, soon you can be thrown into prison. Politics, psychology, culture, education, they all serve society. Religion alone is basically rebellious. But the society has fooled you, it has created its own religions: Christianity, Hinduism, Buddhism, Mohammedanism—these are social tricks. Jesus is antisocial.

Look at Jesus: he was not a very respectable man, could not be. He moved with wrong elements, antisocial elements, he was a vagabond, he was a freak—had to be, because he would not listen to the society, and he would not become adjusted to the society. He created an alternate society, a small group of followers. *Ashrams* have existed as antisocial forces—not all *ashrams*, because society always tries to give you a false coin. If there are a hundred *ashrams* then there may be one, that too only perhaps, that is a real *ashram*. Because that one will exist as an alternative society, against this society, this crowd, against what Jesus calls "they"—the nameless crowd.

Schools have existed—for example, Buddha's Bihar monasteries —which try to create a society that is not a society at all. They create ways and means to make you really and totally free—no bondage on you, no discipline of any sort, no boundaries; you are allowed to be infinite and the All.

Jesus is antisocial, Buddha is antisocial, but Christianity is not antisocial, Buddhism is not antisocial. Society is very cunning: it immediately absorbs—even antisocial phenomena it absorbs into the social. It creates a façade, it gives you a false coin, and then you are happy, just like small children who have been given a false plastic breast. They go on sucking it, they feel they are being nourished. It will soothe them, of course, they will fall into sleep.

Whenever a child is uneasy, this has to be done: a false breast has to be given. He sucks, believing that he is getting nutrition. He goes on sucking, and then sucking becomes a monotonous process; nothing is moving in, just sucking and it becomes like a *mantra*. Then he falls into sleep; bored, feeling sleepy, he goes into sleep. Buddhism, Christianity, Hinduism, and all other 'isms' which have become established religions, are just false breasts. They give you consolation, they give you good sleep, they allow a soothing existence in this torturing slavery all around; they give you a feeling that everything is okay, nothing is wrong. They are like tranquillizers, they are drugs.

Not only is LSD a drug, Christianity is also, and a far more complex and subtle drug which gives you a sort of blindness. You cannot see what is happening, you cannot feel how you are wasting your life, you cannot see the disease that you have accumulated through many existences. You are sitting on a volcano and they go on saying that everything is okay: God in Heaven and government on the earth, everything is okay. And the priests go on saying to you, "You need not be disturbed, we are there. You simply leave everything in our hands and we will take care of you in this world and in the other also." And you have left it to them, that is why you are in misery.

Society cannot give you freedom. It is impossible, because society cannot manage to make everybody absolutely free. Then what to do? How to go beyond society? That is the question for a religious man. But it seems impossible: wherever you move society is there; you can move from one society to another, but society will be there. You can go even to the Himalayas—then you will create a society there. You will start talking with the trees, because it is so difficult to be alone. You will start making friends with the birds and animals, and sooner or later there will be a family. You will wait every day for the bird who comes in the morning and sings.

Now you don't understand that you have become dependent, the other has entered. If the bird doesn't come you will feel a certain anxiety. What has happened to the bird? Why has he not come? Tension enters, and this is not in any way different from when you were worried about your wife or worried about your child. This is not in any way different, it is the same pattern: the other. Even if you move to the Himalayas you create society.

Then something has to be understood: society is not without you, it is something within you. And unless the root causes within you disappear, wherever you go the society will come into existence again and again and again. Even if you go to a hippy community, the society will come in, it will become a social force.

If you go to an *ashram*, society will come in. It is not the society that follows you, it is you. You always create your society around you—you are a creator. Something in you exists as a seed which creates the society. This shows really that unless you are transformed completely you can never go beyond society, you will always create your own society. And all societies are the same; the forms may differ, but the *basic* pattern is the same.

Why can't you live without society? There is the rub! Even in the Himalayas you will wait for somebody: you may be sitting under a tree and you will wait for someone, a traveller, a hunter, who passes by the road. And if somebody enters, you will feel a little happiness coming to you. Alone, you become sad, and if a hunter comes you will gossip, you will ask, "What is happening in the world? Have you got the latest newspaper?" Or, "Give me news! I am hungry and thirsty for it." Why? Roots have to be brought up to light so that you can understand.

One thing: you need to be needed, you have a deep need to be needed. If nobody needs you, you feel useless, meaningless; if somebody needs you, he gives you significance, you feel important. You go on saying, "I have to look after the wife and the children," as if you are carrying them as a burden—you are wrong. You talk as if it is a great responsibility and you are just fulfilling a duty. You are wrong! Just think, if the wife is not there and the children have disappeared, what will you do? Suddenly you will feel your life has become meaningless, because they needed you. Small children, they waited for you, they gave you significance, you were important. Now that nobody needs you, you will shrink because when nobody needs you, nobody pays attention to you; whether you are or not makes no difference.

I have heard: One mental patient was psycho-analyzed, but the psycho-analyst was a very eccentric man—as they almost always are. After two or three years of analysis he told his friend, "This man is in even more trouble than I am, because I go on talking and he never says anything—not even *yes* or *no* has he said for these three years—he simply sits there. And now I am worried what to do. I go on talking and talking and talking, he listens and this has been going on for three years. What to do?"

The friend said, "Then why don't you stop?" But the man could not stop.

And then a second trouble happened: the psychiatrist died. Again he said to the friend, "Now another problem has arisen. First was this, that this man never said anything, *yes* or *no*. I never knew whether he rejected me or accepted me, or whether I was wrong or right. I simply talked and talked and talked, and he listened. Now he is dead, so a second problem has arisen. What to do now?"

The friend said, "If he never talked to you, what is the difference? You go on talking!"

But the man said, "No! But he listened."

The whole of psycho-analysis and its business depends on listening. There is nothing much, there is really nothing much in psycho-analysis, and the whole thing around it is almost complete hocus-pocus. But why? Because a man pays you so much attention, and not an ordinary man—a famous psychiatrist, well-known, who has written many books; many well-known people have been treated by him. You feel good because nobody else listens to you, not even your wife. Nobody listens to you, nobody pays any attention to you, you move in the world as a nonentity, nobody—and you pay too much to a psychiatrist. It is a luxury, only very rich people can afford it.

Why, why do they do it? What do they do? They simply lie down on the couch and talk, and the psycho-analyst listens—but he listens, he pays attention to you. Of course, you have to pay for it, but you feel good. Simply because the other is paying attention you feel good. Out of his office, you walk differently, your quality has changed: you have a dance in your feet, you can hum, you can sing. It may not be forever now—next week you will have to come again to the office—but when somebody listens to you, pays attention to you, he says, "You are somebody, you are worth listening to," he doesn't seem bored. He may not say anything but then, too, it is very good.

You have a deep need to be needed. Somebody *must* need you, otherwise you don't have any ground under your feet—society is your need. Even if somebody fights with you it is okay, better than being alone, because at least he pays attention to you, the enemy; you can think about him.

Whenever you are in love, look at this need. Look at lovers, watch, because it will be difficult if you yourself are in love. Then to watch is difficult because you are almost crazy, you are not in your senses. But watch lovers: they say to each other, "I love you," but deep down in their hearts they want to be loved. To love is not the thing, to be loved is the real thing; and they love just in order to be loved. The basic thing is not to love, the basic thing is to be loved.

That is why lovers go on complaining against each other, "You don't love me enough." Nothing is enough, *never* can anything be enough, because the need is infinite. Hence the bondage is infinite, it cannot be fulfilled. Whatsoever the lover is doing, you will always feel something more is possible; you can still hope more, you can still imagine more. And then that is lacking and then you feel frustrated. And every lover thinks, "I love, but the other is not responding well." And the other thinks in the same terms. What is the matter?

Nobody loves. Unless you become a Jesus or a Buddha you *cannot* love because only one can love whose need to be needed has disappeared.

In Khalil Gibran's beautiful book *Jesus the Son of Man*, he has created a fictitious but beautiful story—and sometimes fictions are more factual than facts: Mary Magdalen looks out of her window and sees Jesus sitting in her garden under a tree. The man is beautiful. She had known many men, she was a famous prostitute —even kings used to knock at her door—she was one of the loveliest flowers. But she had never known such a man—because a person like Jesus carries an invisible aura around him that gives him a beauty of something of the other world, as if he doesn't belong to this world. There was a light around him, a grace, the way he walked, the way he sat, as if he were an emperor in the robes of a beggar.

He looked so much of another world, that Magdalen asked her servants to go and invite him, but Jesus refused. He said, "I am okay here. The tree is beautiful and very shady."

Then Magdalen had to go herself and ask, request Jesus—she could never believe that anybody would refuse the request. She said, "Come into my house and be my guest."

Jesus said, "I have already come into your house, I have already become a guest. Now there is no other need."

She could not understand. She said, "No, you come, and don't refuse me—nobody has ever refused me. Can't you do such a little thing? Become my guest. Eat with me today, stay with me this night."

Jesus said, "I have accepted. And remember: those who say they accept you, they have never accepted you; and those who say to you that they love you, none of them has ever loved you. And I tell you, I love you, and only I can love you." But he would not enter into the house; rested, he left.

What did he say? He said, "Only I can love you. Those others who go on saying that they love you, they can't love, because love is not something you can *do*—it is a quality of your being."

In the state you are, you cannot love; in the state you are your love is false. You simply show that you love, so that you can be loved. And the other is also doing the same. That is why lovers are always in trouble: both are cheating each other, and both feel that they are being cheated. But they never look at themselves and see that they are cheating. Have you really loved any woman, any man? Can you say with your total heart that you loved? No! You never bothered about it, you have taken it for granted that you love. The problem is always the other, you never look at yourself.

Mulla Nasrudin had become ninety-nine years old. And a reporter from a local newspaper came to interview him, because he was the oldest man in the valley. After the interview the reporter said, "I hope that I will be able to come next year also, when you have attained your hundred years, when you have completed your hundred years. I *hope* I will be able to come." Mulla Nasrudin looked at the man wide-eyed and said, "Why not young fellow? You look healthy enough to me!"

Nobody looks at himself: the eyes look at others, the ears listen to others, the hands reach towards others—nobody reaches towards himself; nobody listens, nobody looks. Love happens when you have attained a crystallized soul, a Self. With ego it never happens; the ego wants to be loved because that is a food it needs. You love so that you become a needed person. You give birth to children, not that you love children, but just so that you are needed, so that you can go around and say, "Look how many responsibilities I am fulfilling, what duties I am carrying out! I am a father, I am a mother...." This is just to glorify your ego.

Unless this need to be needed drops, you cannot be a solitary. Go to the Himalayas—you will create a society. And if this need to be needed drops, wherever you are, living in the market place, at the very hub of the city, you will be alone.

Now try to understand the words of Jesus:

"Jesus said: Blessed are the solitary and elect, for you shall find the Kingdom; because you come from it and you shall go there again."

Penetrate each single word: "Blessed are the solitary..." Who is the solitary? One whose need to be needed has dropped; one who is completely content with himself as he is; one who does not need anybody to say to him, "You are meaningful." His meaning is within him. Now his meaning does not come from others—he does not beg for it, he does not ask for it—his meaning comes from his own being. He is not a beggar and he can live with himself.

You cannot live with yourself. Whenever you are alone you become uneasy; immediately you feel inconvenience, discomfort, a deep anxiety. What to do? Where to go? Go to the club, go to the church or go to the theatre or just go shopping—but go somewhere, meet the other. For people who are rich, shopping is the only game, the only sport; they go shopping. If you are poor, you need not enter the shop, you just move on the street looking at the windows. But go!

To be alone is very difficult, very unusual, *extraordinary*. Why this hankering? Because whenever you are alone your whole meaning disappears. Go and purchase something from a shop; at least the salesman will give you meaning, not the thing, because you go on purchasing useless things. You purchase just for the sake of purchase, but the salesman, the owner of the shop, he looks at you as if you are a king. He behaves as if he depends on you— and you know well that this is just a face. This is how shopkeepers exploit: the salesman is not bothered about you at all, his smile is just a painted smile; he smiles at everybody, it is nothing particular for you, but you never look at these things. He smiles and greets and receives you as a welcome guest. You feel comfortable, you are somebody, there are people who depend on you; this shopkeeper was waiting for you.

All over, you are in search of eyes who can give you a certain meaning. Whenever a woman looks at you she gives you meaning. Now psychologists have discovered that when you enter a room— in a waiting room at the airport, or at a station or in a hotel—if a woman looks twice at you, she is ready to be seduced. But if a woman looks once, don't bother her, just forget it. They have made films, and they have been watching, and this is a fact, because a woman looks twice only if she wants to be appreciated and looked at.

A man enters in a restaurant: the woman can look once, but if he is not worthwhile she will not look another time. And woman-hunters know it well, they have known it for centuries. Psychologists have come to know just now, they watch the eyes. If the woman looks again, she is interested. Now much is possible, she has given the hint, she is ready to move with you or play the game of love. But if she doesn't look at you again then the door is closed; better knock at some other door, this door is closed for you.

Whenever a woman looks at you, you become important, very significant; in that moment you are unique. That is why love gives so much radiance; love gives you so much life, vitality.

But this is a problem, because the same woman looking at you every day will not be of much help. That is why husbands become fed up with their wives, wives become fed up with their husbands: because how can you gain the same meaning from the same eyes again and again? You become accustomed to it—she is your wife, there is nothing to conquer. Hence the need to become a Byron, hence the need to become a Don Juan and move from one woman to another. This is not a sexual need, remember, this is nothing related to sex at all, because sex goes deeper with one woman, in deep intimacy. It is not sex, it is not love, absolutely not, because love wants to be with one more and more, in a deeper and deeper way; love moves in depth.

This is neither love nor sex, this is something else: an ego-need. If you can conquer a new woman every day, you feel very very meaningful, you feel yourself a conqueror. But if you are finished with one woman, stuck, and nobody looks at you, no other woman or man gives you meaning, you feel finished. That's why wives and husbands look so lifeless, 'lustless'. You can just look and you can tell from a faraway distance whether the couple coming are wife and husband or not. If they are not you will feel a difference; they will be happy, laughing, talking, enjoying each other. If they are wives and husbands, then they are just tolerating each other.

Mulla Nasrudin's twenty-fifth wedding anniversary came. And he was getting out of his house that day. His wife felt a little peeved, because she was expecting he would do something and he was just moving in a routine way. So she asked, "Nasrudin, have you forgotten what day it is?"

Nasrudin said, "I know."

Then she said, "Then do something unusual!"

Nasrudin thought and said, "How about two minutes of silence?"

Wherever you feel life is stuck, it shows that you may have been thinking it was love. It was not love, it was an ego-need—a need to conquer, to be needed every day by a new man, a new woman, new people. If you succeeded, then you felt happy for a while because you were no ordinary man. This is the lust of the politician: to be needed by the whole country. What was Hitler trying to do? To be needed by the whole world!

But this need cannot allow you to become solitary; a politician cannot become religious—they move in opposite directions. That's why Jesus says: "It is very difficult for a rich man to enter into the Kingdom of God. A camel may enter through the eye of a needle, but not a rich man into the Kingdom of God." Why? Because a man who has been accumulating riches is trying to become significant through wealth. He wants to be somebody, and whosoever wants to be somebody, the door of the Kingdom is closed for him.

Only nobodies enter there, only those who have attained to their nothingness, only those whose boats are empty; whose ego-needs they have come to understand are futile and neurotic; whose ego-needs they have come to penetrate and found to be useless—not only useless but harmful also. Ego-needs can make you mad but they can never fulfill you.

Who is a solitary? One whose need to be needed has disappeared, who does not ask any meaning from you, from your eyes, from your responses. No! If you give your love, he will be grateful; but if you don't give, there is no complaint; if you don't give, he is as good as ever. If you come to visit him he will be happy, but if you don't come he is as happy as ever. If he moves in a crowd, he will enjoy it, but if he lives in a hermitage he will enjoy that also.

You cannot make a solitary man unhappy, because he has learned to live with himself and be happy with himself. Alone, he is sufficient. That is why people who are related to each other never like the other to become religious: if the husband starts moving towards meditation, the wife feels disturbed. Why? She may not even be aware of what is happening. Why does she feel disturbed? If the wife starts to pray, starts moving in the direction of religion and God, the husband feels disturbed. Why?

An unconscious fear comes into the conscious. The fear is that she or he is trying to become sufficient unto herself or unto himself; this is the fear. So, if a wife is given the choice: "Would you like your husband to become a meditator or a drunkard?" she will choose that he become a drunkard rather than a meditator. Given the choice: "Would you like your wife to become a *sannyasin* or to move on wrong ways and go astray?" a husband will choose the latter.

A *sannyasin* means one who is sufficient unto himself, who does not need anybody, who is not in any way dependent—and that gives fear: then you become useless. Your whole existence has been around his need that he needed you. Without you he was nothing, without you his life was futile, a desert—only with you did he flower. But if you come to know that he can flower in his solitariness, then there will be disturbance because your ego will be hurt.

Who is a solitary? And Jesus says: "Blessed are the solitary. . ." people who can live with themselves as easily as if the whole world were there with them, who can enjoy themselves just like small children.

Very small children can enjoy themselves. Freud has a particular term for them: polymorphous. A small child enjoys himself, he plays with his own body, he is auto-erotic, he sucks his own thumb. If he needs somebody else, that need is only for the body; you give the milk, you turn him over, you change the clothes—physical needs. He has really no psychological needs yet. He is not worried what people are thinking about him, whether they think him beautiful or not. That's why every child is beautiful, because he does not bother about your opinion.

No ugly child is ever born, and all children become, by and by, ugly. It is very difficult to find an old man beautiful—rare. It is very difficult to find a child ugly—rare. *All* children are beautiful, all old men become ugly. What is the matter? When all children are born beautiful, they should die beautiful! But life does something. . . .

All children are self-sufficient—that is their beauty; they exist as light unto themselves. All old men are useless, they have come to realize that they are not needed. And the older they grow the more the feeling comes that they are not needed. People who needed them have disappeared; children are grown up, they have moved with their own families; the wife is dead or the husband is dead. Now the world does not need them, nobody comes to their home, nobody pays respect. Even if they go for a walk, nobody recognizes who they are. They may have been great executives, bosses in offices, presidents in banks, but now nobody recognizes them, nobody even misses them—they are not needed. They feel futile, they are just waiting for death. And nobody will bother; even if they die, nobody is going to bother. Even death becomes an ugly thing.

Even if you can think that when you die, millions of people will weep for you, you will feel happy: thousands and thousands will go to pay their homage when you are dead.

It happened once: One man in America planned it—and he is the only man in the whole history of the world to have done it. He wanted to know how people would react when he was dead. So before his death when doctors said that within twelve hours he would die, he declared his death. And he was a man who owned many circuses, exhibitions, advertising agencies, so he knew how to advertise the fact. In the morning his agent declared to all the press, to the radio, to the television that he was dead. So articles were written, editorials were written, phone-calls started coming, and there was much commotion. And he read everything, he really enjoyed it.

When someone dies he is always good, people are so approving.

When you die you become an angel immediately, because nobody thinks it worthwhile to say anything against you when you are dead. When you are alive, nobody will say anything for you. Remember, when you are dead they will be happy—at least you have done one good thing: you have died.

Everybody was paying respects to this man, and this and that, and photographs had come into the newspapers—he enjoyed it perfectly. And then he died, completely at ease that things were going to be beautiful.

Not only in your life do you need others, even in your death.... Think about your death: only two or three persons, your servants and a dog following you for the last goodbye—nobody else; no newspapermen, no photographers, nothing—even your friends are not there. And everybody is feeling very happy that the burden is gone. Just to think about it, you will become sad.

Even in death the need to be needed remains. What type of life is this? Just others' opinions are important, not you? Your existence doesn't mean anything?

When Jesus says, "Blessed are the solitary..." he means this: a man who has come to remain absolutely happy with himself, who can be alone on this earth and there will be no change of mood the climate will not change. If the whole world disappears into a third world war—it can happen any day—and you are left alone, what will you do? Except to immediately commit suicide, what will you do?... But a solitary can sit under a tree and become a Buddha without the world. The solitary will be happy, and he will sing and he will dance and he will move—his mood will not change. You cannot change the mood of a solitary, you cannot change his inner climate.

Jesus says: "Blessed are the solitary and elect..." And these are the elect people, because those who need a crowd will be thrown again and again into the crowd—that is their need, that is their demand, that is their desire. God fulfills whatsoever you ask, and whatsoever you are is just a fulfillment of your past desires. Don't blame it on anybody else—it is what you have been praying for. And remember, this is one of the dangerous things in the world: whatsoever you desire will be fulfilled.

Think before you desire a thing! There is every possibility it will be fulfilled—and then you will suffer. That is what happens to a rich man: he was poor, then he desired riches, and desired and desired, and now it is fulfilled. Now he is unhappy, now he is crying and weeping and he says, "My whole life gone accumulating worthless things, and I am unhappy." But this was his desire. If you desire knowledge, it will be fulfilled: your head will become a great library, many scriptures. But then in the end you will weep and cry and scream, "Only words and words and words, and nothing substantial. And I have wasted my whole life."

Desire with full awareness, because every desire is bound to be fulfilled sometime or other. It may take a little more time because you are always standing in a queue; many others have desired before you, so it may take a little time. Sometimes your desire of this life may be fulfilled in another life, but desires are always fulfilled, this is one of the dangerous laws. So before you desire, think! Before you demand, think! Remember well that it is going to be fulfilled some day—and then you will suffer.

A solitary becomes an elect; he is the chosen, the chosen one of God. Why? Because a solitary never desires anything of this world. He does not need to, he has learned whatsoever was to be learned from this world; this school is finished, he has passed through it, transcended it. He has become like a high peak which remains alone in the sky—he has become the elect, the *Gaurishankar*, the Everest. A Buddha, a Jesus, they are high peaks, solitary peaks. That is their beauty: they exist alone.

The solitary is the elect. What has the solitary chosen? He has chosen only his own being. And when you choose your own being, you have chosen the being of the whole universe—because your being and the Universal Being are not two things. When you choose yourself, you have chosen God, and when you choose God, God has chosen you—you have become the elect.

"Blessed are the solitary and elect, for you shall find the Kingdom; because you come from it and you shall go there again."

A solitary is a *sannyasin*—that is what *sannyasin* means: a solitary being, a wanderer, absolutely happy in his aloneness. If somebody walks by his side it is okay, it is good. If somebody leaves, it is also okay, it is good. He never waits for anybody and he never looks back. Alone, he is whole. This 'beingness', this wholeness, makes you a circle, and the beginning and the end meet, the *alpha* and the *omega* meet. A solitary is not like a line. You are like a line—your beginning and end will never meet. A solitary is like a circle—his beginning and end meet. That is why Jesus says: "...because you come from it and you shall go there again;" you have become one with the source, you have become a circle.

There is another saying of Jesus: "When the beginning and the end have become one, you have become God." You may have seen a picture—it is one of the oldest seals of the secret societies in Egypt—of a snake eating its own tail. That is what the beginning and end meeting means, that is what rebirth means, that is what you becoming like children means: moving in a circle, back to the source; reaching there from where you have come.

"Jesus said: If they say to you..."

"They" means the society, the crowd—those who are not yet elected, those who are not chosen, those who are in constant need of being needed—"they". "If they say to you..." and they will say, because they don't allow anybody to become a solitary. They will haunt you, they will try to press you back, into the society. They will want you to come back to the prison—they cannot imagine how you escaped. And they will feel uncomfortable with you if you become a solitary one. Why? Because the very presence of you makes them doubtful about their own existence; that is the discomfort.

Whenever a Jesus moves amidst you, you become uncomfortable, because if this man is right then you are wrong—and this man walks in such a way that he looks right. If this man is right then what about you? The very movement of a Jesus in the society, and the whole society is in an earthquake—because this man seems so happy, not needing anybody, not being needed, so solitary, so alone and so blissful; and you are almost neurotic, almost mad.

Something is wrong with you, not with this man. You will try in every way to prove that this man is wrong. There are books written against Jesus in which it is proved that this man was a psychological case, a mental case; there are books which prove that this man was neurotic. Who is writing these books? "They"

—they are writing these books, because only if they can prove this man is wrong, neurotic, gone mad, are they at ease. But both cannot be right: if this man is right, then you are wrong.

But what is the need? If this man is neurotic, he is neurotic—what is the need to prove it? Why be bothered? Why bother about him? No, it is because he gives you a doubt about yourself. That is why we have not welcomed such people, never! We have always rejected them when they were alive. We welcome them when they are dead, because then we can paint their faces in our own ways.

Look at the face of the Christian Jesus! It is not even a caricature, not even a cartoon—it is absolutely false. Christians say Jesus never laughed, and I cannot see Jesus in any other posture than laughing. He must have been a laughter; whether you heard it or not is not the point, but he must have been like a laughing, bubbling spring, flowing all over. But the Christians have painted him *as* sad as possible. He looks neurotic as they have painted him; he looks *so* sad that to be in his company will be a burden. Just go in any Christian church and look at Jesus' portrait. Would you like to be with this man for one night completely, in one room? You will say, "This is okay, just this Sunday morning is enough." With this man the whole night? One will start trembling and be afraid. And he is so sad; you are already sad enough—why add more?

Christians have chosen the cross as their symbol, and they have missed the whole point. Jesus talked about the cross and he was crucified, but his meaning was totally different. They have chosen the cross because it shows suffering, and we have been suffering so much that we cannot believe in a laughing Christ. We can believe in a suffering Christ—that is so similar to us, just like us, even more in suffering than us. We understand suffering; the language of sadness, suffering and death we understand. Life we don't understand. That is why there is a Christianity, but around Krishna there could not be any religion.

Hindus worship Krishna, but grudgingly—because he is so contrary to your existence: playing on his flute, dancing with girls, always happy and laughing. He is so much against your existence that you cannot understand him. How can you understand dancing?

You can understand death, you can understand crucifixion—you cannot understand a flute and singing.

Christianity spread like a fire all over the world, and there is not a single worshipper of Krishna. Those who think they are, they are not either, they also have difficulties with Krishna. They have to explain Krishna away in many ways. They cannot believe that this man was dancing with everybody's wife, or that he had sixteen thousand girl-friends. Impossible! There must be some other meaning. So they interpret Krishna in their own ways: that these sixteen thousand girl-friends are not real girl-friends, they are man's nervous system—sixteen thousand nerves. But I tell you, this man had sixteen thousand girl-friends: and this man laughed and sang and danced—he was ecstasy itself. And Jesus was the same; that is why I say his name, 'Christ', may have been derived from 'Krishna'.

Jesus was the same, he was not a sad man. But you cannot understand the language of laughter—no, not yet. For a dancing god, your hearts are not yet ready; the world is not yet a home for a dancing god. Krishna seems impossible, but Jesus seems to be almost the conclusion of your life.

The crucifixion became the symbol, the cross became the symbol, but for Jesus the cross means something absolutely different, and I would like to tell you what it means to Christ.

The cross has two lines, simple lines: one line horizontal to the earth, another line vertical to the earth. That is how the cross is —a cross-road, a crossing point. The horizontal line is time: past, present, future; A, B, C, moving in a line. You live on that line. The vertical line is eternity, the now. It is *always* present; there is no past to it, no future to it. It goes higher and higher and higher; it moves higher, not forward.

Time and eternity meet where Jesus is crucified; that moment where Jesus dies is the now. If you die in the now, you are reborn, you are resurrected. Then there is no death for you, because time disappears and you are eternal. The cross is a symbol of time and eternity meeting. *And that point must be your death*. It cannot be anything else, because when you disappear from the time-world, you become part of eternity. And both cross—where do they cross? Here and now, at this moment they cross.

Now is the moment where the cross exists. But if you go on moving horizontally, in the future, then you miss. If you start moving from this very moment, vertically, you are on the cross; you will die as you are, and you will be reborn—a new birth, absolutely new. And through that birth, no death exists—Life Eternal. To Jesus, the cross was a time symbol: time and eternity crossing. But for Christianity it became a sad death symbol of suffering.

If Jesus had been in India and he had not gone to the Jews, and if we had painted the cross, then the cross would be the same but Jesus would be different. He would be just like Krishna: ecstatic, his face smiling, his whole being smiling, because this is the moment of ecstasy. When time disappears, you die to the world of time and you are reborn to the world of eternity—at that moment you must be ecstatic. That is what Hindus have called *samadhi*.

But Christianity missed. It always happens so because Jesus alive is a discomfort, he is like a worm in the heart, biting you. You have to put yourself at ease. When he is dead, then you can arrange everything *according to you;* then you can paint Jesus according to you—then he is nothing but your representative.

"If they say to you—and they will say—*'From where have you originated?' say to them: 'We have come from the Light, where the Light originated through itself.' "*

"We come from God, we are sons of God; we come from the source of all existence. And the source of all existence has no other source—it is self-originating, it is self-creating. The Father has no other father, the Creator has no other creator to it—the Creator is a self-creating force. ... We have come from the Light, where the Light originated through itself."

"If they ask you: 'What is the sign of your Father in you?' "

They *will* ask—they will ask, "Have you become Enlightened? What is the sign? Have you come to know the Father? Then what is the sign? Give us signs!" because they cannot look directly, they always look at signs—they cannot penetrate directly to *you*. Even when a Buddha is there you ask for signs; even when a Jesus is there you ask for signs: "Show us some sign so that we can understand." And Jesus is there. Is he not a sign enough? No, but that you cannot understand—he transcends you.

People used to come to Jesus and they would ask: "Are you really the One who has been promised? Are you that Chosen One?" And they were asking *him*. They must have been asking his disciples more because "they" are always against the disciples. They are against the Master, but they are against the disciples even more, because the disciples move amongst them more; they live with them, they have to live with them, and they will ask puzzling questions. They will ask, "What is the sign of the Father in you? Make water into wine and we will understand. Or revive this man who is dead, or do something against nature!" Then they will understand.

What did Jesus say? Jesus did not say, "Do miracles and give them signs." What he says is one of the most beautiful things ever asserted. He says:

"Say to them: 'It is a movement and a rest. This is the sign of God in us: a movement and a rest.' "

Very difficult to understand. What does he mean? He says: "We are moving and yet at rest. The contradiction has dissolved in us. Now we are a synthesis of all contradictions: we are talking and yet not, we talk and yet there is silence; we love, yet we don't love, because the need to be loved has disappeared; we are alone and yet amidst you, because you cannot disturb our loneliness. We are in the crowd, but not of the crowd, because the crowd never penetrates us. We live and move in this world, but we don't belong to this world—we may be in it, but this world is not within us."

This is what Jesus says: "It is a movement and a rest. Look at us: we move and yet there is no tension in the movement; we walk but at the center of our being there is no movement because there is no motivation to reach anywhere—we have reached. This is the sign of the Father in us. Look at us! There is no desire and yet we go on working. There is no motivation, yet we go on breathing and living. Look at us: the contradictions have dissolved. We walk, and yet do not; we live, and yet do not. You *see us in time,* and time has disappeared for us—we have entered eternity." But this is the sign of a perfect Master. If you want to look at a perfect Master, this is the sign: movement and rest.

It will be easy for you if a master is moving, serving people, changing the society, creating a great movement for some utopia. It will be easy for you to understand a Gandhi: continuous movement, activity—political, social, religious—and devoted to others. It will be easy, very easy, to see that Gandhi is a *mahatma*, a great soul. It is very easy, because there is only movement, and movement devoted to others. It is service: not moving for himself, moving for others, living for others. Or you can easily understand a man who has retired, renounced the world and moved to a Himalayan retreat—does not speak, remains silent, does not move, does not do anything; no service, no social activity, no religious activity, no ritual—he simply sits there in his silence. You can understand him also: he is at rest.

But both have chosen one polarity. They may be very good people—there are good people—but they are not perfect. They don't show the sign of the Father, because perfection is the sign. They have to be like Jesus: moving, and yet silent.

Movement and rest: living in the world, not renouncing it—and yet totally renounced. Where contradictions meet, the Ultimate appears. If you choose one, you have missed, you have sinned, you have missed the mark. Don't choose! That is why Lao Tzu, Jesus and others say, "Don't choose!" Choose and you miss. Be choiceless—let movement be there, and let rest be there, and let movement and rest rest together. Become a symphony, not a single note. A single note is simple, there is not much trouble.

I have heard about Mulla Nasrudin, that he had a violin, and he continuously created one note on it. The whole family became disturbed, the neighbourhood became disturbed, and they said, "What type of music is this? If you are learning, then learn well. You go on creating one note continuously and it is so boring that even at midday, the whole neighbourhood falls asleep."

Nasrudin's wife said, "This is enough. For months and years we have been listening, we have never seen such a musician! What are you doing?"

Nasrudin said, "Others are trying to find their note, and I have found it. That is why they change: they are still on the way, trying to find the note. And I have found it, so now there is no need —I have reached the goal."

A single note is simple, there is no need to learn much, it is uncomplicated. But a single note misses all that is beautiful, because the higher the complexity, the higher the beauty that appears. And God is the *most* complex: the whole world is in Him, the whole universe meets in Him. So what is the sign of your Father? It can only be a synthesis, it can only be a symphony, where all the notes have dissolved into one.

"Movement and rest" is just symbolic. "Say to them, 'It is a movement and a rest.' "

Try to follow this, try to do it in your life. Extremes are easy to choose: you can move into activity and get lost in it, or you can renounce the activity and get lost in rest. But both will be choices —you will be as far away from God as possible, because God has not rejected anything, He has not renounced anything.

He is in all, He is the All. If you also become the All, not renouncing, not rejecting, without any choice, a choiceless awareness, then you have the sign of the Ultimate, the sign of God.

Beware of extremes! They are the dangerous paths from where one falls. Let both the extremes meet, then a new phenomenon arises—more subtle, more delicate, more complex, but more beautiful.

Eighteenth Discourse

7th September 1974, Poona, India

THE EIGHTEENTH SAYING

Simon Peter said to them:
Let Mary go out from among us,
because women are not worthy of the Life.

Jesus said:
See, I shall lead her
so that I will make her male,
that she too may become a living spirit
resembling you males.
For every woman who makes herself male
will enter the Kingdom.

We will be sailing in rough waters today......

But many things have to be understood—and don't be prejudiced either this way or that, because prejudice makes it almost impossible to understand.

First thing: man and woman differ basically; they not only differ, they are opposites. That's why there is so much attraction. Attraction can exist only between opposites; the similar cannot be very attractive—whatsoever you are, you are acquainted with it. For a man, the woman is the unknown. It attracts, it invokes, it invites; an inquiry arises, a curiosity arises. For woman, the man is the unknown. For man, God penetrates through this world in the shape of woman, because God is the unknown. For woman, man represents the Divine because he is the unknown for her. Hence, the opposite is so significant.

So first thing to be understood: they are different; not only different, but opposites—but they are not unequal, they are equal. Difference is there, oppositeness is there, a polarity is there, but they are not unequal, they are equal. Two opposites are always equal, otherwise they cannot oppose each other.

Second thing to be understood: that the female body exists for a totally different purpose; biologically, physiologically, chemically, it has a different function to fulfill from the male body. And it is so different from the male body, that unless you penetrate into the deeper layers of biology you will not be able to understand the difference. They exist as if in two worlds apart.

422

THE MUSTARD SEED

The woman carries a womb. The very word 'woman' comes from 'man with a womb'. And the womb is so important—nothing is more important than the womb, because a whole life has to come through it. The whole moving phenomenon of life passes through it, it is the very gate into this world. And because of the womb the woman has to be receptive, she cannot be aggressive. The womb cannot be aggressive, it has to receive, it has to be an opening, it has to invite the unknown. The womb has to be a host, the man will be the guest.

Because of the womb being a central phenomenon in the feminine body, the whole psychology of woman differs: she is non-aggressive, non-inquiring, non-questioning, non-doubting, because all those things are part of aggression. You doubt, you inquire, you go in search; she waits, the man will come in search of her. She will not take the initiative, she simply waits—and she can wait infinitely.

This waiting has to be remembered because that will make a difference. When a woman enters into the world of religion she has to follow a totally different path from the man. Man is aggressive, doubts, inquires, goes out of the way to search, tries to conquer everything. He has to, because he exists around an aggressive semen. His whole body exists around a sexuality which has to seek, penetrate.

All the arms that man has created up to now—even the bomb, the H-bomb—they are just projections of the male sex, projections of the penis. The arrow, the gun, or the bomb, they penetrate, they reach, they cross the distance. Even going to the moon, a woman will simply laugh and think it is foolish: "Why go there?" But for man it is worth risking life because it is a sort of penetration —penetration into the mysteries of life.

The more distant the goal, the more appealing. Man will reach Everest, he will reach the moon, he will go further ahead; he cannot be checked, he cannot be prevented. Whatsoever becomes known becomes useless, then it is not interesting. Deeper mysteries have to be penetrated, as if the whole of nature is the woman—and man has to penetrate and know.

Man has created science; women can never be scientific, because the basic aggression doesn't exist in them. They can be dreamers because dreaming is a waiting, it is part of the womb, but they cannot be scientists, they cannot be logical—logic is also aggression. Women cannot be skeptical and doubting; they can trust, they can be faithful, and this is natural to them because it is all part of their womb. And the whole body exists so that the womb can survive in it; the whole body is just a natural device to help the womb. Nature is interested in the womb because through the womb life comes into existence. This gives a totally different orientation to the woman.

For her, religion can be a sort of love, it cannot be a search for truth. The very phrase 'search for truth' is male-oriented. It can be a waiting for the beloved, for the lover; God can be a son, a husband, but God cannot be truth. It looks so bare, flat, dry, dead; there seems to be no life in the word 'truth'. But for man, truth is the most meaningful word. He says, "Truth is God, and if you know the truth you have known all." And the way man is going to follow is to conquer: nature has to be conquered.

Because of these distinctions, this has always been a problem. It arose before Buddha because Buddha's whole method was male-oriented. It has to be so, because to devise methods is again an aggression. Science is an aggression, yoga is also an aggression, because the whole effort is how to penetrate the mystery and dissolve it, how to come to know; the whole effort is how to demystify the universe. That is what knowledge means: we have come to know, now there is no mystery.

Unless mystery dissolves, man cannot rest at peace. The universe *must* be demystified, everything *must* be known, no secret should be allowed to remain a secret. So they, men, devised all the methods: Buddha is a man, Jesus is a man, Zarathustra is a man, Mahavir is a man, Krishna is a man, Lao Tzu is a man. No woman comparable to them has ever existed who devised any methods. There have been women who became Enlightened, but even then they could not devise methods, even then they followed. They cannot because to devise a method, a methodology, a path, an aggressive mind is needed.

Women can wait, and they can wait infinitely, their patience is infinite. It has to be so, because a child has to be carried for nine months. Every day it becomes heavier and heavier and heavier, and more difficult and more difficult. You have to be patient and wait, and nothing can be done about it. You have to love even your burden, and wait and dream that the child will be born. And look at a mother, a woman who is just about to be a mother: she becomes more beautiful, because when she waits, she flowers. She attains a different type of grace, an aura surrounds her because now she is at her peak when she is going to become a mother, the basic function her body has been devised to fulfill by nature. Now she is blooming, soon she will flower.

And look at her dreams: no mother, or a woman about to be a mother, can think that an ordinary boy or girl is going to be born—the unique child is always in her dreams. A few dreams have been recorded: Buddha's mother dreamt, Mahavir's mother dreamt, and in India they have a tradition of recording the dreams of the mother whenever an Enlightened person is born. But I always suspect that this is how every mother dreams. You may not record her dreams—that is another thing, because they are not needed—but every mother dreams she is going to give birth to a god. Otherwise is not possible. Buddha's mother's dream has been recorded, that is the only difference. Your mother's has not been recorded, otherwise it could be known that she was also dreaming of a Buddha, a Jesus, something unique. For it is not a question of giving birth. She is going to be born through it.

Whenever a child is born, not only is the child born—that is one part of it—the mother is also born. Before that she was an ordinary woman; through the birth she becomes a mother. On one side the child is born, on another side the mother is born. And a mother is totally different from a woman: a gap exists, her whole existence becomes qualitatively different. Before that she may have been a wife, a beloved, but suddenly that is no longer so important. A child is born, a new life has entered: she becomes a mother. That is why husbands are always afraid of children.

Husbands basically never like children because a third party enters into the relationship—not only enters, but the third party also becomes the center. And after that the woman is never the same wife, she is different. And after that, if a husband really wants love, he has to become just like a son, because this woman who has become a mother can never be an ordinary wife again. She has become a mother, you cannot do anything about it now. The only thing left is that you become a son to her. That is the only way you can get her love again, otherwise the love will be moving towards her son.

A mother has attained to the peak. It is as if the husband, the lover, was just a means to become a mother. Look at the difference: for a woman seeking to become a mother, waiting to become a mother, the husband, the lover, is just a means. For a husband children are not the goal; the man is seeking a woman to love, a beloved, and if children happen they are simply accidents. He has to tolerate them, they are by the side of the road, they are not the goal where the road ends.

This will make a difference when one moves on the path towards God. The question has been arising again and again. Thousands of women became interested in Buddha, and they wanted to enter on the path, they wanted to be initiated, but Buddha resisted, Buddha tried to avoid it. The reason was that the method was basically male-oriented, and to allow women would corrupt the whole scheme. But he had to yield because he was a man of compassion. And when thousands of women came again and again to be initiated, he yielded, but he said very sadly, "My religion was going to be a living force for five thousand years. Now my religion will only be a living force for five hundred years." Because the opposite had entered, now everything would be a chaos. And this was how it happened, Buddhism disappeared from India within five hundred years. It could not remain a living force, because when a woman enters, many problems enter with her: she brings her womanhood in, and the method is basically for the male.

If you can understand Buddha's standpoint, Jesus will look more compassionate. Then you will not think him a male chauvinist—he was not: he was not for man, against woman. And his method, which the Church has completely lost, can be used by both. And the man who raised the question is the man who created the Church. Simon Peter is the man who created the whole Church, Christianity—and of course he should be the first to raise the question.

"Simon Peter said to them: Let Mary go out from among us, because women are not worthy of the Life."

The Church has remained anti-women: monasteries have existed where men have not allowed any women to enter—woman seems to be the root cause of evil. The stranger always seems to be evil because you cannot understand. If you can understand then something can be done. Woman remains the mysterious, and once a woman enters into your life she starts dominating you. And her domination is so subtle, you cannot rebel against it.

Man has always been afraid of this, so those who are in search of some secret in nature or in God would like to avoid woman, because once she comes, she starts to dominate everything. And she wants your total attention: she would not like a god to be there as a competitor, she would not like the Truth to be there as a competitor; she will not allow any competitor, she is jealous. So if somebody is to seek, it is better to avoid women.

Some young man asked Socrates what he would suggest, whether he should get married or not. And he asked the right man! He thought that he was asking the right man, because Socrates had suffered so much through marriage. He had a wife, her name was Xanthippe, one of the most dangerous women in the whole history of man. And he had suffered a lot: continuously she was nagging and dominating him, throwing things at him. She even poured hot tea on his face, and half his face remained burnt his whole life. So this young man was right to ask this man—he knew. Socrates said, "One must get married. If you get a good wife you will be happy, and if you get a wife like mine you will become a philosopher. In either case you will be profited."

Peter said to them (to his friends and other disciples): "Let Mary go out from among us, because women are not worthy of the Life."

It was dangerous to allow women in—because then territories become blurred, you don't know where you are going, you don't know what is going to happen. Woman symbolizes the mysterious, the unknown, the strange, for man; woman symbolizes the poetic, the dreamy, the illogical, the irrational, the unconscious, for man. Woman symbolizes the absurd. It is always difficult to find any logic in a woman's behaviour. She jumps from one point to another, there are gaps, she is unpredictable.

One day it happened: There was a long fight between Nasrudin and his wife. And at the end, as it always happens, Nasrudin thought he would surrender. It is difficult to fight with a woman. She has to win, otherwise she will create such trouble that it is not worthwhile, the victory is not worthwhile. So Nasrudin thought, "Why waste three or four whole days? And then one has to surrender anyway, so why not surrender now?" So he said, "Okay, I agree with you."

His wife said, "Now it won't help—I have changed my mind."

And those who are in search of God, they have always been afraid because with women you are never certain. And it is not better to make them fellow-travellers—they will create trouble, and the trouble is multi-dimensional. Illogical is their behaviour, unpredictable is their mind. And not only that, there is also always a deep possibility of falling in love, a deep possibility of being attracted to them, a deep possibility of sex entering. And once sex enters the whole path is missed, because now you are moving in another direction. Monks, seekers, have always been afraid; their fear is understandable. And this man Simon Peter was giving the direction for the coming centuries, that the purity of religion would be lost, the rationality would be lost if women were allowed.

So he said: "Let Mary go out from among us..." And Mary was no ordinary woman—the mother of Christ! Even that could not be allowed. "...because women are not worthy of the Life." What life? The life that they were seeking, the Eternal Life. Now try to understand why women are not capable of that life.

The whole focus of the woman is natural, she lives in nature, she is more natural than man. In India, we have called her *prakriti*, the very nature, the earth, the base of all nature. She is more natural; her tendencies, her goals, are more natural. She never asks for the impossible, she asks for what is possible. Man has something in him which always seeks the impossible, it is never satisfied with the possible—just becoming a satisfied husband is nothing. A woman will be happy if she can be just a deeply contented wife, a mother, then her life is fulfilled.

Biologists say there is a reason: in man there is an imbalance physiologically, a hormonal imbalance; woman is more complete, she is like a circle, balanced. They say that in the very beginning the combination of the sperm and the egg from which you come decides whether you will be a male or a female. Twenty-three chromosomes are given by the mother and twenty-three chromosomes are given by the father. If the twenty-three from the mother and the twenty-three from the father make twenty-three symmetrical pairs then there is a deep balance: a girl will be born; the same, they balance, they make a symmetry: a girl will be born. But the father has an odd pair of chromosomes, the XY pair. In the mother it is balanced: XX. So half the sperm contain the X chromosome and half contain the Y chromosome. If a sperm containing the Y chromosome moves and meets the mother egg, then a male will be born, a boy will be born, because there will be an imbalance, an asymmetry: XY.

And you can see this imbalance even on the first day a girl and boy are born: the boy is restless from the very first day, the girl is at ease from the very first day. Even before the first day, even in their wombs, mothers know, because boys are restless; they kick, they do things, even in the womb; a girl simply rests, she sleeps. Mothers can become aware whether a boy is to be born or a girl, because a boy cannot be at rest. A deep restlessness exists in man, and because of this deep restlessness he is always moving and going somewhere, always interested in the distant, in the journey.

A woman is more interested in the home, in the surroundings; a woman is more interested in the gossip of the near neighbourhood. She is not much worried about what is happening in Vietnam, it is too distant; what is happening in Cyprus, it is meaningless. She cannot even conceive why her husband goes on reading about Cyprus: "How does it enter into your life?" And the husband thinks that she is not interested in higher subjects. That is not the point. She is at ease with herself, so only the surroundings interest her. Just if somebody's wife has gone with somebody else, that is the news; or somebody is ill, or a child is born, or somebody is dead. That is news—more personal, more homely; just the neighbourhood is enough.

And a more contented wife or mother will not even worry about the neighbourhood, her own house is enough. She feels perfect, and the reason is biological: her hormones, her cells, are balanced. A man has a restlessness, and that restlessness gives him inquiry, doubt, movement. He cannot be satisfied unless he finds the Ultimate. And even then you don't know whether he will be satisfied or not, whether he will again start inquiring into something else.

This makes a difference. And all religions have existed for the distant.

So whenever a woman comes to a Jesus, she has not come in search of God. No, that distant thing cannot be meaningful for her. She may have fallen in love with Jesus. When a woman comes to Buddha, she has not come to find what Truth is—she may have fallen in love with Buddha; Buddha may have attracted her. This has been my feeling also: if a man comes to me he always says, "Whatsoever you say appears convincing, that's why I have fallen in love with you." Whenever a woman speaks, she never says it the same way. She says, "I have fallen in love with you, that's why whatsoever you say appears convincing."

Peter is rightly afraid that even Mary, the mother of Jesus, will create trouble. You are moving in unknown territory. It is better to remain with the boundaries, definitions. Don't allow women in! You can depend on the male mind, you know how it functions, you know the very working of it. Man functions with the conscious and woman functions with the unconscious. So man can accumulate details, but can never be very deep. Woman cannot accumulate details, but can be very deep in a small, simple fact. Man can attain to knowledge, much knowledge, but not to intense love. Woman can attain to intense love, but not to much knowledge—because knowledge is a conscious phenomenon and love is an unconscious phenomenon.

Said St. Peter: "Let Mary go out from among us, because women are not worthy of the Life."

And all religions have remained against women basically because they were created by man. Nothing is evaluated by this, it is not an evaluation, it is simply because they were created by man. He was afraid of women, he would like his territory to be clear-cut, he would not like women to enter in it.

So all religions have remained basically homosexual, they are not heterosexual. And all religious communities have remained homosexual: monks living in a homosexual society. If they have ever allowed women, they have allowed a secondary status to them: they must not decide anything, they simply have to follow the rules—

whatsoever men have decided to be followed—so that they don't create any trouble. And they have never been given the same importance, the same significance; they have been put aside, given a secondary role. They can be nuns, and they can have their own monasteries, but they will never be important, they will not be the deciding factors.

You cannot think of a woman becoming a Pope, impossible! She will destroy the whole structure, the whole establishment. Because he was thinking in terms of creating an establishment, a Church, a great organization of followers, that's why Peter says: "Women should not be allowed. And we should start with Jesus' mother, because once she is allowed, and if we give this preference because she is Jesus' mother, then other women will enter—and it will be impossible to stop the chaos."

"Jesus said: See, I shall lead her so that I will make her male, that she too may become a living spirit resembling you males. For every woman who makes herself male will enter the Kingdom."

Jesus said, "Don't be afraid. I will lead her so that I will make her male." What does he mean? To make a woman male means to make her unconscious conscious; to bring her inner darkness into the conscious mind, so the unconscious disappears and it becomes a conscious whole; to make her mysteriousness not a stumbling-block, but a stepping-stone. Then there is no problem. That can be done, but a very great Master is needed: a very great Master who is both a male and a female, who has attained to the inner perfection where his own inner male and female have dissolved; who is no longer divided, who has become asexual, who is neither male nor female. Only he can help, because he can understand both.

So Jesus says: "I will make her male."

What is he saying? Is he going to change her body? No, that is not the point. The body is not the point: there are feminine minds even in male bodies, and there are male minds even in feminine bodies. A Madame Curie is possible, and she can be as perfect a scientist and as rational as anybody else; the body is feminine, but the mind is not. And there are males who can be as absurd as any woman. Chaitanya Mahaprabhu was a perfect male, he was a great logician, a philosopher. History would have recorded him as one of the greatest logicians if he had remained with it and stuck to it. But then he renounced all logic, became a madman, started dancing and doing *kirtan* (devotional singing and dancing) on the streets. He became feminine, even his face became feminine, so graceful; even his body followed, he became more curved, curves came to his body. And he started to love God as a beloved, dancing and singing. That has happened.

What is Jesus saying? He is saying that the unconscious of the woman can be changed into a conscious, then she becomes totally different. "And I will do this. See, I shall lead her so that I will make her male." What does he mean by"make her male"?

Males should not think that they are in some higher position. It only means the inner darkness from which a woman lives ordinarily, from which she has to live, because she is more body-oriented. Nature needs her more than man: man is just on the periphery, he is disposable; woman is not disposable.

Man is not needed so much. That's why you don't find fathers in nature. Mothers are everywhere—with birds, animals, fishes, mothers are everywhere—but no fathers. Only in human society do you find the father, because the father is just a formality, a social convention, the father is not a natural phenomenon. Linguists say that 'uncle' is a more ancient word than 'father'; 'father' came into existence very late. When the one man, one woman relationship became established, then the father came. But the uncle was already there because all the males were uncles for the child, nobody knew who the father was. Just as with animals, nobody knows who the father is but all the males are uncles.

There can again be a world where the father disappears, there is a possibility, because the father came into existence with private property. Once there was private property, the father came into existence. Then he not only dominated his private property, he also guarded his private female. Private property is going to dissolve some day or other. Once private property is gone, the father will dissolve.

Already in the West the phenomenon has entered: there are many women alone with their children, the father has been disposed of. This is going to grow more and more. But the mother cannot be disposed of, nature needs the mother more, that's why the mother is a more bodily phenomenon, women are more body-conscious than men. If they take too much time while they are dressing, that is the reason. You may go on honking your horn and they don't come and they don't come. . . .

I once heard one woman: I was sitting in the car and her husband was honking, and she looked out of the window and said, "I have told you a thousand times that I am coming in two minutes!" And she was exactly right, because for one hour she had been saying, "I am coming in two minutes." Why so much time in dressing? She is body-conscious. Man is more mind, woman is more body.

One famous actress said once—when she said it people thought she was very humble, modest, and actresses are not expected to be so—she said, "I know I am not a very beautiful woman, but what is my opinion against the opinion of the mirror? What is *my* opinion against the opinion of the mirror? I know I am not a very beautiful woman, but the mirror says, 'You are the most beautiful'."

They go on standing at the mirror for hours, looking at themselves. A man cannot even imagine what is happening.

Mulla Nasrudin was killing flies one day and he told his wife, "I have killed two women and two men, two male flies and two female flies."

His wife was puzzled, she said, "How did you come to know which was male and which was female?"

He said, "Two were sitting on the mirror."

Women are more body-conscious, more *body*, more *grounded*—that's why they live longer than men, four years longer than men. Hence so many widows: they always exhaust the husband first. One hundred and twenty boys are born to one hundred girls, but by the age of fourteen, twenty boys have died, and nature maintains its balance. Just to maintain the balance, nature gives birth to one hundred and twenty boys per hundred girls, because those hundred girls, by the age of fourteen will still be a hundred, but twenty boys will have disappeared.

If you are so restless, your restlessness dissipates energy. If everything is taken into account exactly, then woman is the stronger sex than man: she lives longer, she is less ill—she may pretend, that is another thing, but she is less ill—more healthy, life is stronger in her, she can resist diseases more easily than man. Look: when it is winter, men are going with their coats and sweaters, and women are moving sleeveless and nothing is happening to them. They have more tolerance, more resistance, they are more protected because they are more body-grounded.

Man lives in his head, he is more mental. That's why more men go mad, more men commit suicide, but less women. Women are not weak, man is more weak because the mind cannot be as strong as the body. The mind entered into existence very late, the body has a long experience. But this body-groundedness becomes a problem when they enter on the path towards God.

In life, in natural life, women are the winners. But a spiritual life is going against and beyond nature. Then their body-groundedness becomes a problem: unless their whole mind becomes conscious, their body-groundedness is not going to leave them, they are so deeply rooted in it. Man is like a bird, flying, and they are like trees, rooted. They get more nourishment, of course, and whenever a bird, a man wants to rest, he has to come in the shade of a woman, under the tree, to be nourished, sheltered. This is good as far as ordinary natural life is concerned, it is helpful, women are the winners there. But when one starts to move beyond nature, then the *very* help becomes the hindrance.

Jesus says: "See, I shall lead her so that I will make her male, that she too may become a living spirit..."

She is a living body so the path is longer for her. Think of three things: the living body, the living mind and the living spirit. These are the three layers. Woman is the living body, man is the living mind, and beyond the two exists living spirit, *atman*. From mind it is a shorter distance to move towards spirit; from body a longer distance has to be travelled. But don't be discouraged by it in any way because in nature everything is balanced. It is difficult because the distance is long, but in another way it is easier, because a woman is a simple phenomenon. Man is very complex and his complexities create trouble.

From the mind the spirit is nearer, but to take a jump from the mind is not easy because the mind goes on creating doubts. A woman can take the jump easily: she is body-rooted, she is trust, she has no doubts. Once a woman falls in love with a man, she can move with him to Hell, she will not care. Once the trust is there, she will follow. That's why a woman can never imagine how a man can deceive so easily, how a man can be so faithless so easily. That's impossible for her to conceive, because she never is. She is always trusting, and she lives with her trust and cannot conceive how a man can be faithless so easily.

So there are difficulties because the body is further from the soul, a gap exists, but there is some help also. That is that woman can take a jump easily. Once she is in love, in trust, she can take the jump. So there have not been many Masters from the world of women, but there have been great disciples. And no man can compete with woman as far as great disciplehood is concerned, because once they trust, they trust.

Look, go through India: you will see Jain monks, and look and see Jain nuns. Jain monks will look just ordinary; their dress is different but they are just ordinary businessmen. If you change their dress and put them in the market you will not find any distinction. But Jain nuns are different: they have a purity; once they trust they have a purity. Look at Catholic nuns! They are different from Catholic priests and Catholic monks. Monks are cunning and you cannot believe whether they are really celibate or not. If they are absolutely foolish, then it is okay, and if they have just a little intelligence they must have found some ways. But nuns? They are celibate, you can depend on them. Once they take the step, they stick to it.

So there are difficulties because the distance is long, but there are also capacities which help because the jump is certain. Once they decide, the jump is taken, then they don't waver. The body knows no wavering, only the mind knows wavering.

"Jesus said : See, I shall lead her so that I will make her male, that she too may become a living spirit resembling you males. For every woman who makes herself male will enter the Kingdom."

This is one part of Jesus' teaching, the other part has not been recorded. The reason may be because there was no woman to record it—this too was recorded by a man. But I know there is another part, and I must tell you so that it is recorded.

In the ultimate culmination, in the crescendo of spiritual being, the male becomes female as much as the female becomes male. It is not one-way, it cannot be, because you are both extremes, opposites. If the woman becomes like man, then what will become of man? He will become like woman, then opposites dissolve.

A woman will have to transform her unconscious into conscious, her irrationality into reasonableness, her faith into an inquiry, her waiting into a movement. And a man will have to do exactly the opposite: he will have to make his movement into a rest, his rest-lessness into a tranquillity, into a stillness, his doubt into trust; and he will have to dissolve his reason into the irrational. Then a super-rational being is born. From both sides they have to move: man has to move from his manhood, woman has to move from her womanhood. Because a mind which is male is half, and the half cannot know the whole. A mind which is female is half, and the half can never know the whole. Both have to move from their static positions, become liquid, melt into each other, become asexual.

Hindus are very clear about it: their term for the Ultimate, Brahma, does not belong to either gender. In English it is difficult because there are only two genders but in Sanskrit they have three genders: one for male, one for female, and one for one who has transcended both. Brahma is the third, neutral gender, and one who reaches Brahma becomes Brahma-like: male will not be male, and female will not be female, their oppositeness will disappear. And only then is being complete; then being is free, then being is liberated.

Jesus must have told the other part also. It has not been recorded because whenever we record, we record according to ourselves. I am saying so many things to you, your mind is continuously record-ing but you will record according to yourself. You will leave out many things and you will not even be aware that you are leaving them out. This is the problem: you may not be aware, you may not be leaving them out consciously, you simply will not record them, your memory will not record them; you will simply drop them, you will record according to yourself.

And in those days it was a greater problem, because Jesus would go on talking, disciples would listen, and the sayings would not be recorded immediately. Sometimes years would pass, sometimes hundreds of years would pass, and the saying would go from one person to another and then it would be recorded. It would have changed completely.

Do one small experiment then you will know: gather twenty friends and sit in a circle. Give a piece of paper to everybody and then write a sentence. The first man in the circle writes a sentence on his piece of paper and says the sentence in the ear of the next one. He listens to the sentence, he writes it on his paper, keeps the paper with him and tells the sentence to the third one. Let the sentence go on being recorded—and you will be surprised. When it comes back to the first person it is not the same sentence; much has changed, much has been added, much has been dropped out. If it can happen within a half-hour's experiment, then when words have been carried in memory for centuries, it is natural that much has changed—the other part is missing.

For a man like Jesus it is not a question of male or female, it is a question of becoming whole. One has to leave his part and reach the Whole. So don't think that you are a male and therefore you have some priority; don't think that you are a male, so God is nearer to you; don't think that you are a male, so you have nothing to do, that you have already done much just by being a male. No, you also will have to become female, just as a female has to become male. You both have to move from your static states and become dynamic, merging into each other. You both have to go beyond the parts and become the Whole.

So I would like to tell you that I will lead the males to become females, and I will lead the females to become males, so that both are dissolved, so that transcendence is achieved and sex disappears, because sex exists on the division. Are you aware of what the word 'sex' means? The original root in Latin means division, to divide. So when you reach God you will be neither males nor females. If you are still a male you are divided—how can you reach the Whole? So don't make this saying a male 'ego-trip', it is not. They have done that in the Church.

Try to understand that the part has to be left so that you can become whole. You should not be identified with any division, so that the Indivisible can enter into you.

"Simon Peter said to them : Let Mary go out from among us, because women are not worthy of the Life."

This is Simon Peter's mind, not Jesus'. And it is bound to be so, a disciple's mind, he is not yet Enlightened, he cannot see the Indivisible, he can only see according to his mind. A disciple is half blind. He has started to see, but not yet completely. A Master is completely open, he can look at both the sides, he can look at all the fragments. A disciple is still in the world of ignorance, of division. This is Simon Peter, his mind. And when Jesus is gone, Simon Peter will become more important than Jesus, because Simon Peter will be more understandable to people—he belongs to the same world.

Peter created the Church, he became the rock—the word 'Peter' means rock. And the whole Church stands, and he really proved to be a very strong rock. Nobody has proved to be such a strong rock, neither a disciple of Buddha nor a disciple of Mahavir has proved to be like Peter, because the Catholic Church is the strongest Church that has ever existed on the earth. But that is why it is more dangerous also: strength in wrong hands. And when a Master is no more, disciples become the masters, they start deciding things. Of course, their attitude can only be a prejudice, a half-understood truth, a half-baked truth. And remember well, a lie is better than a half-truth because the lie can be exposed any day, but you cannot expose a half-truth.

A lie will be thrown some day or other, because you cannot deceive people forever and forever. But a half-truth is very dangerous: you cannot expose it because it carries an element of truth. And this saying is a half-truth: it carries one element, that the female has to become male. But this is a half-truth, and if you make it the whole truth it is very dangerous. The other has to be added to it. That's why I said we would be sailing in rough waters.

I would like to add the other half: every male has to become like the female, because he has also to learn waiting; he has also to learn receptivity; he has also to learn non-aggression, passivity; he has also to learn compassion, love, service—all the qualities of the feminine mind. Then only, when you are whole, neither male nor female, do you become capable of entering into the Kingdom. Then you yourself are God because God is neither male nor female—He is both, or neither.

Remember that other part of the truth also, otherwise you will miss. Nobody is more capable of entering into the Divine, nobody is less capable. There are differences, but on the whole, if you take account of the whole, everybody is *equally* capable of entering into the Divine; everybody, I say, is *equally* capable. But there are foolish people who will always use their negative qualities, then they cannot enter. And there are wise people who will use their positive qualities, then they can enter.

For example: the feminine mind has both qualities, the negative and the positive. The positive is love, the negative is jealousy; the positive is sharing, the negative is possessiveness; the positive is waiting, the negative is lethargy, because waiting can look as if it is waiting and it may not be, it may be just lethargy. And the same happens with the male mind: the male mind has a positive quality that he inquires, goes in search, and a negative quality that he always doubts. Can you be an inquirer without doubt? Then you have chosen the positive. But you can also be a doubtful man without inquiring, just sitting and doubting.

One philosopher in the Second World War went to the front. Then his girl friend's letter and a photograph came as he had been expecting. She was sitting on a beach, one more couple was there in the background, a happy couple, very loving to each other, in an ecstasy, and she was sitting alone, depressed, sad. For a moment he felt very happy that his girl was sad for him, but the next moment the doubt came: "Who is this guy who has taken the picture?" Then he was worried because there must have been one more person who had taken the picture—"Who is that guy?" Then he could not sleep the whole night.

This is how negative doubt functions. A man has a positive quality that he is in search of rest, and a negative quality that he is restless. Because he is restless, there is no need for him to get identified with it. You can use your restlessness as a jumping-board to attain a restful repose. You have an energy, an urge to do something—you can use that urge to become a 'non-doer,' you can use that urge to be a meditator. The negative has to be used in the service of the positive, and each has both. Wherever there is a positive quality, just by the side exists the negative. If you pay too much attention to the negative you will miss; pay much attention to the positive and you will attain.

And male or female, both have to do that. Then happens the most beautiful phenomenon in the world. That phenomenon is an indivisible person, a one, a unity, an inner cosmos; a symphony where all the notes have become helpers to each other, not a noise, but they give rhythm, colour to the whole. They make the whole, they create the whole, they are not against the whole, they are not fragments any more, they have fallen into a unity. This is what Gurdjieff calls 'inner crystallization' or what Hindus have called 'attaining to the Self', and what Jesus calls 'entering into the Kingdom of God'.

Nineteenth Discourse

8th September 1974, Poona, India

THE NINETEENTH SAYING

Jesus said:
A man had guest-friends, and when he had prepared the dinner,
he sent his servant to invite the guest-friends.

He went to the first, he said to him:
'My master invites thee.'
He said: 'I have some claims against some merchants;
they will come to me in the evening;
I will go and give them my orders.
I pray to be excused from the dinner.'

He went to another, he said to him:
'My master has invited thee.'
He said to him: 'I have bought a house
and they request me for a day. I will have no time.'

He came to another, he said to him:
'My master invites thee.'
He said to him:
'My friend is to be married and I am to arrange a dinner;
I shall not be able to come.
I pray to be excused from the dinner.'

He went to another, he said to him:
'My master invites thee.'
He said to him:
'I have bought a farm, I go to collect the rent.
I shall not be able to come. I pray to be excused.'

The servant came, he said to his master:
'Those whom thou hast invited to the dinner have excused
themselves.'

The master said to his servant:
'Go out to the roads, bring those whom thou shalt find
so that they may dine.
Tradesmen and merchants shall not enter the places of my Father.'

Jesus talks in parables. The parables are very simple but very significant. They are not literal so we will have to understand the symbolic meaning of them. These sayings today are concerned with a particular type, not exactly tradesmen and businessmen, but the type. You may not be a businessman but you may be the type; you may be a businessman and you may not be the type.

So remember, there is a particular type and that particular type constitutes almost ninety-nine percent of people: businessmen and traders are all over. They may be doing something else, but their mind is that of a businessman. So first thing to be understood: who is a businessman, who is a trader?

A businessman is one who is busy about non-significant things, who is busy about the trivial, who is busy about the outside, who is busy about things, commodities, but not about himself. He has completely forgotten himself, he is lost in the world. He thinks of money, possessions, but never of consciousness, because consciousness is not a commodity, it can neither be sold nor purchased, it is useless. A businessman is one who is a utilitarian: poetry is meaningless, religion is meaningless, God is meaningless, because they cannot be converted into saleable objects, you cannot earn money through them. And money is the most significant thing for this type. He can sell himself, he can lose himself, he can destroy his whole life, just to accumulate money. This is the first characteristic of the type.

I have heard that two businessmen met in a market. It was the peak of the season, of the year. And one said to the other, "Have you heard that Sheikh Fakhruddin, the clothier, died this morning?"

The other said, "What! In the middle of the season?"

Neither is life meaningful, nor death, only the season. His measurement is money, he measures a man with money; how much you have got, not who you are—that is meaningless. If you have money you are significant, if you don't have money you are nobody. If he pays respect to you, he pays respect to your possessions, never to you. If you lose your possessions he will not even look at you.

Once it happened: A rich man became poor. He was in misery and he was saying to his wife, "I believed that I had so many friends. Fifty percent of them have already left me, and the other fifty percent do not yet know that I have become poor."

All of them are going to leave, they were never with him. You cannot have a friendship with a businessman. No, he is only friendly with the money that you have. The moment money is not there, the friendship disappears—it was *never* with you.

You cannot relate to a businessman, that is impossible: you cannot be a wife, you cannot be a husband, you cannot be a son, you cannot be a father to a businessman, because he relates only to money. Everything else is beside the point, his target is money. If your son starts earning money, the son is valuable; if your father is rich, then he is your father; if he is poor, you would not like people to know that he is your father.

This actually happens every day in life: you will recognize a father who is rich; if he is a poor man or a beggar, you will not recognize him—you recognize only the money. The businessman, the type, cannot love, because love is the most anti-money phenomenon in the world.

Love is concerned with being. Love is a sharing, it is a giving away—not only what you possess, but what you are. A businessman can never be a lover, and a businessman always thinks that lovers are a little crazy, they have gone nuts, they are not in their senses, they are doing nonsense. "Why are you wasting your time? Time is money!" That is what a businessman says.

I have heard about one businessman who purchased one hundred clocks and put them all around his house. Somebody asked, "What are you doing?"

He said, "I have heard that time is money. So the more of it, the better!"

His whole concern is about things, not about persons. Love is concerned with persons, the money-oriented mind is concerned with things. And this type of man is continuously busy; he is never at rest, he cannot be because there is always more and more to be accumulated. There is no end to it.

A man of love can rest. There is a fulfillment when you can rest. But a man after money can never rest because there is no end to it. And there is never fulfillment because money cannot fulfill the soul; the soul remains empty, the inner remains a void. You go on throwing things into it but they never touch your inner emptiness. The more you accumulate, the more you become aware that you are empty, your hands are empty; money is with you but you have lost yourself. Your whole effort is not to look at this fact, because this is very painful.

The businessman runs after money more and more. He wants to completely forget himself in the money; money becomes an intoxicant. He is always busy, a businessman is always busy about nothing. I say about nothing, because in the end it proves nothing. All that you possess proves to be as if you were making drawings on water: they disappear; death comes and your whole effort is nullified. Death negates the businessman.

I would like to tell you that only the businessman dies, nobody else—but he constitutes ninety-nine percent of people. Only the businessman dies because only he accumulates things, and death can snatch things away. Death cannot take your love, death cannot take your prayer, death cannot take your meditation, death cannot take away your God. But a businessman even becomes interested in God if there is some business to be done.

Once it happened: The weather was bad and stormy, and one aeroplane was lost. The fog was so dense that everybody became afraid and fearful. One minister was aboard. Except for him, everybody was weeping, crying, perspiring. The moment was dangerous—any moment, death. Even the pilot was perspiring and nervous. The minister told everybody to kneel down and pray.

All except one businessman, a small man, all kneeled and started praying.

The minister asked the businessman, "Why are you not praying?"

The man said, "Forgive me, Father, because I don't know how to pray. I have never prayed."

And there was no time to teach the man: any moment the plane would be falling, any moment it would crash. So the minister said, "Okay, there is no time left now. So you just behave as if you are in a church."

The businessman walked down the aisle and collected money from people.

The type—even at the moment of death he knows only one way to behave in a church: to collect money; at the last moment money still remains the focus. This is the first thing to be understood, then you will be able to understand these sentences.

Second thing: in this parable Jesus says God's invitation is always there. Many times He comes and knocks, or His messenger comes and knocks at your door. He invites you to come for a dinner, but you are always busy and you cannot go. You want to be excused.

Think about yourself: if a messenger comes and invites you, are you ready to go? You have so many things to do and finish first—and you will never be able to finish them, because there is no end to them. The invitation is rejected. You say, "I would have come, I would have liked to come." but these are all false things. Why can't you accept the invitation? Because more important things are to be done: there is some marriage and you have to go because it is a business relationship; or you have purchased land and you have to go and collect the rent; or something else. God is always the last item on the list of a businessman. And he never comes to the last item—before that, death comes.

God is the most useless phenomenon. People come to me and they ask, "Why meditate? What will we achieve out of it?" They are asking, "What profit? What are we going to achieve out of it?" And if I say, "Nothing," they simply cannot understand. Why are people coming to me? To learn nothing? To attain nothing? The businessman needs something visible, tangible; if he meditates and money starts falling on him, then it is worthwhile; if he meditates and he becomes successful in the world, then it is worthwhile; if he meditates and the illness disappears from the body, then it is worthwhile.

But if you say, "Nothing," or "God"—which means the same, just the words differ, because God is nothing—if you use your measurements that you use in this world, what is God? You cannot categorize Him. Where will you put Him? In what category? How will you label Him? And how will you decide the price? He is nothing, He does not belong to this world. In what way can you use Him? You cannot use Him because God is not a utility, He is an ecstasy.

An ecstasy cannot be used. You can enjoy it but you cannot use it. What is the difference between enjoying and using? You look at a tree, at the green, the sun rising—you enjoy it, but you cannot sell it. You look at a flower, you enjoy it. But the businessman will pluck the flower and go and sell it in the market. You cannot pluck God and go and sell Him in the market. You have tried; that's why temples, mosques, *gurudwaras,* churches exist. This is how the businessman has behaved with God: he has tried to sell Him also and earn something out of it. It is a great business.

And the priest is the businessman turned into a religious man— he is not religious at all. That is why he is always against Jesus, Buddha, Nanak, Kabir: he is against all of them because these people are dangerous, they destroy the whole business. A businessman is not interested in God, in poetry, in prayer, in love, in beauty, in goodness; in ecstasy he is not interested. Just to enjoy means nothing to him. He says, "What profit out of it?"

One millionaire once visited a primitive tribe. When he got down from the train he saw a primitive man lying just on the platform under a tree. The morning was beautiful, very sunny, the air was clean, fresh and cool, birds were singing and the man was resting. The businessman could not tolerate it. He said, "Hey, chief, what are you doing there? It is time to go and earn something!"

The man who was resting opened his eyes and asked, very sweetly, "Why?"

This *why* cannot be understood by a businessman. He said, "Why? To earn some money!"

The primitive started smiling and again asked, "Why?"

This was impossible. The businessman became annoyed and he

said, "Why? To have a bank balance so that you can retire and rest, and then there is no need to work."

The primitive closed his eyes and said, "I am resting now."

This is impossible, resting now is impossible. A businessman postpones rest for the future: "Work here, now. Have a bank balance, then retire, then rest and enjoy!" But that never comes, it cannot come. A businessman can never retire—that is not in the type, that is not the quality of the type. He may retire from one business, but immediately, or even before it, he will manage another, because he cannot rest. He always thinks in the future, he postpones his enjoyment. Remember, a man who is religious enjoys here and now. The Heaven of a religious man is not somewhere in the sky, in the future. No! That is how a businessman looks at Heaven.

The Heaven of a religious man is here and now, *right this moment*. He enjoys it, he does not postpone it, because nobody knows about the future. The future doesn't exist, only the present exists. The future is a fallacy; it is just somehow to console oneself that some day you will be able to enjoy. And *your whole life* you are training yourself not to enjoy, and postponing—even if you enter Heaven.

I have heard, once it happened: Four businessmen entered Heaven. I don't know how they entered—they must have been smuggled in, they must have managed it. Then a saint died who knew those four gentlemen. He entered and he saw them in Heaven, but he was very much puzzled as to what was the matter, because they were bound in iron, they were not free. He couldn't believe it so he asked the gatekeeper, "What is the matter? Because I have heard that in Heaven there is total freedom, why have these men been made prisoners here? Why have you bound them?"

The gatekeeper laughed and he said, "These are four businessmen and they want to get back to the world. And that will not be good. Somehow they got in, but now to leave them to go back to the world, the whole prestige of Heaven will be destroyed. They want to go back, they say there is no business here. What to do? So we had to put them in chains."

A businessman remains a businessman because the type cannot change so easily—unless you become aware of the whole fallacy of postponing, future, money, possessions; unless you become so intense in your awareness that the very intensity burns your type. And if you are not a businessman then you become a religious man.

The invitation comes every day, it knocks at your door every day—*every moment* to be exactly right, it knocks. But you say, "Excuse me, I have to do many more things, and then I will come." Enjoyment, happiness, blissfulness, rest—no, they are not for the business type; he has to do much before he can rest. That is why the invitation was denied. Now try to penetrate this parable. It is beautiful.

"Jesus said: A man had guest-friends, and when he had prepared the dinner, he sent his servant to invite the guest-friends.

He went to the first, he said to him: 'My master invites thee.'

He said: 'I have some claims against some merchants; they will come to me in the evening; I will go and give them my orders. I pray to be excused from the dinner.'"

A dinner is symbolic of enjoying life. And for Christ, dinner was a meditative phenomenon. He always loved his disciples, friends, to come and have a dinner together. Even on the last night, when he was going to be murdered the next day, he had the Last Supper. He enjoyed eating together. And Christianity has raised the whole phenomenon to a religious level. Hindus are completely ignorant of this. Try to understand it.

Animals would like always to eat alone, never together—that is part of animality. If a dog gets a piece of bread, he will immediately escape into some corner. He would not like anybody to be there because the danger exists that the other may take the bread from him. He is afraid, he is fearful; he eats, but eats alone. No animal shares, sharing is absolutely human. And if you try to penetrate into your unconscious you will always find the animal hidden there.

You also don't like to eat with people, you would like to be alone. Look at a *Brahmin* travelling in a train; he will keep his back to all others if he is eating. This is animal-like, he will not invite others. A Mohammedan will invite others, a Christian would like to share, but not a Hindu. Hindus have missed one great thing: the feeling of togetherness and sharing. And when you share food, you become brothers. Why are you a brother to some-body? Because you share the same milk. Otherwise, there is nothing else that makes you a brother to somebody. You share the same breast, you share the same food from the same mother—the mother is the first food.

When you share food you become brothers, and when you share food you are not afraid of the other: a community arises. Hindus have a society but they have no community feeling. Mohammedans, Christians are more community-oriented because they can share their food. And food is very basic in life because you depend on food, you will die without it. Sharing food with others means sharing your life. And Jesus raised it to a status of prayer: you should not eat alone, you should be together while eating. This is a transcendence of the animality in you.

The last night, when he had to depart, he collected his friends, disciples, and they had the Last Supper. Even before death you should go on sharing.

And food is also a symbol of love. Have you observed why you love your mother? Why does so much love exist between the child and the mother? Because mother is the first food: the child has eaten her, the mother has gone into him. And the child becomes aware of the mother first, not as a love-source, but as a food-source. Later on, when he grows in consciousness, then by and by he will feel love for the mother.

Food is first, love follows. And food and love become associated because they come from the same source. That is why if you go to a house and they don't offer you food, you don't feel good: they rejected you, they didn't give their love to you, they were not hosts to you. If they offer food—they may be poor, they may not have much to offer, but they offer whatsoever they have—you have a feeling of well-being; you have been received well, they shared food with you—because food is associated with love.

Whenever a woman loves a man, she would like to prepare his food. She would like to serve it, she would like to see him eat. And if a woman is not allowed to do this she will feel uneasy, because love flows through food. Love is invisible, it needs some visible vehicle. And the quality of food changes immediately: if a woman who loves you prepares your food, it has a different quality. That quality cannot be analyzed by chemists, but it has a different quality.

If a man who is angry, or a woman who is against you and hates you prepares your food, it is already poisoned—because anger, hate, jealousy are poisons in the blood. They have a radiation of their own, and that radiation moves through the hands into the food. If a woman *really* hates you and prepares your food, she can even kill you, unknowingly—no court will be able to catch her. It is very dangerous to live with a woman who prepares your food and hates you; it is slow poisoning. But if a woman loves you, she gives her life through the food, she gives her love through the food. She is moving through the food to you.

Food is very basic. It can be shared, and through its sharing you can leave your animality behind, you can become human. Hindus are one of the oldest societies, but one of the most inhuman societies, just because they have never been concerned with sharing. Rather, they have created all types of barriers in order not to share: a *Brahmin* cannot eat with a *Shudra*; a *Brahmin* cannot eat with a *Vaishya*; a *Brahmin* cannot eat with lower castes and if you cannot eat with the other, you reject the other as human. If you cannot eat with someone, that shows that you think yourself very superior and him very inferior, and a gap exists. That gap is the most inhuman in the world.

Jesus based much of his religion on sharing. He talks many times of God inviting you for a dinner. This man has invited his friends for a dinner. Dinner is an enjoyment, sheer enjoyment of being, of body; enjoying food and forgetting everything is a gratitude towards God.

The servant went to the first, but he said, "Difficult, I cannot come, I pray to be excused."

"He went to another, he said to him: 'My master has invited thee.' He said to him: 'I have bought a house and they request me for a day. I will have no time.' "

A businessman never has time for himself: no time to enjoy, no time to meditate, no time to love. He is always in a hurry. Ambition makes him so feverish that he cannot have any time. If you are ambitious you will have no time, if you are non-ambitious you have eternity at your feet. A non-ambitious man has so much time to enjoy and dance and sing; you cannot conceive of it. An ambitious man has no time. Even to love he has no time, because there is always the future, the bank balance, the money that he can get out of this time if this time is used. A businessman even dreams only of business, thinks only of business.

"He came to another, he said to him: 'My master invites thee.'
He said to him: 'My friend is to be married and I am to arrange a dinner; I shall not be able to come. I pray to be excused from the dinner.'

He went to another, he said to him: 'My master invites thee.'
He said to him: 'I have bought a farm, I go to collect the rent. I shall not be able to come. I pray to be excused.' "

They were all busy, they didn't have any time. Are you also busy? Then you are a businessman. Or have you got some time to waste, to meditate, just to be in the here and now, sing and dance; or to not do anything, just lie down under the tree and enjoy existence? Looks foolish? Then you are a businessman, then you are not religious. But if you feel that it is meaningful, significant, just to be, without any business around, not in any way occupied with anything, unoccupied, then you are a religious man.

Remember, mind needs occupation, constant occupation— because mind cannot exist without occupation.

You must have heard the story: Once it happened, a man revived a ghost, a genie. The genie said, "Only one condition: I will need constant work. If you can supply me constant work, then I will be a servant to you. But if you stop supplying work for me, then you will be in danger—I will kill you immediately."

The man must have been a businessman. He said, "This is what I want! I have got hundreds of servants, but all lazy, nobody wants to work. This condition is good, it is in my favour. I will give you as much work as you like, more than you can do!"

He was not aware of what he was saying and what was going to happen. He came home very happy. Many many ambitions of many many years he told the genie. But within a minute they all were finished and the genie came back. He said, "Now give me other work." Then the man became afraid, because from where to find so much work? Even he, a businessman, could not find it! He gave some other work, the genie came back.

By the morning the businessman was in danger. He ran away

to a Sufi saint and asked, "What to do? That genie will kill me—he has finished all that I can think of!"

The Sufi saint was a mathematician. He said, "Go and tell him to make the circle square. Give him something impossible which cannot be done, otherwise he will kill you."

And the businessman has died since then, but the genie is still trying, he is still occupied.

A businessman has a genie inside and *all* desires are impossible. Not only can a circle not be squared, no desire can be squared either. All desires are impossible. But the same is the condition of the mind: "Give me work, don't leave me empty!" Not that the mind will kill you, but the mind can kill your ego if you don't give it any work. Whenever you have work, you are doing something, you feel very good, you are somebody. Whenever you have no work, when you are not doing anything, your identity is lost, you are nobody.

Just the other day I was reading a book, a book on the *Hare Krishna* movement. The name of the book was *The World of Hare Krishna*. The woman who has written the book writes in it about Dr. S. Radhakrishna, former President of India, as the *late* Dr. Radhakrishna—because whenever a politician is out of work he is already 'late'. She may not know that he is alive, because newspapers suddenly forget about a man who is out of office. Now where is Nixon? Forgotten! Where is Giri? Forgotten, thrown into the dustbin, nobody bothers. Only when they die there will be a little news in newspapers. That is why everybody clings to the post, the work, nobody wants to retire, because once you retire where is your identity? You were somebody, now you become nobody.

The genie of the mind has a condition: "If you give me work I will give you the ego, you will be somebody. If you stop giving me work, you will be nobody. Remember, if I am empty, you are empty—you exist with me." A businessman is a follower of the mind. He goes on giving work, the ego is strengthened, but the soul is lost. It is a suicide, but very subtle.

If you can exist for a few moments without work and still feel grateful to God, if you can be a nobody and still feel grateful and thankful to existence, then you are a religious man. Then your worth does not come from what you are doing, not from there; your worth does not come from your doing, your worth comes from your being; then your worth is not in the bank, it is in you. Then you *are* worthy. The world may not recognize it, because the world recognizes the businessman. The world may forget you completely. You may pass along the street and nobody may wish you good-day. Nobody may look at you, that is possible, that happens, because nobody ever looked at *you*. It was your work that you were doing which was important. Now the work is gone, you are no more there—you have become a nonentity.

But if you can be happy becoming a nonentity, you have become a *sannyasin*, you have entered the other world of the Divine. Now you can enjoy beauty and the full moon, now you can enjoy the greenery of the trees and the ripples in the lake. Now you can enjoy everything, and the Whole is open and inviting you. The invitation is always there but you have no time to look at it. You are always busy and you want to be excused.

For many, many lives you have been saying, "Please excuse me, I cannot come. Somebody is getting married and I have to go there. I cannot come because I have to purchase a house." What are you saying? Life invites you to be ecstatic and you reject the invitation, and then you say, "I am suffering;" then you say, "I have been rejected;" then you say, "Why is there so much pain in life?" You reject all invitations to be happy.

The trees invite you, the moon invites you, the clouds invite you, the river invites you. The whole existence invites you from everywhere, but you say, "Excuse me." The rose invites you and you pass by the side and you say, "Excuse me, I cannot come because I am going to a friend's marriage."

"The servant came, he said to his master: 'Those whom thou hast invited to the dinner have excused themselves, they are not coming.' The master said to his servant: 'Go out to the roads, bring those whom thou shalt find so that they may dine....'"

This has to be understood: the invitation was sent to respectable persons before, to persons who were 'somebodies', persons who had attained some identity with the ego—the President, the Prime Minister; the invitation was sent to 'somebodies', the VIP's. They have refused because they are too busy and they cannot come. Now the invitation is sent to the beggars, to the hippies, to those who are just on the road. This is a very significant thing to be understood: those who think they are very respectable, they miss the Divine.

Even beggars reach and emperors miss, because beggars are always on the road. You invite them and they are ready. They will never say, "Excuse me," they have nothing to be excused from, they are just waiting. You call and they will come, they are just on the road. So the master said, "Go out to the roads, bring those whom thou shalt find..." You will not find respectable persons there: the Mayor and the President and the millionaire. No, you will not find them on the roads, they are never there. You will find beggars, people who have gone astray, people who have nothing to do, just wandering vagabonds—you will find them.

It is very meaningful. Buddha left his palace and became a beggar; Mahavir left his kingdom and became a naked *fakir*, just on the roads; *paribrajaka*, always on the road. What does it mean? Now these people will get the invitation. And they are always ready, they have nothing to make them say, "I cannot come." There is no marriage which they have to attend, they have no house to sell or purchase; they have nothing to do, they are always at rest and at home.

The master said: "Now go out to the roads, bring those whom thou shalt find so that they may dine." Those who are somebody in the world of the ego will always refuse the invitation, because the ego needs constant occupation and it cannot enjoy. It is like a wound: it can suffer but it cannot enjoy; it is not like a flower, it is like a wound. Then those who are like flowers, those who are *already* enjoying; even if they have not received the invitation, they are at dinner; those who have already entered into existence and who are enjoying; those who have no worries and burdens to carry with them—those who are on the road.

It may have been a full moon night.... "Now go and bring nobodies, because God *has* to share." If the VIP's were not coming, then nobodies, but God had to share. And beggars have enjoyed God more than emperors, because they have a quality of being unoccupied. They are not businessmen, they are not utilitarians; they live in the moment, they don't postpone for the future.

I have heard a story about one beggar. A businessman was passing and the beggar asked just for two or three *annas* for a cup of tea. The businessman was in a hurry, as businessman always are. He said, "Next time when I pass I will give it to you. Now I am in a hurry."

The beggar said, "Please, I am not a businessman and I cannot live on promises. Either you give or not, either you say *yes* or *no*, but no future. I am a beggar, I cannot live on promises—there is no future for me."

A businessman lives on promises; his whole life is invested in promissory notes. He has sold his present for some future dream.

And then Jesus says:

"Tradesmen and merchants shall not enter the places of my Father."

The same is the situation as far as God the Father is concerned, and His place, His palace is concerned. If you say, "I will come sometime in the future," you will miss. If you can say, "Right now I am ready, there is nothing to withhold me. I was just waiting for your invitation, and I will start coming towards you," only then will you be able to enter into the Kingdom of God.

How can you reject life's invitations? But you have been rejecting them. What is the mechanism of this rejection? People think that *sannyasins* renounce life. I tell you that is absolutely wrong: only the businessman renounces life; sannyasins enjoy it, they don't renounce it. It looks like a renunciation in the eyes of a tradesman and a businessman, but otherwise, sannyasins simply enjoy it; they are not renouncing anything. They enjoy *more* intensely, that's all. They enjoy so totally that if they die this very moment, there will be no complaint. They will say, "We lived, we enjoyed. Enough!" Even a single moment of the life of a sannyasin is a fulfillment. If he dies, he is happy. But a businessman—even millions of lives and he has not finished his work; the work is such that it cannot be finished.

There is an old story in the Upanishads: One king, Yayati, was dying and he was a hundred years old already. Death came and Yayati said, "Is it not possible that you take one of my sons? Because I have not lived yet. I was so much engaged in the works of the kingdom. I completely forgot that I have to leave this body. I have not *lived*—this is too cruel to take me away, because the whole opportunity is lost. I was serving the people and the kingdom and couldn't live. So be kind!"

Death said, "Okay, you ask your children."

He had a hundred sons. He asked, but the older ones had already become cunning. Experience makes people cunning, calculating. They listened, but they would not budge from their places. The youngest—he was so young, just sixteen—he came near and he said, "Okay."

Even Death felt sorry for the boy, because if an old man of one hundred had not lived, how could this boy of sixteen have lived? He had not even started! Death said, "You don't know, you are innocent. Your ninety-nine brothers, on the other hand, are silent. Some of them have already reached seventy, seventy-five. They are old, and their death is coming sooner or later, it is a question of a few years. But why you?"

The young boy said, "If my father could not live in a hundred years, how can I hope to live? The whole thing is useless! It is enough for me to understand that if my father could not live in a hundred years, even if I live a hundred years there is no possibility to live. There must be some other way to live. Through life it seems that life cannot be lived, so I will try through death. Allow me, and don't create a hindrance."

This is what a sannyasin is saying, "If I couldn't live through the life of the ego, I will live through the death of the ego. So take me!"

The son was taken and the father lived a hundred years more. Then Death came again. The father was again surprised. He said, "So soon? Because I was thinking a hundred years is too long a period, there was no need to be worried. I have not lived yet. I tried, I planned, but now everything is ready and I was just starting to live, and you have come again. This is too much!"

And this happened ten times: each time a son donated his life and the father lived.

When he was one thousand, Death came and asked Yayati, "What is your idea now? Should I take another son again?"

Yayati said, "No, because now I know even a thousand years

is useless. It is my mind, not a question of time. I again and again get involved in the same nonsense, I have become habituated to wasting existence and being. So now it is not going to help."

Yayati has written for the generations to come so that you may remember. He has written: "Even one thousand years I lived, but I couldn't live because of my mind. It is always concerned with the future and I always miss the present. And life is the present."

If you are not here and now, you will go on missing it. The invitation has always been given to you but you were never there, you were never found at home, you were engaged somewhere else. And then you say you suffer, and then you say, "Why so much misery?" And everybody seems to be miserable: those who have lived long, they seem miserable; those who have not lived, they seem miserable. Young people, old people, everybody seems miserable—because the mind is the same.

I once read a sign on a restaurant window. It was written on the window glass: "Don't stand outside and look miserable—come in and be fed up!" So if you stand outside you are miserable, and if you come in you get fed up and you become miserable.

Mind *is* the misery. 'In' or 'out' won't help; one hundred years, one thousand years won't help; one life, many lives won't help—unless you become aware that this very mind that you are carrying, the mind of a businessman, is the barrier. You drop this mind, and *sannyas* happens.

And Jesus says: "Tradesmen and merchants shall not enter the place of my Father."

They will miss by themselves—not that the doors are not open! They will miss by themselves—not that the invitation is not given! The invitation is eternally standing; it is a standing invitation, forever and forever. And the messenger comes every day. Jesus was a messenger, but the Jews rejected him. Buddha was a messenger, the Hindus rejected him. The messenger comes every day, knocks at your door, but you say, "We are engaged."

It happened in Buddha's life: he passed through a village many many times, almost thirty times. And one man was always thinking of going to listen to him, but there was always something or other: the wife was ill, or the wife was pregnant, or there were many people, guests in the house, or there was some business trouble, or something or other. Buddha came and went. The man could not go to see him.

Thirty years, thirty times, Buddha passed through that village. And then one day, suddenly in the morning, when the man was going to open his shop, he heard that Buddha was going to die that day. Then he became aware of what he had been missing, but now it was too late. He ran—Buddha was ten, fifteen miles away—he arrived by the evening.

Buddha had retired. He asked his disciples, "Do you have anything to ask?"

But they were weeping and crying, and they said, "You have told enough and we have not understood even that. We have nothing to ask."

So Buddha asked thrice, as was his habit to always ask thrice, because he said, "You are so deaf, you may miss again and again." He used to say every sentence thrice so that you might hear. Then he went behind a tree. He sat restfully, closed his eyes, and started dissolving into the universe.

Then came this man, running, perspiring, and he said, "Where is Buddha? I have to ask something. And I have waited long."

The disciples said, "You are too late. Buddha passed through your village and we know that he always asked about you, and you never came. Thirty times he passed through your village. He was always near your house; the village is small—just one minute's walk and you would have reached him. And he always asked whether that businessman had come or not, and we had to say *no*. Sometimes *bhikkhus* even went to you and asked, and you said, 'This time it is impossible because it is a season; this time it is impossible because my wife is pregnant; this time it is impossible because guests have come to my house.' And now you have come but it is too late."

It is one of the most compassionate stories: Buddha came out of his meditation, and he said, "He may have erred, but my invitation stands. He may have been late, but I am still alive. So let him ask. I was waiting for him, I was delaying my dissolution because I was hoping he might come now, hearing that I am going to die."

Drop the businessman's mind! Otherwise, you have missed many Buddhas before, you may miss again and again. And it becomes a routine for you to miss, you become habitual. Jesus is right: "Tradesmen and merchants shall not enter the place of my Father." That Kingdom is not for them, because they are not interested in that Kingdom at all, they are interested in the kingdom of this world. Their eyes are focused downwards, they look downwards, they look at the material, at the world. Because of the way their look is focused they cannot look above. Then the invitation goes flat—they hear, but they excuse themselves.

You have chosen the non-essential and you have rejected the essential. You have chosen the worthless, you have chosen that which intrinsically is going to die and you have rejected the immortal. You have chosen the body and rejected the internal, the inner, the consciousness. And whatsoever you choose, you move in that direction.

Be mindful about it. Look at the situation, *and don't start thinking about others:* "That man is a businessman." Look at yourself, because out of one hundred persons, ninety-nine are businessmen. There is every possibility that you will be a businessman. Don't think that you are the exception, because that exception is always totally different. That exception has already entered, he is already dining with God.

Twentieth Discourse

9th September 1974, Poona, India

THE TWENTIETH SAYING

His disciples said to him:
When will the repose of the dead come about,
and when will the new world come?

He said to them:
What you expect has come,
but you know it not.

His disciples said to him:
Twenty-four prophets spoke in Israel
and they all spoke about thee.

He said to them:
You have dismissed the Living One
who is before you,
and you have spoken about the dead.

Jesus said:
I have cast fire upon the world,
and see,
I guard the world until it is afire.

It has happened again and again: Jesus comes, but you don't recognize him; Buddha comes, but you don't recognize him. Why does this happen? And then for centuries and centuries you think about Jesus and Buddha. Then religions are created, then great organizations are created for the one whom you never recognized when he was here. Why do you miss a living Christ? This has to be understood, because it must be something very deep-rooted in the mind, in the very nature of the mind. It is not an individual error, it is not a mistake committed by this man or that man. For millennia it has been committed by the human mind.

The mind has to be penetrated and understood. One thing: the mind has no present, it has only past and future. The present is so narrow that the mind cannot catch it. The moment the mind catches it, it has already become the past. So the mind can remember the past, can desire the future, but cannot see the present. The past is vast, the future also is vast; the present is so atomic, so subtle, that by the time you become aware of it, it is gone. And you are not so aware. A very great intensity of awareness is needed, only then will you be able to see the present. You have to be fully alert; if you are not totally alert, the present cannot be seen. You are already drunk with the past or with the future.

The other day it happened, Mulla Nasrudin came to see me. He hailed a taxi, entered it and said, "Driver, take me to Shree Rajneesh Ashram."

The driver came out of the car very much annoyed because the taxi was standing before 17, Koregaon Park. He opened the door and said to Mulla Nasrudin, "Fellow, we have reached the Ashram. Come out!"

Nasrudin said, "Okay, but don't drive so fast next time."

The mind is drunk. It cannot see the present, that which is before you. The mind is filled with dreams, desires. You don't have a presence of mind. That is why Jesus is missed, Buddha is missed, Krishna is missed, and then for centuries you weep and cry, then for centuries you feel guilty. For centuries you think, pray, imagine, and when Jesus is there you miss. Jesus can be met only if you attain to a presence of mind, such a presence that has no past, that has no future; only such a presence can look into the present. And then the present is eternal. But eternity is in depth, it is not a linear movement, it is not horizontal—it is vertical.

Second thing to remember: you can understand the past, because to understand anything you need time to think, theorize, philosophize, systematize, argue. Then intellectually you can sort things out. But when a Jesus is present, you cannot think—you have no time to think. Mind needs time to think. It gropes in the dark. Somehow it creates a sort of understanding which is not understanding at all. If you have understanding, then you can look directly into a fact and the truth of the fact is revealed. If you don't have understanding, you have to think.

Remember, a man of understanding never thinks, he simply looks at the fact. The very look reveals. A man of non-understanding thinks. It is just like a blind man who wants to go out of this house: before he leaves the house he will have to think, "Where is the door, where is the staircase, where is the gate?" But a man with eyes, if he wants to go out, simply goes out. He never thinks, "Where is the door, where is the staircase, where is the gate?" because he can look, there is no need to think.

If you are blind, then there is much need to think. Thinking is a substitute, it hides your blindness. A man who can see directly never thinks: Jesus is not a thinker, Aristotle is a thinker; Buddha is not a thinker, Hegel is a thinker. A man who is Enlightened never thinks, he simply looks, he has the eyes to look. And the very look reveals where the way is, where the door is, where the gate is, and then he goes.

When Jesus is there the gate is open, but you are blind. There is every possibility that you will ask Jesus himself, "Where is the door? Where is the gate? Where should I go?"

There is a famous painting by William Hunt. When for the first time it was exhibited in London, critics raised a question. The painting is of Jesus, one of the most beautiful: Jesus is standing at a door. The door is closed and it seems that it has remained closed forever and forever, because weeds have grown near it; nobody has opened it, it seems, for centuries. It looks very ancient, tattered, and Jesus is standing at the door, and the painting is entitled *Behold, I stand at the door!* There is a knocker on the door, and Jesus has that knocker in his hand.

The painting is beautiful, but critics always look for some mistake; their whole mind moves to where something is lacking. They did find one mistake: a knocker is there on the door, but there is no handle. So they told Hunt, "The door is okay, Jesus is okay, but one thing you have missed: there is no handle on the door."

Hunt laughed and said, "This door opens inwards"—Jesus is standing at the door of man, his heart. It cannot open outwards, so there is no need for a handle, there is only a knocker. It opens inwards, the door of the heart.

Jesus comes and knocks at your door, but you start thinking. You don't open the door, rather, you may even get scared and bolt it more: "Who knows what type of man is standing outside? Looks like a tramp. And who knows what he is going to do once you open the door?" Once you open the heart you become vulnerable; then you are not so secure and safe. And this man looks an absolute stranger. You cannot trust. That's why when Jesus comes to the door you miss.

First, you are blind, you cannot see, you can only think. Second, you are afraid, scared of the unknown. But about the past you are at ease, because enough time has passed, many people have thought, they have created theories, they have supplied all that is needed. Now you can just look at books—books are dead. But you can think about Jesus and come to a conviction. And then there is no danger either, because even if you open your heart to a book, nothing is going to happen. So millions of Christians go on reading the Bible every day, Hindus go on reading the Gita every day, Buddhists go on reading Dhammapada every day. They repeat in a mechanical way, every day the same again and again. There is no danger because the book is not a fire.

But Jesus is a fire: once you open your heart, you are going to be burnt totally. Once that stranger enters into your heart, the unknown has penetrated into the known. Now your mind as it existed before cannot exist any more; you cannot be the same again. A discontinuity has happened, the past is dead—not even in dreams can it be reflected any more; all that you had accumulated is gone. This man is going to burn you completely, this man is going to be a death! But you are scared because you don't know that after every death there is birth. Greater the death, greater the birth—total the death, total the birth. And this man is going to give you a total death.

You are afraid. Who is this who is afraid? It is precisely that one who is afraid within you who is not you. That is the ego, your accumulation of the past, your identity: you are a man of position, prestige, power, a man of knowledge, respectable. This ego is going to be shattered completely by this man. This ego says to you, "Be alert ! Don't open the door so easily. Nobody knows who this man is. First make sure." And by the time you are sure, Jesus is gone, because he cannot wait at your door forever and forever. It is such a rare phenomenon: the penetration of the unknown into the known, the penetration of eternity into time. The meeting of a Jesus with you is such a *rare* phenomenon that it exists only in certain moments and then it is gone. You miss—you don't have the presence of your mind.

I have heard, once it happened: A miser got fifty thousand *rupees* from the Government, because he was travelling in a train and there was a wreck, and he claimed. His bones were broken, many fractures were there, but he was very happy when he got fifty thousand *rupees*. He walked all over the town telling people the good news, "I have got fifty thousand *rupees* and my wife has got twenty-five thousand *rupees*!"

So one friend asked, "But your wife was also hurt, wounded, in the wreck?"

The miser said, "No! But even in that chaos when the train was in the wreck, in that accident, I had the presence of mind to kick her teeth. She was not hurt at all, but I had the presence of mind to kick her teeth. So she also got twenty-five thousand *rupees*."

In this world, sometimes you use presence of mind—for wrong reasons of course. But when Jesus comes, Buddha comes, you never use presence of mind, because it is dangerous: it is not going to give you something, rather on the contrary, it is going to take everything that you have; you are not going to get twenty-five thousand *rupees* from the insurance or the Government; on the contrary, all the treasury that you have accumulated will simply be washed out. So whenever a Jesus is there you never look at his eyes directly. You look this way and that, you look sideways, you never encounter him. Left and right your eyes move, past and future your mind moves, but just directly, *immediately*, you are cunning. You miss because deep down you want to avoid.

Jesus is a discomfort. To meet him is inconvenient because he shatters your complete adjustment. He makes you aware that you have been absolutely wrong, he makes you feel that you have sinned, you have missed the mark. He makes you feel that your whole life has been a wastage, that you have not reached anywhere, that you have been standing on the same spot for millions of lives—of course you feel uneasy before him, you start shaking and trembling deep inside. The only way is to avoid, and you are very cunning in avoiding. You avoid in such ways that even *you* cannot become aware that you are avoiding. Now try to understand these words.

"His disciples said to him: When will the repose of the dead come about, and when will the new world come?"

Jews have been waiting for centuries for the day when the dead should be resurrected, for the day when a new world order of peace, benediction, a Divine Order will be born. This world is ugly; as it is, it is like a nightmare. And the only way to tolerate it is to hope that some day this should not be so, the nightmare will end; some day this ugly world will disappear and a new world of beauty and truth and goodness will be born. This is a trick of the mind: this is intoxicating, this gives you hope, and hope is the most alcoholic beverage that exists—nothing can compare with it. If you can hope you can remain drunk forever and ever. This gives you a possibility to wait: "This world is not final, this ugliness is not final, this life is not real life. The real life is to come." This is what an irreligious man will think.

A religious man accepts whatsoever is, he is not waiting for something else to happen; he accepts this world as it is, this life as it is. He has a deep acceptance: he is grateful even for this, he is not complaining. He does not say, "This is ugly and this is bad and this is a nightmare." He says, "Whatsoever it is, it is beautiful. I accept it." And *just* through this acceptance he is born, he becomes a new man, *and for him* a new world is there. This is the way to get into the new world. If you simply wait, hoping that some day this world is going to change, it is never going to change—it has always been so. Since Adam and Eve left the Garden of Eden it has remained so.

In China there is a proverb: " 'Progress' is the oldest word." Always, the human mind has been thinking that we are progressing. We are going *nowhere*, the world has remained the same. Details may change, but the substance remains the same; it is again and again a wheel, it moves on the same track.

A religious man is one who accepts this very moment—whatsoever the case is—and through that acceptance he is born anew, the dead is resurrected. This is a rebirth. And when your eyes are different the whole world is different, because the world is not the case, the way you *look* at it is the case. The way you look at it is the case, the way you approach it is the case—your attitude is your world. This world is neutral: to a Buddha it looks like *Moksha*, the ultimate beauty and ecstasy; to you it looks like a hell, the final, the seventh—nothing can be worse than this. It depends on how you look at it.

When *you* are reborn, everything is reborn with you: the trees will be the same, and yet they will not be the same; the hills will be the same, and yet they will not be the same—because you have changed. You are the center of your world, and when the center changes, the periphery *has* to follow because the world is just a shadow around you. If you change, the shadow changes. And those who are waiting, and thinking, that some day the shadow will change, they are fools.

Jews were waiting, as everybody is waiting, for a day to come when the world would be reborn and the dead would be resurrected; there would be peace, eternal peace, and life. So they asked Jesus:

"When will the repose of the dead come about, and when will the new world come?"—they were asking about the future, and this is how you miss Jesus.

Don't ask a Jesus about the future, because for a Jesus no future exists—the whole eternity is present for him. And for a Jesus no hope exists, because hope is a dream. For Jesus, only truth exists, not hope. Hope is a deception, hope is intoxicating; it gives your eyes such a drunkenness, that because of that drunkenness you look at the world and everything is different. For Jesus, only truth, the 'facticity' of it—bare, naked existence—exists; he has no hopes about it. Not that he is in despair—remember, despair is part of the hope.

If you hope in the future, despair will follow in the past. Despair is a shadow of hope: if you hope, you will be frustrated. The more you hope, the more frustrated you will be, because hope creates a dream and then it is not fulfilled. Jesus is not in despair, not in frustration. He never hopes, so everything is fulfilling; he never expects, so everything is as it should be; he never dreams, so there is no failure. Nothing can fail you if you are not after success, and nothing can frustrate you if you are not looking at the future. No! There is no misery if there is no dreaming.

Dreams bring misery, existence is pure ecstasy. Jesus lives here and now, that is the only existence for him. That is why I say it is very difficult for Jesus to meet you, because you are always in the future and he is always here and now. How to meet? The distance is *vast* !

There are two ways. One, Jesus should start dreaming like you— which is impossible, because knowingly you cannot dream. Knowingly there is no possibility for dreaming, because if the knower is there the dream cannot come. The dream comes only when the knower is fast asleep. So Jesus cannot come to your level, that is impossible. Howsoever he tries, it cannot be done. He would like, a Buddha would like, to come exactly where you are to meet you, but it is intrinsically impossible because he cannot fall asleep, he cannot become unconscious, he cannot fall into a dream, he cannot hope. Then where to meet? If he moves into a dream, into the future, then there can be a meeting. But that is not possible, that is impossible. The only possibility is that he should shake you awake.

So Jesus goes on saying to his disciples, "Awake, be alert! Watch, see, look!" He goes on saying, "Be mindful, have presence of mind here and now!" But even disciples ask about the future. They are not looking at Jesus, they are thinking of the future because they have suffered in the past. That is the balance: they have suffered in the past, they will be blissful in the future. This is the balance of their life, otherwise they will go insane.

In ancient days, every emperor had a wise man in his court, and a fool also. Looks absurd—a wise man is needed, but why a fool? To give balance, otherwise the court would be unbalanced. And this is right.

It happened once: A great King had a wise man but not a fool. And things were going wrong, so a search was made and a man was found who was a perfect fool. Perfection is rare: to find a perfect wise man is rare, to find a perfect fool is still more rare. But perfection is beautiful wherever it is. Even a perfect fool has a quality in him that you cannot challenge—perfection. Perfection has its own beauty, it gives a grace. If you want to see what a perfect fool is, read Dostoyevsky's novel *The Idiot*.

A perfect fool was found. The King wanted to test him to see whether he was really worthwhile. So he said to the fool, "Make a list of ten great fools in my court"—there were one hundred members of the court—"Make a list of ten persons, and put the names in order: the greatest fool first, and then the second and then the third. . . ." And seven days time was given.

The seventh day the King asked, "Have you made the list?"

The fool said, "Yes."

The King was curious. He said, "Who is the first?"

The fool said, "You!"

The King was annoyed and he said, "Why? You will have to give me an explanation."

The fool said, "Just yesterday, up to yesterday, I had not filled the first place. To one of your ministers you have given millions of *rupees*, and you have sent him to a faraway country to purchase big diamonds, pearls, and other precious stones. I tell you, that man is never going to come back. You trusted him—you are a fool. Only a fool trusts."

The King said, "Okay. And if he comes, then?"

The fool said, "Then I will cross your name off and put his name instead."

In old courts it was a must, because he gave a balance. Your life is a continuous effort to keep a balance. If you move too much in one direction, balance is lost and there will be illness and disease. Disease means that balance is lost; 'dis-ease'—the very word means imbalance. So when your past is ugly, a long suffering, a tedious phenomenon, a boredom, how will you balance it? You have to, otherwise you will go insane. You balance it by a beautiful future, you paint a romantic picture of the future; it gives a balance.

But Jesus needs no balance because he himself is balance. Jesus needs no wise man and no fool. Your past is like a wise man, because you have gained experience; you have gained wisdom through experience. Your future is like a fool: it dreams. If you don't have any future, what will happen? Suddenly you will go berserk. If you don't have any future, you will go mad.

That is what is happening in the West, particularly in America. Because of the H-bomb, atomic energy, the future is no longer there. If America has become the land of hippies and beatniks and others, the reason is because America is more alert. They used an atom bomb in the Second World War, and America is alert: the future is no longer there, and the past is just a long ugliness, a nightmare. What to do? The future is not there to fool around with, to dream and make a balance: the hippie is born—he has gone berserk, he is not in balance.

A Buddha is also born in a similar way but the method is different; a Jesus is also born in a similar way but the method is different: he simply throws the past, he stops thinking about the future, he stops remembering the past. Then suddenly, he himself is the balance. You cannot unbalance a Jesus, no. You can unbalance anybody who is simply adjusted, but Jesus is not simply adjusted. An adjusted person can be unbalanced by any accident, but Jesus cannot be unbalanced, he cannot go mad, because the very base has changed. He does not live in the past, he does not live in the future.

The disciples ask Jesus about the future. How will the meeting be possible? How will they encounter him? And these are disciples—what about the masses?

"He said to them: What you expect has come, but you know it not."

"What you expect has come: the dead *are* resurrected, they have attained to repose. The new world has entered, it is already here, but you don't know."

Jesus is speaking about himself: "I am the new world, I am the dead resurrected, I am the Life, the very center of life—and I am here, standing before you, and you know it not. You ask questions about the future and the future is here."

He said to them: "What you expect has come, but you know it not!"

In eternity there is no future. The future is part of the present, but because of our narrowness of mind, we cannot see the whole. We are just like a man who has been locked in a room and who looks through the keyhole: he cannot see the whole. Through the keyhole you cannot see the whole—unless you have taken hashish. Otherwise, through the keyhole you cannot see the whole.

I will tell you one story. Once it happened that three men came to a city when the sun was setting. They tried in every way to reach it before sunset, they ran, because the doors would be closed; the moment the sun went down the doors would be closed, and the whole night they would have to remain outside the wall. And it was dangerous—wild animals and murderers and everything. They ran, but they couldn't reach the city in time. When they reached it the doors were closed, the sun had set.

One of them started beating his heart and crying loudly so that the doorkeepers who were behind the wall might hear. He cried loudly, he beat on the door, his hands started bleeding, and he fell in a faint. Another started to search around the wall. There might be some other small door, a back door or some place through which he could enter, or a drainage system or something. The third was a hashish smoker: he simply smoked his hashish, then he looked through the keyhole and he said, "Behold! No need to go anywhere—we can enter through the keyhole!"

That is what happens when you are on a drug trip. This happens: the keyhole seems to be so big that you feel you can even enter the Kingdom of God through the keyhole. Nobody can enter the Kingdom of God through a keyhole. You will remain outside, and when you come to your senses you will laugh about the whole thing.

Think of a man enclosed in a room who can look only through the keyhole: he cannot see the whole outside, he looks at a part. And imagine also that he moves his eye across the keyhole: then one tree comes into vision; he moves his eye, then another tree comes into vision. The first tree has gone out of existence; the first has become past and he thinks it has disappeared. The second tree has become present, and the third, which has not yet appeared, is in the future. He goes on moving his eye: then the second goes into the past and the third appears, and that man thinks—and he thinks logically: "That which I can no longer see is no more, and that which I cannot yet see does not exist yet. Only that which I see exists."

This is what we are doing. And this man will not think that his eye is moving across the keyhole, he will think trees are moving into existence and out of existence. This is what we are saying: we say time moves. Remember, time is not moving, only your mind moves. Where can time move? Have you ever thought? Where can the time move? Because movement needs time again: if your time is moving then another time will be needed, because movement needs time. You come to this house from your house, you take half an hour. You move from one point to another, time is needed. If your time is moving as we think time is moving—like a river, going to the past, coming from the future—then another time is needed in which this time should move. Then you will fall into an infinite regress: then the other time will be moving in some other time. No, that cannot be.

Time is not moving. Rather on the contrary, your mind moves but you cannot see it. It is just like when you move in a train and the train is going fast and you see trees moving, going fast: you are moving in the opposite direction. If you are not allowed to look and observe, you may have the feeling, and sometimes you do have the feeling, when your train starts moving and the other train is standing at the platform, suddenly you think the other train is moving.

For millions of years man has existed on the earth. The earth is moving but nobody became aware of it; everybody thought the sun was moving. Still now, science goes on saying that the earth is moving, but the language has not changed: we say 'sunrise', 'sunset'. The sun never rises, the sun never sets, but still we think as if it does. Even a scientist thinks in the same way. He knows the fact, but the thinking is so deep-rooted that he never thinks that the earth is moving. 'Earthrise', 'earthset'— no, there are no such words; the sun still moves around the earth.

The same fallacy exists about time. Time is not moving, it is eternal. Only your mind moves, and when it moves you have a narrow slit: that which comes before it is the present, that which goes out of it is the past, that which has not come into it is the future. But where can the present move?

The whole thing is absurd if you think about it. How can the present move suddenly into non-existence? How can existence become non-existence? The past is nowhere to be found, it has become non-existence. And how can the future, which is non-existential, come into existence? It looks absolutely absurd. Existence remains existence, non-existence remains non-existence—only your mind moves. And you cannot see the whole, that's why division is created.

Jesus lives in the whole. That is why he says, "What you expect has come, but you know it not. And not only has it come now, what you have been expecting has always been here." That's why Jesus says in some other saying: "Before Abraham was, I am. I have always been here." Your mind says Jesus will come in the future. The same mind denied Jesus because it is impossible for the same mind to have any communication with the present. Hence Jews said, "This is not the right man we are waiting for."

And no one is going to be the right man ever. Whosoever comes will be the wrong man, because it is not a question of man, his being right and wrong, the question is of mind, living in the future, investing in the future. And when Jesus has come, there is no future— then all your dreams drop. Jesus becomes a destroyer of your dreams, and you have invested so much in them that it is difficult, it is very difficult.

One doctor was saying to a drunkard, "You stop now, otherwise your hearing will go, you will not be able to hear."

The drunkard said, "I am not going to stop, because the stuff that I am hearing is not so good as the stuff I am drinking. Even if hearing goes, nothing is lost, because the stuff that I am hearing is not worthwhile."

You have invested so much in the future that the stuff that you are dreaming has become so valuable. It gives you balance against the past, it gives you motivation to move and act, it helps you to run. In fact, it helps you and your ego to be there at all. It is difficult to drop it. So whenever a Jesus comes he will say, "I am here !" And you will say, "No, the wrong man !" The right man never comes, not because he never comes but because you cannot allow him to be the right man. If you once allow that Jesus is Christ, then you have to change immediately. You cannot continue the old pattern, the old style of life has to be thrown. You will have to die and be reborn.

"He said to them: What you expect has come, but you know it not.
His disciples said to him (again the same obsession, again they said): *Twenty-four prophets spoke in Israel and they all spoke about thee."*

This number, twenty-four, is very meaningful, because Hindus think there are twenty-four *Avatars*, Jains think there are twenty-four *Teerthankers*, (ford-makers), Buddhists think there are twenty-four Buddhas, and Jews think there are twenty-four prophets.

Why twenty-four? Why not more or less? Why do they all agree about it? In this world, everything exists in a particular quantity, even wisdom, that too has a particular quantity. And that quantity is such that when one man becomes Enlightened it is difficult for others to become Enlightened immediately. The whole Light is absorbed in that man. You can live in his shadow, he will try and help you in every way, but it becomes difficult.

Hence the phenomenon: Buddha dies, and many disciples become Enlightened when he dies. Mahavir dies, and many disciples become Enlightened after he is no more. The same phenomenon as under a very big tree where small plants cannot survive. A particular quantity exists, and when somebody is like a Christ he absorbs the whole quantity. He is so vast that from everywhere small quantities disappear. He becomes the whole Light. Hence, much mathematics has gone into it, and all those who have been calculating the phenomenon have come up with the number twenty-four. In one

Mahakalpa, from one creation to one annihilation, twenty-four are the possibilities, twenty-four persons can reach the highest peak.

The disciples said to Jesus: "Twenty-four prophets spoke in Israel and they all spoke about thee. And they all said, 'We are only the newsbringers. The real One is to come, the Final, the Ultimate is to come. We bring you only the news.' " That is the difference between a prophet and a Christ. A Christ is the culmination of all aspirations, of all longings, of all the dreams, of all that has been thought about the other world; a Christ is the culminating point, he is the peak, the Everest. A prophet indicates, he points the way, he gives you the news that the One is coming; a prophet is a messenger. Twenty-four prophets had declared that the Christ was coming, the *omega* point, where the whole humanity and the whole consciousness of humanity would come to a peak.

"His disciples said to him: Twenty-four prophets spoke in Israel and they all spoke about thee.

He said to them: You have dismissed the Living One who is before you, and you have spoken about the dead."

"Why bring these twenty-four prophets in? You are not looking at *me*! You are still talking about those twenty-four prophets who are dead. They talked about me, you talk about them—and I am here. They missed me because they were looking in the future, you miss me because you are looking at the past, and I am here!"

"Jesus said: I have cast fire upon the world, and see, I guard the world until it is afire."

This has to be understood very deeply, very consciously. It is very easy to talk about the dead, because you are dead; you have the same quality, you have a similarity to the dead. It is very difficult to look at Jesus because then you have to be alive. Only the same can feel the same, the similar is needed to know. How can you know light if you are darkness? How can you know love, how can you know life if you are not that? Jesus is missed because you are not alive. You live a dull, dead life. Your life is at its minimum, and Jesus' exists at its maximum. You exist as the *alpha* and he exists as the *omega*.

You are just the A and he is the Z, he is the final culmination.

You go on talking, even before him, you go on talking nonsense. It would have been better if the disciples had been silent, it would have been better if they had just remained with him, but they were asking foolish questions. These questions can be answered by a scholar, no need to go to a Jesus. And scholars are always available, they are cheap, there is never any scarcity of them. A Jesus only happens sometimes—at the culminating point of human growth he happens; when the circle comes to its peak he happens. He is rare, and you are asking foolish questions, childish curiosities!

"Twenty-four prophets spoke in Israel and they all spoke about thee."

Jesus simply rejects the whole thing. He says, "Foolish! Don't ask foolish questions. You have dismissed the Living One—in asking the very question, you have dismissed the Living One."

How can one ask a question before a Jesus? One should look, one should drink him, one should eat him, one should allow him to enter one's deepest core, the innermost of your being. One should melt in him, and allow him to melt into you.

And you are asking questions! And you are asking about prophets! They have spoken, now you want confirmation from Jesus. You want a certificate from Jesus, a signature that he also says, "Yes, they spoke about me!" Can't you see Jesus directly? You need a certificate? If Jesus is not enough, what will the certificate do? Even if Jesus says, and he has been saying continuously, "I am the one for whom you were waiting," you go on asking foolish questions again and again. Somewhere deep there is doubt, the question arises out of doubt. The disciple who is asking must be looking at Jesus at that time to see how he responds.

And this is the trick of the mind. If Jesus says, "Yes, I am the One whom all the prophets have declared is coming," then you will think those prophets have also said that one who is the real One will not claim, he will not say, "I am the One." And if Jesus says, "No, I am not that One," then you will go and you will say, "He himself says that he is not the One."

Look at the trick of the mind, how you want to escape from him. People ask, "Have you realized?" If you say, "Yes," they will say, "In the Upanishads it is said that one who says, 'I have realized,' has not realized." If you say, "No," they will say, "Then it is okay.

Then we must go and seek someone who has realized. Why waste time with you?"

The mind is in search of how to avoid, and the question is foolish—that's why Jesus is not answering it. And the question is a trick. In a subtle way, Jesus is saying something else and the disciples are asking something else. He is not answering directly because if he answers directly, whatsoever he says you will leave him.

You are ready to leave him any moment. It is a wonder why you have not left him already, why you go on lingering. Maybe it is the vagueness of his answers, maybe it is his not saying *yes* or *no*. Maybe it is because the way he is speaking you cannot understand and you have not yet decided what to do. If he says, "Yes, I am the One," you become suspicious: "How can one who has realized say, 'I am the One'?"

Said Jesus to them: "You have dismissed the Living One. I am here and you talk about the prophets, the dead. You have dismissed the Living One who is before you, and you have spoken about the dead."

This is continuously happening. If I say something, and you are a Hindu and that is written in your Gita, you nod your head: "Yes, right." You are not nodding to me, you have rejected the Living One; you nod not to me, you nod to your Hinduism and your Gita. You say, "Yes, he must be right because it is written in the Gita." If I say something which is against the Gita you will not nod, you will say, "He must be wrong because it is not written in the Gita." If you look at the Living One, then if I say something which is against the Gita, the Gita will be wrong, not me. If I say something which is written in the Gita, the Gita will be right because I say so.

But this is not the case. If you are a Jew, and if I say something, immediately your Jewish mind gets disturbed. Jews have remained disturbed all through these talks. They are here, many of them are here, and they are disturbed: they have written long letters to me—thirty-page letters—that this is not so. You Jews don't understand. If I say something which goes against your Jewish mind, immediately I am rejected, not the Jewish mind. If I say something which fits, you accept me—but that is not acceptance, you are simply befooling yourself. If I confirm your mind, then you accept me. Your mind remains the center.

This is what Jesus is saying: "You have dismissed the Living One. *Look at me, I am here!* The sun has risen and you are talking about the night when somebody said that soon there would be a sun, but you are not looking at the sun: 'Soon there will be a morning and there will be a dawn, and the darkness will disappear.' You are still talking about those who lived in darkness. You talk about me, *and I am here* and you are not looking at me!" Very difficult to be alert! When the Hindu gets hurt, the Jew gets hurt, the Christian gets hurt, remember it is not you, it is just the conditioning. Put that conditioning aside.

Look how disciples and enemies are similar. They are not very different, a basic difference is not there. Jews said to Jesus, "You are not that One who has been promised forever and ever, because those twenty-four prophets gave some signs to judge by. You are not that One, because we have a criterion from the dead to know the Living One." They said, "We cannot believe in you. Prove it, because these are the signs: make a man who is dead alive, resurrect him!" And Jesus could not even save himself on the cross, so what will he do? How can he resurrect somebody else from death? He could not escape his own death. On the cross it was proved that he was not the promised One.

What have his disciples been doing? They believe that he cured the sick, they believe that he resurrected the dead, they believe that he didn't die on the cross, and that within three days of his death he was seen by a few people.

But both depend on the dead. The criterion is provided by the dead, as if Jesus just has to follow, just follow the twenty-four dead prophets who provided the criterion; as if he is not allowed to be spontaneous. If you say that he never did any miracle, Jews will be happy. They will say, "Yes, that is what we have been saying." And Christians will be unhappy, because once it is proved that he never did any miracle, then he is no longer a Christ.

Christ is not enough unto himself? As he is, he is not a Light? As he is, he is not Truth? As he is, he has not brought a grace, an unknown grace into this world? No, you have a criterion, he should fit your criterion. If he fits, *or if you think he fits*, then it is okay. If he does not fit, *or* if you think he does not fit then he is no longer the right person. The whole thing seems to be the same: both are living with the dead—the disciples and the enemies. Nobody is looking directly, immediately, at the phenomenon that is Jesus.

"He said to them: You have dismissed the Living One who is before you, and you have spoken about the dead.

Jesus said: I have cast fire upon the world . . ."

Why is he saying this? Because the old prophets had said he would bring peace, eternal peace.

He says: "No! *I have cast fire upon the world, and see, I guard the world until it is* completely *afire.* I have not brought any peace."

He contradicts, just to see whether the disciples nod or not; he contradicts to see what they say, how they react. He is not contradicting in fact, because the peace can come only after the fire has been there.

When the world is afire, and the old has been burnt and gone dead, only then can the new arise. The new is always when the old is dead. The old *must* cease to be for the new to be, the dead *must* disappear for the live to appear. The known must go, must give space for the unknown to enter.

He is not contradicting, he cannot contradict; there is no possibility because the prophets were *really* talking about him—but he contradicts the disciples. Many must have left him then because, "The old say he will bring peace, and this man says, 'I have brought fire,' he is just the opposite. We are already in much fire, why bring more fire? We are burning already, the world is already afire, aflame, in misery, in anxiety, in anguish. Why bring more fire? We need peace."

But remember, peace cannot come *as you are*, peace cannot exist for you. It is not a question of peace, it is a question of you: as you are, everything will disturb you; as you are, you will create anguish around you. Anguish is not some accident that happens to you, it is a growth. Just as leaves come on the trees, anxieties come into you—*they are part of you.* You can cut the leaves, but that will not help, that will be just pruning, and instead of one leaf, four leaves will come, there will be more anxiety. Unless you are burnt completely, unless you are no more, the anxiety will come.

Hindus, particularly Patanjali, have used two words for this transformation: one he calls *Sabeej Samadhi,* transformation with a seed; and one he calls *Nirbeej Samadhi,* transformation without a seed. And the first is nothing, *Sabeej Samadhi* is nothing because the seed remains, it will sprout again and again and again; the seed is not burnt. You carry the seed; there is no tree, but the tree will come because the seed is carried by you. You may have suppressed yourself completely, then the tree has disappeared, you have become a seed.

What is a seed? A compressed tree, compressed so much that you cannot see it. But give this seed an opportunity, a situation, the right soil, and the seed will sprout and the whole tree will be there. The seed carries the blueprint, a small seed carries the blueprint of the whole tree. In every detail the seed carries the blueprint: what type of leaves, what type of flowers, what colour, the height, the age—everything is carried in the seed. If you can read the seed, you can make a picture of how the whole tree is going to be.

The tree is just an unfoldment of the seed. Whatsoever you are is not the question; the question is what type of seed you carry within you. Whatsoever you are is just an unfoldment of the seed. You can go cn changing the branches and cutting here and there, but those will all be modifications; you may decorate yourself, but you will not change. And you can decorate your hell, but it cannot become heaven.

Patanjali uses another word, *Nirbeej Samadhi.* He says that unless seedless *Samadhi* is attained, nothing is attained—unless the seed is burnt completely, so all misery, anguish, anxiety is gone because the blueprint has been burnt. This is what Jesus means.

He says: "I have cast fire upon the world. I bring fire to burn you. I am not here to console you, I am not here to solace you. I am here to *destroy* you because your seed is wrong. The seed must be burnt, and when your seed is burnt, when you become empty, only then can the seed of the Divine get into your womb.

Then a new flowering, a new blossoming happens. I have come, cast fire upon the world, and see, I guard the world until it is afire."

And this is a promise. He says, "I will guard it, I will remain here until the whole world is afire."

Whenever a man becomes a Christ or a Buddha, he never disappears. Only *you* disappear, because you are *not* there, you are just an appearance. You come and go, you are a form. You are just like a wave in the sea: you have no substance in you, you are not crystallized. You come and go just like a dream comes and goes. Every night you come and every morning you disappear. Millions of times you come and millions of times you disappear. But whenever a Christ happens.... What does it mean to be a Christ? It means one who has attained the substantial: who is no more the form but who has attained the formless, which cannot disappear; who is no more the wave, who has become the ocean; who cannot disappear.

A Buddha remains, a Christ remains, he remains in existence. That is what is meant by, "I guard the world until it is afire: I will be here." But you couldn't see him when he was in the body, so how will you be able to see him when he is not in the body? And look at the strange phenomenon: many Christians see him with their eyes closed praying, they see a vision—and the nearest disciples could not see him when he was present. What is happening?

These Christs which you see in your prayers are just your imaginations, hallucinations, projections. You have created them, it is your mind. That is why a Christian sees Christ, a Jew can never see Christ, and a Hindu—impossible even to think! A Hindu sees Krishna, he has his own points of imagination, objects of imagination. A Jain can never see Krishna, Mahavir will come to his visions. What is happening? Your mind is imagining. You can play with imagination. This is autohypnotic and it is very pleasant. It is very pleasant, you have created a Christ in you. You feel very happy, but the happiness is just like that of a nice dream. In the morning, you feel very happy because you had a very nice dream. But even if it is nice, it is a dream and useless.

Why is Jesus missed? When he is present, he himself says, "You don't look at the Living One." And then when he is dead, millions of people close their eyes and see him and enjoy him, the same people who crucified him when he was here in the body. The same people go on imagining and thinking about him—because this imagination is not a fire, it is a consolation. It consoles you: "I have seen Christ."

People come to me and they say, "I have seen Christ," and they look at me so that I should say, "Yes, you have seen him." Then they go away very happy—children playing with toys. If I say, "This is foolishness, drop all this imagination!" they feel very unhappy, they never come back to me. Why go to such a man who destroys, destroys your nice dreams?

Christ, when alive, you miss. How can you meet him when he is not there in the body? But again the same phenomenon comes into existence: now Christians talk about Jesus as they were talking in front of Jesus about twenty-four prophets. Now he is dead. Now you talk about the dead and you miss the Living One.

It happened that a Christian came to a Zen monk. He brought the Bible with him and he told the monk, "I would like to read a few sentences from Jesus." And the man to whom he had come was himself a living Master.

The Master laughed and he said, "Okay."

So he read a few sentences from the Sermon on the Mount. Just after two or three sentences, the Master said, "Okay, the man who said these words was an Enlightened One." The man was very happy because Christ had been recognized, and he wanted to read more. He again started reading. The Master said, "Yes, very good. Whosoever said these words was an Enlightened One."

The Christian thanked the Master and went back, completely happy that Jesus had been recognized by a Buddhist—completely missing, because this man was a Christ himself. And the Master had tried twice, thrice: twice, thrice he had said, "Okay!" He was saying, "Keep your book closed. Enough! I have tasted. I say, yes, this man was an Enlightened One."

If this man had really been interested in Truth, hearing this he would have looked at the Master, because he would have wanted to know: "Who is saying that the man who uttered these words was an Enlightened One?" He would have thrown the book. "Why be worried about the dead? Look at this man!" But he went with his book. He must have gone to fellow Christians and he must have said, "Jesus was *really* an Enlightened One. I went to a Buddhist. It is very difficult for a Buddhist to recognize Jesus. This man is very great, he recognized him."

You seek recognition for the dead from the Living One. Remember this, because you may be doing the same.

Twenty-first Discourse

10th September 1974, Poona, India

THE TWENTY-FIRST SAYING

Jesus said:
If you bring forth that within yourselves,
that which you have will save you.
If you do not have that within yourselves,
that which you do not have will kill you.

Jesus said:
Let him who seeks,
not cease seeking until he finds.

And when he finds he will be troubled,
he will marvel,
and he will reign over the All.

And he said:
Whoever finds explanation of these words
will not taste death.

The search is for oneself. Whatsoever you seek, deep down you are seeking yourself in it. That is why the whole outward search proves ultimately futile. You may be seeking wealth, but you are seeking yourself. When you attain to wealth then you will realize the futility of it; wealth is attained but you remain unfulfilled. It was not wealth that you were seeking at all, the direction was wrong: you chose to move further away from yourself, and you wanted to seek yourself.

What exactly is a man seeking through wealth? He is seeking life through wealth, more life, abundant life. The mind says, "Without wealth how can you live?" The mind says, "Without wealth how can you be secure?" The mind says, "Without wealth how will you protect yourself against death?" Wealth is a protection against death, the search is for life. But when you attain wealth, suddenly it is revealed that wealth cannot protect you. And if wealth cannot protect you against death, how can it give you more and abundant life? No, you were seeking in a wrong direction.

Another man is seeking power, prestige. What is he seeking? He is seeking to be omnipotent, he is seeking to be so powerful that death cannot destroy him. But that is deep down, he is not even aware of it. When he attains to power, then the poverty will be revealed.

Hence the paradox that whenever you succeed in this world, you feel ultimate failure. I say again and again that nothing fails like success. If you don't succeed, then the illusion can be maintained,

then you think: "Some day or other I will succeed and I will attain."
But if you succeed, how can you maintain the illusion any more?
You have succeeded, and the inner emptiness remains the same.
Rather, on the contrary, now you can feel it more against the
contrast: the wealth is there all around you, and within the poverty;
light is there all around you, and within darkness; life is all around
you, and within death. That is why whenever a society becomes
affluent, rich, suddenly religion becomes meaningful.

In a poor society religion cannot be meaningful, because people
have not yet failed. Their search still carries meaning, the outward
search. They think if they can get a good house, everything will
be okay; they think if they can get a little money, then everything
will be okay. A poor man can live in illusion, but not a rich man.
And if you see a rich man also living in illusion, remember well,
he is still poor, he has not succeeded yet.

A Buddha leaves the palace, a Mahavir leaves the kingdom. They
succeeded, and success failed them. They became alert that the
whole direction had been wrong, so they took an about-turn, they
moved into totally the opposite direction: they were kings, they
became beggars; they were clothed in the costliest clothes possible,
they became naked. It became a conversion: success fails, and
failure becomes a conversion.

But why does success fail? It fails because you were searching
not for wealth, you were searching not for power, you were
searching not for security and safety; you were not searching for
a house, you were searching for something else. You were searching
for the eternal home from where there is no going away. You were
searching for an eternal rest, you were searching for a peace which
lasts forever, non-temporal. That is what the search is: a search
for the home. It is not a search for any house outside, it is a search
for a state of being where you are at home. You were not searching
for wealth, you were searching for protection against death; you
were searching for a life which no death can destroy.

This life is going to be destroyed. Every moment the fear is there.
How can you live this life when it exists just as if you were standing
on a volcano? Any moment the explosion, any moment you can
be thrown into death. You may live a hundred years, but you will
tremble for a hundred years.

Just a few years ago, scientists started thinking about this problem because now there is a possibility that man's life can be lengthened as much as we want. Within this century it will become possible to change the blueprint in the chromosome in the basic cell. And then you can feed to the basic cell that this body is going to live three hundred years, and then the body will live three hundred years. Right now it lives seventy years because your father and your mother lived almost seventy years; unconsciously they have fed this to the cell. A blueprint is carried by the cell that within seventy years you will die. If we can change the blueprint in the cell, then man can live as long as he wants. This has been one of the greatest dreams: to win over death, to prolong life as long as one wants.

Just a few years back, scientists stumbled upon the fact. Now it can be done, within this century it has become feasible, but a new problem has arisen. They thought that if this could be done, then everybody would be happy and the fear of death would disappear, the anxiety about death would disappear. But no! When they pondered over the problem, they became aware that if a man lives for seventy years, *he is afraid of death for seventy years*. If he lives for three hundred years, he will be afraid of death for three hundred years. Fear will increase, not decrease. How can the fear go? You may live for three thousand years, it makes no difference —only that for three thousand years you are on the volcano, any moment it can erupt, and the fear continues.

The search is for a deathless existence. And that existence is within you, you *are* within you. That's why you cannot touch yourself: hands cannot move inwards, they move outwards, they have been invented to manipulate the outside world; legs cannot travel inwards, there is no need, there is no space to travel; eyes cannot see within, no need—because your being has invented this whole mechanism in order to exist with things, persons, the outside.

Inside, nothing is needed. *Inside*, you are perfect. *Inside* nothing is to be done, everything is as it should be, it is already the case.

The search *is* for this inner being—and that inner being is omnipotent. No power can become a substitute for it. You may become a Napoleon or a Hitler or anybody you imagine, but you will remain powerless. Unless you become a Buddha or a Jesus, you cannot become omnipotent, you cannot be all-powerful. You may become an Einstein or a Bertrand Russell, but you cannot be all-knowing. You may collect information, as much as you can, but your inner ignorance will remain the same, unless you become a Jesus, a Zarathustra—then you become all-knowing.

The search is for omnipotence, omniscience, omnipresence. Remember these three words. They are derived from a Sanskrit root, *AUM*. In Sanskrit, *AUM* is the symbol for the whole universe. It carries three basic sounds: A-U-M. Through these three basic sounds all the sounds have evolved. So *AUM* is the basic sound, the synthesis of all the basic roots. That's why Hindus have been saying that *AUM* is the secret *mantra*, the greatest *mantra*, because it implies the whole Existence.

The three English words, omnipresent, omnipotent, omniscient, are derived from *AUM*. They mean one who has become as powerful as *AUM*, one who has become as knowing as *AUM*, one who has become as present as *AUM*—one who has become universal, one who has become the All. And unless the All is achieved, there cannot be any contentment, there cannot be a deep, ultimate satisfaction. You will remain a beggar, and you will go on begging from one life to another; you will move like a beggar, you cannot be the Emperor.

Now, we should try to penetrate these beautiful words of Jesus. He is saying very strange things.

"Jesus said: If you bring forth that within yourselves, that which you have will save you. If you do not have that within yourselves, that which you do not have will kill you."

Very strange! He says, "If you bring forth that which is already within yourselves; if you allow, if you help that which is already there to grow—the mustard seed, the seed of the Divine, the seed of the Kingdom of God is already there—if you help it to become manifest, to unfold, if you allow it to grow, that which you have will save you. You already have it, it will save you. But if you miss, if you do not have that within yourselves, that which you do not have will kill you."

If you miss it—as I told you, the word 'sin' in Hebrew means missing the mark—if you miss yourself, you are a sinner. It is already there, you carry the mustard seed, but you don't give it to the soil, to the right soil, you don't water it, you have not become a gardener. You carry the seed, dead, encased in the cell, you don't put it into the earth. You are afraid that the seed may die. The fear is true in a sense: the seed will have to die, only the tree will be born. Every unfoldment is a death and a birth. The past has to die, the old has to die, only then is the new born. The seed will have to die—that's why you are afraid, so you protect the seed.

I have heard, once it happened: One King was puzzled because he had three sons, and they were all wise, strong, talented, and it was difficult to decide to whom the father should give the Kingdom, who should be the ruler after him. And he was getting older every day. It was very difficult to decide because they were all equal in every way, they were equally talented. So he asked a wise man what to do. The wise man made a plan and he told the King, "You go on a pilgrimage." And following the wise man's plan, the King called his three sons and gave them the same quantity of certain seeds of beautiful flowers. He told them, "Preserve these seeds as carefully as possible, because your whole life depends on them. When I come back you will have to give me a report of what happened to the seeds." And the King went away.

The first son, he was the eldest, was more experienced in the ways of the world, more cunning and more calculating. He thought, "The best way will be to lock the seeds in a safe because when my father comes, he will ask for the seeds. Exactly as he has given, I will return them to him. And much depends, it seems, on this." So he took every care to find the best of all safes and he locked away the seeds. He carried the key with him twenty-four hours a day because his whole life might depend on the seeds.

The second son thought, "The seeds have to be preserved, but if I lock them up like my elder brother, it may happen that in the iron safe they will get rotten. And my father may say, 'These are not the seeds I gave to you. They have gone rotten, they have become useless.' So what to do?" He went to the market and sold the seeds, which were of rare flowers. He thought, "This is the best way: to sell them, keep the money, and when my father comes, I will purchase seeds again and who will know the difference?

Seeds are seeds. The new seeds I can give to my father, they will be fresh, alive. Why bother about these old seeds? And then, nobody knows when father will be back—one year, two years, three years—he has not given any date, so it may take many years. I need not get worried about the seeds." He sold them and kept the money.

The third son thought, "Seeds have been given—there *must* be some significance in this." He was the youngest, the least trained in the ways of the world, a little foolish, innocent. He thought, "Seeds are meant to grow. The very word 'seed' means a growth, the very word; it is not a goal, it is a bridge. The very word means a reaching towards something. A seed in itself is meaningless unless it grows, unless it becomes something. A seed is just a passing phase; it is not the goal. It is not the final state, it is just like a bridge you have to pass across." So he went into the garden and planted the seeds.

Then the father came after one year and he asked his sons. The first son was very happy because he thought, "The youngest has destroyed them. How can he return the seeds, the same seeds? How can he return them? Now they have become plants and are flowering. And the second has also missed because he has changed the seeds, he has purchased new ones. He went to the market and purchased new seeds."

The second thought, "The first will miss because his seeds will already be rotten, useless, dead. And the third has already missed because the *seeds* were to be preserved—exactly, literally—and he has not preserved them. I am going to win!"

But the third never thought about winning, he was not interested in any victory. He was simply interested in one thing: "Father said the seeds have to be preserved. And seeds are a phase, not a goal. The *only* way to preserve them is to allow them to grow. And now the flowers have come, and soon seeds will be coming in millions." And he was just happy that his father would be happy.

Then the father came and he told the first son, "You are stupid. Seeds are not to be preserved in safety vaults, they are not to be preserved in banks, because if you preserve a seed you kill it. A seed can be preserved only if it is allowed to die into the soil, and allowed to be reborn."

He said to the second son, "You did better than the first, because you understood that the old seeds would die. But the quantity remains the same. And a seed, if preserved, multiplies a millionfold; if a seed is preserved, it multiplies a millionfold. You did better than the first, but you have also missed."

And then he asked the third son who took his father to the garden and said, "I have not preserved them in the safe, I have not sold them in the market, I have thrown them into the ground. These are the seeds, but now they have become plants, and the plants are flowering, and soon there will be many seeds. If you want seeds, I will return them to you a millionfold."

The father said, "You have won! You will be the King of this Kingdom, because the only way to preserve a seed is to allow it to die so that it is reborn."

That is what Jesus says, "If you bring forth that within yourselves, that which you have will save you. If you do not have that within yourselves, that which you do not have will kill you."

But you have not looked at all within, you have not even taken a single glimpse. So whatsoever you have is going to destroy you, it cannot save you. You may have wealth, you may have power, you may have many things of this world, but nothing is going to save you. On the contrary, that weight of the world is going to drown you. You have gathered much weight, and that is what is drowning you already, your boat is half-drowned already. You cannot leave the boat either, because all your possessions are there, you have to carry them to the other shore. But the possessions *belong* to this shore, and they *cannot* go to the other shore. Nobody has ever been capable of taking anything from this world to the other.

When you die, how can you carry anything from this world to the other? When you die your body drops. All that could be carried, could only be carried through the body, and all that you possessed was possessed through the body. When the body drops, the very medium, the very vehicle drops. Then you cannot carry anything from this world, it is impossible. That is why many clever people think, "Don't collect the commodities of the world, just collect knowledge because knowledge can be carried." Remember well: knowledge cannot be carried either because when the body drops, the brain drops, and the brain is the accumulator of knowledge.

Your brain is the computer in which knowledge, information collects. It is also outside: if you take the brain of Einstein out, he will be an ordinary idiot, because with the brain knowledge disappears. But if you take the brain of Jesus out, there will be no difference. He will remain the same because Jesus accumulates awareness, not knowledge.

So there are three types of people: the most outward-oriented, they collect things, but those things cannot be carried to the other shore. Then the second—who are not so outward-oriented, but still outward—they collect knowledge, scriptures, theories, philosophies. They are more clever but still stupid, because knowledge is accumulated in the brain and the brain is part of the body—the innermost part, but still part of the body. And when the body drops, the brain drops. Then there is the third person who accumulates awareness, who cultivates awareness, whose whole life goal is to be more and more conscious.

This consciousness is your innermost self. Only this consciousness goes to the other shore, only this consciousness belongs to the other shore. In this body, both worlds exist: this and that, of matter and of consciousness. And between these two worlds there exists an interlink. That interlink is your knowledge. Drop things and drop knowledge! Just grow more and more in awareness, consciousness, become more and more alert. The more alert, the more you will carry from this world to the other; you will not go like a poor man, you will go rich. In *this* world you may look like a poor man, like a Buddha, like a beggar, a *bhikkhu*, but in the other world you will be like a king, because you will carry only yourself.

It happened, when Pompeii was destroyed by a volcanic eruption, that the whole city was afire in the middle of the night, buildings were falling and people were escaping. Everybody was carrying something or other, because the city was very rich. And people were carrying their richest things: somebody was carrying his gold, somebody his diamonds, somebody his money; scholars were carrying their scriptures, books—whatsoever could be saved they were carrying. But there was only one man who was not carrying anything, just his walking stick. And those who were carrying things were very much disturbed, worried, their whole lives were being destroyed. Only this man was walking amidst the crowd as if he were going for his morning walk. That was his usual routine: at three o'clock in the morning he used to go for a morning walk, and this was the time.

Whosoever looked at him said, "Why? You couldn't save anything? Everything is lost?"

The man said, "I didn't have anything, and all that I have I am carrying."

"Then why are you walking as if you are going for a morning walk? It is such a crisis, whole lives are destroyed, people are ruined!"

The man laughed and he said, "Because whatsoever you have accumulated is of this world—death ruins it, fire burns it. I have accumulated only awareness. It may be a crisis for you, for me it is time for my morning walk."

This man is the mystic, this man is the yogi, this man is the one about whom Jesus is talking.

"If you bring forth that within yourselves, that which you have will save you. If you do not have that within yourselves, that which you do not have will kill you."

If you are poor inside, you may be rich outside, but you are going to be destroyed by your own possessions. If you are rich inside, then don't bother. Then whether you have anything or not, death cannot snatch anything from you. Only awareness transcends death; that is the *only* ray of light in human life which transcends death. Can you die fully aware? That is the only, the *whole* point. But if you have not lived fully aware, how can you die fully aware? Even in life you are so unaware—how can you be aware in death?

Remember that whenever there is too much pain, the body has an automatic mechanism to throw you into unawareness, because otherwise it will be intolerable. Doctors have invented anaesthesia very late, but nature knows anaesthesia, it has always known anaesthesia. Whenever you come to a point when there is too much pain, suddenly you become unconscious, you faint, because it will be intolerable. So the body has an inner thermostat. You may be saying to people, "It is intolerable, my pain is intolerable," but you are wrong because if it is intolerable, you will be unconscious.

There exists no pain which can be called intolerable. All pains are tolerable, all sufferings are tolerable. That is why you remain alert, otherwise you would faint. And death is the *most* painful thing. When death comes, it is the greatest surgery possible, because your whole being has to be taken away, separated from the body with which you have become so much identified and one. It is not cutting a finger, it is not cutting a hand, it is not removing your appendix—it is removing your *whole body* from you. No doctor can do that yet. The whole body is being removed, separated. And you have lived with this body for seventy years, eighty years; not only lived with it, you have lived in identification with it: you thought you were the body. The pain is such that you will become unconscious.

The whole of life is a preparation to be aware in death. That is what a *sannyasin* should do, that is what a seeker should do: *be ready!* Don't lose a single moment, because once lost it cannot be regained again. And the *only* richness that you can get out of it is by being more aware. Do whatsoever, but do it with alertness, awareness. Your lives may be different but your inner search cannot be different, it is the same.

You may be a businessman, you may be a professor, you may be a doctor, an engineer, or a labourer, but it makes no difference. The inner search is the same, and that is how to become more and more conscious. A point comes when you are so conscious that even death cannot make you unconscious. This is what Jesus means: unfold that which is within you. If you have that you will be saved, if you don't have that you will be drowned.

And in another saying Jesus says a very strange thing. He says, "Those who have, they should be given more. And those who don't have, even that which they have will be taken away." Looks absurd! Jesus says, "Those who have should be given more. And those who don't have, even that which they have will be taken away from them."

He is talking about awareness, because awareness attracts more awareness. If you become aware, you become capable of being more aware, every step leads to a further step. If you are not aware, then every step leads you further away.

I have heard: Mulla Nasrudin knocked one night at a door at three in the morning. He was punch-drunk. The landlord opened the window, looked down and said, "Nasrudin, I have told you many times that this is the wrong door, this is not your door. Go to your house and knock there—you are knocking at the wrong door."

Nasrudin looked up and said, "What makes you so certain? Maybe you are looking from the wrong window. What makes you so certain?"

The drunkenness of man is such that it is impossible to think that "I am wrong." The other is going to be wrong. If you suffer in your life, you suffer because you are losing your consciousness somewhere: you are wrong, but you think the other may be looking from the wrong window, you think you are always knocking at the right door.

You have *always* been knocking at the wrong door, because all the doors in this world are wrong—unless you knock at the inner door, which is not part of this world. It moves with you, but it is not part of this world. You carry something within you which *does not* belong to this world. That is your treasure and that is your door through which God can be approached. Jesus says, "Grow in that which you are already carrying." The one ray has already happened: you are *not* aware, or just a little bit; a cloudy aware-ness, a dim light, very dim—you cannot see. But it has happened, that is how you are higher than the animals, even that is not in animals.

The first ray of consciousness has penetrated you, but that ray of consciousness is just a mustard seed, you have to give it soil. What is the soil for it? Hindus have called that soil *satsang*. Go near to those who have grown higher than you, just be near them, in their presence, and your ray of consciousness will become higher and higher—it needs a challenge. But the common tendency of the mind is always to move with inferiors, always to move with people who are even *less* alert than you. Why? Because there you feel superior, there you feel you are somebody.

Everybody seeks the inferior and through this seeking becomes inferior himself. Whenever you reach a man like Jesus you are disturbed, because you cannot assert your superiority here. You *are* inferior, it is not an inferiority complex; you simply are inferior before a Jesus, because your consciousness is nothing. And he is a *light*, so tremendous that you become almost dark before him; even the flicker, the one ray of consciousness seems to be nothing. It has to be so: you take your earthen lamp out in the day before the sun, and what will you feel? As if the earthen lamp, the flame has become dark before the sun. Take your earthen lamp into a dark room and it becomes a sun itself.

Hence the tendency of the mind to seek the inferior. It is just like water: as water always seeks a lower and lower level, mind always seeks the inferior. A husband would not like to marry a woman who is wiser than him, no. He will not marry a woman who is taller than him, no. He will not marry a woman who is older in years than him, no! Why?

Biologically it would be better if a husband married a woman who was at least five years older than him, because then they could die together—because a wife is going to live five years more than a man, she has a longer age-limit. Then there would be no widows in the world—and this is a very sad thing. Biologically it would be the right method that a boy of twenty marries a girl of twenty-five, but the ego feels hurt. Neither would you like to marry a taller girl because the ego feels hurt; you will not marry a wise woman, no!

The mind always seeks the inferior. Look at your friends, why have you chosen them? Deep down, you will find the cause to be this: they are inferior to you, with them you become a great light; otherwise you are an ordinary flame in an earthen lamp. The mind seeks the inferior to prove that it is superior. People even love animals; people who cannot love human beings, how can they love animals? But a dog buttresses you so beautifully, as no person can. Whether you beat him or welcome him, it makes no difference, he goes on moving and waving his tail, he is always welcoming you. He always goes with you wherever you go, you cannot find a better follower than a dog. Why do people enjoy the fellowship of a dog? The inferior helps, you feel you are superior.

Mulla Nasrudin was playing cards with his dog. A man looked, he was surprised—the dog was *really* playing. So he said to Nasrudin, "Nasrudin, you really have a strange and wise dog."

Nasrudin said, "Nothing—he is not so wise as he appears, because whenever he gets a good hand he wags his tail. Not so wise as he looks!"

The mind is always seeking the inferior. And there comes a point when even a dog can sometimes be superior to you. In many ways he is! He is more strong; if he fights you will be nowhere. People go on falling lower, then they seek things, then a car becomes their love object—do whatsoever you want to do and the car cannot do anything—then a house, then objects, possessions. With things you feel like a person, very superior.

Satsang means always choosing the company of the superior. The mind will help you to choose the company of the inferior. Be alert and avoid this, because with the inferior you will become inferior. More and more the ray of consciousness will be lost in darkness.

Always choose the superior, move towards the superior. But your ego will feel hurt. The ego has to be left. *Satsang* means living against the ego, transcending the ego, always seeking the superior. And you want to encounter God, and you are not happy in encountering Jesus and Buddha? How will it be possible then? Because God is the superior-most light, the climax of the whole existence, the flowering of all life. If you always choose the inferior, how can you really desire to enter into the Kingdom of God? You are following a wrong path.

Remember this, and only one point has to be continuously kept in mind and that is: move in circles, with people, with friends, with books, always remembering that something superior is there, so that you can drop your ego; you can feel inferior and drop the ego. Always seek the superior. By and by, one step, another step...you will be able to encounter Jesus. And only if you can encounter Jesus will you be able to encounter God.

This is the meaning when Jesus says, "Except through me, you cannot reach Him." This is the meaning: if you cannot encounter me, how can you think of encountering the Supreme-most? If you encounter the son, then there is the possibility that you may be capable of encountering the Father, because the son is just a representative. *Avatars*, Buddhas, *Teerthankers*, they are just the representatives, they are a light from the Supreme. If you cannot encounter them, if you cannot live with them, if your ego cannot allow them to exist with you, then there is no possibility for the final, Ultimate Truth.

"Jesus said: Let him who seeks, not cease seeking until he finds."

Mind is lethargic, and whenever you move upwards it is more lethargic. If you move downwards it has much energy, because a downward movement needs no effort. It is just water falling from a waterfall, going low, no effort is needed. To reach Hell no effort is needed, you will reach automatically; don't do anything and you will reach. You are already flowing towards lower and lower and lower levels, and the lowest state of your mind is Hell. It is not something outside, it is the lowest rung of your ladder, where all consciousness disappears, you become just like a vegetating phenomenon. But if you start moving higher, upwards, then effort will be needed, much effort will be needed. That is why Jesus says, "Let him who seeks, not cease seeking until he finds."

Many times there will come moments when the mind will say, "What are you doing? Why are you making so much effort? Relax, enjoy, rest!" And if you listen to the mind you will be thrown back. Don't listen to the mind! A seeker should persist and go on making efforts until he finds.

But the saying looks against Zen. It has to be understood, because it is not. Zen Masters say, "Be effortless. Don't make any effort, otherwise you will miss. A slight movement and you have already missed. Be at rest, be totally relaxed, in a let-go, as if you are not, and you will attain." They say, "Seek and you will miss, don't seek and you will find." Jesus' saying looks against Zen. It is not, because as you are you cannot be in a total let-go. Even if you try, even if you relax, activity continues.

Zen is not for you as you are, Jesus is for you as you are. And if you follow Jesus, a moment will come when Zen will be for you. When will that moment come? When you have exhausted all your effort, when you have done everything that can be done, when you have come to the last peak of your effort. Now nothing can be done, now there is no more to do; you have put *all* that you could into it, now nothing is being held back, your whole energy has moved into the effort. *And it is not now that YOU stop!* Because the whole energy has moved into the effort, there comes a stop, there comes relaxation. It happens, a let-go happens—*you cannot do it*. It is just like a man who has been running and running and running, and then comes a moment when he cannot run. Even if you put a bayonet behind him and you say, "Move!" he says, "No possibility!"

I have heard about a frog: he got into a rut on a muddy village road. He went into the rut, but he couldn't get out of it. It was so difficult, he tried and tried—and nothing! His friends helped, they did all that could be done, and then evening was coming, so in a very depressed, frustrated state, they had to leave him to his fate. Next day, the friends were thinking that he must be dead by now, because he was just on the road, in a rut. So they went to see him, and they found him hopping here and there. They asked, "What happened? How could you get out of the rut? It seems impossible, a miracle! How did it happen?"

The frog said, "Nothing! A truck came by and I had to get out. A truck was coming and I *had* to get out!"

The whole effort was not applied when there was no danger. If you can see death, the truck coming by, you will put the whole effort of your being into it, you will get out of the rut. You have been missing because you have been holding back. You do things, you meditate half-heartedly. It is a lukewarm effort, you cannot evaporate through it because there is a particular law: a degree has to be attained, only then does evaporation happen. You do this and that, and you know well that you are half in it. Half in it, nothing can happen. The truck has not come yet, you are in the rut: half of your being wants to get out, but half of your being does not want to get out. You want to be free, but the rut also gives you a certain protection, and the rut also gives you a security, it looks like a home—just getting out seems to require too much effort.

Jesus says, "Seek and seek until you find." Go on making the effort, bring the effort to a climax, to a crescendo, then Zen becomes applicable. If you study Zen in the beginning, you can move in a wrong direction. And that is happening in the West, because people in the West who have written about Zen don't know what effort Zen people have been making before they relax. And it appeals to the lazy mind very much. That is why there is so much attraction for Zen in the West: don't do anything—it appeals, because nothing is needed, you are already the case. It appeals, but it is not going to help.

Much has to be done before you can come to a point where relaxation is possible. And that relaxation is not from *you*, it happens: because the whole energy has moved, nothing remains behind to be restless, a rest comes. And Zen is right, because only in that rest is the Ultimate revealed. And Jesus is right, because that rest comes only when you have put all your energies into effort. Jesus is the first part and Zen is the last part of the same process; Zen is the conclusion, Jesus is the beginning.

And I would suggest to you that Jesus is better for you, because you are all beginners. Zen can mislead you, the very appeal may be for wrong reasons. You may start thinking, "Nothing is to be done, I am okay as I am." You are not okay as you are, otherwise there would be no problem. Why should you come to me? Why should you go to Zen? Why should you seek Jesus? If you are *really* okay, then there is no problem. Then why do you seek? Then why waste your time in seeking? Then everything is useless if you are *really* okay, then there is no Yoga for you, no Tantra, no method. But that is not the case. As you are, something is wrong: you are not happy, you are not blissful, you are not ecstatic; you are a miserable lot, in misery, a deep anguish—your being is ill. No you are not okay, everything is wrong.

Listen to Jesus: "Let him who seeks, not cease seeking until he finds." And only in the end will you find that Zen people are right, because when you have done everything that can be done, effort disappears, effortlessness comes to you. In that repose, in that stillness where there is no movement, no activity, no energy left to do anything, there is *Samadhi*, there is the ultimate door. It happens always in effortlessness, but the effortlessness happens through much effort.

"Seek, and do not cease seeking until you find and when you find you will be troubled..." A very difficult thing.

"And when he finds he will be troubled, he will marvel, and he will reign over the All."

Why, when you find, why will you be troubled? You will be troubled because the thing is so great. It is so vast, infinite, that when you find it for the first time you will be completely lost. When for the first time you become aware of it, it is as if a man who has lived all his life in a dark room, in a dark cell, has been brought into the open sky, into the light of the sun. He will be troubled, his eyes will not be able to open. Even if he opens his eyes, he will be so dazzled that the light will look like darkness.

The first encounter with the Divine is a crisis, because you have lived many, many lives in a wrong way. You have lived many lives so miserably that when bliss happens you cannot believe it, you are troubled. You never expected it, you never knew what was going to happen. You talk about God—do you know? What do you mean? The word 'God' is not God, the theories about God are not God. You may know the definition from the dictionary, from the scripture, but what do you really mean when you say, "I am seeking God"?

I have heard: A small boy was making a picture, a painting, and his mother asked, "What are you doing?"

And he was so absorbed in it, he said, "Wait, don't disturb me—I am making a portrait of God."

His mother said, "But nobody knows how God looks, nobody knows where God is. How will you make a portrait of Him?"

The boy said, "Don't be worried. When I get through, they will know how God looks."

And every seeker is in this situation: you don't know what you are seeking, you don't know what the goal is, you don't know where you are going, why you are going. A deep urge is there, that is right: a deep thirst is there, that is right. But you have never tasted that for which this thirst exists. You move, you grope—when suddenly it happens, you will be troubled.

This sentence shows that Jesus has known. A man who has not known God cannot write this sentence, a man who has not known God cannot say, "When you find Him, you will be troubled." He will say, "Then you will be blissful, absolutely blissful."

Bliss comes, but it comes only when the crisis has settled. God is the greatest catastrophe that you can come across, because you will be shattered completely, you will be no more, you will be thrown into a bottomless abyss, you will become a zero, your whole existence will disappear like vapour. Suddenly you are dispersed like a cloud and the sun rises—the light is too much and the Truth is too much. You have always lived in lies, your whole life has been a fabric woven out of lies and more lies and more lies. You will be shattered, completely shattered. You will die, and God will rise. When the Truth is revealed, you will simply disappear. And Jesus is right, you will be troubled.

Many have come back from this situation, many have left, many have escaped from this situation. And then they never turn back, they become afraid. I have a feeling that people who are atheists are people who somewhere in their past lives have reached this situation, and they became so troubled that they closed their eyes and escaped. Now they don't want to go to that situation again, and the best way is to deny that God exists.

They are like small children. If you say to a small child, "Don't eat sweets, don't eat this and that," and if you force him too much and you make him so afraid that whenever he eats sweets he becomes ill and gets diarrhoea and much trouble comes to him, then look at that small boy: if he moves into the market he will close his eyes; wherever there is a possibility of a sweet shop or something, he will close his eyes. Afraid, he is denying. He is saying, "There is no shop, nothing," because if there is, if sweets are there, then it will be difficult not to become attracted again.

Atheists are those people who somewhere in their past lives encountered this situation, and they became so scared that now they deny, they say there is no God. This denial is based on a deep fear. It is psychological, it is not philosophical.

I have come across many atheists, and whenever I penetrate deep, I have always found that they are the people, who somewhere got so scared that now the very fear of the possibility grips them: if God does exist, then again He will attract them; if God does exist, then again they will start moving. "No! There is no God, no Truth, nothing. Everything is a lie, and the whole of life is just an accident." Then they are at ease, then they can avoid the final catastrophe.

Jesus is right: "And when he finds, he will be troubled..."

And you will also come to this situation. Many of you have sometimes reached, not exactly the point Jesus is talking about, but just somewhere near. And you have come to me, and you have told me, "It is very difficult now, I cannot meditate, I don't want to meditate. A fear grips me, and it looks like it is going to be a death. I have come to you to seek life, not death. But I am scared and there is anxiety: whenever I close my eyes and I move deeper, suddenly I feel as if I am going to die." Many of you have come and told this to me. That is a good sign, that shows you are *really* going deep, that shows that the meditation is happening. Don't escape from there, because there *is* the treasure of the Whole.

Just a little more, and you will come to the point where you will be troubled, so much troubled that your whole being will be at stake—and there is every possibility that you may escape. But if you escape, then for many lives you will not be able to gather courage to go in that direction, you will simply avoid that dimension. When trouble arises in your inner being, be alert. Don't try to escape. Move, go ahead—everybody has to pass through that.

The school to which Jesus belonged, the Essenes, they have a word for that state of trouble. They call it 'the dark night of the soul'. Everybody has to pass through it. Only then does the dawn come, when you have passed the dark night of the soul. The darker the night, the happier you should feel, because the sooner there will be dawn. Soon, out of the womb of this night, a sun is going to be born; soon—it is not very far away. The darker the night, the nearer it is coming. Don't try to escape, because every morning needs a dark night as a womb. The dark night prepares the ground for the morning to be. That troubled state is the womb through which ultimate blessing will be born.

Jesus is right—listen to him and remember him. This is going to come to you, any day this is going to happen to you and the sooner it happens the better. Feel blissful when you feel troubled in your being, not because of any anxiety of this world, but because of the anxiety that comes when Truth is reached, when you are close to it.

The same anxiety is felt near an Enlightened person also. Whenever you go to him, a certain fear grips you. You start trembling inside, you find reasons how to escape, how not to go to this man. You are attracted, but a deep fear rationalizes: how to leave, how not to come to this man? You are not at ease—you cannot be with a Jesus, with a Buddha. And you have to pass through it, it is part of growth.

"And when he finds he will be troubled..."

But *if* he has not escaped, not turned his back and run about in the world, then: "...he will marvel..."

Then he will feel the *mysterium*, the mysterious. Then he will laugh and smile, because out of this night such a beautiful morn! Out of this troubled state, out of this hell and fear and anguish, such a blessing! Out of thorns, such beautiful flowers.

Then: "...he will marvel, and he will reign over the All."

Then he is a beggar no more. When desires disappear—and they disappear only when you have attained to your Self, because all desires are basically desires to attain the Self, the inner consciousness, the innermost—when you have attained the innermost, desires disappear, you are a beggar no more. You have become an emperor, you have become a king: "...and he will reign over the All." Now this whole existence is his Kingdom.

"And he said: Whoever finds explanation of these words will not taste death."

"Whoever finds explanation of these words..." Not explanation *in* words, that won't help. I have explained to you in words; this is not going to make you deathless. No, not explanation in words—explanation in living, in a lived experience. Words never explain, rather on the contrary, they explain away. Only experience can explain, only experience can be the explanation. And Jesus said, "Whoever finds explanation of these words..." That is, whoever finds experience, whoever moves through this troubled state—anxiety, anguish, the spiritual night—and who has marvelled and come to see the *mysterium*, the mysterious.

Rudolf Otto, one of the keenest, profoundest thinkers of this age, has written a very deep, profound book. That book is *The Idea of the Holy*. He uses two words in that book: one is *tremendum*, the other is *mysterium*. When you first reach this troubled spot, the whole thing is such a tremendous phenomenon, it is *tremendum*. You are lost in it, you cannot sort out what is happening; you simply go crazy, as if the mind cannot function. This is the last point up to which mind can function. Now the mind has to be left behind. A *tremendum* happens—an earthquake, an inner earthquake, a volcano erupts: everything of the past is broken and thrown and shattered.

If you can pass through this *tremendum*, then there arises *mysterium*, the mysterious. What is the mysterious? The mysterious is that which cannot be explained in any way; the mystery is that which is blissful, beautiful, ecstatic, but cannot be solved. It is the source of existence—you cannot go beyond it, there is no beyond. You can experience it, but you cannot analyze it. You can know it, but you cannot make knowledge out of it. You can feel it, but you cannot create any *theoria*, any theory, out of it. Hence it is the *mysterium*, the ultimate mystery.

And he said: "Whoever finds explanation of these words will not taste death."

One who has tasted the final mystery of existence will not taste death; death is no more for him. Death exists only because of the mind, death exists only because of the ego, death exists only because you are identified with the body. If you are not identified with the body, if you don't have a mad ego within you, if you are centered in the Self, death disappears. Death is there because you are a *lie*.

If you become true, death disappears. There is no death for the Truth; it is eternal, it is Eternal Life. So this is the vicious circle: because you are a lie there is death, and because of the death you become more afraid, you create more lies around you to protect yourself. Then you get entangled in a vicious circle. One has to be alert and jump out of it.

Death is the problem because ego exists. And ego is the *most* false thing possible, the most illusory thing possible: it is not there—you have to maintain it somehow, it has to be constantly maintained. It is not a real phenomenon. If you leave it even for twenty-four hours, it will die. Twenty-four hours is too long, twenty-four minutes will do—even twenty-four seconds. You have to feed it continuously, you have to pull it up, you have to manipulate it, you have to support it. Your whole life you work for it so that the dream that you are somebody can be maintained. And then in death it has to disappear. Then you feel the fear: you become unconscious, you are reborn in another body in an unconscious state, and the whole vicious circle starts again.

Don't be a lie! Start dropping lies, start dropping masks, be an authentic man. And try to be whatsoever you are, don't try to pretend to be that which you are not, because pretensions won't save you, they are the very burden which is going to drown you. The Truth saves.

Jesus has said: "Truth liberates, Truth saves. Truth becomes Eternal Life." And he said: "Whoever finds explanation of these words will not taste death." And the same I say to you: if you can taste your Self you will not taste death, if you can know your Self you will never know any death.

And that which can save you is already there, but it is a mustard seed. Help it to grow. And the first help that you can give is to help it to die. Don't cling to the seed, because the seed is a bridge, it is not the goal. Help it to die, dissolve, so that the inner life hidden in it is freed and the seed becomes a great tree. Small is the seed, but the tree will be very great. Invisible almost is the seed— and the tree? The tree will become a great refuge. Millions of heavenly birds will take shelter in that tree.

Truth not only saves you, it also saves others through you. Truth not only becomes freedom to you, it becomes a door of freedom for many others also. If you become a light, it is not only your life that will be lighted—if you become a light then you also become a light for millions; many can travel and reach their goal through you. If you become a light, you become a representative, you become a Christ.

I don't want you to become Christians—that is useless, that is a lie. I would like you to become Christs. And you can become Christs, because you have the same seed.

Rajneesh Meditation Centers

MAIN CENTER

SHREE RAJNEESH ASHRAM 17 Koregaon Park, Poona 411 001, Maharashtra, India (tel: 28127).

U.S.A.

CHETNA, P.O. Box 34, Woodstock, New York 12498 (tel: 914-679-6673).

DEVADEEP, 1430 Longfellow St. N.W., Washington, D.C. 20011 (tel: 202-723-2186).

DHYANATARU, 375A Huron Avenue, Cambridge, Massachusetts 02138.

GEETAM, Box 576, Highway 18, Lucerne Valley, California 92356 (tel: 714-248-6163).

MADHU, 3326 Dwight Way, Berkeley, California 94704 (tel: 415-548-6774).

PARAS, 4301 24th Street, San Francisco, California 94122 (tel: 415-664-6600).

PREMSAGAR, P.O. Box 2862, Chapel Hill, North Carolina 27514.

RAJNEESH YOGA INSTITUTE, 3910 El Cajon Blvd., San Diego, California 92115.

SARVAM, 6412 Luzon Avenue, Washington, D.C. 20012 (tel: 202-726-1712).

SATGIT, c/o Ma Anand Rupa, 415 Central Park West, New York, N.Y. 10025.

SHANTIDUTA, 3747 Harpers Street, Houston, Texas 77005 (tel: 713-668-9585).

CANADA

DEVAGAR, 310 Petit Brule, Ste. Madeleine de Regand, P.O. JOP 1PO, Montreal, Quebec (tel: 514-451-0640).

UNMADA, 156 Central Avenue, London, Ontario.